AGE OF SPIRITUALITY:

A SYMPOSIUM

Edited by
KURT WEITZMANN

The Metropolitan Museum of Art, New York

Published in association with Princeton University Press

The exhibition *Age of Spirituality: Late Antique and Early Christian Art, Third to Seventh Century* was made possible by a grant from the National Endowment for the Humanities, matched by a grant from The Andrew W. Mellon Foundation.

Further assistance was received from the Robert Wood Johnson Jr. Charitable Trust.

Under the Arts and Artifacts Indemnity Act, indemnity was granted by the Federal Council on the Arts and the Humanities.

The Metropolitan Museum of Art, New York

Bradford D. Kelleher, Publisher

John P. O'Neill, Editor in Chief

Peter Oldenburg, Designer

Composition by Graphic Composition, Inc., Athens, Georgia
Printed and bound by The Murray Printing Co., Westford, Massachusetts

LIBRARY OF CONGRESS CATALOGING IN PUBLICATION DATA

Main entry under title:

Age of spirituality.

Held in conjunction with the exhibition, Age of spirituality: late antique and early Christian art, third to seventh century, held at The Metropolitan Museum of Art, Nov. 19, 1977–Feb. 12, 1978.
Includes index.
1. Art, Ancient—Addresses, essays, lectures. 2. Art, Early Christian—Addresses, essays, lectures. 3. Christian art and symbolism—Medieval, 500–1500—Addresses, essays, lectures. 4. Jewish art and symbolism—Addresses, essays, lectures. I. Weitzmann, Kurt, 1904–   II. New York (City). Metropolitan Museum of Art.

N5340.A34   709'.01'5   80-11497
ISBN 0-87099-229-5
ISBN 0-691-03956-9 (Princeton University Press)

CONTENTS

PREFACE

WHEN The Metropolitan Museum of Art determined to hold a symposium in conjunction with the exhibition *Age of Spirituality*, it was decided that the program should be structured in accordance with the exhibition's aims and organization. The works of art were displayed so as to appeal not only to archaeologists and art historians, but also to a public interested in seeing the artistic aspects of the age, as well as the broader perspective of its political, economic, literary, theological, and cultural history. Concomitantly, the speakers were chosen from various fields and asked to select topics related to the major realms into which the exhibition was divided.

In dealing with a period that had undergone diverse and, at times, contradictory evaluations, it seemed proper to begin the symposium with an introductory historiographic lecture. This was entrusted to Professor Arnaldo Momigliano, who surveyed the various historical theories about the decline and fall of the Roman Empire, from Gibbon to the present day. The second, and likewise introductory, lecture was consigned to Professor Peter Brown. Professor Brown, who has an extensive sympathy with and understanding of the fine arts, treated social and economic problems in late antiquity.

Two lectures were devoted to the imperial realm. Since within the period of our concern the emperor of Constantinople had achieved political supremacy, it was fitting to ask a Byzantinist to give the historical lecture. Professor Hans-Georg Beck traced Constantinople's rise as a new center in the East from the political point of view, but with full awareness of her slowly emerging cultural, literary, and artistic activities. The complementary art historical lecture was given by Professor Beat Brenk. Concentrating primarily on the earliest phase of Late Antique and Early Christian art, he focused with good reason on Rome, a city then still the artistic center of the Empire.

Professor Ihor Ševčenko, the first of two lecturers discussing the classical heritage, investigated and evaluated the continuation of classical learning and literature in the Christian world. A classical, as well as a Byzantine philologist and historian, Professor Ševčenko is also acquainted with art historical problems. For the second lecturer on the classical heritage, the choice among classical archaeologists was narrowed to those relatively few who were not only familiar with the problems of the continuity of classical art, but who took a positive approach to Late Antique art, rejecting the traditional view of it as a debasement of classical norms. Professor George M.A. Hanfmann, in his diversified writings dealing with all periods from the prehistoric period on, has continually shown a thorough understanding of, and sympathy for, the art of the Late Antique era.

The last three lectures centered on the rise of Christianity. It seemed quite natural that the first speaker be a theologian with an interest in the arts. Thus, the Reverend Massey H. Shepherd, Jr., who dealt with various aspects of the development of Early Christian thought, also discussed Christianity's rather delayed adoption of the visual arts. Christian art began on a modest scale in the third century, but only after the Tolerance Edict of 313 did it burst into full bloom. Architecture immediately became the dominant art, and the great basilicas of Rome its most forceful expression. This necessitated a special lecture on Christian architecture, for which the obvious candidate was Professor Richard Krautheimer, who is particularly qualified to discuss the problem of tradition and innovation in early church buildings. The representational arts, however, then caught up with architecture and began to flourish in every possible medium. Professor Ernst Kitzinger reviewed the debt of Early Christian art to the imperial and classical traditions, along with its development of an independent repertory and style that would become the foundation of medieval art. Professor Kitzinger brings to this task broad experience in every one of the periods involved—the classical, the Early Christian, the Byzantine, and the early medieval.

It should be made clear that the intent of the symposium was not to give a general survey of the various historical fields from the third to the seventh century, but to allow to each speaker freedom to concentrate on any aspect he preferred, and to center on those thoughts that might stimulate further research.

It remains to me to express my personal thanks to every one of the speakers, who graciously agreed to take part in this symposium and cooperated in the preparation of the manuscripts for publication. I also wish to extend my sincere thanks to Thomas P. F. Hoving, former Director of the Metropolitan Museum, who fully supported the symposium and left me a free hand in the layout of the program and the selection of the speakers. I am very grateful also to Philippe de Montebello, present Director of the Metropolitan Museum, for his help in seeing this volume to press.

K. W.

NOTE:
References to objects in the catalogue *Age of Spirituality: Late Antique and Early Christian Art, Third to Seventh Century* appear in the texts of the present papers as [Cat. no. 000], and in the footnotes as Cat. no. 000.

AGE OF SPIRITUALITY: A SYMPOSIUM

KURT WEITZMANN

Introduction

THE EXHIBITION *Age of Spirituality: Late Antique and Early Christian Art, Third to Seventh Century* dealt with a transitional period during which classical art came to an end and Christian art grew from infancy to full bloom. It was one of the main purposes of the exhibition to demonstrate that this change was not abrupt, but that the art of both cultures, the pagan and the Christian, ran parallel throughout these centuries and, indeed, penetrated each other so thoroughly that they must be viewed against a common cultural background. The opinion of past generations of Early Christian archaeologists and art historians, who held that Christianity invented a new spiritual art congenial to the transcendental outlook of the new religion,[1] must therefore be modified. We now understand that this new spiritual element in art was not exclusively a Christian achievement, but was shared by movements within classical culture, especially the mystery religions and gnostic sects. All of these movements, striving toward greater spirituality, started out in their representational arts with the same formal vocabulary—that of the Greco-Roman past—and this vocabulary underwent the same changes in each movement. What is different among them is not style, but subject matter. It was only in the fourth century, when Christianity was firmly established, and in the fifth, when it had developed dogma and liturgy, that Christian art gained the lead in the depiction of an ever increasing spiritualization.

The general change from the comparatively naturalistic style of the Hellenistic and Roman past to one that used more abstract means to achieve a higher degree of spirituality has been very differently judged by art historians and critics over the centuries. It is no exaggeration to say that few periods have undergone such contradictory evaluations. If we can understand the reasons for these varying evaluations, we will gain insight into the nature of the art of the period.

The widely accepted division into classical, medieval, and modern periods began in the Italian Renaissance. Lorenzo Ghiberti was the first to adapt it to art history in his *Commentarii*, written in Florence around 1450. According to Ghiberti, the classical period ended with the reign of Constantine the Great, when the Christians began to destroy classical monuments.[2] Then followed an artistic decline and standstill that lasted until the fourteenth century, when art was regenerated under Cimabue and Giotto. A hundred years after Ghiberti, in 1550, Giorgio Vasari elaborated on the same tripartite view of art history. As Vasari saw it, the *maniera antica* ended with one specific monument, the Arch of Constantine [Cat. no. 58].[3] This monument has remained pivotal to the theory of decline in the second period, a decline characterized by Vasari as the *maniera vecchia*, the "old-fashioned manner." To Vasari, it was not so much the Christians as the invading barbarians from the North who were responsible for the breakdown of good classical art. Following the *maniera vecchia* came the *maniera moderna*, the art of the Renaissance, which revived the *maniera antica*.

Vasari's two criteria for good art were *naturale*, the mastery of nature, and *rinascità*, or *rinascimento*, the revival and copying of good classical models. Obviously, then, as long as these standards prevailed—and they lasted throughout the Renaissance and Baroque, well into the nineteenth century and even the twentieth[4]—the eyes of critics were closed to any art built on values other than closeness to nature.

Yet, when in the course of the nineteenth century artists began to question the singular validity of classical values and embarked on ever quickening changes in style (some of which were not only unclassical but even outspokenly anticlassical), historians, under the impact of the contemporary arts, began to reevaluate the art of the past, in particular that of the period with which we are concerned. The

1

Viennese scholar Franz Wickhoff, for example, discovered an antecedent to Impressionism's fleeting brush technique in the illusionistic miniatures of the Vienna Genesis, the key monument of Early Christian book illumination [Cat. no. 410].[5] When Art Nouveau introduced a new decorative style with abstracting linear design, Alois Riegl, likewise a Viennese, recognized similar principles of abstraction in late classical art, described in his *Industrial Arts of the Late Roman Period*.[6] Here for the first time the Arch of Constantine, the pivotal monument, received an affirmative evaluation, especially its sculpture. Recognizing the style as a transformation within Roman art, Riegl evolved positive stylistic principles, such as symmetry, isolation of figures in a crystalline treatment, rhythm of light and shade, and illusion by optical rather than tactical means.[7] Then the art of Expressionism taught us that distortion of the human figure need not be an indication of artistic incompetence but could be applied intentionally. This realization added another dimension to our understanding of the abstract principles that prevail in the reliefs of the Arch of Constantine. Wilhelm Worringer, in his *Abstraction and Empathy*, considered this abstraction as a *novum*.[8] Departing from Riegl's theory of transformation and development of Roman art, he pointed to the ancient Orient as a source of inspiration, a source transmitted through Christianity, which was itself rooted in the oriental Semitic tradition. However, when modern art turned to total abstraction, art historians turned away from Mediterranean art, which at no time completely abandoned the organic human figure, and found historical antecedents for Christian abstraction in northern European, especially Irish and Anglo-Saxon art.

But even if we were to subscribe to Ghiberti's and Vasari's judgment that good classical style broke down in the time of Constantine, it is at best a half truth. From the third century, which produced the first Christian monuments, to the seventh, when Islam eclipsed classical art, there is no linear artistic development from a relatively naturalistic to an evermore abstract and spiritual style. Rather, there were repeated relapses into a pure classical style, fostered by pagan revival movements under Julian the Apostate and the Roman senate in the late fourth century and also adopted by the Christians;[9] other revivals shared by both cultures occurred in the subsequent centuries. As late as the seventh century, the silver plates from Cyprus with stories from the life of David [Cat. nos. 425–33] display classical forms so lively that, were the plates not surely dated by their stamps to

the reign of Heraclius, scholars would be inclined to (and once actually did) date them much earlier. The coexistence of a classical and an abstract art cannot be explained by social differences or by associating the first with the interests of the upper, humanistically oriented, class, and the second with the folkloric tastes of a wider populace. Not only were abstract forms used in some of the most refined works of art, but the same artist at times applied classical realism and the abstract mode simultaneously in one work. This stylistic duality is seen clearly in the apse mosaic of the Transfiguration at Mount Sinai (p. 92, Fig. 30), executed, as we believe, by Constantinopolitan artists in the time and under the sponsorship of the emperor Justinian, founder of the monastery.[10] Christ's body is rendered flat, motionless, and dematerialized, and his face is geometrically designed. By contrast, in the flanking figures of the prophets Moses and Elijah, the emphasis is on corporeality and a firm stance, while their faces show a liveliness and expressiveness rooted in the tradition of classical realism. In this way, an artist of the highest quality, working simultaneously in two different and even contradictory modes, distinguished between the divine and the human.[11]

Yet, speaking of Christian art in the same breath with Late Antique art, one should be aware that the very existence of Christian art is a phenomenon not to be taken for granted. It took Christianity, an offspring of Judaism, about two centuries to overcome the Second Commandment, "Thou shalt not make unto thee any graven images" (Exod. 20:4). Only after Christianity had become hellenized did it make wider use of Greek art forms, exploiting them to the fullest to propagate the new religion in pictorial language. In the course of time, the picture was elevated to the highest status, equal in importance to the Word. As John of Damascus said, "The image is a memorial, just what words are to a listening ear. What a book is to the literate, that an image is to the illiterate. The image speaks to the sight as words to the ear; it brings us understanding."[12] Clearly, then, this importance extends also to the didactic purpose of the icon. Hans-Georg Beck, however, has qualified John of Damascus' remark, pointing out that we are dealing here with an essentially rhetorical *topos*.[13]

These few introductory remarks about the nature of art from the third to the seventh century should make it clear that, because of the lack of any linear development from comparatively naturalistic to comparatively abstract representations, and, it may be added, because of the subordination of individual expression under clearly defined and traditional thematic programs, an exclusively stylistic approach would not do justice to the very essence of the art. Nor would a geographical approach be appropriate, one that would revive the age-old controversy of Orient or Rome, i.e., of whether Rome or the eastern Mediterranean centers made the more fundamental contribution to the creation of Early Christian art.[14] We know today that the answer must be Orient *and* Rome. But scholarship has still not succeeded in defining clearly the art of the great artistic centers, except for that of Rome. The beginnings of the art of Constantinople remain veiled in uncertainty, and the reasons for this are made clear in Hans-Georg Beck's paper.[15] The art of Alexandria, with its famous catechetical school, and that of Antioch, with its equally famous theological school of biblical exegesis, are still enigmas—less for late classical than for Christian art.[16] Lacking clear stylistic definition for each geographical area, we therefore structured the exhibition and the symposium according to ideological realms, a structure that best reflects the use to which art had been put by political forces and by the competing religions.

We placed the imperial realm at the beginning because in the contest between paganism and Christianity the autocratic rule of the emperor remained the Empire's most stable institution. The emperors used the arts skillfully for the propagation of their prerogatives, prerogatives in no way impaired by the emperor's transformation from a *divus* to Christ's vicar. This applied not only to his portraiture and that of the empress, but also to a wide range of activities revolving around the emperor. He was depicted participating in ceremonial processions, distributing gifts, victorious in battle, celebrating triumphs, demonstrating his prowess in the hunt, or honoring the opening of the circus games with his presence.[17]

The theme of the classical realm centers on the continuity of mythological art. In the Christian era, certain Olympian gods remained more popular than others: Dionysos, Apollo, and Aphrodite survived; and, among the heroes, Heracles and Achilles especially were readily accepted as models of virtue and strength. The mystery cults of Orpheus, Isis, Mithras, and Cybele competed with Christianity, using pictorial language to good effect for the propagation of their beliefs. Although some Christians harbored a smoldering hostility toward these classical cultures, classical art was never entirely obliterated. But its base shrank as it became gradually restricted to the humanistic concern of the educated court officials

and high clergy. Texts, often illustrated, became the chief vehicle of transmission, paving the way for the survival of so much of the classical heritage to the present day.[18] However, in fields where no ideology was involved, such as the sciences, the Christians remained entirely dependent on the pagan tradition and perpetuated it without reservation. Botanical and zoological treatises, medical handbooks, surveying manuals, and engineering texts, often extravagantly illustrated, were still needed [Cat. nos. 178–92].[19]

There is also a secular realm, a neutral region that includes, on the one hand, representations of daily life,[20] where a man's professional activity is more important than his religious affiliation, and, on the other, utensils and ornaments of all kinds, most conspicuously revealing social standing.[21]

The inclusion of a Jewish realm in the exhibition is justified by one monument in particular that is among the most important archaeological discoveries of our century: the third-century synagogue of Dura Europos on the Euphrates [Cat. no. 341], whose walls are covered with extensive stories from various books of the Old Testament.[22] These frescoes are of dual importance. They prove that the Jews, when strongly hellenized, had a very extensive representational art. The frescoes also provide evidence that Christians, when they started to tell the Old Testament stories in pictures, were capable of utilizing an existing tradition.[23]

In the Christian realm, it was our intention to demonstrate that art developed in different conceptual stages. At the very beginning, Christian representational art assumed two modes; the first rendered biblical stories in abbreviated form, restricting such scenes as Moses Striking the Rock [Cat. nos. 381–82] or Christ Raising Lazarus [Cat. nos. 403–404] to their most essential figures, thus concentrating on ideas such as the salvation of the soul;[24] the second depicted narrative stories in full detail and in numerous consecutive scenes.[25] This second mode, already fully developed in the Dura synagogue[26] and adopted also in some contemporary frescoes of the Christian baptistery of Dura [Cat. no. 360][27], is most appropriate to the illustrated book, presumably the medium in which this mode was invented and in which it reached its greatest extension and perfection.

Sporadically in the fourth, but very emphatically in the fifth and sixth centuries, the Greco-Roman tradition of the cult image made a comeback in the Christian world, not in the classical form of a statue of a god or goddess, but as an icon, a cult image, either painted or in flat relief, whose very existence had to be defended by the Christians against accusations of reintroducing idolatry. John of Damascus, writing during the iconoclastic controversy, when the issue was hotly debated, based the defense largely on the doctrine of the Incarnation: "You see that the divine beauty is not set forth in form or shape and on this account it cannot be conveyed by an image: it is the human form which is transferred to canvas [i.e., panels = πίνακπες] by the artist's brush. If therefore the Son of God became man, taking the form of a servant, and appearing in man's nature, a perfect man, why should his image not be made?"[28] Images of Christ, the Virgin, and the saints, and subsequently of the great feasts of the ecclesiastical year, were cast into what one might call a canonical form, permeated by a hieratic quality.[29] The formulations of subject matter as developed in the icon became so predominant, and penetrated other media to such an extent, that one can justifiably speak of an iconic concept that left its imprint on the whole of Early Christian art.

After the Church had achieved temporal power, a rich and ceremonial ritual developed in the spacious houses of worship built for large communities, as is expounded by Richard Krautheimer in the paper published here.[30] The altar became the focus for the celebration of the liturgy or Mass,[31] and on it were displayed the sacred vessels. The same artistry and splendor that once had been bestowed upon the statues of pagan divinities now were lavished on these vessels.[32] Moreover, the liturgy inspired certain representational images, such as the Communion of the Apostles [Cat. no. 547]. In general, the liturgy left so marked an imprint on the arts that Byzantine art especially can be termed a liturgical art *par excellence*.

While it is only natural that in a museum exhibition the objects themselves should absorb the main interest, in this particular exhibition we sought to focus attention on them not exclusively from the artistic point of view, but from as many different angles as possible, the better to stimulate the interrelation of disciplines. However, it must be left to the readers of these symposium papers to follow up the many leads they provide for a more comprehensive understanding of the period, and to make a personal synthesis according to individual interests.

NOTES

1. M. Dvořák, "Katakombenmalerei. Die Anfänge der christlichen Kunst" (1919), in *Kunstgeschichte als Geistesgeschichte*, J. Wilde and K. M. Swoboda, eds., Vienna, 1923, 1928, Chap. I.

2. L. Ghiberti, *I Commentarii*, O. Morisani, ed., Naples, 1947, p. 32.

3. G. Vasari, *Le Vite de più eccellenti pittori, scultori ed architettori*, G. Milanesi, ed., Florence, 1878, p. 224.

4. B. Berenson, *The Arch of Constantine or The Decline of Form*, London, 1954.

5. W. von Hartel and F. Wickhoff, *Die Wiener Genesis*, Vienna, 1895; English translation by S. A. Strong, *Roman Art. Some of its Principles and their Applications to Early Christian Painting*, London, 1900. It is symptomatic that Wickhoff, in analyzing elements of ancient illusionism in the Vienna Genesis, linked the manuscript closely to the Roman tradition of painting radiating from a certain type of Pompeian fresco. Hence, he dated it in the fourth century, while current scholarship has agreed on a sixth-century date. Writing in 1895, Wickhoff could not imagine a continuation of classical illusionism at such a late date.

6. A. Riegl, *Die spätrömische Kunstindustrie*, I, Vienna, 1901.

7. Ibid., pp. 46–51.

8. W. Worringer, *Abstraktion und Einfühlung. Ein Beitrag zur Stilpsychologie*, Munich, 1921, pp. 122–25; English translation by M. Bullock, *Abstraction and Empathy. A Contribution to the Psychology of Style*, London, 1953, pp. 93–96.

9. K. Weitzmann, "Das klassische Erbe in der Kunst Konstantinopels," *Alte und Neue Kunst*, III, 1954, pp. 41–59; reprinted in Weitzmann, *Studies in Classical and Byzantine Manuscript Illumination*, H. L. Kessler, ed., Chicago, 1971, pp. 126–50, under the title "The Classical Heritage in the Art of Constantinople." E. Kitzinger, *Byzantine Art in the Making. Main Lines of Stylistic Development in Mediterranean Art, 3rd–7th Century*, London, 1977.

10. G. H. Forsyth and K. Weitzmann, *The Monastery of Saint Catherine at Mount Sinai. The Church and Fortress of Justinian*, Ann Arbor, n.d. [1973], pp. 11–16 and pls. CIII–CXIX, CXXXVI–CLXXXVII.

11. K. Weitzmann, "The Classical in Byzantine Art as a Mode of Individual Expression," in *Byzantine Art. An European Art. Lectures*, Athens, 1966, pp. 149–77; reprinted in Weitzmann, *Studies in Classical and Byzantine Manuscript Illumination*, pp. 151–75. Similar ideas about the contemporaneity of classical and abstract trends were expounded recently by E. Kitzinger, *Byzantine Art in the Making*.

12. M. H. Allies, *St. John Damascene on Holy Images*, London and Philadelphia, 1898, p. 19. Migne, *PG*, XCIV, col. 1248.

13. H.-G. Beck, *Von der Fragwürdigkeit der Ikone*, Munich, 1975 (Sitzungsberichte der Bayerischen Akademie der Wissenschaften, philosophisch-historische Klasse, fasc. 7), pp. 16–17.

14. J. Strzygowski, *Orient oder Rom: Beiträge zur Geschichte der spätantiken und frühchristlichen Kunst*, Leipzig, 1901.

15. "Constantinople: The Rise of a New Capital in the East," pp. 29–37.

16. Whereas opportunities to excavate Alexandria are very limited because a modern metropolis has been built over the ancient site, Princeton University has carried out extensive, though not exhaustive, excavations at Antioch—excavations that brought to light only a disappointingly small number of Christian objects among the rich findings.

17. A. Grabar, *L'Empereur dans l'art byzantin. Recherches sur l'art officiel de l'empire d'Orient*, Paris, 1936.

18. K. Weitzmann, *Greek Mythology in Byzantine Art*, Princeton, 1951. Idem, "Book Illustration of the Fourth Century. Tradition and Innovation," *Akten des VII. Internationalen Kongresses für Christliche Archäologie* (Trier, 1965), Città del Vaticano and Berlin, 1969, pp. 257–81.

19. K. Weitzmann, *Ancient Book Illumination*, Cambridge, Mass., 1959 (Martin Classical Lectures, XVI).

20. First pointed out by O. Jahn in his study "Darstellungen antiker Reliefs, welche sich auf Handwerk und Handelsverkehr beziehen," *Berichte der Kgl. Sächs. Gesellschaft der Wissenschaften*, Leipzig, 1861, pp. 291–374.

21. A. Riegl, *Die spätrömische Kunstindustrie*, was the first to integrate the objects of the so-called minor arts into the mainstream of artistic production.

22. For the most basic study of this monument, see C. H. Kraeling, *The Synagogue. The Excavations at Dura-Europos. Final Report VIII, Part I*, New Haven, 1956.

23. A series of articles dealing with this problem is conveniently assembled by J. Gutmann in his volume *No Graven Images. Studies in Art and the Hebrew Bible*, New York, 1971.

24. On the theme of what T. Klauser termed the "Kurzszene," see his "Studien zur Entstehungsgeschichte der christlichen Kunst," I–IX, *Jahrbuch für Antike und Christentum*, I–X, 1958–67.

25. K. Weitzmann, *Roll and Codex. A Study of the Origin and Method of Text Illustration*, 2nd ed., Princeton, 1970.

26. K. Weitzmann, "Narration in Early Christendom," *American Journal of Archaeology*, LXI, 1957, pp. 89–91.

27. See the essays by E. Dinkler and H. L. Kessler in the catalogue *Age of Spirituality: Late Antique and Early Christian Art, Third to Seventh Century*, New York, 1979, pp. 396–402 and 449–56.

28. H. Allies, *St. John Damascene on Holy Images*, p. 42. Migne, *PG*, XCIV, col. 1269.

29. For pre-iconoclastic icons, see K. Weitzmann, *The Monastery of Saint Catherine at Mount Sinai. The Icons, I, From the Sixth to the Tenth Century*, Princeton, 1976.

30. "Success and Failure in Late Antique Church Planning," especially pp. 123–31.

31. On the interrelation of art and liturgy, see T. F. Mathews, *The Early Churches of Constantinople: Architecture and Liturgy*, University Park, Pa., 1971.

32. Basic for the study of the altar and the liturgical implements are the various publications by J. Braun: *Der christliche Altar in seiner geschichtlichen Entwicklung*, Munich, 1924; *Das christliche Altargerät in seinem Sein und in seiner Entwicklung*, Munich, 1932; *Die liturgischen Paramente in Gegenwart und Vergangenheit*, Freiburg, 1924; *Die Reliquiare des christlichen Kultes und ihre Entwicklung*, Freiburg, 1940.

ARNALDO MOMIGLIANO

After Gibbon's *Decline and Fall*

I

SINCE HYPOTHETICAL HISTORY has once again become respectable, under the name of counterfactual history, we may allow ourselves a little innocent game that would have been strictly prohibited in the less enlightened days of my youth. We may ask ourselves what the consequences would have been if Edward Gibbon, instead of publishing his *History of the Decline and Fall of the Roman Empire*, in three installments—the first in 1776, the second in 1781, and the third in 1788—had for any reason chosen to publish the complete work in one piece in 1788. According to the best rules of hypothetical history, we must naturally assume that the text would have been exactly the same as it is in the three-installment form. The only variable we want to consider is the absence of partial publication in 1776 and 1781, that is, the publication of the entire text for the first time in 1788. We can posit one certain consequence from our hypothesis—and two probable ones. The one certain consequence is that we would not be here, in this month of November 1977, to celebrate (although a year late) the bicentenary appearance of the first sixteen chapters of the *Decline and Fall*. The second consequence, which I venture to consider only probable, is that students of the *Decline and Fall* would be more inclined to connect it with the French Revolution of 1789 than with the American Revolution of 1776. Whether they would be right (or more right), I leave you to decide. I have myself connected the *Decline and Fall of the Roman Empire* with the decline and fall of the first English empire. The connection certainly occurred to Gibbon himself, at least in a letter, and was current among his friends and enemies, as shown by the famous lines attributed to Charles James Fox: "King George in a fright lest Gibbon should write—the story of Britain's disgrace." Gibbon, however, is not a historian whom one can simplistically connect with contemporary events.

The most intriguing probable consequence of a delayed publication of the first volume is that the two chapters connecting the rise of Christianity with the decline of the Roman Empire would have been much less noticed and commented upon. Discussion would have started in 1789, when clergymen and priests in western Europe had something else to think about. Moreover, these chapters are somehow anomalous in the economy of the whole work. Read in 1776, when they seemed to summarize all that Gibbon had to say about the causes of the decline of Rome, they inevitably gave the impression that Gibbon wanted to expand the thesis already advanced by Voltaire and later repeated by Condorcet: that Christianity had destroyed the most civilized political organism that had ever existed. But with the whole work before our eyes, it is obvious that Gibbon neither considered Christianity the sole cause of the fall of Rome, nor the fall of Rome the sole theme of history. To be more explicit, with the entire text of the *Decline and Fall* before us, we can say that Gibbon was proposing a new and reassuring image of modern civilization. The disappearance of the Western Roman Empire, the tenacious sterility of the Eastern Empire, the movements of the nomads, the rise of Islam, the urban revolution of the Italian *comuni* leading to the renaissance of letters, all were for Gibbon the necessary steps toward the formation of that modern civilization which no barbarian could destroy, because in order to destroy it the barbarian himself would first have to become civilized.

Gibbon cannot, of course, be understood without taking into account his concern for the disappearance of classical pagan culture; the disappearance of that culture's society and of its values in politics, literature, and art—all of which constitute the essence of European humanism. But it would be wrong to dwell exclusively on the classical component in his view of history. Professor J. G. A. Pocock has recently shown that Gibbon used contemporary sociological ideas derived from his friends Adam Smith and David Hume in order to explain the manners of pastoral peoples and to distinguish between religious enthusiasm (which had merits) and fanaticism (which apparently had none).[1] Independently of Pocock, I have myself tried to show that Gibbon's original classicism broke down, *inter alia*, under the impact of the new orientalistic research of the late eighteenth century.[2] Two leading figures in Orientalism made a great impression on him: Carsten Niebuhr, the explorer of Arabia, and Sir William Jones, Gibbon's personal friend, a student of Persian literature, and discoverer, for all practical purposes, of Sanskrit literature and law.[3] Furthermore, there were earlier books, such as De Guignes' *Histoire des Huns*, to guide Gibbon through unfamiliar lands, societies, and languages. Gibbon was barred from knowledge of Herder through lack of German; and if he ever heard of Vico, he must have remained uninterested in this kind of speculative history. But there existed enough serious books either written in, or translated into, French or English to give Gibbon the opportunity to reconsider in earnest what the Hunnish attacks and the Arab conquests, respectively, had contributed to the dissolution of the Western Roman Empire and to the political and cultural conditions of medieval Byzantium. In Gibbon's opinion, Islam also provoked the Crusades, the second manifestation of the suicidal fanaticism of Western Christianity. By looking beyond the borders of the ancient classical world, Gibbon reasserted the validity of Voltaire's dictum (*Essai sur les moeurs* . . . , Introduction) that the Western compilers of universal history, in deference to Jewish prejudices, had forgotten three-quarters of the human race. Gibbon reasserted it, however, in such a way as to lead to the conclusion that the mistakes and wars of both the Christians and their non-Christian opponents had provided the more enlightened men of western Europe with the chance to build a better and more lasting civilization than that of the Roman Empire.

The fact is that the role Gibbon attributed to Christianity in the fall of the Roman Empire evoked noisy disagreement and less explicit, but equally heated, consent immediately after the publication of the first volume in 1776. After 1788, when it became possible to read the complete work, the earlier polemics petered out. No doubt the intellectual atmosphere was different, and attention was directed elsewhere. As the years passed, the *Decline and Fall* became a recognized masterpiece in which even the Romantic supporters of the Christian Middle Ages found little to blame. I am not aware that the chapters on the Crusades produced anything like the scandal caused by the final chapters of Volume I on Early Christianity. For the greater part of the nineteenth century, the steady rise of Gibbon's authority as a historian went together with a substantial indifference to the problem of why the Roman Empire fell.[4] True enough, Burckhardt's *Die Zeit Constantins des Grossen*, which appeared in 1852, was inspired by Gibbon and shared his antipathy toward Constantine and his depreciation of Christianity.[5] But Burckhardt's work was not typical of his time. Nineteenth-century historians were far more interested in discovering whether anything new and good had come out of the fall of the Western Roman Empire than in meditating on the fall itself. The leading historians were Germans, and the Germans had good reason to be pleased with themselves, whether they thought of the Battle of Adrianople or of Waterloo, of Alaric or of Moltke, of Wulfila or of Goethe. To the Protestants in particular, the anti-Christian mood of Gibbon was unattractive because it did not spare the first centuries of Christianity. But it is characteristic that differences of belief did not prevent general admiration for Gibbon's achievements. In an age when narrative historiography was everywhere appreciated and competently practiced—it is enough to remember how well even German historians used to write—Gibbon was valued as the supreme model of the narrative historian. Leaving Burckhardt aside, Gibbon's anti-Christian bias seems to have attracted little attention. Thus, it is not surprising to find that the first great Jewish classical scholar of the nineteenth century, Jacob Bernays, was also the first to plan a book on Gibbon as a historian free from Christian preconceptions.[6] Bernays, by definition a lonely man, became more so in the 1880s when, disliking Bismarck, he turned to England for friendship and hope.

II

To the best of my knowledge, therefore, there is a gap of a good hundred years between the appearance of Gibbon's *Decline and Fall* and the emergence of the great discussion on the causes of the fall of Rome, or of the end of ancient civilization—themes that became central to historical research in the 1880s and 1890s and continued to be debated well into the twentieth century. But if the problem of the decline of civilization was not treated by historians in the century following the publication of Gibbon's work, it was treated by certain great scientists. In 1862, Julius Liebig produced an enlarged edition of his pioneering work of 1840 on the application of chemistry to agriculture and physiology (*Die Chemie in ihrer Anwendung auf Agricultur und Physiologie*). The introduction to the 1862 edition connects the decline of nations to the exhaustion of their soil and, more specifically, of the mineral constituents of the soil, such as potash, soda, and sulphur. Liebig applied this theory to the Roman Empire. Then Emil Du Bois-Reymond, one of the fathers of modern German physiology, proclaimed in an academic speech of 1877 (with reference to Liebig and due mention of Gibbon) that the Romans declined because they did not devote sufficient study to the natural sciences; hence, to save civilization, the need for a Real-Gymnasium in modern Germany, with less Latin and more science.[7]

Whereas Gibbon had been heir to the optimism of the French Enlightenment and had placed the fall of Rome within a perspective of progress, the new discussion that started about 1883–84 did so in a typical *fin-de-siècle* atmosphere. The issue of decadence in general was thus rooted in the social crisis of contemporary Europe. It fell to Verlaine to provide the motto ("Je suis l'Empire à la fin de la décadence") and to Huysmans to produce the prototype of the decadent.[8] But each European nation came to have its own Byzantines, and I understand that even America was not spared them. The periodical *Le Décadent*, edited by Anatole Baju, appeared in April 1886. Mental sanity and political sanity were closely associated in the 1880s, a period that witnessed the beginning of psychoanalysis. Questions of degeneration were a lifelong concern for Cesare Lombroso, the Italian Jew who pioneered the scientific study of crime and combined a sympathy for socialism with a horror of revolutionaries. Lombroso's *Delitto politico e le Rivoluzioni* of 1890 (in collaboration with R. Laschi) developed a theory already outlined in a very famous pamphlet of 1883, *Due tribuni studiati da un alienista*. This theory, which Lombroso called "nuova teoria psichiatro-zoologica delle rivoluzioni," was intended to show that deep historical changes are brought about by madmen, who, being madmen, express what normal people would repress.

It was no accident that Lombroso's son-in-law, Guglielmo Ferrero, wrote a work that, had it been completed, would have extended Lombroso's theories to embrace both the greatness and the decadence of Rome.[9] Ferrero began to publish his *Grandezza e Decadenza di Roma* in 1902, to the delight of Theodore Roosevelt. But for several years before this date, the generic discussion of decadence had already been accompanied by a more specific, detailed, and technical analysis of the decline of Rome. My bibliographical list of these researches begins with a paper by Ludo Moritz Hartmann, the Austrian Jewish Social-Democrat: "Ueber die Ursachen des Unterganges des römischen Reiches," published in *Archiv für soziale Gesetzgebung und Statistik*, II, 1889—the same year in which J. B. Bury produced his earliest remarks on the fall of Rome.[10] Hartmann also published a popular book on the subject in 1903. Whatever the form, the ghost of the present was always behind these theories about the past. Even Thomas Hodgkin, historian of Italy and its invaders, felt compelled to publish in the *Contemporary Review*, LXXIII, 1898, pp. 51–70, an essay with the telling title "The Fall of the Roman Empire and its Lessons for Us."[11]

I would like to treat in greater detail three papers that quickly succeeded each other and are clearly interrelated, because the pleasure they gave me when I first read them has never been exhausted. The earliest is Otto Seeck's "Die Ausrottung der Besten" ("The Elimination of the Best"). It produced a sensation when it appeared in the first volume of his monumental *Geschichte des Untergangs der antiken Welt* in 1895 (the year, incidentally, in which Brooks Adams published his *Law of Civilization and Decay*), although Seeck had already given the outlines of his theory in the *Deutsche Rundschau* of 1892. Seeck maintained that an inverted Darwinism could explain the decline of the ancient world, since the political developments of antiquity had implied a continuous elimination of the best elements of society. Social struggles, external wars, and, later, religious persecutions ended regularly with the murder of the most able and morally serious opponents. Because the elimination of rivals was in the nature of ancient political struggles, it was almost a tautology to conclude that only opportunists saved their skins in defeat. Seeck, contrary to widespread belief, was not a vulgar racist. He was, in fact, one of the very few German historians to recognize the high level of spiritual creativity among Jews throughout the centuries.

In 1900, Julius Beloch undertook to refute Seeck in the *Historische Zeitschrift*, LXXXIV, pp. 1–38. Beloch, however, was not as distant from Seeck as he thought. Beloch, too, in his own way emphasized the elimination of the best, but he put the responsibility for this elimination squarely on the shoulders of the Romans. By destroying Greek liberty, the Romans destroyed the roots of ancient civilization. The Roman soldier who murdered Archimedes in Syracuse at the end of the third century B.C. was the symbol of Rome murdering Greece. In the eyes of Beloch, a German professor transplanted to Rome, Renaissance Florence was the heir of Athens. Both Seeck and Beloch, although purporting to explain the end of ancient civilization—that is, the end of the Roman Empire—discovered the causes in a process that started many centuries before and had its center in Greece rather than in Rome. Through a kind of teleological projection, later shared by Arnold Toynbee, Rome was made to fall in consequence of the decline of Greece—a decline for which Seeck did not even hold Rome directly responsible.

In 1896, between Seeck's and Beloch's papers, Max Weber uttered a very different verdict, one that rigorously limited responsibility for the fall of the Roman Empire to Rome. Weber's original essay, published in the periodical *Wahrheit*, found little immediate echo. But a new version, "Agrarverhältnisse im Altertum," appearing in the *Handbuch der Staatswissenschaften* in 1897 and then again in 1909, became famous. In America, W. L. Westermann underlined its importance as early as 1915 in "The Economic Basis of the Decline of Ancient Civilisation," *American Historical Review*, XX, pp. 723–43. Later, Weber's thesis was put into general circulation by Rostovtzeff, who wrote about it in several places. Weber, in his turn, owed something to Marx and Engels, more specifically to Engels. In *Der Ursprung der Familie, des Privateigentums und des Staates*, Engels had suggested that the decline of the cities and the replacement of slaves by serfs in agriculture were the signs of the end of the ancient world. Nevertheless, what was known of Marx's writing on antiquity at the beginning of this century and what Engels developed out of it was cursory and insufficiently documented. It must not be confused with the later developments in Marxist historiography, which made the transition from antiquity to the Middle Ages a controversial and sensitive field.[12] In Weber's view, ancient Rome, like modern Prussia, had fallen into the hands of a landowning aristocracy hostile to progress and reform. The more the big Roman estates became self-sufficient, the less the cities were capable of paying for their own maintenance. When Rome was compelled to stop its expansion, the normal source of slave supply—conquest—disappeared. Slaves had to be replaced by *coloni*, who reproduced themselves within the structure of ordinary family life and who, consequently, consumed a greater portion of what they produced. This increased the power of the landlords and reduced the wealth of the cities by cutting down their supply of food from the country. City life, which is literally civilization, thus declined with the decline of slavery and the rise of the ancient Junkers. This explanation did not quite satisfy Rostovtzeff, but when he provided his own in *Le Musée Belge*, XXVII, 1923, p. 233, and then again in his great book of 1926, he accepted Weber's major premise that there had been a conflict between city and country in late antiquity. Indeed, in the light of his Russian experience, Rostovtzeff saw a red army of Roman peasants terrorizing the cities, which had lost control of the situation. Rostovtzeff never questioned the assumption implicit in Weber's major premise, that slaves cannot reproduce themselves and must be replaced by *coloni* when external supplies run out. As far as I know, this assumption remained unchallenged (in the case of Roman, not, of course, of American slavery) until Moses Finley exploded it in 1958 (*JRS* 48, pp. 156–64).

A chronicle of theories about the decline and fall could easily continue on this familiar path for a considerable time. It would show American scholars, with the characteristic exception of W. L. Westermann, introducing topics nearer their home ground: race mixture (T. Frank), changes in climate (Ellsworth Huntington), and body exhaustion—the latter first proposed by the Russian-American Vladimir G. Simkhovitch in the *Political Science Quarterly*, XXI, 1916, pp. 201–43. Soon Spengler appeared in Germany to retroject the despair of the conquered nations of the First World War onto the end of other civilizations. Spengler, we remember, moved the great historian Eduard Meyer to a reply that was not total disagreement, and ultimately inspired Arnold Toynbee to outline a competitive "Morphologie der Welt-geschichte." Toynbee, far more subtle in construction (we have gained from him the distinction between inner and external proletariat), faced a question that did not trouble Spengler: how to reconcile a cyclical theory of the rise and fall of civilizations with a religious faith, whether Christian or Hindu.[13]

But I do not intend to go on giving a catalogue of theories on the decline of Rome. I suspect that we have, for different reasons, again lost interest in the problem of why Rome fell—at least in its traditional formulations. At the root of my suspicion is the impression, which I believe to be widely shared, that our problems are incommensurable in quality and quantity with those of Rome in decline. Yet, I would not like to rely on impressions. There are at least three different considerations that make it advisable to reexamine the legitimacy of the question "Why did Rome fall?" The first consideration I shall touch on only briefly, because other people are more competent than I to deal with it. It concerns the very nature of the change that, with characteristic ambiguity, used to be called either "the fall of Rome" or "the fall of ancient civilization," as if the identity of the two terms "Rome" and "ancient civilization" could be taken for granted. The second consideration is suggested by the thesis set out in the first part of this paper, namely, that what moved Gibbon to look for the cause of the decline and fall of Rome is very different from what, a century later, started a new hunt for the hidden cause of this decline. Finally, and rather obviously, there are methodological difficulties in the use of the category of causality in historical research, difficulties that even the least theoretically minded historian has to take into account.

III

I am not, of course, underrating the weight of articulate and well-informed research that still instinctively equates the disruption of the Roman Empire with the end of a better civilization. It is a telling sign of our enduring classicism that our books continue to devote much more space to explaining why the Romans became weaker than why the Germans became stronger. Nobody would dream of explaining the decline and fall of the Incas without explaining what happened in Spain, but this is what classically minded historians still do for Rome. They study the Romans and believe they have understood the Germans as well. However, few people today would take for granted what my teacher Gaetano De Sanctis and his teacher, Julius Beloch—the one a Catholic,

the other a materialist—both took for granted: that the Parthenon was more beautiful than Hagia Sophia and that Plato or even Cicero wrote better than St. Augustine. Most of us enjoy Ammianus Marcellinus and the Venerable Bede more than Xenophon or Livy. Interestingly enough, Bernard Berenson may well remain the last great art critic to take up the defense of classicism against what he called "decline of form" in his 1952 book on the Arch of Constantine.

Politically, we are less and less certain that there is happiness in big bureaucratic states like the Roman Empire. My delight as an Italian is to cover the few miles that separate Verona from Padua, or Pisa from Lucca, or Faenza from Forlì, and to discover a different historical tradition, a different religious and political mood, and, consequently, a different way of insuring the continuity of social life among the often ferocious contrasts of internal factions. To say the least, our ideological sympathies are divided. Theodoric, the first German king of Italy, killed Boethius, the last of the Romans. Even worse, Theodoric was an Arian heretic and apparently an analphabet. But Cassiodorus, his Latin Catholic minister, defined religious tolerance in such a way that French Protestants chose some of his *obiter dicta* as their mottoes during the Wars of Religion: "Religionem imperare non possumus, quia nemo cogitur ut credat invitus" (*Variae* 2. 37); "Cum divinitas patiatur multas esse religiones nos non audemus unam imponere" (*Variae* 10. 26). Several years ago, I enjoyed discovering that Casaubon himself had chosen these mottoes to adorn the frontispiece of his copy of Cassiodorus's *Variae*, preserved in the British Museum Library.[14] Compare Cassiodorus and his master Theodoric with Justinian, the man who destroyed the Gothic rule of Italy only to open the way for the Lombards. I have at last had the leisure to go through all that remains of Justinian's theological writings, which still constitute a sizable quarto. Although prepared by samples for the worst, I was nevertheless surprised by the extravagance of his claim to dictate orthodoxy and present himself as the "*defensor fidei*." One can sympathize with the Roman Pope Agapetus, to whom Justinian nominally offered collaboration in defense of the true faith, but effectively indicated his own will. Pope Agapetus timidly protested: "It is my business not your business, to preach orthodoxy." ("Non quia laicis auctoritatem praedicationis admittimus sed quia studium fidei vestrae patrum nostrorum regulis congruens confirmamus atque roboramus."[15])

Justinian's ear for Latin was probably not up to

appreciating the irony of the Pope's hint. If Justinian's ambition to reconstruct the Roman Empire had been fulfilled—and it came very near to realization—it would have introduced into Western Christianity imperial supervision of religious thought, from which the Germans saved us. The spectacle of Justinian heaping insults upon Origen, a long dead martyr of the Christian faith and one of the most genuine metaphysical thinkers of any time, remains exemplary, with the additional touch that Justinian or his advisers often took for pure Origen what was actually the interpretation of Origen by Euagrius Ponticus. I prefer not to choose between the German king who killed Boethius and the Roman emperor who damned Origen's works on the assumption that Origen's body (or whatever represented Origen's body) was safely damned in hell. Therefore, I am not sure that the fall of Rome implied decline.

What is more, I am also not sure that the fall of Rome implied decline for all the educated Christians who witnessed it. Ambivalence of attitude toward the Roman Empire is an essential feature of Christian thought both before and after Constantine. Early Christian thought was particularly sensitive to Rome's oppression of individual nations. The eighth Sibylline book and the commentary on Daniel by Hippolytus of Rome contained emphatic remarks on this point. Later, St. Augustine was ready to admit that from the Christian point of view there was no difference between an immense empire and small national states. Augustine, in fact, seems to imply that small states were less likely to be founded on *latrocinia*. Orosius made the even more momentous admission that perhaps a providential hand had guided the invaders into the Empire so that they could be brought into contact with Christianity. The birth of Christian literature in Syriac, Coptic, Armenian, and other languages, showed that the need for self-expression in their native tongues was very real among Christians.[16] Christianity had derived from Judaism a strong emotional respect for local and national roots.

After Constantine's conversion, the temptation to see the Roman Empire as the instrument provided by God for the salvation of mankind was no doubt irresistible. Eusebius and his followers developed this argument, and Christian emperors soon began to perform miracles and to discover holy relics. A Christian bishop had no difficulty in recognizing at the right moment that "vere Dominus propitius est imperio Romano," to quote St. Ambrose (*Epistles* 61. 6). But the system of Christian values and beliefs remained impervious: it did not merge with the system of imperial values. When pagans pointed to the disasters that had followed the Christianization of the Empire, the Christians reacted with indignation. However, not even indignation against such accusations could induce Augustine and Orosius to identify the ethics of Christianity with those of the Empire. The paradox of the situation was that even after having conquered the Roman Empire the Christians remained what they had been from the beginning—critics of imperial ideology.

Rather than taking commonly known texts, let us consider a work that only recently came to light. It amplifies the Augustinian defense of Christianity against the pagans who accused Christians of ruining the Roman Empire. For various reasons, this text has not yet been properly appreciated, although under the title *Anonymus contra Philosophos* it occupies about four hundred pages in a volume of the Latin series *Corpus Christianorum*, which appeared in 1975. The text was discovered and published in Spain from a manuscript preserved in Valencia by A. E. Anspach in the unpropitious year 1942. He attributed the text to the period between 525 and 550. A few years later, in 1949, B. Blumenkranz noticed that the text was also preserved in the Bodleian Library in a Rawlinson codex, together with another treatise, obviously by the same author, against the Jews. Blumenkranz gave reasons for believing that the author belonged to the twelfth century—which immediately distracted the attention of students of the ancient world.[17] In fact, Blumenkranz's arguments, notwithstanding his immense competence in this subject, were never cogent, and I am satisfied that Diethard Aschoff, the new editor of the treatise *Contra Philosophos* in the *Corpus Christianorum*, is likely to be right in returning to the sixth-century date.[18] Both treatises—the anti-pagan and the anti-Jewish—are *florilegia* from St. Augustine of a type that was common in late antiquity and perhaps most common precisely in the early sixth century. The *Contra Philosophos* transforms some of the main arguments of *De Civitate Dei* into a dialogue, with additions from other Augustinian (or pseudo-Augustinian) works, most notably the *Enchiridion* and the *De Consensu Evangelistarum*. The principal pagan opponents of St. Augustine, from Scipio Nasica, Varro, and Cicero, to Apuleius, Porphyry, and Iamblichus, are made to argue personally with St. Augustine and, needless to say, are knocked down one after another. The confrontation, which starts with the specific question whether Christianity damaged the political structure of the Empire, involves all pagan thought, but turns mainly on the value of Neoplatonism. The whole work is a lively and well-organized restatement of St. Augustine's philosophy, made at a time when both the decline of Rome and the value of Platonism were living issues. In the early sixth century, many pagans, Zosimus among them, asked questions about the responsibility of the Christians for the decline of Rome; and many Christians, such as Boethius, were sufficiently attracted by Neoplatonism to succumb to it. Thus, in the *florilegium*, St. Augustine is made to reassert that the Christians have done nothing to weaken the Empire. At the same time, St. Augustine is shown once again unable to accept imperial values, as he restates the Christian's primary concern for the salvation of the individual soul.

IV

It was from Christian polemics against pagan intellectuals, no less than from pagan intellectuals themselves, that Gibbon learned the relevance of Christian ethics to any inquiry about the fall of Rome. His point of view, therefore, has an immediate relation to the self-awareness of late Roman intellectuals—a relation missing in the studies of Hartmann, Seeck, and later scholars who searched for the causes of the fall of Rome. Clearly, it would not be difficult to collect complaints in ancient texts about taxation, the barrenness of the land, the infertility of mankind, and, above all, despotism. But these complaints were nothing new in the late Roman Empire. None was a central issue in the fourth and fifth centuries, as the victory of Christianity certainly was, both for the ruling class that brought it about and for the intellectuals who witnessed and recognized the slow sinking of the Empire. Gibbon's strength is that he relies on the self-awareness of the late Romans, or at least of some influential groups of them. He is one of those rare historians—like Thucydides or Guicciardini or Tocqueville—who put their finger on something both characteristic and vital for the actors themselves. Much history, of course, happens beyond the borders of self-awareness, but this does not make it less important to define the explicit problems of an age.

It is also evident that Gibbon did not succeed in placing his chapters on Christianity at the right point for the right purpose. They come too early in his narration, they do not keep to the main theme of the relation between Christianity and Empire, and they do not show with sufficient coherence the process of formation of the new Christian organization within the imperial structure. In a memorable page of chapter 20 (the chapter on the conversion of Constantine), Gibbon observed: "When Constantine embraced the faith of the Christians, he seemed to contract a perpetual alliance with a distinct and independent society" (ed., J. B. Bury, II, p. 315). This remark is not made the center of the story, as it should be. Most curiously, even Augustine's *De Civitate Dei* is only appreciated, or rather dismissed, in a brief footnote: "His learning is too often borrowed, and his arguments are too often his own, but the whole work claims the merit of a magnificent design, vigorously, and not unskilfully, executed" (chapter 28, ed., Bury, III, p. 211, note 86). I have sometimes wondered whether Gibbon ever read through *De Civitate Dei* or whether he absorbed its principles indirectly. As Carl Becker taught us long ago, St. Augustine's treatise is not only the foundation of Gibbon's specific notion of the inherent conflict between Christianity and the Roman Empire, but also the root of all the historical thought of the Enlightenment. The route by which Augustinianism reached Gibbon, however, is a very tortuous one that has still to be mapped in detail. Bossuet and Voltaire are only two of the intermediate stations.

Once admitted, however, these deficiencies of Gibbon's may turn out to constitute another point in his favor. His thesis, precisely because it recognizes an authentic state of mind among late Latin men, avoids the most obvious objections that any search for causes in history is likely to raise. With this point, I have reached the third and last section of my exposition.

There is no need here to go into theoretical subtleties. Ultimately, Rome fell because it was conquered. German tribes took over the western part of the Empire, and, if we want a cause, this is it. We may dignify this cause by calling it the military superiority of the conquerors. But the truth is that we do not want to accept such a cause since we rightly feel that it does not make the situation meaningful: it is really too obvious or too trivial to explain what happened. A great historian, André Piganiol, re-proposed the military cause after the last World War because he was justly angry with the Germans, and he abandoned it when he was less angry.[19] So we go on searching for *real* causes, with all of the emphasis on the word "real." And soon we learn that there is nothing easier to find than *real* causes. Anything that makes a situation meaningful can be turned into a cause, either in isolation or in conjunction with other elements. Heavy taxation, decline of cities, incompetence or corruption among civil servants, barbarization of the army, race mixture, transition from slavery to serfdom, and even plagues (as has been most recently and authoritatively suggested[20]) are important features of the late Roman situation that can be called causes of the decline of Rome, if we so wish. But what would we gain from calling them causes? To make them causes, we should have to put the various elements of the situation in a certain order and to show that element A—say, the barbarization of the army—is the cause of element B—say, heavy taxation—which, in turn, is the cause of element C—say, the corruption of the civil servants. If we embark on this operation, we shall be told by the first fellow historian we meet that element C (the corruption of the civil servants) may be turned with minimum effort into the cause of element B (heavy taxation), which then looks like the cause of element A (the barbarization of the army) because it stands to reason that you cannot use as soldiers those whom you want as taxpayers. One causal series may look slightly more probable than the other, but plausibility is not a ready criterion for judgment when the situation is extremely complex and many elements are available for different combinations.[21]

Historians, one must admit, were not created by God to search for causes. Any search for causes in history, if it is persistent, as in the case of the fall of the Roman Empire, becomes comic—such is the abundance of causes discovered. And this really ends the matter. What we want is to understand the change by analyzing it and giving due consideration to conscious decisions, deep-seated urges, and the interplay of disparate events. But we must have a mental picture, a model of the whole situation as a term of reference, and here, I submit, is where Gibbon helps us because he understood that late antiquity meant the replacement of paganism by Christianity.

If what we want is to understand the fall of the Roman Empire in the West, we must somehow include all the elements I have mentioned and, no doubt, many others. As the Marxists saw, the decline of slavery and the rise of serfdom are important features. Yet, I would still maintain—as I first did in 1935 in my article on the Roman Empire for the *Enciclopedia Italiana* and then in 1959 in my introduction to the volume *The Conflict Between Paganism and Christianity in the Fourth Century*—that Gibbon offers the framework to include the other elements; the more so because he never succeeded in turning Christianity into *the* cause or even the main cause of the fall of the Empire. What he understood was a situation. It was a situation in which Constantine rec-

ognized the power of an organization that controlled the life and thought of the most assertive and expansive group of Roman citizens: the Christians.

We must go further along the path indicated by Gibbon. The Christian Church had become a state within the state, just as in early Rome the plebs had become a state within the state. It had its own hierarchy, its own rules, its own beliefs, and its own loyalties. Like the early plebs, the Christian Church offered increasing opportunities for leadership to those who were excluded from the ruling class. Indeed, what characterized the late Christian plebs, as it had characterized the early urban plebs of Rome, was the proximity of its leaders to the grassroots. Instead of the Roman provincial governors coming from the center and having a limited period of residence in the provinces, the Christians most often elected local people as bishops for life. Yet the new Christian plebs, like the ancient urban plebs, were prepared to give a chance to aristocrats, if the aristocrats were ready to join the ranks of the Church. For a late Roman aristocrat, conversion was, in social terms, the equivalent of *transitio ad plebem*. This was the reality with which Constantine decided to come to terms and not just out of sheer calculation.[22]

An empire built on such a dual organization of state and church was never going to be the same as the old one. There is no point in asking whether the Christian regime accelerated or slowed down the inability of the Roman army to stand up to the barbarians, or whether it increased or reduced the burden of taxation. But we do know that whatever happened in the fourth and fifth centuries had to be fitted into a new frame. The Christian communities practiced proselytism, did not tolerate dissent, obeyed their local spiritual leaders more willingly than their political administrators and governors, and were expected to care more for the certainties of the next life than for the uncertainties of this one. Even if they increasingly relied on monks and priests to keep the peace of God, there were moments in which the Christian laymen could not escape their personal liabilities toward God. The significant point is not that Sozomenus (*Hist. Eccl.* 9. 1, 2) could tell his readers that "piety alone is enough to save the kings." This sentence was, to say the least, ambiguous. If taken to refer to earthly prosperity, it would only too quickly be contradicted by experience. It did not need Machiavelli to discover that wars are not won by prayers.

Truly characteristic of the Christian Empire is what Hilary of Arles says of St. Honoratus, the bishop of Arles who died in 430. St. Honoratus belonged to a consular family, but out of love for truth did not seek the "vain honors of his relatives": "pro amore veritatis iam suos non optabat."[23] He preferred a bishopric to a consulship. The classical world had known the choice between *vita activa* and *vita contemplativa*, not between two *vitae activae*, one for the state, the other for the Church. That is why the emperor Julian's letter to the high priest Theodorus about the pagan clergy is such an important document of the decline of paganism.[24] Here Julian accepts almost entirely the Jewish and Christian assumption that priesthood has a place of its own in society, a place that must be kept apart from political magistracies. The difference even extends to what a priest is forbidden to read: no novels, no treatises by Epicurus or Pyrrhon. I may be old-fashioned, but I cannot help accepting the traditional view that Julian was capable of defending paganism only by making it as similar as possible to Christianity. When the choice is offered, when you can choose between being a bishop and being a consul, you are no longer an ancient man, you are a medieval one.[25]

NOTES

1. J. G. A. Pocock, "Gibbon's Decline and Fall and the World View of Late Enlightenment," *Eighteenth Century Studies*, X, 1977, pp. 287–303.

2. "Eighteenth-century Prelude to Mr. Gibbon," *Gibbon et Rome*, P. Ducrey, ed., Geneva, 1977, pp. 57–70.

3. Jones was not, however, a warm admirer of the first volume of Gibbon's history. See his *Letters*, G. Cannon, ed., Oxford, 1970, I, p. 212.

4. I do not know of a general study of Gibbon's reputation. Some basic facts are in S. T. McCloy, *Gibbon's Antagonism to Christianity and the Discussion that it has provoked*, Chapel Hill, 1933, and, of course, J. E. Norton, *A Bibliography of the Works of E. Gibbon*, London, 1940. Cf. M. Baridon's admirable thesis, *Edward Gibbon et le mythe de Rome*, Paris, 1975. For Gibbon in Germany, important evidence appears in J. Bernays, quoted below, note 6. For Italy, see my essay "Gibbon from an Italian Point of View," *Daedalus*, Summer 1976, pp. 125–35. (The issue was devoted to Gibbon and has been reprinted by Harvard University Press, 1977, under the title *Edward Gibbon and the Decline and Fall of the Roman Empire*.) The contents of my paper are misunderstood in E. Badian's review of the Harvard volume in *The New York Review of Books*, October 13, 1977, p. 8. Further details on the Italian reception of Gibbon may be found in my paper "Edward Gibbon fuori e dentro la cultura italiana," *Annali Scuola Normale Pisa*, ser. 3, VI, 1976, pp. 77–95.

5. On Gibbon and Burckhardt see, above all, W. Kaegi, *J. Burckhardt*, Basel, 1956, III, pp. 350–421. Also S. Mazzarino, "Politologisches bei J. Burckhardt," *Saeculum*, XXII, 1971, pp. 25–34. Burckhardt's presuppositions are in many aspects actually remote from Gibbon's. Kaegi was unable to find references to Gibbon in the mass of notes Burckhardt prepared for the writing of his book. But this may simply mean that he was already well acquainted with Gibbon.

6. J. Bernays, *Gesammelte Abhandlungen*, Berlin, 1885, II, pp. 206–54. Cf. p. 227: "so wenig wie Gibbon gehöre ich einer der christlichen Religionsgenossenschaften an."

7. Du Bois-Reymond's speech was reprinted in his *Reden*, I, Leipzig, 1886, pp. 255–57.

8. Verlaine's sonnet (now in *Jadis et naguère*) was originally published in *Le Chat Noir*, May 26, 1883. Verlaine later gave to Baju his *Ballade pour les Décadents* (now in *Dédicaces* under a changed title). See, in general, A. E. Carter, *The Idea of Decadence in French Literature, 1830–1900*, Toronto, 1958. K. W. Swart, *The Sense of Decadence in Nineteenth-Century France*, The Hague, 1964. Max Nordau's *Entartung* appeared in 1892.

9. In 1854, half a century before the publication of Ferrero's work, Renan was ready to exchange the whole of America for a small-size Italian town like Pisa or Siena ("Channing," *Oeuvres Complètes*, Paris, 1947–62, VII, p. 279). But Ferrero was ambiguous both on ancient Rome and America: in *Grandezza e Decadenza di Roma*, Milan, 1902, I, p. 489, he compared Caesar to a Tammany Hall boss. His later work, *La Ruine de la civilisation antique*, Paris, 1921, is dominated by a different outlook, the crisis of the "principe de légitimité."

10. Compare Bury's early statements in *History of the Later Roman Empire*, 1889, I, chap. 3, and in his essay "Rome and Byzantium," *Quarterly Review*, CXCII, 1900, pp. 125–55 (cf. *Selected Essays*, 1930, pp. 231–42), with the *History of the Later Roman Empire* of 1923, I, pp. 303–13. See also D. S. Goldstein, *American Historical Review*, LXXXII, 1977, p. 901.

11. In this article, Hodgkin, for all his optimism about the future of the British Empire, found its weakness in the economic exploitation of India.

12. Weber must also have studied with care Ludo Hartmann's paper. Hartmann's emphasis on the *"soziale Frage"* in the Roman Empire had lent an independent expertise to the development of Marxist themes. Marxism very soon made important contributions to the study of Christian origins. But although the social analysis of Christianity was in the long run bound to affect the interpretation of the decline of the Roman Empire, the earlier research by F. Engels and K. Kautsky had not succeeded in connecting the two points. This is particularly evident in Kautsky's *Die Entstehung des Christentums*, 1908; English translation by H. F. Mins, *Foundations of Christianity*, 1925. Here there is an imbalance between the generalizations on the slave-holding system over several centuries and the narrower study of the primitive Christian communities. Kautsky no longer shared Engels' notion that the victory of Christianity was a prefiguration of the victory of socialism, but he did share Engels' inability to see that Christianity created a hitherto unknown rivalry within the Empire between civil and religious society. See the contemporary discussion by R. von Pöhlmann, *Aus Altertum und Gegenwart*, 2nd ed., Munich, 1911, I, pp. 346–84.

13. The various theories about the decline and fall of Rome are treated in *Der Untergang des Römischen Reiches*, K. Christ, ed., Darmstadt, 1970, with introduction and bibliography.

14. Cf. A. Momigliano, *Tra Latino e Volgare. Per Carlo Dionisotti*, Padua, 1974, pp. 615–17.

15. Justinian's theological writings have recently been reprinted, although not in an entirely satisfactory way, by M. Amelotti and his collaborators, Milan, 1972–77.

16. An introduction to these literatures is contained in B. M. Metzger, *The Early Versions of the New Testament*, Oxford, 1977.

17. Blumenkranz argued his thesis in *Revue du Moyen Age Latin*, V, 1949, pp. 193–96 and *Les auteurs chrétiens latins du Moyen Age sur les Juifs et le Judaïsme*, Paris, 1963, p. 52.

18. D. Aschoff has not yet published his evidence, but see the introduction to his edition (*Anonymi Contra Philosophos*, Turnholt, 1975) and "Kritische Bemerkungen zu einer wenig beachteten Edition eines Augustinkompilators der Spätantike," *Scriptorium*, XXVI, 1974, pp. 301–08.

19. Cf. Piganiol's *Histoire de Rome*, 1st ed., Paris, 1939 (Collection Clio), pp. 512–13, and 5th ed., Paris, 1962, p. 522. Curiously, there are also contradictions between these two passages!

20. W. H. McNeill, *Plagues and Peoples*, New York, 1976.

21. If some guidance is required on the difficulties of historical causation, it can be found, for example, in G. H. von Wright, *Explanation and Understanding*, Ithaca, 1971, and in the book by Rex Martin (von Wright's partial pupil), *Historical Explanation*, Ithaca, 1977.

22. For an original and recent examination of the social attitudes and of the economic level of the Christian communities of the first three centuries, see R. M. Grant, *Early Christianity and Society*, San Francisco, 1977.

23. Hilaire d'Arles, *Vie de Saint Honorat*, M.-D. Valentin, ed., Paris, 1977, chap. 4, frg. 2.

24. Julianus, *Oeuvres complètes*, J. Bidez and F. Cumont, eds., Paris, 1924, I, 2, ep. 89.

25. No bibliography is attempted here, either on Gibbon or on the decline. But reference should at least be made to some old companions. W. Rehm, *Der Untergang Roms im abendländischen Denken*, Leipzig, 1930. S. Mazzarino, *La fine del mondo antico*, Milan, 1960. L. White, *The Transformation of the Roman World. Gibbon's Problem after Two Centuries*, Berkeley, 1966. In more recent years, L. Cracco Ruggini has illuminated many aspects of Gibbon and the decline: "Pubblicistica e storiografia bizantina di fronte alla crisi dell'impero romano," *Athenaeum*, LXI, 1973, pp. 146–83; "Zosimo ossia il rovesciamento delle storie ecclesiastiche," *Augustinianum*, XVI, 1976, pp. 23–36. H.-I. Marrou's posthumous little book, *Décadence romaine ou antiquité tardive*, Paris, 1977, appeared too late to be used in this lecture, but I have known Marrou's thoughts and, indeed, his noble mind from long acquaintance. Carl Becker's interpretation of eighteenth-century historiography has been subtly reasserted by L. Krieger, "The Heavenly City of the Eighteenth-century Historians," *Church History*, XLVII, 1978, pp. 279–97.

PETER R. L. BROWN

Art and Society in Late Antiquity

ANY HISTORIAN who comes to speak on art and society in late antiquity is likely to find himself in the position of a general who has advanced impetuously too far ahead of his troops. For the relation between the study of Late Antique art and the writing of Late Antique history is a peculiar one. The Late Antique period has come to interest us primarily by reason of the puzzling quality of Late Antique civilization. Between A.D. 300 and 600, within the relatively stable social and political environment of the late Roman Empire, one form of civilization, with which we have tended to identify ourselves wholeheartedly—the civilization of the classical ancient world—was replaced by something disturbingly different.

The charge of having declined through having departed from the ideal of classical antiquity rests heavily on the Late Antique period. To rebut such a charge, the historian has been forced to face up to the problem of the nature of change in a traditional civilization. He has had to develop an insight into the aims and the positive achievements of a culture plainly different from that of the classical world, and yet so plainly continuous with it as to be open to frequent invidious comparisons with a supposedly "superior" predecessor. He has to make intelligible and to communicate without the rhetoric of "decline and fall" the process by which a civilization as seemingly complete in itself as that of classical antiquity changed into the impenitently postclassical world of late antiquity.

Consideration of Late Antique art has played a quite outstanding role in the reassessment that has enabled us to treat late antiquity as a period in its own right. The art historians of this century have elaborated clear and dispassionate criteria with which to judge the artistic changes of the postclassical world,

and they have not hesitated to bring into their assessment of Late Antique art a willingness shared by cultivated men of our century to look with more tolerant eyes on the nonclassical and the exotic.

Thus, on the crucial issue of the quality of Late Antique civilization and the nature and pace of the changes by which it became so different from its classical predecessor, the history of Late Antique art has come to be the arbiter of elegance. We have learned to expect that any study of the culture and society of the period that wishes to claim to be something more than a useful contribution to erudition must, in some way, reflect the ability to seek out meaningful criteria, to sense the complexity of the processes by which one style changes into another, and, above all, to treat divergences from classical norms with serenity of judgment. This kind of judgment has been the hallmark of a small, but distinguished, band of historians of Late Antique art in Europe and America.

If we turn, therefore, to the work of a master of such scholarship, the late Henri Irénée Marrou, we meet an author whose vivid eye and unfailing musical sensitivity to the quality of change within a continuous tradition gave warmth and a concrete "presence" to even the most dry and seemingly remote products of the late classical schoolroom. Marrou's work was marked throughout by a willingness to allow the art of the age to speak loudly and clearly about the changes that he could trace with such *finesse* in other areas. Those who have found in the *Retractatio* to his *Saint Augustin et la fin de la culture antique*, first published in 1949, a new starting point for their own meditations on what was really happening in the period after A.D. 300, will remember the long passage with which he concluded his plea to regard late antiquity as a period in its own right, rather than as an age of "decadence," or as a rarefied harbinger of the Middle Ages.

> Let us take the most concrete case: the plastic arts. Look at the great bronze head of Constantius II in the Museo dei Conservatori in Rome. Faced by a work of art that embodies so many new values . . . who would be content to talk in terms of "decadence," to treat this "portrait" (even the word "portrait" is misleading) as an unsuccessful imitation of models of the age of Augustus? Who, then, looking at the porphyry sarcophagi in the Vatican Museum would be satisfied with comparing these with the reliefs on the Ara Pacis? Or who would judge the triumphal mosaics of the Christian basilicas of Rome in the light of the frescoes of Pompeii . . . ? No: the art of the late Roman Empire is something new. . . . The same judgment holds good for the civilization and culture of the fourth century as a whole.[1]

Yet once this debt of gratitude is stated, the historian must go on to admit his limitations. The art of late antiquity has provided a vivid and readily communicable paradigm for the central problem of the period—the relation between change and continuity in Late Antique civilization. But to be inspired by a paradigm drawn from a neighboring discipline is a very different matter from claiming to be proficient in that discipline itself. Having enthusiastically followed the lead given by the art historian, the student of Late Antique society finds, only too soon, that he has got out of his depth: he looks back with justifiable dismay at the distance that separates him from the sheer bulk and the problematic nature of the surviving artifacts of late antiquity.

Furthermore, to use the art of late antiquity largely as a paradigm has tended to limit our perception of what is, perhaps, its most challenging feature—an exuberant diversity. There is a tendency among historians of late antiquity, only too faithfully betrayed in the choice of illustrations available in most modern publications, to adhere to a narrow, almost "canonical," selection of works of Late Antique art. A few dramatic illustrations of departures from the classical tradition, and a few tantalizing instances of the preservation of classical standards at unexpectedly late moments in Late Antique history, command the attention of the scholar and the general reader.

What the social historian can do is to take these artifacts, some of which we have often met before in photographs and have now had occasion to see magnificently arranged in this exhibition, and attempt to place them back into the living context of the Late Antique world. We can permit this world to breathe, for a moment, its own, unfamiliar air. By frankly allowing oneself to be bewitched by so much of the beauty and vigor of this art and by asking in what social setting it was first shown, the historian may stumble upon one of the most tantalizing features of Late Antique civilization itself. For in much of Late Antique art there is a splendidly un-self-conscious humanity, whose cumulative effect comes as a challenge to us, accustomed as we have become to a narrow canon of illustrations that stress the abstract, the majestic, or the otherworldly features of late antiquity. This quality of unalloyed delight seems to elude neat divisions between "pagan" and "Christian," "religious" and "secular," "classical" and "nonclassical." It is a reminder of the bedrock of shared humanity in a civilization that, for all its dramatic changes, was firmly held in the rhythms of Mediterranean life and that continued to draw, for secular as well as for religious purposes, on a long-established Mediterranean imagery to express common human needs and hopes—triumph, pleasure, and the yearning to "put off the cares of this life."

To set the works of Late Antique art in their social context involves something more than a feat of archaeological reconstruction, by which each detached fragment is fitted into its correct position. The attempt reveals something of the nature of Late Antique art itself. For this is an art whose most striking feature is that each artifact assumes a context and is fully intelligible only within such a context. Thus, the objects that we now see in an exhibition of Late Antique art are merely so many silent "stills" from what was once a film full of sound and movement.

Let us, therefore, look at a few of the main features of Late Antique society as these affected the way in which the visual arts were orchestrated.

We are dealing with a civilization in which, over large areas of the Mediterranean, the towns had survived, but had changed in style of life and structure. Much of Late Antique art is the art of the Greco-Roman city in its last, strange burst of vigor. The city remained the center of attention for Late Antique men because in one vital respect it had not changed. As always in the ancient world, the city continued to enjoy an importance quite out of proportion to its economic capacity. It was the backdrop against which the upper classes of the Empire acted out the long, intense play of wealth and power, and insured that they and their dependents ostentatiously enjoyed the amenities of civilized living. In the Late Antique suburban villas around Antioch, the local magnates still laid out mosaics declaring their intention to exercise, within the city, virtues dear to ancient man: *megalo-psychia*, civic generosity, and *apolausis*, the public enjoyment of the good things of life.[2]

A town, therefore, was less a center of production than a carefully nurtured oasis of civilized living. As Constantine wrote to his praetorian prefect about the small community of Orcistus in Galatia:

> For emperors such as ourselves, whose active concern it is to found new cities, to give back their ancient glory to those established long ago, and to restore to life those that have seemed to die, this request is most welcome. For they have claimed that their settlement has, for a long time, flourished with all the splendor of a town: it boasts magistrates holding annual office, it is frequented by civic dignitaries, its plentiful population call themselves "citizens." It is well placed at the joining of four highways, each provided with an official staging post. . . . And water is abundant there. There are baths, public and private; and the town is decorated with statues of the emperors of old. . . .[3]

Unimpressive though Orcistus might seem to us, by ancient standards it deserved to be a town.

Throughout the Late Antique period, to "renew" a city was the most praiseworthy achievement of the powerful.[4] The emphasis on renewal should not be seen merely as a nostalgic concession to the ideals of the classical past; nor need we assume that the "renewed" city had literally stood in ruins. "Renewal" might be no more than a token repair: in the sixth century A.D., a Cretan "renewed" his city by repairing the floor of one cistern.[5] In the eastern Mediterranean, throughout the Late Antique period, there was no lack of men anxious to leave their mark on their community by such gestures. The extent of Late Antique secular building in the Aegean cities of Sardis and Ephesus continues to take the archaeologist by surprise, as does the steadily expanding register of impressive churches, which came to cover the eastern provinces of the Empire from Asia Minor to the Negev.[6] The cumulative evidence for constant building activity, secular as well as ecclesiastical, is bound to modify the sheltered, inward-looking impression of Late Antique art that consideration of a few isolated artifacts might convey. This is not an art of remote shrines or of secluded palaces and country villas. Behind so much of it we can sense the weight of masonry piled up by a governing class determined that the towns and their immediate neighborhood should remain the well-lit stage on which they acted out their power and their culture.

The urge to build, in late antiquity as in earlier periods, grew from the bottom up. Building was part of the manner in which highly competitive local aristocracies had always both sought prestige and, at the same time, judiciously plowed back into the local community a portion of the profits of indecent success. A new building, therefore, registered new power and, at the same time, was an acceptable form of insurance premium against the risks accompanying new power. A well-to-do farmer who built a public bath at Serğilla in northern Syria in the fifth century stated quite frankly that, by such a gesture to his fellows, he had "chased away envy."[7]

The governing classes of the Late Antique world seem at first sight to be totally different from those oligarchies of civic grandees who, in the second century A.D., had decorated their cities with such seemingly effortless generosity. In fact, it was merely the structure of these classes and the nature of their recruitment that had changed. The need to display wealth in an urban setting and to ward off unpopularity among insecure and ambitious men was frequently present throughout the Late Antique period. In the fourth century, there were many imperial officials anxious, on their own account, to leave their mark on the towns of Africa, Greece, and the Aegean.[8] These were joined at the end of the century by the Christian bishops. Such men were hardly urban notables in the style of the Antonine age: their religion was comparatively new and their churches were often the first of their kind. Yet, by the undemanding standards that could make a city even of Orcistus, the late fourth and fifth centuries were a period of urban "renewal" under Christian patronage.

Bishops had not only to provide for newly expanded congregations. They were like their lay equivalents—men anxious to register their new position in Roman society and constantly threatened by rivals. Those who had come from upper-class backgrounds immediately brought with them the ancient reflexes of their class. As early as the reign of Constantine, we find the bishop Cyril Celer of Laodicaea Combusta in Phrygia describing his achievements:

> having been made bishop by the will of Almighty God; and having administered the episcopate for twenty-five years with great distinction; and having rebuilt from its foundations the entire church and all the adornment around it, consisting of stoa and tetrastoa and paintings and mosaics and fountain and outer gateway; and having furnished it with all the construction in masonry and, in a word, with every-

thing; and being about to leave the life of this world; I made for myself a plinth and a sarcophagus on which I caused the above to be engraved, for the distinction of the church and of my family.[9]

By the late fourth century, Alexander, the bishop of Tebessa in North Africa, could build a formidable pilgrimage shrine and proudly boast:

> This is not the work of any nobleman, but redounds to glory of the name of Alexander the bishop.[10]

In the controversy-ridden world of the mid-fifth-century Eastern Empire, the bishop who wished to survive had to pay in the ancient insurance premiums against the risks of success. Theodoret of Cyrrhus wrote in his own defense:

> When was I ever obnoxious to the many illustrious residents here? It is on the contrary well known to your excellency that I have spent a considerable part of my ecclesiastical revenues in erecting porticoes and baths, building bridges, and making further provision for public objects.[11]

When Theodoret built his church to house the relics of the apostles Peter and Paul, the ceremony of dedication was a bid to get the civic notables solidly behind him, quite irrespective of their beliefs:

> It was my wish to summon you [he wrote to one] to the feast of the holy Apostles and Prophets, not only as a citizen, but as one who shares both my faith and my home. But I am prevented by the state of your opinions. Therefore I put forward no other claims than those of our country. . . . This participation no difference of sentiment hinders.[12]

Not unnaturally, "lithomania" was the besetting sin of great bishops. Theophilus of Alexandria, for instance, broke with his second-in-command, the *economus* Isidore, because Isidore, knowing Theophilus, had kept back from him the money that a noblewoman had donated to buy clothes for the poor: Theophilus would have sunk it in stone.[13] In the sixth century, the emperor Justinian was forced to legislate against laymen who built churches without providing them with sufficient endowments to support a clergy and the running costs of the liturgy: the ancient reputation of *ktistés*, "founder," had been all that such donors had wanted.[14] Justinian's law assumes a background where prestige continued to be measured in stone.

Thus, faced by Christian works of art in late antiquity, we should be careful to look at the dedicatory inscriptions. These were carved on the portals of churches or, in the case of the more important ones,

were placed in mosaics, where the donor is shown holding the church, or they ring the splendid silverwork patens and chandeliers associated with the liturgy of the churches. Around the scenes that hold the attention of the art historian, such as the Communion of the Apostles on the Riha paten at Dumbarton Oaks [Cat. no. 547], we are plainly intended to see the inscription, carefully worked around the edge:

> For the peace of the soul of Sergia, [daughter] of John, and of Theodosius, and for the salvation of Megalos and Nonnous and their children.[15]

Such inscriptions take us into the human context that imbued each work of art and that gave it meaning to contemporaries. For beneath the Christian formulae—"in accordance with prayer," "for the repose of the soul," "for the remission of sins"—we can sense the unabated energies and the insecurities of the little groups of ruling families throughout the Empire, who continued to litter the landscape of the Mediterranean with amazing new buildings and to fill the treasuries of the churches with precious objects.

The emperor merely stood at the top of a pyramid of competitive builders. As in Hellenistic and Roman times, the emperor was no more than the urban benefactor writ large. If the majority of the Late Antique buildings best known to us—from Diocletian's Baths in Rome to Justinian's Hagia Sophia in Constantinople—are imperial, this merely registers the crushing superiority of the resources available to the emperor. Whenever direct comparisons are possible, they illustrate this clearly. Private persons, even Christian bishops with the accumulated wealth of their churches behind them, competed with "conventional" armaments against a patron who worked on a "nuclear" scale. Constantine could contribute 3.7 tons of silver and 300 kilograms of gold to the churches of Rome at a time when the bishop, Sylvester, contributed 55 kilograms of silver and one-third of a kilogram of gold.[16]

Yet, the cumulative impression, at least for the eastern Mediterranean, is of a society where the overpowering wealth of the emperors never extinguished private urges. Wealth and the motivation to spend were both present. So also was a principal prerequisite for rapid building: manpower. If anything, the eastern Mediterranean appears to have suffered not from a manpower shortage, but from something equally dangerous in a primitive economy—a population rise, or possibly, an increasing maldistribution of the population.[17] In the fifth and sixth centuries, as in the Northern Europe of the late thirteenth century, we have the sense of great buildings made possible by a weight of population pressing dangerously on the available resources. The decision to build was a moment of good cheer for a region condemned by shortage of land and the rhythms of a Mediterranean climate to months of unemployment.[18] When Bishop Porphyry began to build a great church at Gaza,

> the construction went ahead from day to day with great speed and enthusiasm. For no worker went short on his wages, but the bishop, as an act of public generosity—*philotimoumenos*—gave a bonus to the laborers. . . .[19]

We must set some of the greatest building works of the Late Antique period against this harsh background. Constantinople in the early sixth century was full of underemployed immigrants from the provinces.[20] There is little wonder that the city exploded in the great Nika, or "Victory," riot of 532. Justinian's ambitious building program formed one aspect of his anxious attempt to control the urban populations of the Empire. And the motivations that led to the rebuilding of the Hagia Sophia after the riot were as mixed as those of all other rulers placed in similar situations, from the emperor Augustus to the eighteenth-century sultan Moulay Ismail of Morocco:

> The Emperor is wonderfully addicted to building: yet it is a question whether he is more addicted to that, or pulling down, for they say if all his Buildings were now standing, by a moderate computation, they would reach to Fez, twelve leagues off; and those who have been near him since the beginning of his Reign, have observed him eternally building and pulling down, shutting up doors and breaking out new ones in the Walls. But he tells them this is done to occupy his People; for says he, if I have a Bag full of Ratts, unless I keep that Bag stirring they will eat their way through. . . .[21]

The unflagging urge to build, seen against a permanent urban backdrop, is an aspect of the civilization of late antiquity that we have come to appreciate recently, as our archaeological evidence for the eastern provinces of the Empire increases. It is closely related to a further aspect of Late Antique life: the careful elaboration and redefinition of the ceremonial life of the towns.

This aspect of late Roman life, as it is shown most clearly in the ceremonials of the imperial court, has recently been the subject of a series of most illuminating studies.[22] What emerges increasingly is that these are *urban* ceremonies: as a fourth-century rabbi said, "It is in the cities that the majesty of the king is shown."[23] Far from being conducted in the sheltered solemnity of a palace, late Roman ceremonial assumes an urban backdrop—the town gates of the city that the emperor visits, the open audience hall where the emperor receives his subjects, the imperial box in the circuses that adjoined all imperial palaces, of which the Hippodrome of Constantinople is the best known.[24] These ceremonials can hardly be called "court" ceremonies. They grew from the streets up. As with his buildings, so in the ceremonial surrounding his person, the emperor was the urban *philotimos*, the openhanded man of power. Hence, the ceremonies associated with the traditional demonstrations of local status by private citizens were merely absorbed into the imperial ceremonial. In cities where the local aristocracies remained strong, such as Rome and Antioch, or were increasingly overshadowed by the Christian bishop, as in Alexandria, this ceremonial was never limited exclusively to official and imperial occasions.[25]

In relation to imperial ceremonies, it has been pointed out that these were occasions on which sight and sound and even, we must remember, the magic of smell that meant so much to ancient men, were orchestrated into a single, satisfying whole:

> For the panegyrics [the speeches delivered on such occasions] bring out one aspect of the classical perception of a basic harmony between the different arts: visual and verbal expression were meant to go hand in hand.[26]

We should look with care at the way in which the works of art connected with imperial ceremonial or with the great *tableau vivant* of the Christian liturgy fitted into a single whole. What we now see are only so many fragments detached from a ceremonial setting whose core has vanished.

To take an obvious example, the carved frieze around the Arch of Constantine [Cat. no. 58] shows various ceremonial occasions: the emperor setting out, arriving, speaking in public, distributing largess. Each detail on this frieze, however, assumes an awareness of a closely knit complex of works of art that played a part in the ceremonies. In all such ceremonies, we begin with architectural settings that could range from the overwhelming decor of early fourth-century Rome, to the palaces, gates, and circuses of the new capitals at Trier and Constantinople,[27] to the cramped imperial residence of a little Near Eastern town on the road to the Persian frontier where, the emperor Julian complained, the inhabitants had overdone their ceremonial greeting with too much incense![28] We continue with magnificent gifts to privileged persons, such as the Missorium of Theodosius [Cat. no. 64].[29] The same ideas are clearly condensed in the seemingly random detail of the small gold coins issued for such occasions.[30]

What we now see was once part of a single whole, where many works of art converged with the spoken or sung word to create a single impression. In this situation, no work of art had to say any more than it was intended to say in its correct place and time. Just as the shared idiom of the classics could enable a speaker to set the tone of a whole train of thought with the help of one half line of Homer or Vergil, so the hand of God, the arch of a palace, or the position of a figure in relation to the top and bottom registers of a panel would be sufficient to set the scene in its correct context. For the rest, the speaker could assume a tissue of verbal and visual associations that have not survived in their full richness, but that were no less precise for being widespread and un-self-conscious. As Charles Pietri has recently written regarding the growth of the iconography of Sts. Peter and Paul in fourth-century Rome,

> Avant de rechercher les élaborations subtiles et réfléchies d'une ecclésiologie, l'enquête doit commencer par ces manifestations plus collectives et spontanés.[31]

Late Antique art is not an erudite or an esoteric art. But it is the art of a city, and an art that assumed onlookers who could supply the associations "triggered off" by a few clear pointers. One example, a fragment from Eunapius, an early fifth-century historian, enables us to appreciate how little of the *tableau vivant* of urban life has come down to us, for it refers to the painted billboards on which the emperor depicted his triumphs.[32] It also reveals a population that was expected to react to any change in the common meanings of Late Antique official art.

> Perses, prefect in [New] Rome, brought the good fortune of the Roman Empire into contempt and mockery. He set up many small billboards in the middle of the stadion, and wanting to express the imperial deeds in a picture, he made a laughing stock of his message and secretly held up what he had written to ridicule by means of the picture. For the picture showed nothing of the courage of the emperor, the strength of the soldiers or the course of an open and just war—merely a hand, as if coming out of the clouds, with the inscription: "The Hand of God chases away the barbarians."[33]

Yet to place too much emphasis on the imperial and the ecclesiastical aspects of the art of late antiquity is to allow its most tantalizing feature to slip between our fingers. The art of the emperors and of the Church was plainly a public, official art. But what has also survived in great quantities is the art of private persons—above all, of the aristocracy that, as courtiers, administrators, and great landowners, dominated late Roman society. And we have to explain the full-blooded secularity, expressed in continuing pagan imagery, of so many Late Antique works patronized by this aristocracy. To treat these works as survivals from an unregenerate pagan past, or as products of mindless traditionalism in the choice of motifs, or as a succession of self-conscious classical "revivals" taking place only in conservative circles is to misunderstand the power and the social relevance of much of the secular art of late antiquity.

We are dealing with an elusive phenomenon, one that had been building up for centuries in the Roman Empire: the continuation and re-formulation of paganism to create something new—a frankly secular heraldry of success.[34] The "classical" and the "pagan" tradition in late antiquity is not an inheritance of the past that gradually lost momentum. If anything, it took a new lease on life by being shaken, like the pieces of a kaleidoscope, into a different pattern to serve the needs of a different, postclassical society. The postclassical society of the fourth century saw the rise to power of a new class of magnates, men who had accumulated more wealth and power than had their more evenly balanced peers of the classical period. The traditional urban landscape in and around the cities was dominated by their new palaces.[35] In the countryside, too, their villas were maintained with a splendor equal to a townhouse.[36] The great estate and the joys of the hunt complemented the more urban theater in which their power was shown.[37] The many Late Antique mosaics from the floors of such palaces and villas, and the astonishing textiles that have survived in the dry sands of Egypt, give some idea of the splendor of the buildings with their curtained colonnades.[38] There is a colorfulness, a fantasy, and a frank use of pagan themes whose very robustness comes as a surprise.

Yet, it should hardly come as a surprise. The new elites of the late Roman world may have lived in a "postclassical" society; but it was not a "*non*classical" society. They still breathed the air of the classical world, and to expect them to breathe any other would be like expecting the inhabitants of this planet to dispense with breathing oxygen. To the Late Antique world, the classical tradition was not what it has become for us, a distant ideal that could be "revived" or imitated at will: it was simply the only tradition that was known to work.[39] And it was irreplaceable, largely because it contained so many of the mythological motifs that still summed up more appositely than could any other available tradition the high moments, the hopes, and the turning points in the life of the *homme moyen sensuel.*[40]

Why this should have been so in an age that saw the final establishment of Christianity as the major religion of the Mediterranean world always remains something of a puzzle, especially so to anyone confronted with the uninhibited use of pagan mythological scenes in Late Antique art. In order to explain it, we have to explain an "air-pocket" in Late Antique Christianity. Throughout the Late Antique period, Christianity was a strict, "otherworldly" religion only for a minority of monks and, with far greater difficulty, some clergymen and a few quite exceptional laymen who had opted to follow the teachings of Christ in their entirety.[41] The remainder of the faithful were frankly accepted to be "men of this world"—*kosmikoi, saeculares.* The clergy and the few ascetic heroes might bring into their lives a touch of the otherworld; but the *kosmikoi,* the men and women caught in the hard disciplines of mundane life, were left by their leaders to find their own, strictly secular, ways of expressing how they stood in this world.[42] It was not the business of the monks and bishops to offer a more Christian version of worldly life. They could only offer its antithesis—a life committed to the otherworld. Thus, the perfectionism of the few full adherents to the Christian message left behind them a moral vacuum that the majority of average Christians filled with gusto from the traditions that lay at hand. The secularity of large areas of the society of the Christian Roman Empire, therefore, stood massively intact.

As a result, the Late Antique period was an "age of spirituality" only for a small, and frequently disapproving, minority. For the majority of the inhabitants of the Christianized Empire, and especially for those successful enough in the world to afford the heavy outlay involved in patronizing the arts, it was a time when they enjoyed as best they could the centuries-old traditions of urban life. Take, for example, Edessa, the oldest Christian city in the Near East, but one that lay on the periphery of the culture of the classical Greco-Roman world. As late as the end of the fifth century, the secular life of this successful frontier city of the Eastern Empire could only be expressed in terms borrowed from the old pagan culture. This is how a monk observed his undoubtedly Christian fellows behaving on one festival:

> Whilst these things were taking place, there came round again the time of that festival at which the heathen tales were sung; and the citizens took even more pains about it than usual. For seven days previously they were going up in crowds to the theatre at eventide, clad in linen garments, and wearing turbans, with their loins ungirt. Lamps were lighted before them, and they were burning incense, and holding vigils the whole night, walking about the city and praising the dancer until morning, with singing and shouting and lewd behavior.[43]

For such men, the classical tradition, despite its overpowering pagan associations, was simply part of the hard-won skill of living in a Mediterranean environment. The traditional images had become part of a neutral technology of life. It would be as unreal to expect the leaders of Late Antique Christianity to have successfully "Christianized" this tradition in their art and literature as it would be to expect modern men to "Christianize" the design of an automobile or to produce a "Marxist" wrist watch. Thus, when pagan motifs were used in the works of art they commissioned, the aristocrats of the Late Antique world were usually as insensible to their former religious overtones as were the English country gentlemen who, over a thousand years later, shocked Puritan writers by turning yet again to the unfailing reserves of classical imagery in order to decorate their tombs in a manner that did justice to their social status:

> And which is worse, they garnish their Tombes nowadays, with the pictures of naked men and women; raising out of the dust, and bringing into the church, memories of the Heathen gods and goddesses, with all their whirligiggs: and this (as I take it) is more the fault of the Tombe makers, then theirs who set them aworke.[44]

What is important to note, therefore, is not that the motifs of Late Antique art remained largely pagan and were constantly reiterated, often by known Christian patrons, but exactly which motifs were mobilized most frequently and for what purpose. The common theme of so much of the classical imagery of late antiquity is triumph and good living. It is an imagery that was retained and amplified so as to make plain the *phantasia,* the "pomp and circumstance," of the wealthy—hence, the frequency of hunting and circus themes. For in town and country alike, the hunt and the circus were the theater in

which ancient men performed in public the play of
fortune and success.[45] The moments of contained
competitive violence that were acted out in the circus, in the form of wild-beast shows and chariot races,
were essential to the life of the Late Antique city.
They were more than random sporting occasions.
Symbolized in these games was the good fortune of
the magnates in general, and of the greatest magnate of them all, the emperor. A mystique of imperial success, totally non-Christian in expression yet
unconnected with the ancient forms of classical pagan worship, came to be associated with the chariot
races in the Hippodrome of Constantinople.[46]
Christian clergymen were allowed to attend these
hauntingly pagan occasions because, as a later can-
onist observed, the emperor was always present and,
consequently, no harm need come to a tender
Christian conscience.[47]

Altogether, one cannot resist the impression that
many ancient themes were subtly orchestrated and
simplified in the Late Antique period, and that, if
anything, a stronger current runs through them. Isolated figures have a majesty that is often lacking in
the previous mythological tradition. "Personifications" in Late Antique art are not airy abstractions:
they add the weight of personality to deeply held
ideas. Thus, the figures of the Tyche, the "Good Fortune" of the individual cities of the Empire, gained
in supernatural "presence" [Cat. nos. 153–56].[48] Such
figures stepped confidently into a gap that had
opened up in men's minds between a very remote
Christian God and a city whose vicissitudes still mattered to them. The "inconsequential talk" that a sixth-
century monk might indulge in continued to hinge
on "agitation in the city, its peace and its prosperity";[49]
and when this peace was disrupted in early seventh-
century Thessalonike, the inhabitants were reas-
sured not by a vision of St. Demetrius, but by the
appearance at his side of Lady Eutaxia, the personification of good order, bringing to bear the full weight
of her almost divine power.[50] It is the same with
more private images. The Hestia Polyolbos now at
Dumbarton Oaks once hung as the symbol of the
good fortune of a great Egyptian nobleman's house.
She may strike us as "a document of a dying paganism," but she does not seem to have grown pale.[51]
The art of late antiquity makes plain that she had
come to stay. As long as the secular framework of the
later Empire survived intact, the new classes that
gained predominance within it needed an imagery
with which to express their hopes and ambitions.
Hence, the paradox that pagan motifs and new forms

of ceremonial intimately connected with the pagan
past were recurrently injected into the life of a self-
confident Christian aristocracy. A generation after
public paganism had declined in the cities in the
early fourth century, the feast of the Kalends of
January—a feast previously limited to Rome in the
classical Roman Empire—spread from one end of
Romania to the other.[52] It spread because it was a
feast connected with a new ceremonial of power: the
entry into office of the consuls, whose ceremonial
status had been vastly expanded by Constantine. It
was associated with the formal receptions and the
gift-giving that linked the great men to their clients.
The celebration was not a feast of the gods, but a
feast of men entering unashamedly into the enjoyment of power and prosperity. It lasted through the
centuries, deep into the Middle Ages, to disturb the
Christian bishops with annual reminders of the
natural "man of the world" and his aspirations, expressed with all the full-blooded ceremoniousness of
the Late Antique city, splendidly untinctured by the
new faith.

Yet, the Christian bishops were very often the
brothers and the uncles of the men who displayed
their power with such exuberance.[53] They shared
the same Mediterranean culture and created for
themselves similarly extroverted ways of showing the
majesty of their new religion. The great celebrations
of Easter, especially if they coincided with the dedication of a new church, were a faithful echo of the
openhanded *euphrosyne*, the "good cheer," expected
of an urban magnate. Porphyry of Gaza

> gathered the monks of the neighborhood together, a
> thousand of them, and the other pious clerics, laymen
> and bishops and held good cheer—*epoiésen euphrosy-*
> *nén*—all the days of Easter. And it was as if one could
> see the angelic choirs, not only during the service in
> the church, but around the banqueting table. . . . For
> after meat, psalms were chanted, and hymns followed
> the drinking.[54]

Very often in the sixth century, the two strands coincided. The secular good fortune of the little communities of the eastern Mediterranean was held to
depend to such an extent on the vicarious intercession of monks and clergy that at Qasr el-Lebya the
Tyche of the city, symbol of urban prosperity, could
appear inside the church.[55]

In many ways, Late Antique Christianity was not
"otherworldly" in the rarefied sense that is usually
associated with this period. For this "otherworld"
was no abstraction; it was a precise place, paradise.
The solemn liturgy, the blaze of lights, the shimmer-

ing mosaics, and the brightly colored curtains of a Late Antique church were there to be appreciated in their entirety. As with imperial ceremonials, these trappings should not be detached from one another.[56] Taken altogether, they provided a glimpse of paradise. For this reason alone, one should not make too much of the reservations that Early Christians are supposed to have had about the representation of human beings, nor of the later lifting of this inhibition with the cult of icons.[57] To do so would be an error in perspective. The representational elements in Late Antique Christian mosaics are a subject of absorbing interest to us. But these elements would have been swamped in the overwhelming impression conveyed by the building, its overall decoration, and its liturgy. In a Late Antique church, the processional movements, the heavy silver of the sacred vessels and the bindings of the Gospel books [Cat. nos. 531–41] as they flashed by on their way to the altar, the mysterious opacity of the curtains shrouding the entrance (even if the curtain itself might have been woven with frankly secular scenes[58]), these things in themselves were the visual "triggers" of a Late Antique worshiper's sense of majesty.

Indeed, it is in such terms that Late Antique sources describe their churches. To these writers, churches are not iconographical puzzles. They are *ho topos*: the "place," where it was possible to share for a moment in the eternal repose of the saints in paradise. Light seems trapped in the churches.[59] The blaze of lamps and gold mosaic recapture the first moment of Creation: "Dark chaos is fled away."[60] They are heavy with incense, which brought into this world a touch of paradise, conceived as a mountain covered with trees in full bloom.[61] Their floors even attempt to catch the same sense of ease and release from care that forms such a poignant theme in the private mansions of the great from Hellenistic times up to the establishment of Islam and beyond: one church could even be described as a meadow blooming with flowers.[62] In the northern Syrian church of Ḥuarte, Adam sits with imperial serenity among the beasts in a paradise regained.[63] Two churches, the one near the dangerous mountains of Isauria and the other set up by its bishop, "a man of subtle mind," in Apamea, a city with a tradition of philosophical leisure, have mosaics depicting the coming of the Kingdom of Peace among the wild animals scattered on the floor.[64] Christians hoped to find in their shrines a "place of fulfillment and sweet perfume,"[65] the echo of a rest beyond the grave in what was still a very classical landscape—because it was a human and a Mediterranean one, "in a grassy place by refreshing waters, whence pain and suffering and groaning have fled."[66]

NOTES

1. H. I. Marrou, *Saint Augustin et la fin de la culture antique: Retractatio*, Paris, 1949, p. 693. See now his *Décadence romaine ou antiquité tardive?*, Paris, 1977.

2. E. Patlagean, *Pauvreté économique et pauvreté sociale à Byzance*, Paris, 1977, pp. 181–96. D. Levi, *Antioch Mosaic Pavements*, Princeton, 1947, p. 304.

3. *Fontes Iuris Romani Anteiustiniani*, S. Riccobono, ed., Florence, 1968, I, p. 462.

4. L. Robert, "Epigrammes du Bas-Empire," *Hellenica*, IV, 1948, p. 14, note 5.

5. A. C. Bandy, *The Greek Christian Inscriptions of Crete*, Athens, 1970, p. 63, no. 33.

6. P. Brown, *The Making of Late Antiquity*, Cambridge, Mass., 1978, pp. 29 and 111–12 for bibliography. C. Lepelley and B. Beaujare, "Du nouveau sur les villes de l'Afrique romaine au temps de saint Augustin," *Revue des études augustiniennes*, XXIII, 1977, pp. 422–31. H. C. Butler, *Early Churches in Syria*, Princeton, 1929. J. Lassus, *Les sanctuaires chrétiens de Syrie*, Paris, 1947. G. Tchalenko, *Les Villages antiques de la Syrie du Nord*, Paris, 1958. A. Ovadiah, *Corpus of the Byzantine Churches in the Holy Land*, Bonn, 1970 (Theophaneia, XXII).

7. *Inscriptions grecques et latines de la Syrie*, A. Poidebard and R. Mouterde, eds., IV, Paris, 1955, no. 1490.

8. L. Robert, "Epigrammes du Bas-Empire," pp. 35–114.

9. *Monumenta Asiae Minoris Antiqua*, W. M. Calder, ed., Manchester, 1928, I, p. 89, no. 170.

10. E. Diehl, *Inscriptiones Latinae Veteres Christianae*, Berlin, 1925, I, no. 1825. See now J. Christern, *Das frühchristliche Pilgerheiligtum von Tebessa*, Wiesbaden, 1976.

11. Theodoret, Epistle 81, B. Jackson, ed., New York, 1892 (Select Library of Nicene and Post-Nicene Fathers).

12. Theodoret, Epistle 68, B. Jackson, ed.

13. Palladius *Dialogus de vita Johannis* 6, Migne, *PG*, XLVII, col. 22.

14. Justinian *Novella* 67, R. Schoell and W. Kroll, eds., *Corpus Juris Civilis*, III, Berlin, 1928.

15. Handbook of the Byzantine Collection, Dumbarton Oaks, Washington, D.C., 1967, p. 17, no. 61.

16. C. Pietri, *Roma Christiana*, Paris, 1977, I, p. 84.

17. E. Patlagean, *Pauvreté économique . . .* , pp. 426–27.

18. *Inscriptions grecques et latines de la Syrie*, A. Poidebard and R. Mouterde, eds., V, Paris, 1959, no. 1999.

19. Marc le Diacre *Vie de Porphyre* 83, H. Grégoire and M.-A. Kugener, eds., Paris, 1930, pp. 65–66.

20. Justinian *Novella* 80, R. Schoell and W. Kroll, eds. E. Patlagean, *Pauvreté économique . . .* , pp. 179–81.

21. J. Windus, *A Journey to Mequinez*, London, 1725, pp. 115–16. See P. Brunt, "The Roman Mob," *Past & Present*, XXXV, 1966, pp. 14–16.

22. See, for example, S. G. MacCormack, "Latin prose Panegyrics: tradition and discontinuity in the late Roman Empire," *Revue des études augustiniennes*, XXII, 1976, pp. 29–77, esp. p. 42.

23. *Pesikta Rabbati*, M. Friedmann, ed., Vienna, 1880, p. 95a.

24. J. H. Humphrey, "Prolegomena to the Study of the Hippodrome at Caesarea," *Bulletin of The American School of Oriental Research*, CCXIII, 1974, pp. 2–45. V. Popović and E. L. Ochsenslager, "Der spätantike Hippodrom in Sirmium," *Germania*, LIV, 1976, pp. 156–81.

25. As is shown in the case of the translation of relics by Christian bishops. See N. Gussone, "Adventus-Zeremoniell und Translation von Reliquien," *Frühmittelalterliche Studien*, X, 1976, p. 128.

26. S. G. MacCormack, "Latin prose Panegyrics . . . ," p. 46.

27. Ibid., pp. 42–43.

28. Julian, Epistle 58, W. C. Wright, ed., *The Works of the Emperor Julian*, III, Cambridge, Mass., 1953.

29. R. MacMullen, "The Emperor's Largesses," *Latomus*, XXI, 1962, pp. 159 ff.

30. H. Mattingly, "The Imperial 'Vota'," *Proceedings of the British Academy*, XXVI, 1950, pp. 155–95 and XXVII, 1951, pp. 219–68.

31. C. Pietri, *Roma Christiana*, p. 317.

32. One dearly wishes that the pictures of pantomimes, charioteers, and wild-beast fighters that cluttered and obscured the imperial images in public places had also survived. For references to these scenes, see *Codex Theodosianus* 15. 17, 12, T. Mommsen, ed., Berlin, 1954.

33. Eunapius, fragment 178, C. Mueller, ed., *Fragmenta Historicorum Graecorum*, IV, Paris, 1868.

34. The process by which the cultic associations of pagan motifs came to be eclipsed by their use as status symbols had been long underway in the Roman Empire. See Tertullian *De idololatria* 8.4: "Frequentior est omni superstitione luxuria et ambitio. Lances et scyphos facilius ambitio quam superstitio desiderabit. Coronas quoque magis luxuria quam sollemnitas erogat"; A. Reifferscheid and G. Wissowa, eds., *Corpus Christianorum*, II, 2, Turnholt, 1954. Cultivated Christians could take part as competitors in festivals in the third century. See L. Robert, *Hellenica*, XI–XII, 1960, p. 424: "Le fait est à noter, et on peut penser que . . . le côté 'spectacles' s'emportait à cette époque sur le sens cultuel des cérémonies."

35. P. Brown, *The Making of Late Antiquity*, pp. 49 and 116.

36. R. Paribeni, "Le dimore dei potentiores nel Basso Impero," *Römische Mitteilungen*, LV, 1940, pp. 144–54. E.B. Thomas, *Römische Villen in Pannonien*, Budapest, 1964. M. Cagiano de Azevedo, "Ville rustiche tardoantiche e installazioni agricole altomedioevali," *XIII Settimana di studi del Centro di studi sull'alto Medio Evo*, Spoleto, 1966, pp. 663 ff.

37. H. Brandenburg, "Bellerophon christianus?" *Römische Quartalschrift*, LXIII, 1968, pp. 49–86. K. M. D. Dunbabin, *The Mosaics of Roman North Africa: Studies in Iconography and Patronage*, Oxford, 1978.

38. V. Gervers, "An Early Christian Curtain in the Royal Ontario Museum," *Studies in Textile History in Memory of Harold B. Burnham*, V. Gervers, ed., Toronto, 1977, pp. 56–81.

39. This is well put by J. Christern, *Frühchristliches Pilgerheiligtum*, p. 260: "Die Situation der Spätantike war ja anders als z.B. die des 19.Jhts, in dem man für verschiedene Bauaufgaben den jeweils passend erscheinenden Stil wählen und anwenden konnte; vielmehr gab es für die Wahl der Stilmittel grundsätzlich nur eine Alternative: entweder verzichtete man auf architektonischen Schmuck, oder man griff, wenn Aufwands- und Repräsentationsformen erforderlich schienen, zum klassischen Formapparat; er war der einzige, der dafür zur Verfügung stand."

40. See J. Fink, "Mythologische und biblische Themen in der Sarkophagplastik des 3. Jahrhunderts," *Rivista de Archeologia Cristiana*, XXVII, 1951, pp. 167–89.

41. N. H. Baynes, "The Thought World of East Rome," *Byzantine Studies and other Essays*, London, 1960, pp. 26–27.

42. P. Brown, "The Rise and Function of the Holy Man in Late Antiquity," *Journal of Roman Studies*, LXI, 1972, pp. 97–100: A. H. M. Jones, *The Later Roman Empire*, Oxford, 1964, I, pp. 979–85.

43. *The Chronicle of Joshua the Stylite*, W. Wright, ed., Cambridge, 1882, pp. 20–21, 30.

44. J. Weever, *Ancient Funerall Monuments*, London, 1631, cited in A. Ludwig, *Graven Images*, Middletown, Conn., 1966, p. 57.

45. H. Brandenburg, "Bellerophon christianus?" pp. 71–72. K. M. D. Dunbabin, *The Mosaics of Roman North Africa*, pp. 46–108.

46. A. Cameron, *Circus Factions*, Oxford, 1976, pp. 157–92 and 201–34.

47. Theodorus Balsamon *Comment. in Canones*, Migne, *PG*, CXXXVII, col. 593 B.

48. S. G. MacCormack, "Roma, Constantinopolis, the Emperor and his Genius," *Classical Quarterly*, XXV, 1975, pp. 131–50.

49. *Barsanuphe et Jean de Gaze: Correspondance*, L. Regnault and P. Lemaire, trans., Solesmes, 1972, p. 317.

50. *Miracula Sancti Demetrii*, Migne, *PG*, CXVI, col. 1268 A.

51. P. Friedländer, *Documents of Dying Paganism*, Berkeley and Los Angeles, 1945, pp. 1–26.

52. M. Meslin, *La fête des Kalendes de janvier dans l'empire romain*, Brussels, 1970.

53. A. Rousselle, "Aspects sociaux du recrutement écclésiastique au IVᵉ siècle," *Mélanges de l'Ecole française de Rome*, LXXXIX, 1977, pp. 333–70.

54. Marc le Diacre *Vie de Porphyre* 92, p. 71.

55. A. Grabar, "La Mosaïque de pavement de Qasr el-Lebya," *Comptes Rendus de l'Académie des Inscriptions et Belles Lettres*, June 1969, pp. 264–82.

56. T. F. Mathews, *The Early Churches of Constantinople: Architecture and Liturgy*, University Park, Pa., 1971.

57. For a long overdue and effective refutation of this view, see M. Murray, "Art and the Early Church," *Journal of Theological Studies*, n.s. XXVIII, 1977, pp. 303–45.

58. M. Murray, "Art and the Early Church," p. 340. V. Gervers, "An Early Christian Curtain," pp. 68–72.

59. *Inscriptiones Latinae Veteres Christianae*, I, no. 1770.

60. *Inscriptiones Latinae Veteres Christianae*, I, no. 1769 A.

61. Gregory of Tours *Libri Historiarum* 2. 31, Migne, *PL*, LXXI, col. 226, on the baptism of Clovis: "talemque ibi gratiam adstantibus tribuit, ut aestimarent se paradisi odoribus collocari."

62. Gregory of Nyssa *Encomium in Theodorum*, Migne, *PG*, XLVI, col. 737 D.

63. M.-T. and P. Canivet, "La mosaïque d'Adam dans l'église syrienne d'Hūarte (Vᵉ s.)," *Cahiers archéologiques*, XXIV, 1975, pp. 49–60.

64. M. Gough, "The peaceful Kingdom," *Mélanges A.M. Mansel*, Ankara, 1974, pp. 411–19. J. C. Balty, 'L'évêque Paul et le programme architectural et décoratif de la cathédrale d'Apamée," *Mélanges d'Histoire ancienne et d'archéologie offerts à Paul Collart*, P. Ducrey, ed., Lausanne, 1976, pp. 31–46, esp. 41–44.

65. *Miracula Sancti Demetrii*, Migne, *PG*, CXVI, col. 1213 C.

66. J. Doresse and E. Lanne, *Un témoin archaïque de la liturgie copte de S. Basile*, Louvain, 1960 (Bibliothèque de Muséon), p. 28.

HANS-GEORG BECK

Constantinople:
The Rise of a New Capital in the East

CONSTANTINOPLE and her splendor: a fascinating and almost misleading topic; so fascinating that not a few Byzantinists and art historians, praising the glory of the city, apparently forget some essential laws of history—for example, that even the rise of Constantinople must have taken time, that it did not burst forth with Constantine the Great, pacing the far-reaching new circuit of his foundation under divine guidance. And there are other scholars who ask if it is really true that this city, from its beginnings, was radiating, that from its beginnings it was the pivot of politics, the center of art and erudition, and the source of Christian life in the East.

The validity of the question is self-evident.[1] Rome was not built in a day; nor was Constantinople, though it is surprising how rapidly she developed into a big city of worldwide importance. For some of the local Byzantine historians this development approaches a wonder. But the wonder may be reduced to a less miraculous dimension by taking into consideration that Constantine's city was built on older foundations. Forgetting the fabulous city of the ancient King Byzas and the Megarean Byzantion, let us turn to the important events that took place in the reign of the Roman emperor Septimius Severus.[2] It is true that in 196 he destroyed the old Byzantion because she had fought on the wrong political side. But soon after this catastrophe, the emperor realized the outstanding value of the city's geographical location in the midst of a new political constellation.[3] Septimius Severus and his successors therefore began to rebuild the city and to give her quite a different, almost an imperial, dimension. With a new wall they doubled the area, and with new buildings sought to answer the needs of imperial representation. There

was the Tetrastoon, a spacious stoa, later called Augusteion; the Kynegion, a circus for animal hunts; large baths—the so-called Baths of Zeuxippus; and a huge hippodrome to compete with the Circus Maximus in Rome.

All these buildings, characteristic of an opulent Hellenistic town, were already there when Constantine arrived. Around them he focused his own plans. From the beginning, the older imperial structures formed the center of Constantine's new foundation, and he envisioned an imperial palace, a senate house, and perhaps a big church to complete the architectural ensemble. Despite Constantine's reliance on his predecessors' accomplishments, one cannot diminish the merit of his own achievements. On the contrary, he succeeded in enlarging the area of the city by at least two-hundred percent, so that ultimately it was but little smaller than the area of Rome within the Aurelian walls. Nevertheless, Constantine had at best eight or ten years in which to execute his plans. And in this period, regardless of what the panegyrists may claim, Constantinople was not finished. Many buildings—churches, palaces, baths, and so on—were finished by his successors. The first Hagia Sophia, for instance, should be attributed to Constantius rather than to Constantine. The vast baths, the so-called Constanti(ni)anae, were begun after Constantine's death. Even the final consecration of the Church of the Apostles did not take place before 370. In short, the local authors of the *Patria Konstantinupoleos* took pains to attribute to Constantine far more buildings than he was actually able to initiate or complete.

Still, there is no doubt that the contractors and masons of Constantinople had much to do, and that they could pile up orders. Money was readily available because the whole treasury of Licinius had fallen into Constantine's hands.[4] But what about the artists? Although I would not exceed my limits and speak of Constantinian art, I suspect that artists had less to do than one would like to suppose. The verdict of St. Jerome is well known: "Constantinopolis dedicatur paene omnium urbium nuditate" ("Constantinople was dedicated by denuding almost all the other cities").[5] Jerome had a sharp tongue, but it is not easy to refute him on this point. He had, after all, spent several years in the city. Moreover, his "nuditate omnium urbium" was taken up by a witness of quite another turn of mind, Eusebius of Caesarea: "The sanctuaries of the other cities were denuded," he tells us, and the new city was full of brazen votive offerings that had been brought to Constantinople from the provinces. Eusebius thinks—or pretends to think—that all of these works of art had been displayed in Constantinople so that Christians could more easily insult the dethroned deities.[6] He mentions the Delphian tripod, two statues of Apollo, and several statues of the Muses. Furthermore, there is also the famous anonymous description of the eighty statues in the Baths of Zeuxippus.[7] Perhaps they were already in place before Constantine. But if it was the emperor who installed them, it is not likely that about the year 330 he would have ordered eighty new statues of pagan heroes and deities. In other words, these statues, too, must have been fetched from somewhere outside Constantinople. I think that in the beginning, and perhaps until the reign of Theodosius I, the attraction of the new capital for an artist in many cases lay less in the availability of employment than in the opportunity to see and study the art of the past in a kind of grand museum. At least this was true insofar as sculptors were concerned. Architects and builders probably had more to do in Constantine's time, although it should be noted that a lot of them seem to have done sloppy work. Authors of the following generation, at any rate, are surprised by the rapid turn of the new buildings and the necessity to repair them so soon;[8] the decades of scaffoldings apparently were not yet over.

The population of Constantinople grew enormously. Construction of the necessary housing and facilities was aided by considerable financial aid from the government, at least until the second half of the century. Senators of Rome were invited to come, and there can be no doubt that some families followed the invitation—certainly not members of those old

gentes, who were especially proud of the mores maiorum, but more likely those who, economically or politically, had gone bankrupt. They were enticed by the privileges granted by the emperor. Constantinople guaranteed them a new material start and, at the same time, a new prestige. Other people sought contact with the court and the bureaucracy, applying for positions in the administration. Adventurers came, fortune hunters, tradesmen and craftsmen, artists and doctors, beggars and schoolmasters. Most of them may have hoped to get a chance. But even when the chance did not appear, they stayed on, increasing the proletarian masses, which from the beginning must have amounted to a considerable part of the population.

Then the inevitable happened: the area became too small and the emperors started to extend the city limits. Already since 384, new walls including a new area were ventilated. In the meantime, houses were built on drained swamps and on pilework near the coast.[9] Under the emperor Theodosius II, new walls were finally built, not exclusively for protecting the barracks of the garrison, but also for protecting the defenseless suburbs.[10] Indeed, by the year 400, Constantinople probably could boast a population of two hundred thousand. Thus, we have to deal with a considerable urban development. The question is whether the development of Constantinople as a predominant political center was keeping pace with this urban development. In answer, it is obvious that the political importance of the city was dependent on the stabilization of the imperial court and the imperial administration within the city itself, that is, on the "domestication" of the Domus Augusta, which thus far had been a wandering comitiva, a retinue of the emperor in his role as commander of the wandering exercitus Romanus. And it is surprising how long it took until this process came to an end.

How many months or years Constantine himself spent in his new capital is difficult to determine. With some hesitation, I would say perhaps half of his remaining years, although probably even less. The actual residence of his son Constantius between 338 and 350 was not Constantinople, but Antioch. Then he left for Milan, returning after some time to Antioch. Constantinople, as far as we know, saw her emperor only occasionally and then only for brief periods. For the emperor Julian, Constantinople was hardly more than a transit station on his way from Paris through the Balkans to Antioch. Valens can be found everywhere, but seldom in Constantinople. It seems as if the city could not play a part in his life, and the city probably knew it. Theodosius I, from 380 to 387, shuttled between Thessalonike, Adrianopolis, Sirmium, Aquileia, Verona, and, once in a while, Constantinople. From 387 to 391 Theodosius remained in the West. Only from 391 to 394 may Constantinople be called his residence. He then returned to Rome and soon moved on to Milan, where he died in 395. It is only with the son of Theodosius, the emperor Arcadius, that the court begins to stay in Constantinople more or less permanently or, as Synesius put it, "that the emperor clings to this city."[11] But for nearly seventy years before, the future of the city trembled in the balance, and it sometimes seemed as if Antioch or Milan would win the race.

With regard to Constantinople as a religious and ecclesiastical center, the year 381 would seem to be of decisive importance. In this year, a synod of bishops met in Constantinople at what was later called the Second Ecumenical Council. The third canon of the synod runs as follows: "The bishop of Constantinople has the primacy of honor (*proteia times*) after the bishop of Rome, because this city is the New Rome." Some scholars maintain that this decision was quite an obvious one for Eastern Christianity. I cannot agree. That Constantinople, an imperial city, was taken out of the ecclesiastical jurisdiction of the metropolis Heraclea—if she ever belonged to it—is not surprising. But Constantinople's newly won precedence over Antioch and even Alexandria, though only honorary, is quite another, more serious, thing. Antioch could merit precedence by virtue of the canonical Acts of the Apostles, which relate that St. Peter stayed within her walls. Antioch eventually regarded St. Peter as her first bishop, thus claiming the apostolicity of her see, one that chronologically preceded even the apostolicity of the see of Rome, apostolicity in these times being the decisive point.[12] Alexandria held that the evangelist Luke was the founder of her church, a tradition soon overlapped by another one, namely, that it was the evangelist Mark who had converted the city to Christianity. Based on these pretensions of apostolicity and backed by the old cities' enormous political and economic weight, which defied competition by any other Eastern town, the two sees hitherto had played a greater part in ecclesiastical affairs than had Constantinople. Indeed, Constantinople is mentioned only occasionally in contemporary ecclesiastical annals. The see of Constantinople does not turn up in the lists of the famous First Ecumenical Council of Nicaea; not one synod gathered there whose canons were worthy to be collected; nothing could be found that might have justified any primacy. In Alexandria, the theology of the divine Logos had been created, and Antioch could boast of her own sober theological line. A Constantinopolitan contribution to the theological development does not exist. Gregory of Nazianzus, bishop of Constantinople during the council of 381, as a theologian belongs to Asia Minor. The Arian party in Constantinople insulted him as an intruder who, in addition, spoke a provincial Greek.[13] The big names during the Arian quarrels are all to be found outside of Constantinople. And when Theodosius I restored Nicene orthodoxy, he did not refer to the faith of Constantinople, but rather to the faith of Rome and Alexandria.[14] Before Gregory of Nazianzus, only one outstanding name—Eusebius of Nicomedia—ranks among the bishops of Constantinople, and the city was already his third bishopric, and then for but a few years. As a whole, the ecclesiastical history of Constantinople in the fourth century is an imbroglio and a rather insignificant one at that.

In one sense, fourth-century religious life is better represented by monasticism than by the ecclesiastical hierarchy. But when we consider Constantinopolitan monasticism, the results remain to a certain degree equally dubious.[15] The fifteen monasteries founded by Constantine the Great in less than seven years are creations of the imagination as are the monasteries founded by his mother, Helen. The historical beginning of monasticism in the second half of the century is rather strange and controversial. Flight from the world—Constantinople *was* the world—apparently played a smaller part than the attractiveness of the capital. The delight in meddling with politics in Constantinople developed much more quickly than in the back country of Alexandria. Whereas the religious achievements of Alexandrian monks are conspicuous, the contributions of Constantinopolitan monks to this field are meager. There is nobody in Constantinople like Euagrius Ponticus, author of a sublime system of spiritual life, which he created in the desert and for the desert. Nor can we find in Constantinople those *Apophthegmata Patrum*, the "Sayings of the Fathers," that are the definitive expression of spiritual concentration, the very nourishment for hungry souls who could not be satisfied by dry, dogmatic formulas. One is tempted to see this monasticism in the light of an event at the Council of Chalcedon in 451, when eighteen abbots of Constantinople signed a petition in favor of a monophysite heretic. The fathers at the council, apparently surprised by the large number of Constantinopolitan abbots, examined the signatures and discovered that only three belonged to genuine abbots of genuine monasteries. Some of the others could not be identified at all—perhaps they were "dead souls"—and the rest turned out to be vagabonds, impostors, or simple guardians of small chapels.[16]

Concerning the religious life of "the people," general statements are extremely dangerous. To sum up some impressions is simply inadequate, so I will limit myself to one point only. Gregory of Nazianzus, ordered to convert Constantinople from Arianism to orthodoxy, was soon captivated by the city and its inhabitants. However, analyzing his lack of success in the first months, he found out that the real problem was not so much the Arian resistance, but the totally unreligious and secular attitudes of the population. Of course, all the preachers of the time intentionally exaggerated for the sake of rhetorical amplification. But Gregory was really fond of the city, and he wanted to show his congregation in the best light. Still, he had to admit that the overwhelming interests of the inhabitants were concentrated less on questions of Christian life or Christian faith than on an inopportune pride in their city—on showpieces, races, and on the display of sumptuousness.[17]

Yet, in the end, I would not say that Constantinople was without ecclesiastical importance. But the point of reference was not the Church as such, or the bishopric. It made a deep impression that the Empire should be centered around a Christian city, Constantinople, rather than heathen Rome. But the practical impulses were focused less on a spiritual center than on the bureaucracy, the court, when it was in residence, and the emperor. One of the startling secondary phenomena of the new system, which I would like to call "political orthodoxy," was that again and again many provincial bishops, sneering at the decisions of the competent synods, even ecumenical ones, appealed to the emperor. They attempted to get a hearing, for which they had to travel to the capital and wait until the emperor saw fit to give them audience. In the meantime, they consulted the bishop of Constantinople, who could advise them on how to handle the greedy people in the imperial antechambers, how to offer the proper bribe. The Constantinopolitan bishop was profiting from this situation, while the emperor, often overburdened by the fussiness of the petitioners and by the intricacy of their cases, may have asked his bishop to pass sentence. And in many cases the bishop probably did not propose such a sentence without having gathered the visiting bishops to discuss the matter with them. The nucleus of what later became the Permanent Synod can thus be ascertained rather early. In other words, without any innate right, the bishop of Constantinople could reap where he had not sown.

This, I think, was the background of the canon on the primacy of honor voted to Constantinople in 381. After the council's decision, the Constantinopolitan bishop could no longer be outflanked, and was owed a certain amount of deference. There is no hint of apostolicity. The legend that St. Andrew was the first bishop of the city did not emerge before the sixth or seventh century. So the argument is a purely political one: Constantinople is the New Rome. The synod ceremoniously phrases a dry matter of fact. Perhaps the canon was introduced by the bishops of Asia Minor, in an effort to counterbalance the power of Alexandria. Since the bishop of Alexandria did not attend the council, Alexandrinian opposition could be ignored. And if the canon was passed after the death of the bishop of Antioch, which took place during the council, any opposition from this side could only have been weak.

The bishops of Constantinople did not rest content with a primacy of honor. John Chrysostom, bishop of Constantinople from 389 to 404, began to exploit the canon far beyond its juridical scope. No one will doubt that Chrysostom was a great saint, but here we must point to some less saintly features of his character. Out of the primacy of honor, he began to create a primacy of jurisdiction—a genuine patriarchate—over large parts of Europe and Asia Minor. And he succeeded, at least for the moment, although the measures he took annoyed even his friends. Meanwhile, Alexandria recovered from a temporary weakness and landed a hard blow by accusing Chrysostom of misconduct in office. Involved in a lawsuit, Chrysostom had to leave his see. But his successors did not give in, nor did Alexandria. Fortunately for Alexandria, one of Chrysostom's successors, Nestorius, provided an opportunity for discrediting the very faith of the Constantinopolitan see. The Council of Ephesus in 431, where Nestorius was condemned, was the great success of Cyril of Alexandria and the gloomy defeat of Constantinople. Even Emperor Theodosius II, at his wit's end, thought that now he had to support Alexandria rather than his own capital. Fortunately again—but this time for Constantinople—Dioscorus, successor of Cyril, overstrained the new prestige of his see and turned half the Orient against him. Thus, the Council of Chalcedon in 451 finally voted once more for Constantinople. The famous twenty-eighth canon, ratified against the will of the pope's legates, changed the primacy of honor into a primacy of jurisdiction, and in this way legalized the encroachments of Chrysostom. The patriarchate of Constantinople was now an established fact.

To sum up: Constantinople became a genuine ecclesiastical center only in 451, that is, more than 120 years after the foundation of the city. From this vantage, the year 381 was merely a promising prelude. But the success of 451 was called into question again and again, by Rome as well as by Alexandria. For long decades, Alexandria continued to oppose Constantinople, whose bishop was helpless even when backed by the emperor, for the emperor himself was helpless in the face of Egyptian resistance. The Constantinopolitan primacy had a conspicuous congenital defect in the lack of a genuine ecclesiastical and spiritual basis, and this defect resulted in an unbalanced interdependency between Church and Empire, disadvantageous more often for the patriarch than for the emperor, although in the long run even the emperor had to pay a high price.

As far as learning and scholarship are concerned, it is unlikely that Constantinople was at an early stage a leader in this field. Founders of cities, especially of Late Antique cities, commonly are occupied by the architectural image of their foundation, by hippodromes and galleries and municipal institutions. Constantine himself is a good example. Even though some *grammatikoi* probably settled down and opened a school in the early days of Constantine's rule, Constantine did little or nothing to encourage such enterprises. He founded no university, library, or scriptorium. And the Bible manuscripts he commissioned were not copied in Constantinople, but rather at Caesarea in Palestine, where the library of Origen provided the best texts. Moreover, these Bibles were not destined for an imperial library; they were to be given as presents to different churches.[18]

Themistius, in his praise of Constantius, complains in cautious words about Constantine's inactivity in the field of scholarship.[19] It was left to Constantius to remedy this lack of imperial patronage. He organized an imperial scriptorium with a chief and a staff of copyists for the purpose of copying the rather deteriorated manuscripts of the ancient authors. In codicological terms, they transferred the texts from the old papyri onto parchment.

Whether the activity of the scriptorium was as expansive as Themistius tries to insinuate is, however, another question.[20] He uses the well-known device of amplification by specification. After referring to "a lot of ancient authors," he then presents a long list of their names. This does not and cannot mean that books by all of these authors really were on the scriptorium's schedule, and still less that each title was actually copied. One should not, therefore, deduce from the list of Themistius a huge mass of new manuscripts.

More important, the employment of copyists, however limited, presupposes that a sufficient number of manuscripts was available for copying—that there was, in other words, a basic library, the size of which remains unknown, at least for the fourth century. The stock of this library was enriched by Julian, and later emperors made new provisions. Valens, for example, appointed three Latin and four Greek *antiquarii*, as well as other people, for the daily work. Such a staff suggests that by Valens' time the collection must have been a considerable one. On the basis of this evidence, scholars have concluded that Constantinople had finally found her prominent place in literature and civilization. Although I would like to agree, I have some reservations, which a short digression may illuminate.

In 1468, Cardinal Bessarion bequeathed his famous library to the city of Venice. There, he hoped, the learned Greek refugees might exploit his manuscripts for their humanistic studies.[21] The Venetian senate promised to house this legacy in the best room of the Doges' palace. In 1469, Bessarion's library, which included nearly five hundred Greek manuscripts, arrived in Venice. But the senate lost interest in the bequest, disregarding the promise to make it accessible. Between 1472 and 1476 the codices were made available only four times. In 1485, the room where the books had been stored was needed for other purposes, so the cardinal's whole library was packed up in cases and kept under lock and key. Seven years later, after the pope threatened the Venetians with anathema, the cases were reopened. But, at the same time, the senate decreed that no codex could be borrowed without the consent of three-fourths of the senators, violators being subject to a fine of five hundred ducats. A building for the library was planned in 1515, begun in 1536, and finally finished in 1588. It is hard to comprehend that all of this took place in the period we call the Renaissance.[22]

But let us return to Constantinople. A library was

there. But was it a public library or only a treasury of books, where now and then an emperor or a courtier could enter and feel bookish? Could any qualified person enter and read and make notes? We have no answer. Nonetheless, the scantiness of the literary production in Constantinople does not favor very optimistic suppositions.

The library in Constantinople burned down in 475.[23] On this occasion, Malchus, a contemporary historian, informs us that the library had contained 120,000 "biblia." No modern scholar is willing to accept such a number. It depends, however, on the definition of the word *biblion*. If taken to mean a codex, the number is incredible. But *biblion* understood as a literary unit, even as an autonomous chapter of work, is well attested and would not strain the limits of our credulity.[24]

The history of the library in the following years is rather obscure. Some sources imply that the emperor Zenon and the *praefectus urbi* Julian restored the library. But, in my opinion, the two or three epigrams that mention a house of the Muses, and so on, remain equivocal—they need not refer to the library known as the Museion—and later scholia are no real help.[25] It is hard to believe that the emperor Justinian should have been very eager to collect ancient pagan manuscripts, considering his persecution of heathen teaching and heathen professors.[26]

The teaching profession in Constantinople is the next topic. There can be no doubt that by the fourth century schoolmasters had arrived in Constantinople, and that by about 350 private schools had become established institutions in the city. The teachers were paid by the pupils, or, rather, by their parents, if payment was made at all. At first, the government did not interfere. But, after a while, the competitive struggle among the schoolmasters became more and more violent, and they seem to have sought some kind of governmental approbation. A special class of teachers slowly emerged, teachers who left behind them the masses of the poor *grammatikoi* and had a special right to be called *magistri*. These *magistri* were entitled to teach publicly and were favored by the government, perhaps now and then even paid by it. Under Theodosius II, this system was brought to an end and stabilized. In his constitution of 425,[27] he confined private teaching to private houses; all public teaching by private professors was forbidden. The only place where public teaching, controlled and salaried by the government, was permitted was the "*auditorium Capitolii*." Thus, we are told, a university had been created. Whether the word "university,"

impressive though it may be, is accurate does not matter. More important is the question I have already asked about the library. Did this university work? Was it a center of learning and successful students? As matters stand, it is more or less impossible to distinguish between professors of this new university and other teachers in the city. So I will treat the two categories together, leaving out the *grammatici linguae latinae*. We can then deal with a series of professors whose names we know and who taught grammar, literature, rhetoric, some introduction to the Aristotelian *organon*, and so on. Half of these professors are names only. Some are mentioned by the "Suda" in the tenth century, along with the titles of some of their works. But most of these professors' texts are lost. What remains, for example, is an introduction to rhetoric by a certain Troilus, a *Peri lexeon* by Ammonius, which is a revision of an older text, and similar trifles. During a period of more than two hundred years, therefore, the only outstanding names in the scholarly life of Constantinople are Libanius and Themistius. Libanius left after a short time for Asia Minor; Themistius is more interesting. In a manner that accorded with the special climate of the capital—which Libanius could not stand—Themistius combined a political career with a kind of political teaching along the ideals of the ancient Greek *paideia*.[28] His numerous enemies felt that he betrayed the Hellenistic tradition to the new Roman trends. For this reason, Eunapius, in his *Vitae sophistarum*, refused to give Themistius a place in the *legenda aurea* of the true and authentic philosophers of the time. Themistius was not able to form an *école* out of his thoughts.

Of course, one can argue that the losses of Late Antique literature are considerable in all parts of the ancient world, and that such a loss is not necessarily due to a lack of quality. But Athens, Alexandria, Antioch, and Caesarea were certainly in no less danger than Constantinople, and perhaps even more so. Yet, the scholars of these cities and others in the East left behind them a body of works far more impressive in number than the poor heritage of Constantinople—whatever the "connoisseurs" of classical literature may think of it. Palladas, Colluthus, Nonnus, Joannes Philoponus, Procopius Gazaeus, Zosimus, Proclus—all the important names of these centuries are non-Constantinopolitan. To be sure, Constantinople may rightly boast of the great historian Procopius of Caesarea, and the city also produced some good epigrammatists. But neither Procopius nor the epigrammatists belonged to the caste of professors and teachers. They were, rather, lawyers and officers, most of whom had acquired their erudition outside of Constantinople. The main center of learning and scholarship from the fourth to the sixth centuries was not Constantinople. Such centers could be found in Athens, Alexandria, and some minor Eastern towns where not only conventional rhetoric, grammar, and philosophy were taught, but even a certain amount of mathematics and science—at least in Alexandria. And poetry still had a home. By comparison, Constantinople had little to contribute. The story of Libanius, one of the toughest defenders of classical learning, suggests why. He had opened a school in Constantinople, but after a few years grew disappointed and left for provincial Nicomedia. In his opinion, the atmosphere of the capital did not favor learning: one had to compromise too much, and there was too much ambition and professional envy.[29]

As for the students who graduated from Constantinople's schools, very few of them can be numbered among the outstanding scholars of the time. In these centuries, theological interests, associated as they were with Aristotelian logic and Neoplatonic philosophy, played a considerable role in education. Yet, among the dozens of names that have an enduring place in the annals of patrology, there are not even six who could rightly be called alumni of Constantinople. The overwhelming majority came from Asia, from Syria, from Palestine, and from Egypt.

In the sixth century, Antioch was impoverished by Persian raids and then destroyed by earthquakes; the school of Athens was breathing its last, due to Justinian's hatred of this "Sleeping Beauty"; and the verve of Alexandria was endangered by the fanaticism of the patriarchs and of the monks they mobilized. Constantinople could profit by these circumstances, and she did. But she had to pay a high price: Constantinople had to forego the very energy and eloquence that for so long had characterized the school of Alexandria; she had to say farewell to the esoteric tunes of Athens; she had to be deferential to her emperor's asthmatic mentality. The old fertile soil of Alexandrinian erudition had to be left fallow.

With some apprehension, I would risk the thesis that this final, and to a certain degree unnatural, formalization of the ancient literature and erudition was due not only to Christian influence in general, but as well to the special atmosphere during the reign of Justinian, the most Christian emperor, under whom a "paganizing" professor or scholar could no longer breathe. I do not mean the kind of profes-

sor or scholar who trusts in the Olympian or chthonic deities, but rather a man not completely satisfied by stylistic delicacies or an exquisite vocabulary, who would like to find his own identity and explain his aspirations in the context of ancient literature, in the attitudes of the classical authors. Such a man is not an *ens rationis*, not even in the early Byzantine centuries. He is, rather, like Synesius of Cyrene or, in later times, Pico della Mirandola, Erasmus of Rotterdam, and Thomas More. Being Christians, these men realized that grace presupposes nature, and nature involves myth, at least for a transcendental understanding. Myth is immortal. As Sallustius said in the fourth century: "This never happened, but it never ceases to exist." The pagan deities survived into the Christian era, if only as dirty demons and mischievous devils. The defenders of Christian doctrine could rest content with battling paganism, but in so doing they missed the transparency and the range of the myth. They did not see beyond simple personifications and mythological fairy tales because they were blind to paganism's immanent, though intermediate, values, where life and nature represented themselves in concentrated symbols inviting *theoria*— that is, an insight that involves identification.[30] It creates a special feeling of closeness, a counterbalance to a nominalistic world view and to a spiritualism that can no longer hear the flute of Pan and the song of the Muses.

I would not say that in sixth-century Constantinople there was no one who found the myth attractive—Agathias certainly did. But whereas in Alexandria a well-preserved and viable heritage of classical and mythical ideas could be combined with some new Christian intellectual trends, Constantinople was behind the times. By the time she became aware of her new role in the field of scholarship, she had no great scholars within her walls. The mediocre people Constantinople nurtured were not eager enough to resume the old, already endangered traditions. And if there was still some nostalgic residue, Justinian's tough religious politics put an end to it. Thus, the final monopoly of the city as a center of scholarship was not the result of its own achievement: it was due to the decay of the Eastern cities and was won at the cost of the final, but in itself unnecessary formalization.

It must seem as if I aimed exclusively at diminishing and slandering the importance of Constantinople. I would like to do her justice, but this can be done only by going beyond the topics just treated.

The foundation of Constantinople was for the East, and especially for the Greek East, the signal of a revaluation of all the traditional values. Through this new city, the Roman Empire and Roman power drew menacingly closer to the East than ever before, especially because it emphasized the Eastern Empire's specific Roman and Latin character. The citizens of the old Greek towns, until then proud of their seeming autonomy, had to realize that the *polis*, in the traditional meaning of the word, was now gone. Constantinople herself was no *polis*. Themistius, justifying his politics of "*ralliement*," tried to suggest it was, but nobody believed him, least of all Libanius. The new city was not living on old traditions with local autonomy. The hundreds and thousands of immigrants were certainly a motley crew, irreverent before the pre-Constantinian heritage of their new home. The city had no old temples of significance, no traditional festivals around famous sanctuaries, no old aristocracy. She was a parvenu, but a parvenu with a huge amount of self-confidence and selfishness, and with a future. On the whole, the city was not "*à la recherche du temps perdu*," like so many other cities in the East, and it was not dreaming of classical attitudes and of classical *paideia*. Constantinople was just trying to make its fortune. If intellectual training was sought, it was primarily a juridical training, Roman jurisprudence, because such a training was the best recommendation for a career in the imperial administration. Libanius tells us that many young people left their small, drowsy towns for such a career. But the champions of the old Greek way of life saw this profession as the very enemy of Greek *paideia*, and not without just cause.

Herein lies one of the most important reasons why Constantinople was so late in competing with the other centers of Greek learning. This competition simply did not have priority. First of all, Constantinople had to compromise with, and make a cultural adjustment to, Roman mentality in every respect, even so far as the architectonical and artistic appearance of the city was concerned. She had to find a middle road between Greek political engagement and the Roman imperial concept; between the arbitrariness of the local Eastern churches and the Roman view of a *religio licita*, controlled by a *pontifex maximus*; and, finally, between a "rhetorical" and a "legal" mentality. That Constantinople arrived at such a compromise is her greatest achievement—an achievement, however, that could not be accomplished without losses on both sides. But the new distance from the old Greek ideals was not greater than the distance from the old Roman views. Thus, a new center was created, impoverished and impoverishing at the same time. It was precisely this "pauperism" that guaranteed survival.

When the great breakdown and the big losses in the midst of the seventh century were a matter of fact, Constantinople still was there. She sent artistic and cultural vibrations to isolated provinces, when these themselves were unable to act on their own account. By her military power, Constantinople gave life to provincial towns, which even with better economic endowment and with more autonomy would not have managed to survive. Eventually, she even amassed a storehouse of learning—enough to preserve scholarship and literary standards beyond the Dark Ages. Every future renaissance could rely on it.

NOTES

1. Cf. G. Dagron, *Naissance d'une capital. Constantinople et ses institutions de 330 à 451*, Paris, 1974. P. Lemerle, *Le premier humanisme byzantin*, Paris, 1971. These two books are basic and I am much indebted to the authors, although on some minor points I cannot agree completely.

2. J. Miller in *Real-Encyclopädie der klassischen Altertumswissenschaft*, III, 1897, cols. 1116–50, s.v. "Byzantion."

3. E. Gren, *Kleinasien und der Ostbalkan in der wirtschaftlichen Entwicklung der römischen Kaiserzeit*, Uppsala and Leipzig, 1941.

4. Julian *In laudem Constantii* 6 (Bidez, p. 18). Nevertheless, the whole empire had to pay heavy taxes. See Sozomenus *Hist. Eccl.* 2, 3, 5, J. Bidez and G. C. Hansens, eds., Berlin, 1960, p. 52.

5. St. Jerome *Chronicon ad annum 330* (Helm, *Eusebius Werke*, VII, p. 232).

6. Eusebius *Vita Constantini* 3. 54, F. Winkelmann, ed., Berlin, 1975, pp. 107–08. Cf. Socrates *Hist. Eccl.* 1. 16, Migne, *PG*, LXVII, col. 117.

7. *Anthologia Palatina* 2, H. Beckby, ed., 1957–58, I, pp. 168–93.

8. Cf. Zosimus *Historia nova* 2. 32, F. Paschoud, ed., Paris, 1971, I, p. 105. Zosimus is biased, but cf. Themistius *Orationes* 3, Schenkl-Downey, eds., Leipzig, 1965, pp. 66–67, and *Orationes* 11, ibid., p. 227. As for the carelessness of the constructors, note that in 385 a fifteen-year liability for the architects and their heirs was decreed; see *Cod. Theodosianus* 15. 1, 24.

9. Sidonius Apollinaris *Carmina* 2. 30 ff., in *Monumenta Germaniae Historica*, Auct. Antiquissimi, VIII, pp. 174–75. Cf. *Patria Konstantinupoleos*, II, Preger, ed., Leipzig, 1907, pp. 184–85.

10. R. Janin, "Deutéron, Triton et Pempton," *Echos d'Orient*, XXXV, 1936, pp. 205–19.

11. Synesius *De regno*, Migne, *PG*, LXVI, col. 1073.

12. Cf. F. Dvornik, *The Idea of Apostolicity in Byzantium and the Legend of the Apostle Andrew*, Cambridge, Mass., 1958, pp. 39–105.

13. Gregory of Nazianzus *Orationes* 33. 8, Migne, *PG*, XXXVI, col. 224.

14. *Codex Justinianus* 1. 1, 1, P. Krüger, ed., Berlin, 1954.

15. G. Dagron, "Les moines de la ville: Le monachisme à Constantinople jusqu'au concile de Chalcédoine (451)," *Travaux et Mémoires*, IV, 1970, pp. 229–76.

16. *Acta Conciliorum Oecumenicorum* 2. 1, E. Schwartz, ed., Berlin, 1933, pp. 310–11.

17. Gregory of Nazianzus *Orationes* 36. 12, Migne, *PG*, XXXVI, col. 280.

18. C. Wendel, "Der Bibelauftrag Kaiser Konstantins," *Zentralblatt für Bibliothekswesen*, LVI, 1939, pp. 165–75.

19. Themistius *Orationes* 4, Schenkl-Downey, ed., I, p. 86.

20. Ibid., pp. 82–89.

21. The deed of Bessarion's bequest is published in T. Gasparini Leporace and E. Mioni, *Cento codici Bessarionei*, Venice, 1968, pp. 101–03.

22. Cf. L. Mohler, *Kardinal Bessarion als Theologe, Humanist und Staatsmann*, I, Paderborn, 1923, pp. 408–15.

23. Joannes Zonaras *Epistome historiarum* 14. 2, T. Buttner-Wobst, ed., Bonn, 1897, pp. 130–31.

24. B. Atsalos, *La terminologie du livre-manuscrit à l'époque byzantine*, Thessalonike, 1971, I, pp. 69–74.

25. *Anthologia Palatina* 16, nos. 69–71, H. Beckby, ed., IV, p. 338.

26. *Codex Justinianus* 1. 5, 18; 1. 11, 10.

27. *Codex Theodos.* XIV, 9, 3.

28. G. Dagron, "L'empire romain d'Orient au IVᵉ siècle et les traditions politiques de l'hellénisme: Le témoignage de Thémistios," *Travaux et Mémoires*, III, 1968, pp. 1–242.

29. Libanius *Autobiography* 34–42, A. F. Norman, ed., London, 1965, pp. 24–32.

30. Cf. F. Boll, *Vita contemplativa*, 2nd ed., Heidelberg, 1922. Simone Weil, *Lettre à un religieux*, Paris, 1951.

BEAT BRENK

The Imperial Heritage of Early Christian Art

THE THEME of this lecture is Janus-faced—and Janus-faced, too, is scholarly research into the imperial heritage of Early Christian art, because classical archaeologists as well as art historians have striven for clarification of the thorny problems involved. Among the archaeologists who have gathered together individual observations, Gerhard Rodenwaldt, Richard Delbrueck, Edmund Weigand, and H. P. L'Orange are among the most notable.[1] André Grabar, the Byzantinist and art historian, succeeded in making the first overall view in his memorable book, *L'Empereur dans l'art byzantin*, a book that has recently appeared in a second edition.[2] On the whole, those involved in studying the problem have concentrated their efforts mainly on proving that Christian images were derived from pagan, imperial themes. But the question of the chronological evolution of imperial topics in Christian art has not been posed to this day—even though it would be of capital importance to know at what time and in which artistic medium and surrounding an imperial theme first appears. Indeed, the importance of the imperial language of imagery for Christian art cannot be evaluated until it has been possible to work out an exact chronology for the specific types of images. The pieces of evidence that contribute to the formation of a possible chronology are extremely complicated, and to relate them would be impossible in an article. Thus, I shall try, rather, to demonstrate some typical cases. I shall make a strict differentiation between cases in which imperial influence *can* be assumed and those in which it *must* be assumed. Only the latter are fruitful for historical analysis. In addition, Roman imperial art is certainly not the principal source of inspiration for Early Christian art, but only one of the many sources. It would not be honest of me to avoid placing this fundamental fact at the beginning.

In the time before Constantine, the relationship between Christians and imperial art can best be defined with the help of the acts of the interrogation and martyrdom of St. Cyprian in 257–58. The last sentence reads: "The most holy martyr Cyprianus suffered on the 14th of September under the emperors Valerianus and Gallienus, in truth under the reign of our Lord Jesus Christ, to whom is honor and glory forever and ever, Amen."[3] These acts of martyrdom were dated in the Roman manner, that is, the names of the ruling emperors were given, as well as that of Christ, who was said to be ruling in truth (*regnante vero*). Thus, Christ's reign is placed on a higher level of importance than that of the Roman emperors, and this indicates that in pre-Constantinian times Christians looked down on imperial art. However, immediately after the Edict of Milan in 313, the first elements of imperial imagery infiltrated Christian art. The year 313 was a turning point. From then on, imperial elements gradually and in a halting fashion penetrated Christian art.

After Constantine, official Roman art gradually forfeited its religious content, and for this reason it could be received, untainted, into Christian art. It was no longer necessary to pay reverence to the emperor. If official state art were to have been directed toward an emperor to whom Christians would have been required to pay sacrifice, then such an art would have been discredited in the eyes of the Christians, and found unworthy of imitation. Constans did away with sacrifices to the emperor in the year 341.[4] Gratian and Theodosius finally withdrew state support from the imperial cult.[5] The emperor Theodosius, in whose reign there gradually developed an official

FIG. 1. Dogmatic sarcophagus. Peter taken captive, detail of soldier.

The Vatican, Rome (Photo: Brenk)

FIG. 2. Arch of Constantine, Rome. *Profectio* relief, detail of soldiers.

(Photo: after Giuliano, *Arco di Costantino*, fig. 41)

discrimination against orthodox paganism, gave up all claim to the title of *pontifex maximus* (Zosimus *Hist. nova* 4. 36, 5). The undermining of pagan religious thought and, with it, of Roman triumphal art that the Christian emperors initiated is one of the chief prerequisites for the acceptance of such themes into Christian art. To the Christian way of thinking, the emperor was supposed to be the representative on earth of *their* God; not until this association became firmly fixed was it possible for imperial representational imagery to be made legitimate for Christians.[6] In addition, the experience of the triumph of Christianity over paganism put imperial triumphal art out of action, as far as the impression it previously produced is concerned. Victories were now achieved not with the help of the old gods, but rather in the name of Christ. From the time of Constantine onward, triumphal art was addressed to a new figure, namely, Christ as King and as the victor over death. And this Christian triumph could be most appropriately expressed with the formulae of imperial art.[7]

If we now turn to the monuments themselves, we can pass over those of pre-Constantinian times. For until the Battle of the Milvian Bridge in 312 and state recognition of Christianity in 313 the influence of imperial representative art on the world of Christian imagery was inconsequential.

The first Christian monument that unequivocally shows imperial influence is the so-called Dogmatic sarcophagus in the Vatican, which was found underneath S. Paolo fuori le mura.[8] The upper panels depict the Creation of Adam and Eve, the Miracle at Cana, the Multiplication of the Loaves and Fishes, and the Raising of Lazarus. Below, we find the Adoration of the Magi, Christ healing the blind, Daniel in the lions' den, Peter denying Christ, Peter being taken captive, and Moses striking the rock. Particularly noteworthy is the scene in which Peter is taken captive. Like Moses, Peter carries a staff.[9] Two soldiers (Fig. 1) wearing mantles (*chlamys*), trousers (*bracae*), and caps (*pileus pannonicus*) grasp the apostle's arms. In the *profectio* relief on the Arch of Constantine (the departure from Milan, Fig. 2), many soldiers in the train are clad in fur caps and mantles like those in the sarcophagus.[10] They are the *apparitores* or *officiales* who played an important role in the persecution of Christians, for which reason this kind of Constantinian soldier also appears on the Dogmatic sarcophagus. In other words, Peter's being taken captive was comprehended as a scene from the history of the persecution of Christians. The conception of this image can only have arisen in a workshop that was in operation both for the emperor and for the Christians.

Furthermore, the heads on both monuments share

FIG. 3. Dogmatic sarcophagus. Daniel scene, detail of unidentified figure.

The Vatican, Rome (Photo: Brenk)

FIG. 4. Arch of Constantine, Rome. *Adlocutio* relief, detail of senator.

(Photo: after Giuliano, fig. 46.)

FIG. 5. Dogmatic sarcophagus. Christ healing the blind, detail.

The Vatican, Rome (Photo: Brenk)

FIG. 6. Arch of Constantine, Rome. Personification of Autumn.

(Photo: after Giuliano, fig. 29)

FIG. 7. Sarcophagus with Victories.
The Walters Art Gallery, Baltimore (Photo: Brenk)

the same kind of roughened beard and fur cap, and the similarity extends even to the facial types, with fish-bubble motifs on the foreheads and wrinkles above the nose between the eybrows. In addition, certain heads on the sarcophagus have mustaches whose ends are rolled up like a snail's shell (Fig. 3), just like those on the Arch of Constantine (Fig. 4). A third comparison shows the youthful Christ with his hair parted in the middle, symmetrical locks on his forehead, and vertical locks on his temples (Fig. 5)— a design virtually identical with the personification of Autumn on the Arch of Constantine (Fig. 6).[11] Christ's hairstyle has thus been taken over from a putto in a cycle of the Seasons. It follows from this analysis that the Dogmatic sarcophagus was made in the same workshop that also produced reliefs for the Arch of Constantine. In imperial art, the Seasons represented prosperity, or *felicitas mundi*, for the entire empire, a prosperity that grew with each victory of the emperor. On the Dogmatic sarcophagus, however, the principle of cosmic flourishing was transferred to Christ. The *felicitas mundi* was no longer applied to the emperor but to Christ, who, in the Christian scheme, had brought about such prosperity. Here, a chapter in the history of salvation becomes apparent, an outlook that prepared the way for Orosius' theology of Augustus.[12]

We will not go further into the purely art historical consequences that result from such confrontations for other sarcophagi would have to be taken into account. Nevertheless, the quintessence of such a study is quite remarkable. Between 312 and 315—that is, shortly after Constantine's Edict of Milan—sarcophagi of highly placed Christian state officials were, for the first time, made in the imperial workshops of Rome. This had not happened before 312. We see that the owner of the Dogmatic sarcophagus was a highly placed personage just from the enormous dimensions of it. At 2 meters 67 centimeters long and 1 meter 30 centimeters high, it is one of the largest extant Christian sarcophagi. Unfortunately, we do not know who the owner was, but we may suppose that he was close to the emperor. In sum, the work signals the acceptance of Christian sarcophagus sculpture once and for all as an official medium. On the emperor's order, a Roman workshop executed scenes of battle and of ceremonial representation on an arch of triumph, and on the order of a state official the same workshop created sarcophagi with a similar repertory of forms and motifs. This workshop also created the new effigy of Christ with a hairstyle taken from the personifications of the Seasons.

In what follows, we shall continue to refer to sarcophagus sculpture. Although even after the Edict of Milan it remained a half-private, half-ecclesiastical category of art, no examples of official church art of the pre-Theodosian period are known—a fact that presents us with as yet unsolved problems. For example, it would be important to know if fourth-century official church art departed from more private funeral art, and which of these two types stood closer to pagan triumphal representation.

Among all the Early Christian sarcophagi, it is those with Passion scenes that were influenced by Roman triumphal art. The foundation for this process was provided by the theologians of the fourth century, who more and more often called Christ *basileus* or "king."[13] Eusebius designated Christ as a *kosmokrator, megas basileus*, and *pantokrator* (*Hist. eccl.* 10. 1, 1).[14] Christian teaching becomes a *basilikos nomos*, an imperial law. Christ's death on the cross was not a painful defeat, but a victorious triumph over death. Because of its outward appearance, the cross presented a certain similarity to the *tropaeum*, the pagan victory sign—a comparison already made by Justin Martyr (*Apol.* 1. 55, 3), Origen (In *Ioann.* 20. 36), and Minutius Felix (*Oct.* 29. 7). So it was, then, that on the sarcophagi with Passion scenes, the pagan *tropaeum*[15] became combined with the *labarum* and refashioned to form the actual cross, while the Chi Rho was refashioned into a crown of laurels. The composition is derived from pagan sarcophagi, such as the third-century sarcophagus with Victories in the Walters Art Gallery in Baltimore (Fig. 7). Both Victories bear a *labarum* in the form of a cross, and the *tropaeum* is represented by a palm tree on which there rests a shield with the *gorgoneium*. Below, two female captives are sleeping; these two figures can be seen again on the Vatican columnar sarcophagus,[16] where they are transformed into the two soldiers sleeping at Christ's grave. The two soldiers designate the Christian composition as a representation of the Resurrection. The representation, however, does not merely describe the Resurrection process itself, but rather shows it to be an immanent victory over death. In this connection, it is interesting to observe that the scene was already created in Constantine's reign. It appears for the first time on a two-zoned, fluted sarcophagus, hitherto unpublished, in the Royal Ontario Museum in Toronto (Fig. 8).[17] The Resurrection scene leans very heavily on pagan *tropaeum* scenes. Because the Christian image so clearly reflects official imperial thought, its conception cannot be traced back to a Christian sarcophagus workshop. It is thus conceivable that there was a monumental aulic model for the Resurrection composition, the more so since it was very influential for centuries to come.[18] Some of the other scenes from later times which clearly derive from *tropaeum* images of Constantine's day are the Crucifixion on the Monza ampullae and the apse mosaic in Sto. Stefano Rotondo [Cat. no. 524 and Cat. fig. 77], even though the Resurrection elements have disappeared from these monuments.

FIG. 8. Two-zoned sarcophagus. Resurrection, soldiers and cross.

Royal Ontario Museum, Toronto (Photo: Brenk)

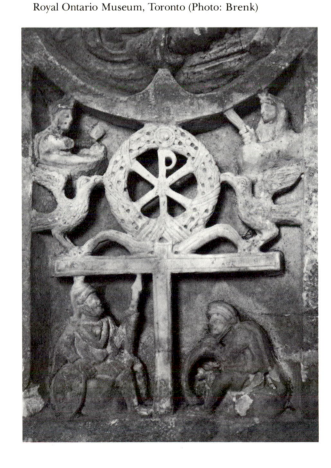

FIG. 9. Frieze sarcophagus. Christ treading on a
   lion and snake.

   Gerona (Photo: after Sotomayor, pl. 18)

FIG. 10. Sarcophagus fragment. Christ treading on
   a lion and snake.

   Museo Oliveriano, Pesaro (Photo: Brenk)

Let us now turn to the enthronement images. It
has always been maintained that the scene of Christ
treading on a lion and a snake—a scene taken from
Psalm 91:13—was inspired by imperial images. Eusebius' description of an encaustic painting in the
vestibule of the palace in Constantinople is continually brought up to support this belief. The painting
depicted the emperor and his sons standing on a
dragon, which the emperor is piercing with a lance.
The dragon was the symbol of political enemies—in
this case, probably Licinius.[19] In the meantime, the
first known example of the representation of Psalm
91 in art appears on an early Constantinian frieze
sarcophagus in Gerona (Fig. 9), a monument perhaps created before 312.[20] Christ is standing on a
lion that is encircled by a snake. Inasmuch as Christ
strides over a lion and viper and crushes them (*am-
bulabis et conculcabis*), the scene can be considered a
biblical illustration. But we do not have the slightest
inducement to suppose the influence of triumphal
art. Chronologically, the next monument to treat the
same theme is a sarcophagus fragment in Pesaro
(Fig. 10), which can already be dated after 350.[21]
The same curious motif of a snake entwining a lion
is found here as well, and we assume that it belongs
to a specific iconographical tradition. New in this

representation is the depiction of Christ enthroned,
not on a *cathedra*, to be sure, but rather on a *solium*,
whose armrests end in lion-head knobs. Here the enthronement no longer corresponds to the Psalm text;
instead, the artist used as a point of departure the
kind of enthronement scene that occurs on monuments of triumphal art, as well as in philosopher
scenes.[22] Not until the early sixth century, in the famous mosaic located in the Archbishop's chapel in
Ravenna, does Christ appear as *imperator*, treading
on lion and snake.[23] In the mosaic, Christ is even
clad as a soldier, as he is later in the Stuttgart Psalter[24] —two cases in which the influence of imperial
triumphal art is not to be disputed.

It has further been maintained that the frontally
enthroned Christ accompanied by apostles must have
been inspired by corresponding imperial images.[25]
However, here too there are other sources that up to
now have been overlooked. For example, we must
recall scenes of philosophers gathering, such as that
on the Gallienic Philosophers' sarcophagus, wherein
the main philosopher sits frontally and is flanked by
two listeners.[26] Although some modern authors want
to characterize the frontal pose as a stylistic tool of
imperial art, the problem of the frontal pose is extremely complex in late antiquity.[27] In late Roman

art—even as early as the first century—not only imperial images, but also scenes of worship, of philosophic gatherings, and of private daily life could be composed frontally. Thus, we have no particular reason for interpreting every catacomb or sarcophagus scene depicting Christ and the apostles as a reflection of lost monumental art.

It would be equally difficult to postulate an imperial prototype for a sarcophagus lid in The Metropolitan Museum of Art. One of the oldest Christian monuments, datable around 300, it represents an enthroned Christ separating the sheep from the goats (Fig. 11).[28] The subject is taken from the parable of the Last Judgment in Matthew 25:31–46. But the frontal composition and the symmetry occur here in the framework of a purely bucolic scene. Thus, both the Gallienic relief in the Vatican and the sarcophagus lid from New York show very clearly that frontal images exist within philosophical and bucolic contexts for which no direct prototypes in imperial art can be established. On the other hand, the enthronement scene on the sarcophagus of Junius Bassus (Fig. 12) would be inconceivable without an imperial model.[29] Christ, enthroned on a *solium* over the *caelus*, the personification of the heavens, derives directly from the figure of the emperor enthroned over the *caelus* on the Arch of Galerius in Thessalonike.[30] Proclus once called Christ τοῦ ἐπουρανίου βαδιλεύς[31] and he is also the *kosmokrator*.[32] This highly significant composition lives on in an Apocalypse scene from the Moutier-Grandval Bible, a work of the Carolingian school in Tours, where the *caelus* is framed by the symbols of the four evangelists.[33]

A much greater influence was exerted by the image of Christ enthroned on a globe. The earliest examples do not predate 350. An apse composition from Sta. Costanza [Cat. fig. 74][34] and a fresco in the new catacomb on the Via Latina[35] constitute the first examples of this iconographical motif—a motif that still lives on in the sixth century in S. Vitale, Ravenna[36] and, in Carolingian times, in the Lothar Gospels from Tours.[37] On Roman coins, the globe signified that part of the world which could be ruled over, strategically and politically.[38] It was called the *orbis*. Correspondingly, the emperor was called the *rector orbis*. There are also coins from a still earlier period with the genius *populi* and Roma. Although Roma does not actually sit on the globe, she at least rests her foot on it.[39]

The emperor Augustus reigns over the terrestrial globe in a memorable description by Ovid (*Metam.* 15. 858–60): "Jupiter controls the heights of heaven

FIG. 11. Sarcophagus lid. Christ separating the sheep from the goats.

The Metropolitan Museum of Art, New York, Rogers Fund, 24.240 (Photo: Brenk)

FIG. 12. Sarcophagus of Junius Bassus. Christ enthroned.

St. Peter's, Rome (Photo: Deutsches Archäologisches Institut).

and the kingdoms of the triformed universe; but the earth is under Augustus' sway. Each is both sire and ruler."[40] Here, the realm of the emperor and that of the gods are neatly separated. Not only Jupiter rules over the ether; in some illustrations, Sarapis, too, appears over the globe.[41] Gradually, the emperor was also seen as ruler of the heavenly sphere. The Commodus bust in the Palazzo dei Conservatori in Rome marks a milestone in this development, for the bust of the emperor, disguised as Heracles, is enthroned over the heavenly globe.[42] But if we recall the Sarapis bust, it is clear that this kind of enthronement scene did not have to be inspired only by imperial images. The globe as a throne had become a common formula—a *topos*—not exclusively reserved for the emperor.

The more the pagan religious content disappeared from triumphal art, the faster Christian art adopted imperial formulae (*topoi*). On the Arch of Constantine, emperors still make sacrifices—Licin-

ius to Apollo and Heracles, Constantine to Diana.[43] In the Theodosian era, a Christian representational art developed out of this religiously inspired triumphal art. The base of the column of Arcadius in Constantinople, for instance [Cat. no. 68], is the first triumphal monument with Christian emblems (the Chi Rho).[44] The Theodosian era signifies a turning point because, for the first time in the history of Roman triumphal art, it was Constantinople rather than Rome that became the focal point. The most visible signs of such a change can be seen in various pieces of imperial architecture in Constantinople: the Forum Tauri with the triumphal Arch of Theodosius from the year 386; the triumphal column; and, finally, the base of the obelisk at the Hippodrome from the year 390 [Cat. no. 99]. These triumphal monuments are closely related to official statuary sculpture, of which many examples survive in Constantinople, beginning in the Theodosian era. Moreover, from the fifth century on, carved capitals should

FIG. 13. Apse mosaic.

Sta. Pudenziana, Rome

also be mentioned in discussing the central role of Constantinople. All the newly created capitals after the year 400 owed their existence to the initiative of that metropolis and document the Roman imperial tradition. At the same time, these monuments testify to a new, highly qualified aulic style, which was inspired by Asia Minor but exerted an influence far beyond Constantinople.

This aulic style appears in Christian art as well, and not mainly in the private realm of funeral art, but in the official realm of ecclesiastical art. This ecclesiastical art, which was promoted by the clergy and the episcopate, is not preserved in the pre-Theodosian period. We are thus faced with one of the most intriguing gaps in the history of fourth-century art. But the earliest monuments of official church art known to us demonstrate that it is the heir of imperial triumphal art.[45] The first surviving church mosaic of an official nature is that of Sta. Pudenziana in Rome (Fig. 13), from the period around 400.[46] Christ sits like an emperor on a throne set with gems and fitted out with purple cushions. The golden tunic with purple stripes (*clavi*) and a golden nimbus designate Jesus as both a king and a god. The entire composition can be better understood through a text from St. John Chrysostom's second homily on Matthew, 1:

> You will see the *king* himself, seated on the *throne of that unutterable glory*, together with the angels and archangels standing beside him, as well as the countless legions of the ranks of the saints. This is how the *Holy City* appears.... *In this city is towering the wonderful and glorious sign of victory, the cross*, the victory booty of Christ, the first fruit of our human kind, *the spoils of war of our king*.[47]

The fact that St. John Chrysostom does not mention the apostles, but only the angels, is of little importance. The Heavenly City, with Christ as king on the regal throne and with the cross as a sign of victory, is described as it is seen in the mosaic. The text is nothing but a contemporary paraphrase of the mosaic and represents, in and of itself, a documentation of the Church fathers' reception of the imperial vocabulary.

Another early and important example of the aulic style of Constantinople is a relief from the late fourth century, acquired only a short time ago by the Berlin Museums (Fig. 14).[48] It represents a cushioned throne on which lie a diadem and a *chlamys*. From above, a dove descends toward the throne. Below, two deer look up to it reverently. The throne is without doubt the kingly throne and the diadem and cape regal attributes. The dove is a sign for Christ, the deer signify the believers. In the broadest sense, the composition can be interpreted as a pictorial symbolization of the Kingdom of Christ. But it has been known for a long time that this particular image of an empty throne was already widely disseminated in Roman pagan art.[49] Since the throne was an object of religious worship for the Romans, the image must have originally appeared to the Christians as especially pagan and therefore worthy of suspicion, before it finally gained acceptance in a Christian context. Once this throne was claimed by Christ and provided with Christian symbols, it could be located in a prominent place: at the zenith of the triumphal arch in Sta. Maria Maggiore, dated 432–40 (Fig. 15).[50] Once again, a royal diadem lies on the throne. Also included, however, are the cross and the scroll of the Seven Seals (Rev. 5:1), as well as busts of the two chief apostles, Peter and Paul. As representatives of the Church the saints pay homage to Christ, who is evoked by the cross and the diadem. This image of homage to the empty throne at the top of the triumphal arch in Sta. Maria Maggiore is inconceivable without the model of triumphal art. Moreover, the composition of the triumphal arch as a whole, with the mosaics set in stripes, has its source in Roman triumphal art—for example, the Arch of Galerius at Thessalonike.[51] The composition of the triumphal arch in Sta. Maria Maggiore is, in other words, the Christian counterpart of the Arch of Galerius; or, to express it differently, it is the Christian staging of the pagan *arcus triumphalis*. In the apex of the inside walls of the Sta. Maria Maggiore arch we can find the christogram with Alpha and Omega;[52] "rho" is joined with "chi" in such a way that we have to read *pax*. Not the pagan *pax Romana*, but rather the *pax Christiana*. The cultural deputation of the Roman Empire becomes a mission serving the Christian idea.[53]

The throne and the *pax* monogram on the triumphal arch in Sta. Maria Maggiore grew out of the state political ideology of the Romans, clad in Christian garments and subordinated to the Christian doctrine of salvation. Other specific scenes on this triumphal arch were also strongly influenced by imperial iconography. Grabar was able to show that the specific form of the Adoration of the Magi—with the child on the throne and the two women sitting on the left and right—was influenced by the consular diptych of Halberstatt, made in 417.[54] The form of the throne is identical on both monuments. In Sta. Maria Maggiore, the diptych's personifications of Rome and

FIG. 14. Hetoimasia relief.

Staatliche Museen, Berlin (Photo: after Brandenburg, *Römische Mitteilungen*, 1972, pl. 66)

FIG. 15. Hetoimasia.

Sta. Maria Maggiore, Rome (Photo: Brenk)

Constantinople become the Virgin and the personification of the Church of the Gentiles, the *ecclesia e gentibus*. The Adoration of the Magi in Sta. Maria Maggiore is the most striking example of the rendering of a Christian scene with the vocabulary of imperial art. But this is a singular case. The usual iconography of the Adoration of the Magi is not based on imperial models, and the image in Sta. Maria Maggiore exerted no influence on later monuments.

The fact that four guardian angels were added to the picture in Sta. Maria Maggiore may also be explained with the help of imperial art. (The motif appears again in the Adoration scene in S. Apollinare Nuovo in Ravenna, where Mary, seated with the

Christ child, is flanked by four guardian angels.[55]) The angelic guards and the gem-studded throne characterize Jesus as the royal sovereign reigning over the *orbis Christianus*. Royalty, however, signified divinity, too, and at this point a theological component is added to our problem. In 428, Nestorius, the archbishop of Constantinople, held that Christ's human and divine natures were separate—that is, that Christ could not have been born as God. Official opinion was expressed on this matter at the Council of Ephesus in 432.[56] The Council confirmed earlier dogma, which held the human and the divine natures of Christ to be inseparable. On the triumphal arch in Sta. Maria Maggiore, Christ's divine nature received special emphasis because Roman theologians believed that Nestorius had denied it. But this was a misunderstanding. What Nestorius did say was: "I do not believe in a two- or three-month-old God."[57] This remark must have irritated Roman theologians to such an extent that they put the Christ child on a royal throne in Sta. Maria Maggiore, the better to demonstrate that even as a child, Christ had been divine. Thus, in the arch of triumph in Sta. Maria Maggiore, triumphal vocabulary is put totally in the service of theology.

These perceptions, however, should not be taken as binding for the entire mosaic cycle in Sta. Maria Maggiore. Since I have discussed the manifold possibilities of the use of triumphal iconography in my monograph on that church, I will make my remarks on this subject brief. One may perceive a certain significance when Abraham appears on horseback at the meeting with Melchisedek, holding out his right hand and greeting like an emperor. Nevertheless, Abraham is not pictured in imperial guise, as he is, for instance, on the relief depicting the Clementia of Marcus Aurelius, but merely as a man of God in a tunic and a *pallium*.[58] The artist, therefore, took the representation found in the Clementia relief simply as a formula. Such a procedure becomes even clearer in the scene from the life of Joshua, where Joshua is rendered like a Roman commander-in-chief, wearing a *chlamys* and accompanied by two attendants. This compositional scheme—that is, with the emperor standing frontally and walking in profile—already appears on the S. Marco column.[59] And the scene of Pharaoh, dramatically drowning while the Israelites pass through the Red Sea, finds its parallel in the Battle of the Dacians on the Column of Trajan. In both representations, a cut-off bust is to be found in the upper part of the picture.[60] Still, the adoption of the infant Moses by Pharaoh's daughter is not represented like a Roman adoption. In the Roman ritual, the emperor tends to stand with his hand on his adoptive son's shoulder, as on the Ephesian relief, now in Vienna, where Hadrian adopts Antoninus.[61]

When viewed together, these observations immediately show that for the designer of Sta. Maria Maggiore, the points of reference were of a very disparate nature. He certainly did not have the slightest theological motivation in representing Abraham or Joshua as a Roman emperor. Joshua, a biblical figure, was not comparable to the Roman emperor, for he was victorious as a result of a divine promise. At Sta. Maria Maggiore, narrative Roman triumphal art is used as a point of departure for artistic and ideological reasons.[62] Because of its vast richness of figures and compositional types, this art was particularly well suited to the design of Christian cycles: it offered an arsenal of representative motifs, which were most welcome to the artists who had to depict cycles from the Old Testament for the first time. It will already have occurred to the careful observer that in Sta. Maria Maggiore it was never whole scenes that were adapted from Roman narrative triumphal art, but rather only selected details.

Other kinds of sources, such as mythological painting in the Greco-Roman tradition, were available to the decorators of Sta. Maria Maggiore. But as far as triumphal art is concerned, the artists probably utilized formulae found in existing pattern books. Such pattern books were also used around 400 by the illustrators of an Old Testament manuscript, the so-called Quedlinburg Itala fragments, and of the Vatican copy of Vergil's *Aeneid* [Cat. nos. 424, 203].[63] With some justification, it has been supposed that both of these manuscripts were illustrated in the same workshop. The studio that employed these pattern books thus worked simultaneously for ecclesiastical and pagan patrons.

The mark of imperial iconography in Christian art is recognizable in different ways. As a rule, artists drew upon Roman triumphal art in cases where it was necessary to emphasize the kingly rule of Christ. The fact that Christ was seen as a king also implied his divine nature. In order to represent Christ's kingdom in art, triumphal images of the past and present were appropriated. Yet, this process does not begin until after 313. The first Christian theme to be presented with imperial formulae is the Resurrection of Christ, seen on sarcophagi with Passion scenes beginning in the late Constantinian period. In the second half of the fourth century, various kinds of enthronement images from imperial art entered the Christian repertory. And these were the scenes that exerted the most powerful influence on medieval art: Christ on the throne, and on the *caelus*. In the Theodosian era, the *hetoimasia* becomes the embodiment of the idea of enthronement—that is, the empty throne, taken over from pagan art, as the symbol of ruling. The mosaics in Sta. Maria Maggiore are the first official ecclesiastical monument to show the effects of triumphal art in all its breadth and refinement. On the triumphal arch, the kingdom of Christ appears, while in the nave, triumphal motifs are employed mainly as artistic devices. The cycle of Abraham, Isaac, and Jacob includes only two allusions to imperial iconography,[64] whereas the cycle of Moses and Joshua draws largely upon Roman triumphal *topoi*. The *raison d'être* for the use of imperial imagery is in almost every case a different one, even though the royal and divine nature of Christ and of Christ's antetypes in the Old Testament were always in evidence. The influence of imperial art should not be overestimated, for together with Greco-Roman mythological and funerary iconography it represents just one of the many sources of Christian iconography.

NOTES

1. G. Rodenwaldt: "Ueber den Stilwandel in der antoninischen Kunst," *Abhandlungen der Akademie der Wissenschaften, Berlin, philosophisch-historische Klasse*, 1935, 3, pp. 1–27; "Zur Kunstgeschichte der Jahre 220–270," *Jahrbuch des deutschen archäologischen Instituts*, LI, 1936, pp. 82–113; "Römische Reliefs: Vorstufen zur Spätantike," *Jahrbuch des deutschen archäologischen Instituts*, LV, 1940, pp. 12–43; "Sarkophagprobleme," *Römische Mitteilungen*, LVIII, 1953, pp. 1–26. R. Delbrueck, *Die Consulardiptychen und verwandte Denkmäler*, Berlin, 1929 (Studien zur spätantiken Kunstgeschichte, II); *Antike Porphyrwerke*, Berlin, 1932 (Studien zur spätantiken Kunstgeschichte, VI); *Spätantike Kaiserporträts von Constantinus Magnus bis zum Ende des Westreiches*, Berlin, 1933 (Studien zur spätantiken Kunstgeschichte, VIII). E. Weigand, "Die spätantike Sarkophagskulptur im Lichte neuerer Forschungen," *Byzantinische Zeitschrift*, XLI, 1941, pp. 104–46 and 406–46. H. P. L'Orange and A. von Gerkan, *Der spätantike Bildschmuck des Konstantinsbogens*, Berlin, 1939 (Studien zur spätantiken Kunstgeschichte, X). H. P. L'Orange, *Apotheosis in Ancient Portraiture*, Cambridge, Mass., 1947.

2. A. Grabar, *L'Empereur dans l'art byzantin. Recherches sur l'art officiel de l'empire de l'Orient*, Paris, 1936; 2nd ed., 1971.

3. L. Koepp, "Antikes Kaisertum und Christusbekenntnis im Widerspruch," *Jahrbuch für Antike und Christentum*, IV, 1961, pp. 58–76; reprinted in *Das frühe Christentum im römischen Staat*, R. Klein, ed., Darmstadt, 1971, pp. 302–36; *Acta proconsularia cypr.* 6, C. S. E. L., W. Hartel, ed., III, p. 3: "passus est autem beatissimus Cyprianus martyr die octava decima kalendarum Octobrium sub Valeriano et Gallieno imperatoribus regnante vero domino nostro Iesu Christo cui est honor et gloria in saecula saeculorum. Amen."

4. J. Geffcken, *Der Ausgang des griechisch-römischen Heidentums* (1929), 2nd ed., Darmstadt, 1963, p. 97.

5. Ibid., p. 145. L. Koepp, "Antikes Kaisertum und Christusbekenntnis," p. 335.

6. L. Koepp, "Antikes ¹Kaisertum und Christusbekenntnis," p. 333.

7. J. Kollwitz, *Oströmische Plastik der theodosianischen Zeit*, Berlin, 1941, pp. 45–50.

8. F. W. Deichmann, G. Bovini, and H. Brandenburg, *Repertorium der christlich-antiken Sarkophage*, I, Wiesbaden, 1967, no. 43.

9. E. Dinkler, "Die ersten Petrusdarstellungen. Ein archäologischer Beitrag zur Geschichte des Petrusprimates," *Marburger Jahrbuch für Kunstwissenschaft*, XI, 1939, pp. 40–49 and 57–66, figs. 15 and 24.

10. H. P. L'Orange and A. von Gerkan, *Der spätantike Bildschmuck*, pp. 43–45 and 52; pl. 3a. For the Arch of Constantine, see also Cat. no. 58.

11. Ibid., pp. 154, 156, 159 and pl. 35c. F. Gerke, *Christus in der spätantiken Plastik*, 2nd ed., Berlin, 1941, pp. 24–27 and figs. 22–23.

12. I. Opelt, "Augustustheologie und Augustustypologie," *Jahrbuch für Antike und Christentum*, IV, 1961, pp. 44–57. B. Brenk, *Die frühchristlichen Mosaiken in S. Maria Maggiore zu Rom*, Wiesbaden, 1975, p. 22.

13. J. Kollwitz, "Das Bild von Christus dem König in Kunst und Liturgie der christlichen Frühzeit," *Theologie und Glaube*, I, 1947, pp. 95–117. K. Wessel, "Christus Rex, Kaiserkult und Christusbild," *Archäologischer Anzeiger*, 1953, pp. 118–36. P. Beskow, *Rex Gloriae. The Kingship of Christ in the Early Church*, Stockholm, 1962. L. Koepp, "Antikes Kaisertum und Christusbekenntnis," p. 321.

14. J. Kollwitz, "Christus als Lehrer und die Gesetzesübergabe an Petrus in der konstantinischen Zeit," *Römische Quartalschrift*, XLIV, 1936, pp. 45–66, esp. pp. 57–59.

15. J. Kollwitz, *Oströmische Plastik der theodosianischen Zeit*, p. 151. E. Dinkler-von Schubert in *Lexikon der christlichen Ikonographie*, IV, Freiburg i. Br., 1972, cols. 361–63, s.v. "Tropaion."

16. F. W. Deichmann et al., *Repertorium der christlich-antiken Sarkophage*, I, no. 49.

17. A full publication by the author is forthcoming.

18. A. Grabar, *L'Empereur dans l'art byzantin*, pp. 194 and 239–41. Idem, *Christian Iconography. A Study of Its Origins*, Princeton, 1968, pp. 38–39. W. Kellner in *Lexikon*

der christlichen Ikonographie, I, cols. 456–58, s.v. "Christogramm." A. Alföldi, "The Helmet of Constantine with the Christian Monogram," *Journal of Roman Studies*, XXII, 1932, pp. 9–18.

19. A. Grabar, *L'Empereur dans l'art byzantin*, p. 237. Idem, *Christian Iconography*, p. 40.

20. M. Sotomayor, *Sarcofagos romano-cristianos de España*, Granada, 1975, pp. 35–37 and pl. 18.

21. B. Brenk, "Zwei Reliefs des späten 4. Jahrhunderts," *Acta ad archaeologiam et artium historiam pertinentia*, IV, 1969, pp. 51–60.

22. Ibid., p. 51, note 1. E. Panofsky, *Tomb Sculpture*, New York, 1964, figs. 97b and 128.

23. F. W. Deichmann, *Ravenna. Hauptstadt des spätantiken Abendlandes. Kommentar*, I, Wiesbaden, 1974, p. 203. Idem, *Frühchristliche Bauten und Mosaiken von Ravenna*, Baden-Baden, 1958, fig. 217.

24. B. Brenk, *Tradition und Neuerung in der christlichen Kunst des ersten Jahrtausends*, Graz, Vienna, and Cologne, 1966 (Wiener byzantinistische Studien, III), p. 198, fig. 74.

25. A. Grabar, *L'Empereur dans l'art byzantin*, pp. 197–98. A monument that seems to support Grabar's view is the so-called Barberini terracotta in the Dumbarton Oaks Collection. A careful check of the inscription at the top reveals the following reading: U I C.O(R?)I. Furthermore, the stamp on a tessera in the left-hand side of the enthroned judge need not necessarily be read as a Chi Rho and therefore permits an interpretation other than solely Christian. I doubt whether the low quality of the terracotta relief reflects imperial art; its Christian origin is difficult to prove. See A. Grabar, *Christian Iconography*, p. 44, fig. 113. M. C. Ross, *Catalogue of the Byzantine and Early Mediaeval Antiquities in the Dumbarton Oaks Collection*, Washington, 1962, I, no. 91, pl. L.

26. A. Grabar, *Die Kunst des frühen Christentums von den ersten Zeugnissen christlicher Kunst bis zur Zeit Theodosius I*, Munich, 1967, fig. 50.

27. G. Rodenwaldt, "Ara Pacis und S. Vitale," *Bonner Jahrbücher*, CXXXIII, 1928, pp. 228–35. Idem, "Zur Kunstgeschichte der Jahre 220–270," pp. 93, 94, 107, and 108. Idem, "Römische Reliefs," pp. 38–39. H. P. L'Orange and A. von Gerkan, *Der spätantike Bildschmuck*, pp. 198–99 and 201. J. Kollwitz, *Oströmische Plastik der theodosianischen Zeit*, pp. 59 and 102. E. Will, *Le Relief cultuel gréco-romain*, Paris, 1956. T. Hölscher, *Victoria Romana*, Mainz, 1967, pp. 88–90, 117–21, 124–25, and 130–31. H. Zaloscer, "Die Frontalität—Form und Bedeutung," *Alte und moderne Kunst*, XV, 1970, pp. 2–13.

28. Cat. no. 501. B. Brenk, *Tradition und Neuerung*, pp. 38–39 and 218–19, fig. 1.

29. Cat. no. 386. F. W. Deichmann et al., *Repertorium der christlich-antiken Sarkophage*, I, no. 680. A. Grabar, *Christian Iconography*, p. 43, fig. 111.

30. Cat. fig. 10. A. Grabar, *Christian Iconography*, p. 43, fig. 110.

31. J. Kollwitz, *Oströmische Plastik der theodosianischen Zeit*, p. 146.

32. J. Kollwitz, "Christus als Lehrer," pp. 56–57. See also the Velletri sarcophagus, where Pluto and Prosperina are enthroned under the *caelus*, reproduced in B. Andreae, *Studien zur römischen Grabkunst*, Heidelberg, 1963, pl. 5 and pp. 26, 69.

33. K. Hoffmann, "Sugers anagogisches Fenster," *Wallraf-Richartz Jahrbuch*, XXX, 1968, pp. 57–88; A. Schmid in *Die Bibel von Moutier-Grandval, Brit. Mus. Add. Ms. 10546*, Bern, 1971, pp. 178–84. H. L. Kessler, *The Illustrated Bibles from Tours*, Princeton, 1977, pp. 69 ff. and fig. 107.

34. J. Kollwitz, "Christus als Lehrer," pp. 59–62. A. Grabar, *L'Empereur dans l'art byzantin*, p. 204. Idem, *Christian Iconography*, p. 42 and fig. 104. The Christian *traditio legis* scene was often compared to the Missorium of Theodosius I in Madrid, but the main features of the two scenes are, in fact, totally different. In the *traditio legis*, Christ is always standing upright, while Peter approaches solemnly from the right side in order to receive the scroll. In functions, the scroll is unparalleled in pagan Roman art, serving as a legal document with far from readable letters handed over by Christ. The text of the scroll ("dominus legem dat, dominus pacem dat") explains the content of the scene. While the scroll became fashionable in Christian iconography, it disappeared from Roman everyday life. The question of how this peculiar scroll originated is as yet unsolved. The only comparable monument is the Probianus-Diptych in Berlin. W. N. Schumacher, "Dominus legem dat," and "Eine römische Apsiskomposition," *Römische Quartalschrift*, LIV, 1959, pp. 1–39 and 137–202. M. Sotomayor, "Ueber die Herkunft der 'Traditio legis,'" *Römische Quartalschrift*, LVI, 1961, pp. 215–30.

35. A. Ferrua, *Le pitture della nuova catacomba di Via Latina*, Vatican City, 1960, p. 69 and pl. CVIII.

36. F. W. Deichmann, *Frühchristliche Bauten und Mosaiken von Ravenna*, pl. 351. Idem, *Ravenna. Haupstadt des spätantiken Abendlandes. Geschichte und Monumente*, Wiesbaden, 1969, p. 241.

37. W. Koehler, *Die karolingischen Miniaturen*, I, 2. *Die Schule von Tours. Die Bilder*, Berlin, 1933, pp. 240–45, 335–36, and pl. I, 98b.

38. T. Hölscher, *Victoria Romana*, pp. 41–47.

39. Ibid., p. 43.

40. "Iuppiter arces temperat aetherias et mundi regna triformis, terra sub Augusto est; pater est et rector uterque."

41. W. Hornborstl, *Sarapis*, Leiden, 1973, pp. 261–62. Idem, "Museum für Kunst und Gewerbe. Erwerbungen der Antikenabteilung in Jahre 1974," *Jahrbuch Hamb. Kunstsamml*, XX, 1975, p. 152.

42. W. Kähler, *Rom und seine Welt*, Munich, 1960, pp. 331–32, pl. 228. W. Helbig, *Führer durch die öffentlichen Sammlungen klassischer Altertümer in Rom*, 4th ed., Tübingen, 1966, II, pp. 306–07.

43. H. P. L'Orange and A. von Gerkan, *Der spätantike Bildschmuck*, pp. 168, 172, and pl. 41b.

44. A. Grabar, *Christian Iconography*, p. 46, fig. 128.

45. The adoption of imperial triumphal art could not, however, have taken place immediately after 313. The symbolic image of the Resurrection with the *labarum* on late Constantinian sarcophagi is the first scene that reflects an early phase of interrelation between imperial art and ecclesiastical iconography (see notes 16 and 18, above). About 370 there followed the two apse mosaics in the mausoleum of Sta. Costanza at Rome (see note 34, above).

46. A. Grabar, *L'Empereur dans l'art byzantin*, p. 196. Idem, *Christian Iconography*, p. 72, fig. 172. E. Dassmann, "Das Apsismosaik von S. Pudenziana in Rom," *Römische Quartalschrift*, LXV, pp. 67–81.

47. Migne, *PG*, LVII, cols. 23–24.

48. H. Brandenburg, "Ein frühchristliches Relief in Berlin," *Römische Mitteilungen*, LXXIX, 1972, pp. 123–54.

49. A. Alföldi, "Insignien und Tracht der römischen Kaiser," *Römische Mitteilungen*, L, 1935, pp. 3–158, esp. pp. 134–135. A. Grabar, *L'Empereur dans l'art byzantin*, p. 199. J. Engemann, "Zu den Apsis—Tituli des Paulinus von Nola," *Jahrbuch für Antike und Christentum*, XVII, 1974, pp. 21–46, esp. pp. 42–46.

50. B. Brenk, *Die frühchristlichen Mosaiken in S. Maria Maggiore*, pp. 14–19 and 37–39.

51. Ibid., p. 2. W. F. Volbach, *Early Christian Art*, New York, 1961, pls. 2–3.

52. H. Karpp, *Die frühchristlichen und mittelalterlichen Mosaiken in S. Maria Maggiore zu Rom*, Baden-Baden, 1966, pl. 5.

53. B. Brenk, *Die frühchristlichen Mosaiken in S. Maria Maggiore*, pp. 34–35 and 37. J. Kollwitz, *Oströmische Plastik der theodosianischen Zeit*, p. 47.

54. A. Grabar, *L'Empereur dans l'art byzantin*, pp. 227–28. B. Brenk, *Die frühchristlichen Mosaiken in S. Maria Maggiore*, pp. 24–27 and 42–44, figs. 12 and 48.

55. F. W. Deichmann, *Ravenna. Hauptstadt des spätantiken Abendlandes*, pp. 146–49.

56. B. Brenk, *Die frühchristlichen Mosaiken in S. Maria Maggiore*, pp. 47–49. M. Anastos, "Nestorius was orthodox," *Dumbarton Oaks Papers*, XVI, 1962, pp. 119–40.

57. B. Brenk, *Die frühchristlichen Mosaiken in S. Maria Maggiore*, p. 48; ὅτι ἐγὼ σιμηνιαῖον καὶ τριμηνιαῖον θεὸν οὐχ ὁμολογῶ.

58. Ibid., pp. 53–56. H. Karpp, *Die frühchristlichen und mittelalterichen Mosaiken in S. Maria Maggiore*, pl. 29. E. Kitzinger, *Byzantine Art in the Making*, London, 1977, p. 72 and figs. 132–33.

59. B. Brenk, *Die frühchristlichen Mosaiken in S. Maria Maggiore*, pp. 147 ff. and figs. 42–44.

60. Ibid., pp. 84–87 and 173, fig. 51, and color pl. 3. F. B. Florescu, *Die Trajanssäule*, Bonn and Bucharest, 1969, pl. XVIII.

61. H. Karpp, *Die frühchristlichen und mittelalterichen Mosaiken in S. Maria Maggiore*, pl. 85. I. Scott Ryberg, "Rites of the State Religion in Roman Art," *Memoirs of the American Academy in Rome*, XXII, 1955, p. 133 and fig. 72.

62. E. Kitzinger, *Byzantine Art in the Making*, pp. 72–73, speaks of "an emphatic, demonstrative and surely deliberate appropriation or assimilation of the pagan past. The evocation of an illustrated epic in the nave mosaics is part of this. . . . The Bishop of Rome . . . asserted his claim as the true and rightful heir of the Caesars. . . . It is not simply a carry-over from the late fourth-century 'Renaissance.' It is a counter move, a conscious and programmatic appropriation of the past." The Vatican Vergil, however, reflects the same triumphal vocabulary as is found in S. Maria Maggiore, and was surely not produced for ecclesiastical purposes. The fact that pagan *and* ecclesiastical cycles of the late fourth and fifth centuries use formulae from Roman triumphal iconography may also be interpreted as a mere artistic development.

63. J. de Wit, *Die Miniaturen des Vergilius Vaticanus*, Amsterdam, 1959. H. Degering and A. Boeckler, *Die Quedlinburger Itala-Fragmente*, Berlin, 1932.

64. H. Karpp, *Die frühchristlichen und mittelalterlichen Mosaiken in S. Maria Maggiore*, pls. 25 and 74.

65. Ibid., pls. 97, 108, 113, 128, 133, 138, 143, 148, 153, and 155.

IHOR ŠEVČENKO

A Shadow Outline of Virtue:
The Classical Heritage of Greek Christian Literature (Second to Seventh Century)*

THE EARLIEST OBJECTS in the *Age of Spirituality* exhibition date roughly from the mid-third century. At about the same time, Origen, the most learned of the Early Christian writers, was refuting the arguments of the pagan philosopher Celsus, who had attacked Christianity some seventy years earlier. Origen, being a proper scholar, quoted his adversary verbatim; thus we know exactly what Celsus said of the Christians. "Their injunctions," Celsus reported, "are like this: 'Let no one educated, no one wise, no one sensible draw near . . . ; but as for anyone ignorant, anyone stupid, anyone uneducated, anyone who is a child, let him come boldly'," for it was patent that the Christians "wished to attract" and were "able to convince only the foolish, dishonorable, uneducated and stupid."[1] Elsewhere Celsus spoke of Christian servants in large households, of "wool workers, cobblers, fullers and total ignoramuses and country yokels," some of whom even tried to turn their masters' children away from their schoolteachers.[2] If we are to believe Celsus, Christians were not only lower class, but ignorant of pagan intellectual values, and hostile to them as well.

In his refutation, Origen did not meet these accusations head on: he even admitted that some Christians were unlettered, and hostile to teachers who instructed children in the "improprieties of the comedy and the licentious poems in iambics."[3] Origen himself was against at least some varieties of classical literature.

Both Celsus' attack and Origen's defense are somewhat puzzling, for neither quite reflects the

---

*This is a slightly revised text of a lecture delivered at The Metropolitan Museum of Art on November 21, 1977. A word on bibliography: the second volume of E. Norden's *Die antike Kunstprosa . . .* , Leipzig and Berlin, 1909, esp. pp. 451–573, still remains the classic on our subject. It is more difficult to quote recent comprehensive introductions for the benefit of the general reader. Of W. Krause's *Die Stellung der frühchristlichen Autoren zur heidnischen Literatur*, Vienna, 1958, only the section "On the General Attitude of the Greek Patristics Towards Pagan Literature," pp. 59–88, is of broader appeal. Outstanding general works of recent date that come first to mind deal with the world of major pagan ideas and with their reflection in Christian thought, rather than with continuity in the use of literary genres, motifs, and devices, which will be this essay's main concern. See C. N. Cochrane, *Christianity and Classical Culture . . .* , London, New York, and Toronto, 1944. E. von Ivánka, *Hellenisches und Christliches im frühbyzantinischen Geistesleben*, Vienna, 1948. M. L. W. Laistner, *Christianity and Pagan Culture . . .* , Ithaca, 1951, esp. pp. 49–73. W. Jaeger, *Early Christianity and Greek Paideia*, Cambridge, Mass., 1961 (important). A. Wifstrand, *L'Eglise ancienne et la culture grecque*, Paris, 1962. E. von Ivánka, *Plato Christianus. Übernahme und Umgestaltung des Platonismus durch die Väter*, Einsiedeln, 1964. H. Chadwick, *Early Christian Thought and the Classical Tradition*, New York, 1966 (excellent). Still, these works can be consulted with profit for our purpose. See also H. Hunger, *Reich der Neuen Mitte. Der christliche Geist der byzantinischen Kultur*, Graz, Vienna, and Cologne, 1965, esp. section V, "Science and Culture Striking a Balance Between Pagan and Christian Components," pp. 299–369. O. Gigon, *Die antike Kultur und das Christentum*, Gütersloh, 1966. Gigon clearly saw that Christian literature was written by the educated for the educated from the post-Apostolic times onward. F. Novotný, *The Posthumous Life of Plato*, Prague, 1977, pp. 74–78, 122–50, 177–94. A number of observations relevant to our subject can be found in H. Hunger's "On the Imitation (μίμησις) of reality of their time. By about 178—the presumed date of Celsus' attack on Christianity—a number of Christian apologists had already published works directed toward the educated pagans in high stations, including the emperor Marcus Aurelius himself. In these works, the apologists freely quoted from the classical poets, pre-Socratic philosophers and, of course, from Plato. On the other hand, if Origen wanted to show that Christians of about 249—the presumed date of his treatise *Against Celsus*[4]—could equal the philosophical and scholarly achievements of the pagans, he had but to point to himself.

Like most polemics, Celsus' strictures against Christians of his time were exaggerated and anachronistic.[5] When we turn farther back, however, to the beginnings of Christianity, we find his assessment to be valid, for the earliest documents of Christian doctrine—the Gospels and some writings of the apostolic fathers, do in fact reflect little of the intellectual values of the educated classes in the Greco-Roman world. To be sure, literary and Church historians remind us over and over again of the three classical quotations in the Epistles of St. Paul and in the Acts of the Apostles: one sententious saying from either Euripides or Menander, a comic writer of about 300 B.C. ("evil communications corrupt good manners"); and one line each from the poets Epimenides (a pre-Socratic writer) and Aratus.[6] And students of Hellenistic Judaism and of Greek philosophy point to

the beginning of the Gospel of St. John with its use of the term *Logos*, or to the chapter in the Acts that relates St. Paul's sermon in the Areopagus of Athens and mentions the words "Stoics," "Epicureans," and the "Unknown God."[7]

We might also remember, however, what the Acts say about St. Paul just prior to his encounter with pagan philosophers. In Athens he had first contacted the Jews of the local synagogue, no doubt to study the Old Testament with them in the Greek translation—the Septuagint—as he surely had done in Thessalonike and Beroea on his way to Athens.[8] The fact is that the point of literary reference for the earliest Christian literature was the Septuagint. It was used not only for direct quotations, but also as a stylistic model, even by an author who was a Gentile, who used Greek sources, and who knew how to write literary Greek. I have in mind the evangelist Luke, whose semitisms are in fact imitations of the Septuagint.[9] The Septuagint—a Jewish text in Greek— was the Homer of the Gospels and, along with the Gospels themselves, of the earliest Christian literature.

Things were quite different some three hundred fifty years later. About the middle of the fifth century, the Greek Psalter, the most frequently read part of the Septuagint, was translated into Homeric verse;[10] a life of a saint—St. Cyprian—was rewritten in hexameters by the Christian empress Eudocia;

Antiquity in Byzantine Literature," *Dumbarton Oaks Papers*, XXIII-XXIV, 1969–70, pp. 17–38, reprinted in the same author's *Byzantinische Grundlagenforschung*, London, 1973. Cf. further J. Dummer, "Die Stellung der griechischen christlichen Schriften im Rahmen der antiken Literatur," *Das Korpus der griechischen christlichen Schriftsteller*, Berlin, 1977 (Texte und Untersuchungen zur Geschichte der altchristlichen Literatur, CXX), pp. 67–76. Among more popular essays, see J. Geffcken, "Antike Kulturkämpfe," *Neue Jahrbücher für das klassische Altertum, Geschichte und deutsche Literatur und für Pädagogik*, XXIX, 1912, esp. pp. 603–11 (old, but readable on account of its vigor). M. Pohlenz, "Die Antike und das frühe Christentum," *Antike und Abendland*, I, Hamburg, 1944, pp. 42–54 (excellent). C. Mohrmann, "Les relations entre culture profane et culture chrétienne aux premiers siècles de notre ère," *Revista Portuguesa de Filologia*, XII, 1962–63, pp. 1–16. L. A. Frejberg, "Vizantijskaja poèzija IV–X vv. i antičnye tradicii," in S. S. Averincev, ed., *Vizantijskaja literatura*, Moscow, 1974, pp. 24–76. Idem, "Antičnoe literaturnoe nasledie v vizantijskuju èpoxu," in L. A. Frejberg, ed., *Antičnost' i Vizantija*, Moscow, 1975, pp. 123–35. Cf., finally, the few but informative pages by S. Gero, "Christianity and Hellenism from the First to the Fourth Century," *Didascalos*, V, 1975, pp. 123–35. For good bibliographical introductions to the

early centuries of our subject, cf. G. Glockmann, *Homer in der frühchristlichen Literatur bis Justinus*, Berlin, 1968 (Texte und Untersuchungen zur Geschichte der altchristlichen Literatur, CV), pp. ix–xvii and esp. 3–17, and N. Zeegers-Vander Vorst, *Les Citations des poètes grecs chez les apologistes chrétiens du IIe siècle*, Louvain, 1972, pp. ix–xlix. For Second Sophistic, whose precepts were followed by Greek fathers of the fourth and later centuries, cf. the bibliography by G. Kennedy and M. Barnard in G. W. Bowersock, ed., *Approaches to the Second Sophistic*, University Park, Pa., 1974, pp. 30–34. For special points concerning literary genres and individual authors, cf. the relevant entries in the (still incomplete) *Reallexikon für Antike und Christentum*, Stuttgart, 1941–. It is a pity that the outstanding catalogue raisonné on the survival of the classics compiled by a number of luminaries under the auspices of the Warburg Institute covers only the years 1931–33. Cf. H. Meier, R. Newald, and E. Wind, eds., *Kulturwissenschaftliche Bibliographie zum Nachleben der Antike, erster Band, die Erscheinungen des Jahres 1931*, Leipzig and Berlin, 1934 (Kraus Reprint, 1978), esp. pp. 134–50, 158; and The Warburg Institute, ed., *A Bibliography of the Survival of the Classics, Second Volume, The Publications of 1932–33*, London, 1938 (Kraus Reprint, 1978), esp. pp. 152–66. In my own references preference will be given to sources and to recent secondary literature.

authentic Homeric lines were put together by the same empress and others and made into *centos*, "quilts," or a continuous narration, in order to render, among other things, Gospel stories and parts of Genesis in epic diction;[11] and in two different works, one pagan, one Christian, the last great poet of antiquity, Nonnus, applied the epithets "virginal" and "shunning the nuptial bed" equally to Pallas Athena and the Virgin Mary.[12]

This was a remarkable development. In terms of Atticism, the literary doctrine that had been growing in influence since the middle of the first century B.C., the early Christian writings had nothing classical about them. But in terms of the Second Sophistic, a literary doctrine that was the heir to Atticism and that was still in force in the fourth century A.D., much of the literature of that century written in high style was classical in form, even if Christian in content. Hellenism, vanquished by Christianity, conquered its victor in turn. This paraphrase of the Horatian line sums up the story of the most refined strand of Christian literature in the early centuries. The decisive events in this story happened within two hundred years, roughly between A.D. 150 and 350.

Antique literature first entered Christian letters on a large scale in the writings of the second-century apologists. We know about a dozen of those authors by name, and can still read more than half of them.[13] The diffusion of Christianity among the pagan educated classes must have been rapid enough by the second half of the second century to produce these apologists, for they seem to have been converts rather than products of upward social mobility within the Christian community: we know for sure that four of them had once been pagans.[14] With the appearance of educated and well-to-do converts—of Christians who, far from being slaves, owned them[15]—a dialogue with pagan intellectuals could be carried on within a common frame of reference. Naturally enough, this frame of reference had to be predominantly pagan.

In order to prove the absurdity of polytheism and the immorality of Greek mythology, defenders of Christianity such as Justin Martyr, Tatian, Athenagoras, Theophilus, and Clement of Alexandria had to adduce concrete examples. These were most commonly drawn from the epic, tragic, comic, and philosophical poets—from Homer, Euripides, Menander, Orpheus, Hesiod's *Theogony*, Sophocles, Callimachus, Pindar, Aeschylus, Empedocles, Aratus (St. Paul's source), Aristophanes, or Solon—in that order of frequency.[16] Substantively, there was little point in the apologists' dwelling on the atrocities and obscenities of mythology, upon Kronos devouring his own children, or Aphrodite's adulterous liaison with Ares, for pagans of Emperor Marcus Aurelius' philosophical sophistication did not in any case take these stories literally. But the practice of citing these offensive acts was nevertheless useful to the apologists as a kind of literary apprenticeship. While proving the absurdity and disarray of the Greek pantheon, one could learn a great deal about Greek mythology.

The apologists pursued two further lines of argument with the help of pagan literary sources. The first aimed at countering the objection that the Christian religion was a recent invention. They connected the Christian message with that of the Old Testament; from there it was a simple matter to show by quotations from ancient poets, from Herodotus and from Hellenistic historians, that Homer, and even his predecessor Orpheus, came later than Moses, that consequently the Pentateuch was more venerable than the *Iliad*, and that the names of the Greek gods were of recent date. It followed—and this was the second argument—that any doctrinal agreements between the Old Testament and Greek wisdom were the result of plagiarism committed by such Greek poets and philosophers as Orpheus, Hesiod, even Pindar and Plato.[17] This particular variety of argument was not a Christian discovery, but was borrowed, quotations and all, from the Jews, who had had to face the problem of harmonizing Hellenism with their own religion centuries before the Christians did.[18] At any rate, in order to prove the Greeks' alleged dependence on the Old Testament, the apologists had to, and did, produce many antique quotations.

We may quibble with the first apologists' performance as *litterati*. With the exception of Clement of Alexandria, they seem not to have felt quite sure of themselves, for they were great show-offs and sought out obscure passages for their quotations. At least one fragment of Euripides is preserved today only because it was quoted by the apologist Athenagoras ("Zeus, if he really exists in Heaven . . . "),[19] and a detail concerning the modesty displayed by Aeneas' wife at the time of the sack and burning of Troy is known only through Clement of Alexandria.[20]

These bits may in fact have been spurious,[21] or the result of faulty memory, but even if they are genuine, the classical erudition of the apologists should not dazzle us. It was not drawn from the sources themselves (except perhaps for some of the dialogues of Plato), but from anthologies upon which the pagans of the time depended for their quotations as well. Clement of Alexandria has twenty-six quotations from Menander, eighteen of which he shares with other, roughly contemporary writers, including Plutarch, Galen, Epictetus, and the fifth-century anthologist Stobaeus. Obviously, it was an anthology, rather than Menander's originals, that also served as Clement's source.[22] Another of the poetic sources on which the apologists openly relied was not classical at all, even if it was written in hexameters. This was the collection of the Sibylline oracles. Second only to Homer and Euripides as a quarry for quotations, the oracles were Judeo-Christian forgeries, their older parts dating from between the second century B.C. and the second century of our era.[23]

Contemporary pagan authors were also quoted, but not by name—since they were not yet classics, there was no point in parading them; their writings would simply be quietly absorbed or plagiarized. In the second century, a Christian compiler using the name of Sextus reworked a pagan collection of ethical sayings, a collection also drawn upon by the contemporary Neopythagoreans and, later, by the great enemy of Christianity, Porphyry.[24] Clement of Alexandria cribbed from Musonius Rufus, the popular Cynic-Stoic philosopher of the first century A.D.[25]

The more or less skillful use of Greek literature to expose the weaknesses of the Greek religion still did not imply approval of it. By about the year 200, the absorption of classical thought and letters into Christian culture was considerable, but it was by no means a foregone conclusion—the signs were in fact ambiguous. Some of them pointed toward reconciliation. Clement of Alexandria, who was at home with classical rhetorical and grammatical devices, was also imbued with late Platonic and Stoic philosophical concepts; no wonder he explained away the passages in St. Paul's Epistle that held the wisdom of this world to be foolishness by saying that what St. Paul was condemning was bad philosophy, such as that of the Epicureans, and not Greek philosophy in general.[26] But other signs were pointing in the opposite direction. Many writings of Origen were a step backward from those of his teacher, Clement: in his surviving *Sermons* and *Commentaries*, Origen quoted not a single Greek poet.

Foremost among the acts of defiance against the system of antique literary and artistic values was the *Discourse to the Greeks*, written by the formidable Tatian some twenty-five years before Clement of Alex-

andria wrote his *Protrepticus*. Aristides, the earliest of the apologists whose works are still extant, had divided the peoples of the world into barbarians, Greeks, Jews, and Christians.[27] Tatian recognized only two of these categories: the Greeks, keepers of pagan culture, and the barbarians—and he identified himself with the latter. Greek poetry corrupts the soul, but learning from the barbarians is laudable. To imitate Attic dialect—a must for the *litterati* of his time—is no better than to speak Doric. The study of Attic diction, syllogisms, dimensions of the earth, the course and the physical nature of the sun, are vain occupations and mere verbiage. Tatian recounts how he came across barbaric writings, unpretentious in style and more ancient than the wisdom of the Greeks (we already know that he was referring to the Old Testament), and how he believed in them. He said goodbye to the bombast of the Romans and the nonsense of the Athenians and espoused "our barbaric philosophy." He, "a native of the land of the Assyrians," became a philosopher after the fashion of the barbarians.[28] In pages contrasting the virtues of Christian women with those of their pagan counterparts, Tatian attacked Greek poetesses—a dozen of them, beginning with Sappho. He also disdained the sculptors who had made statues of those morally reprehensible females and other depraved men and women.[29]

When he wrote his *Discourse*, Tatian, this Tertullian of the Greek East, may already have been a heretic.[30] If not, he became one soon afterward—a fortunate thing for the survival of Sappho and of classical letters in general. But even if Tatian had remained orthodox, his rigor might have impeded his chances of success. To be sure, Tatian's attitudes lived on among a few later orthodox writers. These writers may have been less familiar than Tatian with the cultural and literary heritage of antiquity; in any case, they too rejected it, and saw in it not only an abomination dear to idolaters but also a source of Christian heresy—Epiphanius of Cyprus (d. 403) was the prize example of such a stance. He thundered against Stoics and Platonists without ever reading them, and quoted Homer—some of whose lines he must have learned in school—only from second hand.[31]

However, as time went on, the signs pointed more and more firmly toward Christian acceptance of pagan writers and of classical literary forms. These clearer signs were already present on the eve of the triumph of Christianity. For Methodius (d. ca. 311), probably the bishop of Olympus on the southern coast of Asia Minor, Homer was no longer a plagiarist of Moses, but an equal to the prophet Isaiah.[32] About 300, Methodius wrote a treatise on chastity. He cast it in the form of a dialogue imitating Plato's *Symposium*;[33] and he blended Homer so skillfully with his own occasional verse that we may be sure he knew the poet intimately. Methodius identified the dragon of Revelation with the Chimera, quoted the verses of the *Iliad* that dealt with the Chimera and her slayer, Bellerophon, and added another verse in which he changed "the gods'" into "the Father's." This he did in order to continue with an elegiac distich of his own, in which Christ the Lord made his appearance.[34] Methodius not only implied in his verses, but expressly said in the prose sentences that followed upon them, that Christ had slain "her," i.e., the Chimera, who stood for the devil. We can thus assert that for Methodius Christ was the new Bellerophon. The passage helps us explain the appearance of Christ and Bellerophon, side by side, on the recently discovered Hinton St. Mary mosaic pavement that Professor Hanfmann treats elsewhere in this volume.[35]

Methodius, incidentally, was among the earliest Christian authors to discuss the lines of the *Odyssey* in which Odysseus, attached to the mast of his ship, listened to and withstood the song of the Sirens. The mast with its yardarm was interpreted as the tree of Christ, that is, the cross; the faithful, attached like Odysseus to that mast, should withstand the temptations and heresies of this world. This Christian literary allegory enables us to understand the message of the bronze lamp that takes the form of a ship with the figure of Odysseus attached to its mast [Cat. no. 199].[36]

In literature, the final triumph of conquered Hellenism came half a century after Methodius and after the triumph of Christianity. We owe it mainly to the Cappadocian fathers, above all to Gregory of Nazianzus (d. 390) and Basil the Great (d. 379). With them came the saturation of Christian elite writings with classical elements.[37] To concentrate on Gregory, literary antiquity made itself at home in all the genres he practiced—epistolography, epigram, even the homily, that cousin of the antique diatribe, so reluctant to imitate all its pagan relative's traits.

In Gregory's homilies, mythology was no longer a working tool, wielded to disparage paganism. By his time, paganism was collapsing by itself. Gregory's mythological passages merely constitute a badge of distinction bearing the same relation to a working tool that the Phi Beta Kappa insignia bears to a key.

But the pretense might still be there. In Gregory's homily on the Epiphany, for instance, he stated that the Christian mystery of that feast was not like the pagan mysteries, which were the work of demons. He then went on to enumerate those pagan mysteries and stories at such length that his account takes up two columns in Migne's *Patrologia Graeca*.[38] Clearly, Gregory's information was given for its own sake. It was, in addition, so rarefied and allusive that by the early sixth century it required a specialized commentary. This commentary on the mythological passages in at least five of Gregory's homilies, which was the subject of a monograph by Professor Weitzmann, was not only widely read (about 142 manuscripts still exist), and translated into Syriac and Armenian at an early date, but also occasionally illustrated.[39] Whether or not Gregory had set out to whet the mythological curiosity of his readers, he had certainly succeeded.

I shall produce one more example from the homiletic genre. The closing passages of Gregory's sermon for the Sunday after Easter are devoted to the praise of awakening Nature. In form, this praise is an *ekphrasis*, that is, to use the technical definition of antique oratory, "a narrative speech bringing its subject before the eyes" of the listener.[40] As a genre, the *ekphrasis* had a number of subdivisions, of which one was "of the Seasons."[41] Gregory's text is precisely that, an *ekphrasis* of Spring, whom he already calls the Queen of Seasons. We are invited to "see" the cloudless sky, the limpid springs, the fragrant meadows, gamboling lambs, diving dolphins; we are shown the husbandman ploughing with a yoke of oxen, the shepherd playing—melodiously, of course—upon the syrinx; we follow the busy bee building the hexagonal—yes, hexagonal—honeycomb for our sake; we admire the birds building their nests; finally, we view a spirited horse galloping, in the rhythms of a Homeric quotation, out of our sight toward a river, in whose waters he then admires his own reflection.[42]

Gregory's praise of the bee echoes the antique, or at least the non-Christian, admirers of that insect, for the bee is not mentioned in the New Testament at all. In conclusion of his praise, Gregory exclaims, "would that we, too, the apiary of Christ, should take unto ourselves this example of wisdom and love of labor." After the description of the chirping birds, he observes: "Everyone is singing the praise of God with inarticulate utterances"—the oxymoron being in the best antique rhetorical style. We are grateful to Gregory for these two tags reading "made in Christianland," which he tactfully appended to his *ekphrasis*, but we are not fooled. For one thing, we remember that Gregory's pagan friend, Libanius, also wrote an *ekphrasis* of Spring. For another, the associations that come to mind from the visual realm are those of a floor mosaic in a fourth-century villa, not those of the Church of St. Mamas in Caesarea where the sermon was preached.[43]

A Byzantine commentator on this sermon surmised that St. Basil was listening to Gregory on that Sunday after Easter.[44] If he was, he must have savored every bit of the sermon's closing part, for Basil himself could turn out a bucolic *ekphrasis* second to none. Take his letter addressed to Gregory, in which he describes his rural retreat in the Pontus. Again we see a tall mountain covered with multifarious trees and watered by clear streams; it is bordered by ravines and a river, in whose deep whirlpool we all but perceive a multitude of fish. We feel the cool breezes; we learn that Basil had no time to admire the flowers and songbirds (but he recorded them, just the same); we stand amazed at the fertility of the land and the wealth of wild goats, deer, and hare that it sustains.

Of Christianity, there is but a little trace: God is twice mentioned, once in the phrase "God willing"; there is one reference to "tranquility" (*hesychia*) by which, however, Basil means not the Neoplatonic or monastic variety of detachment and contemplation so familiar to him, but the kind always sought by city dwellers, the peace that comes from the absence of other people. On the other hand, Basil says that his retreat is even better than the island of Calypso, "the beauty of which Homer appears to admire," and the letter closes with a reference to Alcmaeon and the Echinades, the latter of which I had to look up in order to catch his drift.[45]

Basil died some twenty years after having described his retreat, and some time afterward Gregory delivered the funerary eulogy in honor of his lifelong friend. In it, he followed the classical blueprint: opening with the *topos* of modesty, he touched upon Basil's country of origin, and then turned to Basil's lineage, which he compared to the great houses of antiquity, of Pelops, Alcmaeon, and Heracles. He did this by using the device of *paraleipsis*, or "leaving out," that is, by saying that he was not going to indulge in such a comparison, although if he had indulged in it, Basil would have come out on top. When the time came to speak of Basil's early education, Gregory compared the relationship between Basil and his father, who had tutored him, to that between Achilles and his teacher, the centaur Chi-

ron; he did it, however, without directly mentioning either of these figures.

Further on, Gregory compared himself and Basil to Orestes and his faithful companion Pylades, and he gave the palm of victory in moral science to Basil over Minos and Rhadamanthys, the incorruptible judges of the pagan netherworld. He alluded to the goddess Diana by quoting one of her rare epithets; he also used the verb "to kill strangers," a cognate of which occurs in Euripides' *Iphigenia at Tauris*, just in order to allude to Iphigenia's sacrifice. When Gregory applied to Basil one of his many borrowed Homeric phrases, he did so, he said, "so that I may fully Homerize him." When Gregory quoted his favorite line from Pindar, it was almost verbatim; but when he quoted from a psalm of David, he paraphrased it so as to render it in more elegant Greek.[46]

In addition to his famous eulogy, Gregory wrote a full dozen funerary epigrams on Basil. He was quite attracted to epigrams, leaving us about two hundred fifty of them in all, mostly epitaphs or poems connected with the desecration of graves.[47] In the epigrams, Gregory made use of two registers, as it were, the classical and the Christian, and he played on them, sometimes simultaneously, as when he appealed to Heracles and three more obscure figures from antiquity and bade them yield to his mother Nonna, the "bearer of Christ";[48] and sometimes he applied the two registers in sequence.

If the person addressed was a priest or otherwise intensely Christian, such as Basil the Great or Nonna, Gregory's verses written for them contained clearly Christian references: the power that caused the death of the person eulogized was the Trinity, Christ the Lord, or an angel of brilliance.[49] If, however, those honored did not belong to that restricted category, even if they had been Christians in life, they were celebrated in terms for which one can easily find parallels in pagan poets or pagan epigrams on funerary stones. Here are a few instances. The Christian Sophist Prohaeresius had been astounding the whole world with his speeches until the day he died; now that he had died, Athens was no longer famous, and Gregory invites young men to desert the city of Cecrops—which is an elegant way of saying "Athens" again. Nonna, Gregory's deceased mother, "lives on among the blessed"—this is Christian enough, but the expression itself was taken over from the Hellenistic poet Callimachus. The brother of St. Basil drowned, the victim of an "envious" river—an antique motif.[50] After death, other Christians "sink below the earth" or "depart to

Hades," and so even Gregory's own brother, Caesarius. The tomb of Gregory's young cousin is called "this Elysian place"; that cousin died unwed, or, in Gregory's terms, "Eros had not lit the torch for his bridal chamber." In a dialogue over this same youth's dead body, Graces and Muses swear never to create a statue like him among men—that is, never to produce another man like him. Our author even pretended to believe that a living lady could be immortal, and that the ghosts of the dead dwelled beside their tombs.[51]

In my own imaginary museum of visual counterparts to Byzantine letters is a group of small late third-century classicizing marbles from Asia Minor [Cat. nos. 362–68]. They represent—again with characteristic duality—busts of secular patrons and scenes from the story of the prophet Jonah. These marbles I place next to Gregory's "two-register" epigrams, with their mixture of pagan and Christian references.[52] Epigrams, a small form, were a genre in which antique models could be imitated most successfully.

We observe the same duality in another genre where brevity was a virtue, namely, in Gregory's correspondence. When he upbraids a young Christian destined for a high government career, he quotes the New Testament once and the Old Testament four times. But when he needs a favor from the pagan ex-governor of Cappadocia, he writes him a letter in which he quotes Pythagoras with approval and adds that he is glad to realize that his correspondent has been an imitator of that wise man from Samos.[53]

Two mechanisms assured that pagan literary culture would enter Christian letters. The first of them was school. When it came to general education, as opposed to the strictly confessional one, Christians did not create programs of their own: their children learned their reading from Homer and the poets. Papyri from Egypt teach us that long after the triumph of Christianity, children practiced their spelling with the names of the pagan gods. Adult Christians taught in secular schools: Origen started his teaching career in such a school around the year 200 at the age of seventeen, and in 268 a priest professed Hellenic rhetoric at Antioch. Almost exactly a century later, the Christian Sophist Prohaeresius, whom we have already met, taught both Christians (perhaps even Gregory of Nazianzus and Basil) and pagans at Athens. From what we learn from one of these pagans, Prohaeresius' grateful and admiring biographer Eunapius, the master's rhetorical technique did not differ from that of any other teacher

of his time and had nothing Christian in it. It followed that Gregory of Nazianzus and Basil, who spent long years during their late teens and early twenties at school in Athens and elsewhere, learned pagan letters there, and in a curriculum that resembled the later seven liberal arts.[54]

The second mechanism, which was surely in operation until the fifth century, was the open intercourse between Christian and pagan men of letters. We should not be too impressed by Libanius' pique at Emperor Constantius who allegedly snubbed pagan *litterati*, by his tearful plea for the preservation of pagan temples, by Gregory of Nazianzus' invectives against the pagan Julian the Apostate, or by stories—true though they were—of the destruction of the Serapeum and the melting down of the statues of pagan gods at Alexandria in 391. We should remember that antipagan imperial laws of the time still recommended preservation of pagan statues for their artistic value, that about the year 400 Lausus, a high Christian official of Constantinople, was allowed to gather a private collection of famous statues, including, so we are told, the Cnidian Aphrodite of Praxiteles,[55] and that at the beginning of the fifth century there was still no Christian church of any size in the center of Athens.[56]

Except for the writing of history, the triumph of Christianity brought no significant change in the development of Christian literature and, for most of the fourth century, no state-inspired difficulties for the adherents of the old world view. No radical change occurred in fourth-century cultural ideals because no radical change occurred in the composition of the elite.[57] In such a world, if Christians could teach the pagans, then pagans could teach the Christians coming to them with Christian letters of recommendation, and both could remain in literary exchange. Pagans—including Libanius—were among the recipients of letters and epigrams by Gregory of Nazianzus;[58] the emperor Julian corresponded with Prohaeresius and was even ready to exempt him from the strictures of his own anti-Christian education law of 362;[59] Gregory of Nyssa praised Libanius' brilliance and entreated him not to be discouraged, but rather to continue his rhetorical output;[60] and in one of his earliest works, John Chrysostom copied several passages from Libanius almost word for word.[61] No wonder that in the fifth century, the Church historian Socrates firmly believed that Chrysostom, Gregory of Nazianzus, and St. Basil had been pupils of Libanius;[62] and we still possess a correspondence (in twenty-six letters) in which Libanius and Basil admire each other's Atticizing style, exchange offprints, indulge in mythological allusions, and invoke the Muses.[63] The correspondence is a forgery, but an early one; it was read in the fifth century by the future heretic Severus, who was said to have been led to Christian literature through it.[64] The fact that the correspondence includes authentic letters by Gregory of Nyssa and by a pagan Sophist writing to him shows that the forger had the right sense of the period and realized that sophisticated writers of the time, whether Christian or not, shared the same literary tastes.[65]

Now we can better understand the Christian intellectuals' reaction to Emperor Julian's edict of 362.[66] The effect of the edict was to prohibit Christian professors from explaining pagan authors in school. In the professors' opinion, this was tantamount to depriving them of any teaching matter whatsoever, for they could not conceive of teaching on the basis of literary genres other than the classical ones. Instead of turning to the New Testament, as Julian suggested,[67] they tried to transpose the Scriptures into an antique form or genre: the Old Testament was rendered in hexameters or iambics; the New Testament, transformed into Platonic dialogues—or so at least the Church historian Socrates tells us.[68] When Julian's law was repealed soon afterward, these surrogate teaching tools were no longer of use. Socrates did not regret their disappearance, for he preferred the original pagan Greek works. He must have dreaded being excluded from the intercourse with these works so much that he even misunderstood the letter, if not the intent, of Julian's measure, for he asserted that the emperor's law had prohibited Christians, not from teaching, but from *being educated in*, Greek literature.[69]

If we were to scrutinize all that Gregory of Nazianzus wrote, his other sermons, letters, and poems, whether in hexameters, in elegiac distichs, in iambics, or in anacreontic verse, we would be able to furnish proof of how greatly Gregory the rhetor and the poet depended on contemporary pagan literary practice with respect to vocabulary, syntax, figures of speech and thought, and how much he depended on the exercises he had learned in school for his mythological apparatus and for his mastery of antique poetical language and meters.[70] The same proof, extended to the use of Platonic dialogue, could be furnished for the other two Cappadocian fathers, St. Basil and St. Gregory of Nyssa. But I have made my point, and I am almost ready to leave the Cappadocian fathers. Almost, but not quite, for I wish to

devote a few more words to the discrepancy between their literary practice and their theoretical pronouncements on literature. The former is all of a piece; the latter are ambivalent. The fathers speak out of both sides of their mouths.[71]

In their literary use of two registers, the pagan and the Christian, the fathers turned to the classical register as often as, if not more often than, the Christian one. But they also delivered themselves of statements that might have been expected to come only from *engagé* adherents of a total ideology. Soon after 362, Gregory of Nazianzus learned that Gregory of Nyssa, previously ordained as a reader in the Christian Church, had decided to become a professional teacher of rhetoric. Gregory of Nazianzus was genuinely shocked. In a letter, he granted that his correspondent from Nyssa would make a perfectly Christian rhetorician, but, after all, one had to observe some decorum. Would his friend, being a moral man, agree to be a boxer—a disreputable occupation—and to perform in public just because he was a moral man? Gregory exhorted his friend to give up the idea of teaching.[72] Some time later, a certain Adamantius, teacher of rhetoric, asked Gregory of Nazianzus for his handbooks on the subject. In his reply, Gregory called rhetoric a game and Christianity the true culture, and he agreed to sell his rhetorical library to Adamantius, with the proceeds to go to the poor.[73]

Faced with pronouncements such as these, we are nonplussed. We notice in passing that the letters to Gregory of Nyssa and to Adamantius contain the same unannounced quotation from Hesiod's *Works and Days*, and that in the second letter Gregory, out of habit, as he himself says, rattles off the themes of rhetorical exercises used in school, such as the descriptions of the battles at Marathon and Salamis. But we still do not clearly see how the same man who thought that teaching pagan programs in school was a shameful occupation for an ecclesiastic of the lowest rank could write a classicizing epigram on the Christian teacher Prohaeresius and pen a note recommending a Christian child to the attention of the pagan teacher Libanius.

This ambivalent attitude of the Cappadocians toward pagan rhetoric and its rules appears most clearly in their prefaces to a number of eulogies of the saints—that is, works that are among the earliest specimens, or at least precursors, of Byzantine hagiography. The fathers knew the classical plan of a eulogy by heart. It required, among other things, a disquisition on the hero's native city, lineage, and circumstances of birth. Since Christian heroes were different from pagan ones, however, should they not be praised in a different fashion? "The divine school knows not the law of eulogies . . . , that law requires that the native city of the person eulogized be praised and his lineage scrutinized. . . . But why am I any better if my city has been victorious over an enemy, or if its location is favorable?"[74] "We are not going," exclaimed St. Basil in his homily on St. Mamas, "to praise Mamas according to the laws of secular eulogy; we shall not speak of his illustrious parents and ancestors—a horse is not swift because his sire was a racer."[75] Gregory of Nyssa expressed the same sentiments. In his eulogy on St. Ephrem, he decided not to follow the secular plan (which, however, he outlined in detail); he would weave the wreath of his discourse out of things by which the saint himself became conspicuous in life.[76] The new rules stressed simplicity, the saint's achievements and, of course, the unadorned truth. Why imitate secular makers of myths and put up a screen of beautiful words around truth? She is naked and comes without a lawyer; Mamas was a poor shepherd, that is all.[77]

We have only to read the actual texts of eulogies by Gregory of Nyssa to realize that these noble promises of creating new norms for the Christian encomiastic genre came to naught. Many of his eulogies, including some that contain programmatic statements against the antique encomium, follow the laws of that encomium down to the last detail.[78] New genres are difficult to create, as everybody knows who has ever attempted to write an innovative report to the trustees. The Cappadocian fathers were caught in the web of pagan literary conventions of their time, and knew it, but they were unable to extricate themselves. Nor were they willing, for classical literature was a part of them. Yet that very literature did reflect a refuted and rejected ideology. What should one do? The answer was given by Gregory of Nazianzus in one chapter of his eulogy for Basil, by Gregory's cousin in a poem, and by Basil in a special homily addressed "To Young Men," really boys of about sixteen, about "How They Might Profit from Pagan Literature."[79]

In substance, Gregory's and Basil's message was that one should proceed selectively. It was all right for St. Basil's young man to study antique authors: he should admire classical poets when they described the deeds of virtuous men and shun them when they described the machinations of wicked people, just as Odysseus shunned the song of the Sirens—again we might remember the bronze lamp [Cat. no. 199].

Basil repeated his point with many variations and seasoned it with appropriate commonplaces. Like a bee collecting nectar only from certain flowers, the reader should retain only certain passages, those in agreement with the truth, and pass over the rest. Poetic descriptions of quarreling and dissolute gods were to be avoided; nor were the orators' lying tricks to be imitated. In short, antique literature was useful only insofar as it sent the reader in pursuit of virtue. One of Basil's precepts was to be repeated countless times by Christian humanists of the Byzantine Middle Ages and the Western Renaissance: the study of classical texts, properly selected for their moral utility, has a propaedeutic value; it provides preliminary training before the student is ready to approach the mysteries of the Holy Scriptures.[80]

Was it a precept or an excuse? I imagine St. Basil would have grown very angry if he had been asked this question. Yet he would have to agree that, on the evidence of his address "To Young Men" alone, the times of the early apologists were far behind. In the address, Basil mentioned Moses only once, not to show that the plagiarists Homer and Plato had gotten their wisdom from him, but to say that Moses himself was a pupil: he learned the sciences of the Egyptians before turning to matters divine. And Basil never directly blamed Homer for his indecent stories. All Homeric poetry, he said, was a praise of virtue. He dared not present this statement as his own opinion, attributing it to "someone knowledgeable in such matters," but it was clear that he had made it his own, for at another point of the treatise, he announced that he would rely on the writings of pagan authors for drawing "a shadow outline of virtue" for his young listeners.[81] Of the at least five quotations from the Gospels in Basil's tract none is literal. In all cases Basil transposed the words of the Scripture into high style and amalgamated their simple messages with his own Attic elegance.[82] Of course, when it came to Euripides, Theognis, and Solon, Basil quoted them verbatim.[83]

So much for the shiny side of the coin. We should now take a brief look at the reverse.

When we dealt with the apologists and the Cappadocian fathers, we were moving mainly among educated writers of high station and among refined literary genres. Before his conversion, Tatian had been an itinerant Sophist, that is, a teacher of eloquence with a philosophical bent. We know from Philostratus, a biographer of such Sophists, that this calling enjoyed a considerable social prestige in the latter half of the second century. We can infer a comfortable social status for Clement of Alexandria, the last of the apologists. He was able to travel widely in quest of education. He was annoyed by the interiors of bedrooms in the mansions of the rich in his city (they were adorned with erotically arousing depictions of the gods)—which proved that he had at least seen them. In his treatise entitled "Which Rich Man Can Be Saved," Clement explained to his audience that St. Matthew's passage about the necessity of selling all one's goods and of following the Savior need not be taken literally, only allegorically. It was no sin to be born rich.[84] Clement, it seems, was reassuring the wealthy, and may have been a fellow member of the establishment.

As for SS. Basil and Gregory of Nyssa, to mention two prominent names from our second period, we have no need to draw inferences. We know they were scions of an old family of Cappadocian landholding magnates,[85] sons of a Christian teacher of rhetoric, and for a time friends of Libanius, the most famous pagan teacher of their time. Christian writers like these were led to adopt pagan literary devices by both their education and their social standing. To have done so was not the only imaginable choice that they could have made, but it was a historically likely choice and, above all, an easy one. In the field of letters, at least, class was thicker than ideology.

The picture changes when we step some rungs down the social ladder or turn to genres whose classical pedigree is either less direct or nonexistent. When we read, say, an early fifth-century Christian metric epitaph from Cappadocia, open the late fourth-century *Life of St. Anthony* by St. Athanasius, the early fifth-century *Lausiac History* of Palladius, or the "Sayings of the Fathers" relating the exploits of fourth- and early fifth-century Egyptian hermits, or when we leaf through the world chronicle by Malalas, written in Antioch and Constantinople in the sixth century, or savor a stanza in the Acathist Hymn to the Virgin from the same century, we are disappointed in our search for classicisms. In the epitaph, for instance, we deplore the spelling errors and barely recognize the intended meter. In the literary texts just cited, we find little understanding of classical culture and little respect for it. In the *Life of St. Anthony* we read how the hero, an illiterate Copt ignorant of the Greek tongue, put the "Hellenic" philosophers—that is, Greek-speaking educated pagans—to shame through an interpreter.[86] In Malalas we find a tidbit stating that Cicero and Sallust

were poets,[87] and the author of the Acathist Hymn made fun of the "polybabbling orators," who were unable to express the mystery of the Incarnation, and bade the Virgin rejoice, for the "writers of myths were withered" and she had broken the "webs of the Athenians"—probably the very philosophers with whom St. Paul disputed on the Areopagus.[88]

Faced with those disappointments, we can choose one of two courses of action. We can declare our initial search for classical vestiges in these sources to have been superficial, and we may renew it, trying harder the second time. To be sure, we shall obtain some results. In the literary epitaph from Cappadocia with which I started my list of disappointing examples, we shall find, appended to the hopeless verses, a perfectly copied line from the *Iliad*.[89] Looking further into literary epigraphy, we shall be able to produce the queen of Early Christian inscriptions, discovered less than a hundred years ago, that of Abercius. Abercius' epitaph, preserved partly on stone and partly in a saint's life, dates from about 200. It was composed for this Phrygian bishop in hexameters, and it alludes, in terms of pagan mystery cults, to Christianity—so obscurely, however, that some scholars of the past century held it to have been the profession of an adherent of a pagan cult, such as that of Attis. At the end, our inscription contains the pagan formula, later adopted by Christians, that prescribed a fine for violation of the grave.[90]

Scrutinizing further references to St. Anthony in other literature, we would be able to point out that an edifying piece inserted under his name into a collection of monkish stories is in fact an adaptation of Epictetus' popular Stoic Manual of the second century A.D.[91] We would also detect in other early lives of saints, even in those that do not affect a high style, the use of antique devices. These lives, we would find, adhered to the same blueprint made for a pagan laudation by Menander, the third-century theoretician of rhetoric, which had been so closely followed by the Cappadocians. Finally, even if we have to concede that the structure of the Acathist Hymn to the Virgin is ultimately inspired by Syriac models, we might contend that Greek homilies in rhythmical prose were the other source of the hymn's literary inspiration, and state that these homilies also followed the devices of Greek pagan oratory.[92]

Such a second try, however, has not regained very much ground. I propose, therefore, to adopt another course of action and to view the Early Christian Greek literature of the third to the seventh century not as one entity, but as several of them—several Christian Greek literatures, as it were. The classical component was strongest in works produced for the pagan market by Christian authors imbued with the basic cultural assumptions of the educated pagans; and later, in works written predominantly for Christians, by authors imbued with a Christian high-style literary tradition that had been formed by the fourth century. To be sure, classical or contemporary pagan literary culture was present, through osmosis, in writings coming from less refined pens, beginning with the New Testament. But starting about 400, a vast literary production was forthcoming for the internal, mostly monastic, market, a production in which the osmosis from the classical world was hardly perceptible. Nonclassicizing genres evolved that were practiced regardless of the educational level of their authors. We have only to think of John Moschus' *Spiritual Meadow*, a collection of monastic stories datable about 600, culled by their author from three continents. Moschus must have been fairly educated, for he was a traveling companion—perhaps even a chaperon—of Sophronius the Sophist, i.e., a man who at some time had been a professor of letters. Yet, hardly a classical allusion can be found in the stories of the *Spiritual Meadow*: their world is that of the Scriptures, of the orthodox and the heretics, and no longer of the Christians and pagans. The linguistic differences in this world are between popular Greek and Semitic languages, not between Atticism and Solecism. Moschus does use the technical term for "studying" employed in the university parlance of his time, but he uses it not to describe attending a course in philosophy or medicine, but to mean spending an hour in spiritual meditation.[93]

To judge by the number of surviving manuscripts, some products of the nonclassicizing Christian prose literature had a clientele at least as wide as the one reading some works of the most popular classicizing fathers: while the correspondence of Gregory of Nazianzus is preserved in some 1600 codices, and the *Hexaemeron*, St. Basil's treatise on the first six days of creation, in some 120, the *Spiritual Meadow* by Moschus is still to be read, in full or in part, in some 150 manuscripts.[94] That parity disappears when we come to religious poetry. There are hundreds upon hundreds of copies of the Acathist Hymn to the Virgin, a *kontakion* in its form, for this hymn occurs not only in the dozen collections called *Kontakaria*, but also in the multitude of liturgical books called *Triodia*, *Horologia*, and *Menaea*. But contemporary high-style poems to the glory of the Virgin Mary, composed in Constantinople in Greek iambics or Latin hexameters, have come down to us only in single manuscripts.[95]

The heyday of the *kontakion* falls between the time of the exquisite, classicizing archangel ivory in the British Museum and that of the Sinai icon of the Virgin with the Hellenistic angels behind her [Cat. nos. 481 and 478]. This poetic genre is the greatest original creation of Byzantine literature. It is not a product of simple piety; its strictly observed correspondences from strophe to strophe are more complicated than are elegiac distichs, let alone iambics following one upon another in monotonous lines. But, as we have already seen, in its structure and devices the *kontakion* owes no direct, and only some indirect, debt to Greek antiquity. We may speculate that in terms of classical culture, the greatest writer of *kontakia*, Romanos the Melode, would hardly meet with the approval of his contemporary, Paul the Silentiary, the courtier of Justinian and author of an *ekphrasis* of St. Sophia in hexameters.[96] For if Romanos knew the names of Plato, Aratus, Demosthenes, and Homer, he used them solely to make unflattering puns.[97] Yet, Romanos, in whom later Byzantine biographers saw a Jewish convert from Beirut, practiced a new literary form, and Paul the Silentiary did not.

The classicizing strand in Greek Christian literature continued to have outstanding practitioners until the Arab invasions: it was not to disappear from that literature so long as Byzantium existed. In the seventh century, George of Pisidia sang the victories of the emperor Heraclius (d. 641) and his lieutenants over the Sassanian Persians or the Avars and the Slavs. He could not resist punning on the name of Heraclius, whose labors he declared to be more imposing than the twelve labors of Heracles. He praised Homer, and referred to Odysseus in such a recondite fashion that his latest editor took it for a reference to the devil.[98] In his poetry, however, he used hexameters sparingly and gave preference to iambics, most of which could be read both in antique fashion and in the new way that suited the development of seventh-century Greek. George's iambics were only a few steps removed from the Byzantine dodecasyllable, and he pointed to the Byzantine future rather than to the classical past.

Theophylact Simocatta, a secretary of Heraclius, is another prominent literary figure of the first half of the seventh century. It could be claimed that he was the most classicizing of all the writers discussed here. Theophylact opened his *Universal History* with a dialogue between Queen Philosophy and her daughter History, in which formally not the slightest hint of Christianity can be found. The emperor overthrown by Heraclius is called the Calydonian boar, a dissolute centaur, and finally Anytus, one of the accusers of Socrates. The patriarch of Constantinople is mentioned, for Theophylact was his literary protegé, but he is called "a hierophant of magnanimity." Philosophy, no longer aware of the Christian interpretation of Odysseus and the Sirens, wishes to be another Odysseus herself, in order to listen to that Siren, History.[99] Theophylact also composed a fictitious correspondence, in which intellectuals, peasants, and harlots—yes, in a seventh-century Christian work—exchanged eighty-five letters in a setting so totally pagan and a style so preciously Attic that in the nineteenth century one letter was mistakenly printed among the works of Isocrates.[100] In his perfection, Theophylact was the first literary antiquarian of the Christian East. Antiquarians are people who know that periods cherished and imitated by them are dead.

It so happens that some of the most spectacular objects of our exhibition—the David plates and the Vienna silver bucket with six pagan deities [Cat. nos. 425–33 and 118]—are contemporary with George of Pisidia and Theophylact Simocatta.[101] Chronologically, these pieces are also among the latest on display. The organizers of the exhibition stopped with the seventh century not because they had read Greek literature or remembered the dates of the Arab invasions, but because artistic evidence dictated to them the choice of that chronological limit.

When new and vigorous literary forms, not greatly indebted to antiquity, stand side by side with antiquarian playthings like the letters of Theophylact Simocatta, or when the Cleveland tapestry with the Virgin or the portrait of Mark the Evangelist inscribed in Coptic [Cat. nos. 477, 498] stand side by side with the silver bucket with pagan deities, devoid of any Christian content, this is an overdue signal that the unity of antique culture is a matter of the past. After the year 650, Greek literary antiquity was ready to be reborn in various renaissances and humanisms.

Many factors made these rebirths possible. I will suggest only one of them here, for it will bring me back for the last time to the Cappadocian fathers.

The Cappadocian fathers put a limited seal of approval on antique literature, which they conveyed, not through their theoretical pronouncements—Basil's address "To Young Men" was much less popular in Byzantium than its Latin translation was to become in the fifteenth-century West, which had never heard anything like it before[102]—but through the power of their own literary output. Within a century of their own lifetimes, the Cappadocian fathers became Christian classics in their own right. We have fifteen hundred manuscripts of Gregory of Nazianzus' *Orations*. Fourteen commentators known to us by name—more than one for each century of Byzantium—explained his prose, and among other things, his classical allusions. At least two lexica—one for his prose, another for his poetry—were in existence before the tenth century; they, too, interpreted his Atticizing words and classical realia, terms such as the "academy," the "lyceum," and the "fire of Aetna."[103] Practically all of Gregory's epigrams were included in the manuscript of the *Palatine Anthology*,[104] where they stood side by side with those collected by Hellenistic scholarly poets living around the time of Christ. Finally, Psellus, an eleventh-century Byzantine humanist, wrote two treatises in which he discussed the style of Gregory in terms of antique theory and enumerated that father's classical models, Isocrates and Demosthenes, among others.[105]

All this meant that the absorption of the classics by such men as Gregory of Nazianzus or Basil mattered a great deal in shaping the educated Byzantine's attitude toward these very classics throughout the life of Byzantium. Without the intellectual climate and reflexes produced by such an attitude, neither the scholarly antiquarianism nor the sheer power of the eternal Greek spirit could have ensured the survival of antique Greek literature.[106]

NOTES

1. Origen *Contra Celsum* 3. 44 and 6. 12, M. Borret, ed., Paris, 1968, 1969 (Sources Chrétiennes, CXXXVI and CXLVII), pp. 104, 4–11 and 206, 6–8. For the English rendering of these and subsequent passages, I adopt, with some modifications, the translation by H. Chadwick, *Origen: Contra Celsum . . .* , Cambridge, 1953 (2nd ed., 1965), pp. 158 and 325.

2. *Contra Celsum* 3. 55, M. Borret, ed., pp. 129–30, 4–28. Cf. H. Chadwick, *Origen*, pp. 165–166.

3. *Contra Celsum* 3. 58, M. Borret, ed., p. 136, 20–26. English translation in H. Chadwick, *Origen*, p. 167.

4. For the respective dates of Celsus' *True Doctrine* and Origen's refutation of it, cf., for example, P. Merlan in *Reallexikon für Antike und Christentum*, II, 1954, col. 954, s.v. "Celsus" and P. Nautin, *Origène, sa vie et son oeuvre*, Paris, 1977, pp. 376 and 381.

5. For a good characterization of Celsus' attack on Christianity as "a religion of the stupid and of stultification," and on the Christian mission as an enterprise carried out in "the basement of social life," cf. C. Andresen, *Logos und Nomos, die Polemik des Kelsos wider das Christentum*, Berlin, 1955 (Arbeiten zur Kirchengeschichte, XXX), esp. pp. 167–78. Nevertheless, Andresen assumes (against others), that Celsus was aware of Christian apologists (and even depended on Justin Martyr), but usually suppressed his awareness of them for polemical reasons. In this work of suppression, Celsus was not quite successful, however, for on at least two occasions he admitted that there existed intellectually advanced individuals among the Christians. Cf. *Contra Celsum* 4. 48 and 5. 65, M. Borret, ed., pp. 306, 3–5 and 174, 11–13. English translation in H. Chadwick, *Origen*, pp. 223 and 314.

6. 1 Cor. 15:32 (= Frg. 187 in A. Koerte, *Menandri quae supersunt*, II, Leipzig, 1959, p. 74; Frg. 218 Kock); Tit. 1:12; Acts 17:28. Cf., for example, N. Zeegers-Vander Vorst, *Les Citations des poètes grecs*, pp. 19–21, and, most recently, R. Renehan, "Classical Greek Quotations in the New Testament," in *The Heritage of the Early Church, Essays in Honor of . . . G. V. Florovsky*, Rome, 1973 (*Orientalia Christiana Analecta*, CXCV), pp. 17–46. Clement of Alexandria had already identified these quotations. See *Stromateis* 1. 59, 2–4 and 1. 91, 4–5. (Clement calls Menander's line a tragic verse; cf. also G. Glockmann, *Homer in der frühchristlichen Literatur*, p. 54). The sources are also identified in John Chrysostom, Migne, *PG*, LXII, cols. 676–77 (Epimenides, Aratus) and in Socrates *Hist. Eccl.* 3. 16, Migne, *PG*, LXVII, cols. 421D–424A (here the Menandrian line is ascribed to Euripides).

7. John 1:1; Acts 17:18 and 23. On Hellenistic and hellenized Jewish antecedents of the Acts passage and of St. John's *Logos*, cf., for example, M. Pohlenz, "Die Antike und das frühe Christentum," pp. 46–47. W. L. Knox, *Some Hellenistic Elements in Primitive Christianity*, London, 1944, esp. pp. 43–44. W. Eltester, "Der Logos und sein Prophet," *Apophoreta. Festschrift für Ernst Haenchen*, Berlin, 1964 (Beiheft zur Zeitschrift für die neutestamentliche Wissenschaft und die Kunde der Alten Kirche, XXX), esp. pp. 121–23. Against the Greek cultural background of John 1:1, A. J. Festugière, *Observations stylistiques sur L'Evangile de S. Jean*, Paris, 1974, esp. pp. 124–41.

8. Acts 17:1–3, 10, 17.

9. H. F. D. Sparks, "The Semitisms of St. Luke's Gospel," *Journal of Theological Studies*, XLIV, 1943, pp. 129–38; reprinted in *Studies in the Septuagint: Origins, Recensions, and Interpretations*, New York, 1972, pp. 497–506. E. Plümacher, *Lukas als hellenistischer Schriftsteller*, Göttingen, 1972, pp. 38–51 and 138–39. N. Turner, "The Quality of the Greek of Luke-Acts," *Studies in New Testament Language and Text. Essays in Honour of George D. Kilpatrick . . .* , Leiden, 1976 (Supplements to Novum Testamentum, XLIII), pp. 387–400. For a stress on Hellenistic traits in Luke's Acts, see also M. Dibelius, *Aufsätze zur Apostelgeschichte*, 4th ed., Göttingen, 1961, esp. chaps. 2, 8, and 9.

10. The paraphrase is ascribed to Apollinarius of Laodicea, a contemporary of Julian the Apostate. See *Apollinarii metaphrasis psalmorum*, A. Ludwich, ed., Leipzig, 1912. For date and authorship, I adopt the view of J. Golega, *Der homerische Psalter. Studien über die dem Apollinarios von Laodikeia zugeschriebene Psalmenparaphrase*, Ettal, 1960 (Studia Patristica et Byzantina, VI), esp. pp. 169–77, who attributes our text to an anonymous author from Alexandria, writing ca. 460–70. As a sample of the sacred text clad in Homeric garb, I quote the English rendering of the paraphrase of Psalm 52 (Ludwich, ed., pp. 107–08) made by Jeffrey Featherstone:

'God there is not,' said the foolish one in his breast:
By their deeds they have perished contriving things vile;
Of the doers of righteousness not a one is left.
From Heaven the Immortal One espied the human race
To observe who it was sought after God the Lord.
But all have turned aside, in evils all confounded:
Of the doers of righteousness not a one is left.
Those thoughtless of Good, ever conspiring with Folly,
Have devoured my people even as wholesome bread;
Senseless, they have forgotten to entreat God the King.
Sore afraid they were when there was no use for fear:
All their bones were scattered, they who catered to men,
And, scorning them, the Immortal One brought upon them shame.
Who shall bring from Zion succour unto Israel?
When God hath changed His people's day of servitude,
Then let Israel rejoice without bound.

Although "Apollinarius" intends to adhere to Homeric vocabulary as closely as possible, he also uses general epic words and phrases, some attested in Apollonius of Rhodes and Nonnus, but not in Homeric epic or hymns. Cf. ll. 3 and 7——ἐργατίνης; l. 4—βρότεον φῦλον; l. 8—συμφράδμονες ἄτης; l. 9—ϑρεψήνορα; and l. 10—Θεὸν βασιλέα.

11. *Eudociae Augustae . . . Carminum Graecorum Reliquiae . . .*, A. Ludwich, ed., Leipzig, 1897; see pp. 96–98 for the story of Eve and the serpent. For Eudocia's lost transpositions into epic verse of the Octateuch, Zachariah, and Daniel, cf. Photius *Bibliotheca*, cods. 183 and 184, also quoted in *Eudociae Augustae, . . .* (Ludwich, ed., pp. 13–15). In the fourth-century Latin West, too, epic *centos* (this time from Vergil) were produced to paraphrase the Gospels; somewhat later (ca. 390), the Psalms were transposed into Latin hexameters by Paulinus of Nola (d. 431).

12. Compare Nonnus *Dionysiaca* 27. 114, R. Keydell, ed., Berlin, 1959, II, p. 55: "παρθενικὴ φυγόδεμνος ἀνέτρεφε Παλλὰς ἀμήτωρ," with his *Paraphrasis S. Evang. Ioannei*, B.2 (A. Scheindler, ed., Leipzig, 1881, p. 17, 9–11): "παρθενικὴ Χριστοῖο θεητόκος ἵκετο μήτηρ . . . παιδοτόκος φυγόδεμνος. . . ." Cf. also *Dionysiaca* 4. 30 and 48. 803, R. Keydell, ed., Berlin, 1959, I, p. 85 and II, p. 501 for παρθενική. For stylistic parallels between *Dionysiaca* and the paraphrase of John's Gospel, cf. J. Golega, *Studien über die Evangeliendichtung des Nonnos von Panopolis . . .*, Breslau, 1930 (Breslauer Studien zur historischen Theologie, XV), 28–62.

13. A convenient list is to be found in N. Zeegers-Vander Vorst, *Les Citations des poètes grecs*, pp. 15–18, with the latest chronological data. The essentially preserved texts (sometimes in only one manuscript!) are by Aristides, Justin Martyr, Tatian, Athenagoras, Theophilus, Pseudo-Justin, and Clement of Alexandria. (The latter is counted among the apologists here on the strength of the date of his *Protrepticus*, ca. 200.)

14. Tatian, Justin Martyr, Theophilus, and Clement of Alexandria.

15. Athenagoras *Legatio pro Christianis* (delivered in 177), 35, E. Schwartz, ed., Leipzig, 1891 (Texte und Untersuchungen zur Geschichte der altchristlichen Literatur, IV), 2, p. 45, 12–13: "Yet, we do own slaves; some of us have more, some fewer of them." H. Kreissig, "Zur sozialen Zusammensetzung der frühchristlichen Gemeinden im ersten Jahrhundert U. Z.," *Eirene*, VI, 1967, pp. 91–100, argues for the presence of well-off members of liberal professions in Christian communities of the first century. Cf. also L. W. Barnard, *Athenagoras, a Study in Second Century Christian Apologetic*, Paris, 1972 (Théologie historique, 18), p. 149.

16. See the statistics in N. Zeegers-Vander Vorst, *Les Citations des poètes grecs*, pp. 32–33. For statistics on poets and prose writers quoted by Greek fathers of the first four centuries, cf. W. Krause, *Die Stellung der frühchristlichen Autoren*, pp. 131–37; cf., however, objections to Krause's results in G. Glockmann, *Homer in der frühchristlichen Literatur*, pp. 6–7.

17. Justin Martyr *First Apology* 44. 5–8 and 59–60, J. K. T. Otto, ed., Iena, 1876 (Corpus Apologetarum Christianorum, I), pp. 122–24 and 158–62. Tatian *Oratio ad Graecos* 29, 31, and 36–41, E. Schwartz, ed., Leipzig, 1888 (Texte und Untersuchungen zur Geschichte der altchristlichen Literatur, IV, 1), pp. 30, 5–7; 31–32, 37–43. Theophilus *Ad Autolycum* 3. 21, R. M. Grant, ed., *Theophilus of Antioch ad Autolycum*, Oxford, 1970, p. 128. Pseudo-Justin *Cohortatio ad Gentiles* 9–10, 14, 20–22, 26, 29, 33, 35, J. K. T. Otto, ed., Iena, 1879 (Corpus Apologetarum Christianorum, III), pp. 42–48, 70–80, 88–90, 100–102, 110, and 112–14. Clement of Alexandria, too, derived the thought of Greek philosophers from that of Old Testament prophets. Cf. *Stromateis* 1. 17, 87, 1–3 and 1. 22, 150, 1–5, with quotations from Aristobulus and Numenius of Apamea. According to Clement, even the "miserable" Pindar was inspired by Proverbs 9:17; see *Paedagogus* 3. 11, 72, 1, C. Mondésert, ed., Paris, 1970 (Sources Chrétiennes, CLVIII), p. 141. For a reflection of the plagiarism theme in Gregory of Nazianzus, cf. *Oration* 43, Migne, *PG*, XXXVI, col. 528B–C. (The Elysian fields of the Greeks are an image of paradise, taken over from the Books of Moses.) The argument survived as late as the seventeenth century. Cf. the learned François Combéfis in Migne, *PG*, XVIII, col. 160D: *ut sunt nostra et sacra longe profanis Graecorum antiquiora.*

18. The Jewish theory of plagiarism went back to the mid-second century B.C.; both Philo and Josephus Flavius subscribed to it. A good summary of the problem (with bibliography) appears in N. Zeegers-Vander Vorst, *Les Citations des poètes grecs*, pp. 180–84. Cf. also K. Thraede in *Reallexikon für Antike und Christentum*, V, 1962, cols. 1242–46, s.v. "Erfinder II."

19. Fragment 900, in Athenagoras *Legatio pro Christianis* 5, E. Schwartz, ed., pp. 5, 25–26.

20. Clement of Alexandria *Paedagogus* 3. 11, 79, 5, C. Mondésert, ed., p. 154. Clement held the modesty of Aeneas' wife up to Christian women in order to exhort them to modesty in dress.

21. Such is certainly the fragment 1025 of Sophocles ("One, one in truth is God . . . "), quoted by Clement of Alexandria in *Protrepticus* 7.74, 2, C. Mondésert, ed., Paris, 1949, p. 139, and in *Stromateis* 5. 14, 113, 1–2; and by Pseudo-Justin *Cohortatio ad Gentiles*, 18, J. K. T. Otto, ed., p. 68. This fragment is probably a Jewish forgery created earlier than the first century A.D. Cf. N. Zeegers-Vander Vorst, *Les Citations des poètes grecs*, pp. 188 and 199–201. Of course, Clement may have believed fragment 1025 to have been authentic.

22. R. M. Grant, "Early Christianity and Greek Comic Poetry," *Classical Philology*, LX, 1965; on Clement, esp. pp. 161–63. On Theophilus' use of anthologies and handbooks, cf., for example, R. M. Grant, *Theophilus of Antioch Ad Autolycum*, pp. xi–xii.

23. Cf. N. Zeegers-Vander Vorst, *Les Citations des poètes grecs*, pp. 32 and 201–05. *Sibyllinische Weissagungen*, A. Kur-

fess, ed., Nördlingen, 1951, Commentary, *passim*. For a good recent summary of views on chronology and attribution of individual books of oracles to Jewish and Christian authors respectively, see A.-M. Denis, *Introduction aux pseud-épigraphes grecs d'Ancien Testament*, Leiden, 1970, chap. XIV, pp. 111–22.

24. *The Sentences of Sextus. A Contribution to the History of Early Christian Ethics*, H. Chadwick, ed., Cambridge, 1959, esp. pp. 138–62. About the year 400, Rufinus translated this Christian reworking into Latin, and drew the ire of St. Jerome who thought that "Sextus" was a pagan.

25. *Musonii Rufi reliquiae*, O. Hense, ed., Leipzig, 1905, apparatus to 64, 3–4; 65, 1–2; 65, 7–66, 1; 96, 7–10; 99; 14–100, 3; 102, 4–6; 103, 1–3; 104, 1–2 and 4–10; 106, 8–9; 107, 9–10; 109, 1–8; 110, 4–6 and 9–12; 112, 4–9, for quasi-literal borrowings by Clement. Cf. also M. Spanneut, *Le Stoïcisme des pères de l'église, de Clément de Rome à Clément d'Alexandrie*, Paris, 1957, pp. 106–12. Clement never acknowledged these borrowings, no more than he acknowledged his debt to Musonius' pupil, Epictetus (d. ca. 130). Cf. M. Spanneut in *Reallexikon für Antike und Christentum*, V, 1962, cols. 634–40, s.v. "Epiktet." Cf. also H. I. Marrou, *Clément d'Alexandrie. Le Pédagogue*, Paris, 1960 (Sources Chrétiennes, LXX), I, pp. 51–52 (with bibliography). Idem, in *Reallexikon für Antike und Christentum*, III, 1957, cols. 1001–02, s.v. "Diatribe."

26. Cf. *Stromateis* 1, 50, 1 and 5–6, discussing 1 Cor. 3:19 and Col. 2:8. Cf., in general, R. E. Witt, "The Hellenism of Clement of Alexandria," *The Classical Quarterly*, XXV, 1931, pp. 195–204. M. Pohlenz, "Klemens von Alexandreia und sein hellenisches Christentum," *Nachrichten von der Akademie der Wissenschaften in Göttingen*, philol.-hist. Klasse, 1943 (N. F., I, 5), pp. 103–80. H. I. Marrou, "Humanisme et christianisme chez Clément d'Alexandrie d'après le *Pédagogue*," in *Recherches sur la tradition platonicienne*, Vandoeuvres and Geneva, 1955–57 (Fondation Hardt. Entretiens sur l'Antiquité classique, III), pp. 180–200 (brilliant and best for our purpose). H. B. Timothy, *The Early Christian Apologists and Greek Philosophy*, Assen, 1973 (paraphrases Clement's passages on the uses of pagan philosophy).

27. Aristides *Apology*, E. Hennecke, ed., Leipzig, 1893, p. 7.

28. Tatian *Oratio ad Graecos*, 1, 12, 26, 28, 29, 35, and 42, E. Schwartz, ed., pp. 2, 16–17; 14, 2–4; 28, 16–20; 29, 7–10 and 13–15; 30, 4–11; 35, 5–8; and 43, 8–12.

29. Tatian *Oratio ad Graecos* 33–34, E. Schwartz, ed., pp. 34–36. The purpose of Tatian's "artists' catalogue" was to prove the moral superiority of Christianity, especially of the Christian women "philosophers," i.e., women leading chaste lives. Cf. R. C. Kukula, "*Altersbeweis*" und "*Künstlerkatalog*" in *Tatians Rede an die Griechen*, Vienna, 1900, esp. pp. 15–16. Tatian's hostility towards pagan philosophical culture did not keep him from absorbing some of its tenets (especially the Stoic ones). Cf. A. F. Hawthorne, "Tatian and his Discourse to the Greeks," *Harvard Theological Review*, LVII, 1964, esp. pp. 175–81.

30. I follow R. M. Grant, "The Date of Tatian's Oration," *Harvard Theological Review*, XLVI, 1953, pp. 99–101 in dating the *Discourse* to 177–78.

31. See, in general, W. Schneemelcher, in *Reallexikon für Antike und Christentum*, V, 1962, cols. 909–27, s.v. "Epiphanius von Salamis." On ἑλληνικὴ παιδεία having blinded Origen's mind and caused him to spew forth the venom of heresy, cf. Epiphanius *Panarion*, haer. 64. 72, 9, K. Holl, ed., Leipzig, 1922 (Die griechischen christlichen Schriftsteller der ersten drei Jahrhunderte, XXXI), p. 523. On Epiphanius' quoting Homer only indirectly, cf. J. Dummer, "Epiphanius von Constantia und Homer," *Philologus*, CIX, 1975, pp. 84–91, esp. p. 90. Dummer asks whether Epiphanius had ever *read* Homer in the full text and answers with a *non liquet* (p. 91). He may be too cautious. Epiphanius—who, after all, writes literate, if simple, prose—must have gone to some *grammaticus* and there read at least the opening passages of Homeric epics in the original. In any case, at the very beginning of the preface to his *Panarion* (Panarion, prooem. 1. 3, K. Holl, ed., Leipzig, 1915, p. 169), he says that pagan writers and poets about to compose a work would invoke "some Muse." Epiphanius must be alluding to the first lines of the *Iliad* and *Odyssey* respectively, rather than to the apologist Theophilus, 2. 8, R. M. Grant, ed., pp. 36–38. For all that, it must be granted that Epiphanius never *quoted* Homer except in passages that he had lifted from other Christian authors.

32. Implied by parallel quotations from Homer and Isaiah in Methodius *Convivium* 4.3, N. Bonwetsch, ed., Leipzig, 1917 (Die griechischen christlichen Schriftsteller der ersten drei Jahrhunderte, XXVII), p. 49, 3–5, and H. Musurillo, ed., Paris, 1963 (Sources Chrétiennes, XCV), p. 134. Homer's equation with the prophet Isaiah is noted in H. Rahner, *Griechische Mythen in christlicher Deutung*, Zurich, 1945, pp. 401–02 and in V. Buchheit, "Homer bei Methodios von Olympos," *Rheinisches Museum für Philologie*, XCIX, 1956, pp. 23–24.

33. Συμπόσιον ἢ περὶ ἁγνείας. On this dialogue, cf., on the one hand, M. Hoffmann, *Der Dialog bei den christlichen Schriftstellern der ersten vier Jahrhunderte*, Berlin, 1966, pp. 121–30 (superficial imitation of Plato), and, on the other, B. R. Voss, *Der Dialog in der frühchristlichen Literatur*, Munich, 1970 (Studia et Testimonia Antiqua, IX), pp. 102–15 (creative adaptation of Plato). Cf. also T. A. Miller, "Mefodij Olimpskij i tradicija platonovskogo dialoga," in L. A. Frejberg, ed., *Antičnost' i Vizantija*, pp. 175–94.

34. Methodius *Convivium* 8. 10 and 12, N. Bonwetsch, ed., pp. 92, 4–9 and 97, 3–13, and H. Musurillo, ed., pp. 224 and 234. Discussed in V. Buchheit, "Homer bei Methodios von Olympos," pp. 24–28. The Homeric lines used by Methodius were *Iliad* 6. 180–83.

35. Cf. p. 85, figs. 19, 20, below.

36. For Methodius' allegory, see his *De autexusio*, N. Bonwetsch, ed., pp. 145, 3–146, 17. Discussed in V. Buchheit, "Homer bei Methodios von Olympos," pp. 19–22. For Odysseus, the mast, and the Sirens in both

pagan Neoplantonic and Christian allegory (Christians being heirs of Neoplatonism), cf. H. I. Marrou, Μουσικὸς ἀνήρ, Grenoble, 1937, pp. 172–77, who wrongly denies the Christian character of motif. P. Courcelle, "Quelques symboles funéraires du néo-plantonisme latin . . . ," *Revue des Études Anciennes*, XLVI, 1944, pp. 65–93. H. Rahner, *Griechische Mythen*, esp. "Odysseus am Mastbaum," pp. 414–86 (the story of the motif in patristic writings). J. Carcopino, *De Pythagore aux Apôtres*, Paris, 1956, pp. 192–99 (a good summary). Since the Odysseus motif discussed here occurs in funerary art, could not the Richmond bronze lamp in our exhibition have been destined for the tomb of a wealthy person?

37. For studies treating the Cappadocian fathers' debt to antique literary practices, see L. Méridier's excellent *L'influence de la seconde sophistique sur l'oeuvre de Grégoire de Nysse*, Paris, 1906. M. Guignet, *Saint Grégoire de Nazianze et la rhétorique*, Paris, 1911. E. Fleury, *Hellénisme et Christianisme. Saint Grégoire de Nazianze et son temps*, Paris, 1930, esp. pp. 55–99. P. Gallay, *Langue et style de Saint Grégoire de Nazianze dans sa correspondance*, Paris, 1933. Y. Courtonne, *Saint Basile et l'hellénisme . . .* , Paris, 1934. J. Mossay, *La mort et l'au-delà dans Saint Grégoire de Nazianze*, Louvain, 1966 (on pagan literary techniques used by Gregory in treating this universal theme). R. R. Ruether, *Gregory of Nazianzus. Rhetor and Philosopher*, Oxford, 1969, esp. chaps. II and IV, Appendix I, and bibliography. The essay by H.-G. Beck, *Rede als Kunstwerk und Bekenntnis—Gregor von Nazianz*, Munich, 1977 (Sitzungsberichte der Bayerischen Akademie der Wissenschaften, philosophisch-historische Klasse, fasc. 4), sketches a brilliant psychological portrait of a man who expressed his inner self through rhetoric. See further V. Pöschl, H. Gärtner, and W. Heyke, *Bibliographie zur antiken Bildersprache*, Heidelberg, 1964, pp. 106–08 and 174–79. For the unpublished dissertation by J. Lercher, cf. note 71 below.

38. Gregory of Nazianzus *Oration* 39, *In Sancta Lumina*, Migne, *PG*, XXXVI, cols. 336D–341A.

39. For *Scholia* by Pseudo-Nonnus, see Migne, *PG*, XXXVI, cols. 985–1058 (scholia to *Or.* 4 and 5), and 1057–72 (selections from scholia to *Or.* 43 and 39). For the full Greek text of the scholia to *Or.* 39, cf. now S. Brock, *The Syriac Version of the Pseudo-Nonnus' Mythological Scholia*, Cambridge, 1971, pp. 159–72. Brock also published and rendered into English the Syriac translation (done in the sixth century and reworked in the seventh) of Pseudo-Nonnus' scholia to the four *Orations*. Ibid., pp. 12–15, on the Armenian version (seventh century or later), which contains scholia to *Or.* 24, and on the Georgian translation, unpublished by 1971. Cf., further, F. Lefherz, *Studien zu Gregor von Nazianz. Mythologie, Überlieferung, Scholiasten*, Bonn, 1958, pp. 113–24, esp. p. 120 on manuscripts. K. Weitzmann's *Greek Mythology in Byzantine Art*, Princeton, 1951, esp. pp. 6–92, offers English translations of the scholia to *Or.* 39 and 43. The illustrations to Pseudo-Nonnus seem to originate in the ninth and tenth centuries (Weitzmann, p. 92).

40. For an example roughly contemporary with Gregory and Libanius, see Aphthonius *Progymnasmata* 12, H. Rabe, ed., Leipzig, 1926, p. 36, 22–23.

41. Ibid., p. 37, 6–7.

42. Gregory of Nazianzus *Oration* 44, *In Novam Dominicam*, Migne, *PG*, XXXVI, cols. 617C–620C. The Homeric allusion is to the *Iliad* 6. 506–10 = 15. 263–67. Cf. also a reference to the same passage in *Or.* 43, Migne, *PG*, XXXVI, col. 529B.

43. For Gregory's two Christian tags, cf. *Or.* 44, Migne, *PG*, XXXVI, col. 620B. For the motif of the bee in classical literature, cf. J. H. Waszink, *Biene und Honig als Symbol des Dichters und der Dichtung in der griechisch-römischen Antike*, 1974 (Rheinisch-Westfälische Akademie der Wissenschaften, Vorträge G 196). Waszink leaves Christian antiquity out; see p. 6. For the same motif in patristic literature, cf. P. Rech, *Inbild des Kosmos. Eine Symbolik der Schöpfung*, I, Salzburg and Freilassing, 1966, pp. 308–32 and 583–86. See also L. Koepp in *Reallexikon für Antike und Christentum*, II, 1954, cols. 279–81, s.v. "Biene." For Libanius' *Ekphrasis of Spring* see R. Foerster, ed., *Libanii Opera*, VIII, Leipzig, 1915, pp. 479–82. Libanius describes cloudless skies, clear springs, fragrance, lambs, calm sea, work in the fields, and singing birds. The one motif that Libanius offers but Gregory suppresses is the sexual awakening of nature in spring.

44. Nicetas of Heracleia (ca. 1080), Migne, *PG*, CXXVII, col. 1434A (Latin translation only). On Nicetas as scholiast, cf. F. Lefherz, *Studien zu Gregor von Nazianz*, pp. 139–40.

45. Basil *Letter* 14, Y. Courtonne, ed., Paris, 1957, I, pp. 42–45; R. J. Deferrari, ed., London and Cambridge, Mass., 1961 (Loeb Classical Library), I, pp. 106–11. For the latest treatment of the concept of *hesychia* (meaning both "solitude" and "inner peace") in St. Basil, cf. A. Guida, "Un nuovo testo di Gregorio Nazianzeno," *Prometheus*, II, 1976, esp. pp. 206–10. The Echinades were islands in the Ionian Sea. For other fathers and Christian authors (fourth to sixth century) who produced *ekphraseis*, cf. G. Downey in *Reallexikon für Antike und Christentum*, IV, 1959, cols. 932–43, and A. Hohlweg in *Reallexikon zur byzantinischen Kunst*, II, 1967, cols. 43–47, both s.v. "Ekphrasis."

46. Gregory of Nazianzus *Oration* 43, *In Laudem Basilii*, Migne, *PG*, XXXVI, cols. 493A–497B, for the immensity of the rhetorical task at hand; 497B–500B, on lineage, and the use of *paraleipsis*; 509A–C, on education *not* by a vainglorious centaur; 525B, on Orestes and Pylades; 528B, on Minos and Rhadamanthys; 504B–C, for Diana ἐλαφηβόλος, and for ξενοκτονεῖν; 520A, on "Homerizing"; 521B, for the quote from Pindar's *Ol.* 6. 1; 509A–B, for the paraphrase of Psalm 138:16.

47. On Gregory's epigrams, cf. for example, R. Keydell in *Reallexikon für Antike und Christentum*, V, 1962, pp. 541–46, s.v. "Epigramm." Epigrams on Basil are numbered 2 to 11.

48. Cf. *Anthol. Palat.* 8. 29, in, for example, P. Waltz, ed., *Anthologie Grecque*, VI, Paris, 1944, p. 43; W. R. Paton, ed., *Greek Anthology*, II, London and Cambridge, Mass., p. 414 (Loeb Classical Library; reprinted 1970).

49. *Anthol. Palat.* 8. 3 (Trinity); 8. 41 and 141 (Christ); 8. 54 (angel).

50. *Epitaph* 5, Migne, *PG*, XXXVIII, col. 13A on Prohaeresius. *Anthol. Palat.* 8. 66, for the echo of Callimachus (*Epigr.* 10. 4, ed. Pfeiffer) and 8.157, for the envious river.

51. *Anthol. Palat.* 8. 106, 123, and 97, on Caesarius; 130, for the Elysian place; 127, for Eros' torch; 128, for the dialogue of the Graces and Muses; 120, for the belief in the immortality of Livia; and 205, for the ghosts of the dead.

52. To say this is to follow Mario Praz who, in his 1967 Mellon lectures, ably revived the proposition that there exists a "general likeness among all the works of art of a period," a fact as remarkable, and as incontrovertible, as is the bumblebee's ability to fly. Mario Praz, *Mnemosyne. The Parallel between Literature and the Visual Arts*, Princeton, 1970 (Bollingen Series, XXXV.16), esp. pp. 54–5.

53. Juxtapose Gregory's *Ep.* 206 to Adelphius with *Ep.* 198 to Nemesius, P. Gallay, ed., Berlin, 1969, pp. 149–50 and 143–44. On these two addressees, cf. M.-M. Hauser-Meury, *Prosopographie zu den Schriften Gregors von Nazianz*, Bonn, 1960, pp. 23 and 128.

54. For the best introduction to the topic "education and Christianity," cf. H. I. Marrou, *Histoire de l'education dans l'Antiquité*, 2nd ed., Paris, 1950 (7th ed., 1971), pp. 421–31, as well as 268–82, and 380–86. G. Bardy, "L'Église et l'enseignement au IVᵉ siècle," *Revue des sciences religieuses*, XIV, 1934, pp. 525–49 and XV, 1935, pp. 1–27 is still useful. On Basil and Gregory as students of Prohaeresius, cf. Socrates *Hist. Eccl.* 4.26, Migne, *PG*, LXVII, col. 529A. For Eunapius on Prohaeresius, see *Vitae Sophistarum* 10.1–8, G. Giangrande, ed., Rome, 1956, pp. 63–79. For the program of Basil's studies at Athens, cf. Gregory of Nazianzus *In Laudem Basilii*, chap. 23, Migne, *PG*, XXXVI, col. 528A–B.

55. Cf., for example, C. M. Bowra, "Palladas and the Converted Olympians," *Byzantinische Zeitschrift*, LIII, 1960, esp. pp. 4–7. The *loci classici* are Socrates *Hist. Eccl.* 5. 16, Migne, *PG*, LXVII, 604B–605B, and *Codex Theodosianus* 16. 10, 8, 10, and 15. On Lausus, see Cedrenus *Hist.* I., Bekker, ed., Bonn, 1838 (Corpus scriptorum historiae Byzantinae, XXXIII), p. 564, 5–19; a late source.

56. J.-M. Spieser, "La Christianisation des sanctuaires païens en Grèce," in *Neue Forschungen in griechischen Heiligtümern*, 1976 (Deutsches Archäologisches Institut, Abt. Athen), esp. p. 310.

57. The key word in this sentence is "radical." I must report that the late A. H. M. Jones was of a different opinion: to him, religious change coincided with a social change.

Cf. his "The Social Background of the Struggle between Paganism and Christianity," in *The Conflict between Paganism and Christianity in the Fourth Century*, A. Momigliano, ed., Oxford, 1963, pp. 17–37.

58. Cf. *Letters* 24 and 38 (to Themistius) and 236 (a two-liner recommending a student to Libanius), P. Gallay, ed., pp. 23, 33–34, 169. For epigrams on the tomb of Martinianus, the prefect of Rome, see *Anthol. Palat.* 8. 104–17. It must be granted, however, that the majority of Gregory's literary acquaintances were Christians.

59. See Julian's *Letter* 31, in J. Bidez, *L'Empereur Julien, oeuvres complètes*, I, Paris, 1924, pp. 58–59. It is unlikely that *Letter* 32, "To Basil the Great," was in fact addressed to the Cappadocian father. On Julian's offer to exempt Prohaeresius, cf. St. Jerome's Chronicle *sub anno II Iuliani*, in J. K. Fotheringham, ed., *Eusebii Pamphyli Chronici Canones*, London, 1923, pp. 324, 26–325, 2.

60. *Letter* 14. 6–8, G. Pasquali, ed., 1959, pp. 47, 19–48, 12.

61. Cf. quasi-literal parallels between passages in Chrysostom's *Comparatio regis et monachi* and Libanius, adduced in C. Fabricius, *Zu den Jugendschriften des Johannes Chrysostomos. Untersuchungen zum Klassizismus des vierten Jahrhunderts*, Lund, 1962, pp. 120–21.

62. Socrates *Hist. Eccl.* 4. 26 and 6. 3, Migne, *PG*, LXVII, cols. 529A and 665A. Modern scholars dispute Socrates, or suspend judgment on his reliability. Cf., for example, the discussion in P. Petit, *Les Etudiants de Libanius*, Paris, 1957, esp. pp. 40–41, and in A. J. Festugière, *Antioche païenne et chrétienne. . .*, Paris, 1959, pp. 409–10. However, Socrates may be right concerning St. Basil, if Letter 13 of Gregory of Nyssa to Libanius is genuine. In this letter, Libanius is explicitly called a teacher of Basil; see G. Pasquali, ed., pp. 45, 23–24 and 46, 8–10. Pasquali assumes that the letter is authentic. In view of young John Chrysostom's textual borrowings from Libanius, C. Fabricius, *Zu den Jugendschriften des Johannes Chrysostomos*, p. 22, note 1 makes a good case for John's having been a student of Libanius.

63. R. Foerster, ed., *Libanii Opera*, XI, 1922, pp. 572–97.

64. Zacharias Scholasticus *Life of Severus*, M.-A. Kugener, ed., Paris, 1903 (Patrologia Orientalis, II, 1), p. 13.

65. On the spurious character of the correspondence, see, among others, R. Foerster, ed., *Libanii Opera*, IX, 1927, pp. 197–205 (all letters but two are false or pseudepigraph). Cf. P. Maas, *Zu den Beziehungen zwischen Kirchenvätern und Sophisten*, Berlin, 1912 (Sitzungsberichte der könig l.-preuss. Akad. d. Wissenschaften Berlin, fasc. 43 and 48, 1912), pp. 987–99, and esp. pp. 1112–23 for letters of Gregory of Nyssa in the correspondence. Maas considered eleven of its letters to have been authentic, the rest false.

66. Cf., J. Bidez, *L'Empereur Julien, oeuvres complètes*, I, 2, pp. 72–75 (no. 61), and 44–47, as well as the excellent discussion in G. W. Bowersock, *Julian the Apostate*, Cambridge, Mass., 1978, pp. 83–85.

67. Cf. J. Bidez, *L'Empereur Julien, oeuvres complètes*, I, 2, p. 75, 8–11.

68. *Hist. Eccl.* 3. 16, Migne, *PG*, LXVII, col. 417C–419A.

69. Cf. *Hist. Eccl.* 3. 12 and 3. 16, Migne, *PG*, LXVII, cols. 412B, 420B, 421B.

70. For Gregory's poetry, cf. the evidence in B. Wyss, "Gregor von Nazianz. Ein griechisch-christlicher Dichter des 4. Jahrhunderts," *Museum Helveticum*, VI, 1949–50, pp. 177–210, esp. pp. 186–97. Wyss's point of departure is classical norm; hence his inclement judgment on Gregory's poetry, a judgment belied by the charm of Wyss's own translations.

71. For a succinct collection of relevant patristic passages, cf. H. Fuchs in *Reallexikon für Antike und Christentum*, II, 1954, esp. pp. 351–55, s.v. "Bildung." For the dichotomy between St. Basil's official attitude toward Hellenic philosophy and science (complete condemnation) and his practice (abundant use of both), cf. E. [= D.] Amand de Mendieta, "The Official Attitude of Basil of Caesarea as a Christian Bishop Towards Greek Philosophy and Science," *The Orthodox Churches and the West . . .* , Derek Baker, ed., Oxford, 1976, pp. 25–49. The microfilm of the typewritten dissertation by J. Lercher, *Die Persönlichkeit des heiligen Gregorios von Nazianz und seine Stellung zur klassischen Bildung (aus seinen Briefen)*, Innsbruck, 1949, reached me too late to be used here. The work appears to be compilative.

72. *Letter* 11, P. Gallay, ed., pp. 13–14.

73. *Letter* 235, P. Gallay, ed., pp. 168–69. The learned Origen, too, is said to have sold his books on literature and philosophy.

74. St. Basil *Homily on the Martyr Gordius*, Migne, *PG*, XXXI, col. 492B-C.

75. Migne, *PG*, XXXI, col. 592A.

76. Migne, *PG*, XLVI, col. 824A–B.

77. Migne, *PG*, XXXI, col. 593A. Praise of literary simplicity and unadorned truth, contradicted by practice, is as old as the apologists. Cf. Athenagoras *Legatio* 33, E. Schwartz, ed., p. 44, 3–4: "our [achievements] reside not in practicing literature, but in showing and teaching by deeds." Cf. also Tatian *Oratio ad Graecos* 31–32, E. Schwartz, ed., p. 32, 22–33.

78. For a good analysis of Gregory of Nyssa's eulogies, cf. L. Méridier, *L'influence de la seconde sophistique*, pp. 227–51.

79. Gregory of Nazianzus *Oration* 43, chap. 11, Migne, *PG*, XXXVI, cols. 508B–509A. Pseudo-Gregory of Nazianzus (in fact, his cousin, Amphilochius of Iconium), Poem 8, *Ad Seleucum*, vv. 33–61 and 240–50, Migne, *PG*, XXXVII, cols. 1579–81 and 1592–93. Basil *Homily* 22. The latest edition of this homily, with a commentary offering the improved text of F. Boulenger (1935; reprinted, 1965), is by N. G. Wilson, *Saint Basil on Greek Literature*, London, 1975. Among the several English translations, see *Saint Basil, The Letters*, IV, R.–J. Deferrari and M. R. P. McGuire, eds., London and Cambridge, Mass., 1934 (Loeb Classical Library), reprinted 1970, pp. 379–435. The date of *Homily* 22 is unknown (the seventies?). The interesting proposal by Ann Moffatt to connect it with Julian's legislation of 362 ("The Occasion of St. Basil's *Address to Young Men*," *Antichthon*, VI, 1972, pp. 74–86) is to be met with caution, for Basil (b. ca. 330) presents himself in our text as a man quite advanced in age. Yet, if he wrote ca. 362, he would have been barely past thirty. It has been asserted, too pointedly, that Basil, when he wrote "To Young Men," was interested more in the salvation of their souls than in classics. Cf. S. Giet, *Les Idées et l'action sociales de Saint Basile*, Paris, 1941, pp. 217–32. Cf. also E. Amand de Mendieta, "The Official Attitude of Basil of Caesarea," pp. 25–27. H. Fuchs, "Die griechische christliche Kirche und die antike Bildung," *Die Antike*, V, 1929, esp. pp. 111–15. John Chrysostom's "Address on Vainglory and the Right Way for Parents to Bring Up Their Children" (English translation of this homily in M. L. W. Laistner, *Christianity and Pagan Culture*, pp. 85–122) is of little use for our purposes here.

80. "To Young Men," 4, 3–11 and 34–36; 8, 1–5; 5, 41–48, for the reference to a bee; 4, 19–28 and 30–32, on dissolute gods and lying orators; 6, 1–7, on good letters and the pursuit of virtue; 2, 37–39 and 44–46, and 7, 38–40, on the propaedeutic value of pagan letters. These references correspond to F. Boulenger, ed., Paris, 1935, pp. 44–45, 52, 46, 49, 43, and 51, respectively.

81. "To Young Men," 3, 8–15, on Moses; 5, 25–38, on Homer; 10, 1–4, on drawing "a shadow outline of virtue." F. Boulenger, ed., pp. 44, 47, and 59 respectively. I lifted the expression σκιαγραφίαν τινὰ τῆς ἀρετῆς from Basil and used it in the title of the present essay. Basil, needless to say, had lifted it from Plato's *Republic* 365c. 4.

Basil's leniency toward Homer was not shared by Gregory of Nazianzus. In his first invective against Julian (a work only a few years earlier than Basil's homily "To Young Men"), Gregory poured scorn on Hesiod's and Homer's treatment of the gods, showed that the device of allegorical interpretation of Homeric myths was unworkable, and demonstrated that pagan stories about gods (including those in Homer) could not be adapted to ethical teachings. Cf. *Oration* 4, chaps. 115–22, Migne, *PG*, XXXV, cols. 653A–661C. There were polemical reasons in the passages just quoted for Gregory's hostile stance toward Homer. But the general reason is to be sought in the ambivalence that the fathers displayed while facing the pagan literary canon as both conventional and *engagé* intellectuals. In the Latin world of letters, this ambivalence is paralleled by St. Jerome's, and particularly St. Augustine's, inconsistent attitude towards Vergil. In one passage, Jerome rejected Vergil:

quid facit . . . cum evangeliis Maro? Still, he taught *Maronem suum* in a secondary school at Bethlehem. Augustine quoted almost one hundred Vergilian lines in *De Civitate Dei*, but spurned Vergil in the *Confessions*. In an early work, he called Vergil "our poet"; twenty years later, he called him "their poet." See H. Hagendahl, *Latin Fathers and the Classics. A Study on the Apologists, Jerome and Other Christian Writers*, Göteborg, 1958, pp. 309–28, esp. pp. 310 and 326. Idem, *Augustine and the Classics*, II, *Augustine's Attitude*, Göteborg, 1967 (Studia Graeca et Latina Gothoburgensia XX:II), pp. 445–63, esp. pp. 449, 454, 456.

82. "To Young Men," 7, 34–35 (cf. Matt. 5:39); 7, 37–38 (cf. Matt. 5:44); 7, 44–47 (cf. Matt. 5:28); 7, 52–53 (cf. Matt. 5:34); 9, 64–66 (cf. Rom. 13:14). F. Boulenger, ed., pp. 51, 52, and 57.

83. Cf. "To Young Men," 5, 48–50, quoting Solon; 7, 22–24, quoting Euripides; 5, 53–54 and 9, 110–11, quoting Theognis. F. Boulenger, ed., pp. 48, 50, 58.

The story of the triumph of Hellenism in fourth-century Christian letters has been sketched here with the help of the Cappadocians, with only an occasional mention or two of their great Antiochene contemporary, John Chrysostom. This is because the writings of the Cappadocians tell that story more fully. To be sure, Chrysostom's mastery of the devices of the Second Sophistic is beyond doubt; and the purity of his Atticism has been admired or acknowledged by critics from Isidore of Pelusium in the fifty century to Wilamowitz in the twentieth, even though—as recent quantitative research has shown—Chrysostom was not an extreme purist, but wrote a standard classicistic Greek. But the paucity of classical allusions and quotations in Chrysostom, when measured both against his own immense output and the wealth of such allusions and quotations in Gregory of Nazianzus and Basil, who wrote less, gives food for thought. Even if it does not necessarily prove that Chrysostom the graduate of a pagan school was less familiar with the classics than were the Cappadocians, it suggests that Chrysostom the pupil of the monks valued the classics less. In his moral rigorism, the Antiochene father resembles an Atticizing Epiphanius of Cyprus more than he does Gregory of Nazianzus or the Basil who wrote "To Young Men." To confirm this impression, we have only to read Chrysostom's pedagogical "Address On Vainglory" and his *Adversus oppugnatores vitae monasticae*. Cf., on the one hand, T. E. Ameringer, *The Stylistic Influence of the Second Sophistic on the Panegyrical Sermons of St. John Chrysostom*, Washington, 1921 (*passim*; pp. 20–28 are too optimistic on Chrysostom's tolerant attitude towards Hellenic letters); and, on the other, P. R. Coleman-Norton, "St. Chrysostom and the Greek Philosophers," *Classical Philology*, XXV, 1930, pp. 305–17. Idem, "St. Chrysostom's Use of the Greek Poets," ibid., XXVII, 1932, pp. 213–21. A. J. Festugière's remarkable *Antioche païenne et chrétienne. . .* , esp. chaps. V and VI (on the two educations and cultures, pagan and Christian), pp. 181–240. C. Fabricius, *Zu den Jugendschriften des Johannes Chrysostomos, passim*, esp. pp. 17–18 (older bibliography), 118–42 (classical idioms, quotations and allusions), and 142–49 (Chrysostom wrote standard classicistic Greek).

84. On the lewd pictures, see *Protrepticus* 4. 60, 1–2, C. Mondésert, ed., Paris, 1949, pp. 123–24. On the allegorical meaning of Mark 10:17–31 and the good uses of wealth, *Quis dives salvetur*, 5, 16, 18, and 26.

85. Cf. T. A. Kopecek, "The Social Class of the Cappadocian Fathers," *Church History*, XLII, 1973, pp. 453–66, for the considerable amount of land held by the families of Basil and Gregory of Nyssa. Kopecek argues, along with others, that the Cappadocians descended from curial aristocracy. See also R. Teja, *Organización economica y sociál de Capadocia en el siglo IV, segun los Padres Capadocios*, Salamanca, 1974 (Acta Salamanticensia, Filosofia y Letras, LXXVIII), pp. 36–37, 81–82, and 92.

86. Athanasius *Vita Antonii*, chaps. 72–80, Migne, *PG*, XXVI, cols. 944B–956A. To a sophisticate of Gregory of Nazianzus' caliber, Athanasius was a man of limited literary culture: cf. *Oration* 21, Migne, *PG*, XXXV, col. 1088B.

87. *Chronographia*, L. Dindorf, ed., Bonn, 1831 (Corpus scriptorum historiae Byzantinae, XIV), p. 212, 18–19.

88. Cf. strophe 17 of the Acathist Hymn in *Fourteen Early Byzantine Cantica*, C. A. Trypanis, ed., Vienna, 1968, p. 36 and pp. 22–23 for the "webs of the Athenians."

89. For the recently discovered epitaph from Kemerhisar, cf. N. Thierry, "Un problème de continuité ou de rupture. La Cappadoce entre Rome, Byzacce et les Arabes," *Académie des Inscriptions et Belles-lettres*, Comptes rendus, January-March 1977, pp. 114–16 and fig. 15. The epitaph's metrical structure is so bad that the editor did not recognize it; otherwise, she would not have mistaken the epic pronoun μιν for the first syllable of a ghost name Μινύων. The epitaph consists of two elegiac distichs and a final verse, culled correctly from Homer (*Iliad* 16. 457=675). The whole should be read as follows:

Γνώριζε τόδε σῆμα, ὁδοιπόρε· ἐνθάδε κεῖται
  Εὐθυμία ἀγαθὴ, σωφροσύνης ἀγάιτις [i.e. ἀγέτις].
Τοὔνεκα μιν υῶν πανυπέρτατος, ἔξοχος ἄλλων,
  Αθηνίων τίμησε, μητέρα τὴν πινυτήν,
τύμβῳ τε στήλη τε· τὸ γὰρ γέρας ἐστὶ θανόντων.

This, I submit, means: "Acknowledge this monument, passerby. Here lies good Euthymia, leader in temperance. For that reason Athenion, the most distinguished [the eldest?] of sons, superior to others, honored her, the prudent mother, with a grave and a stele; for this is the reward of the dead."

90. For the text, see A. Dieterich, *Die Grabschrift des Aberkios*, Leipzig, 1896. *S. Abercii Vita*, T. Nissen, ed., Leipzig, 1912, esp. pp. 53–54. Cf. H. Strathmann and T. Klauser in *Reallexikon für Antike und Christentum*, I, 1950, cols. 12–17, s.v. "Aberkios." W. M. Calder, "Early Christian Epitaphs from Phrygia," *Anatolian Studies*, V, 1955, esp. pp. 25–26.

91. Pseudo-Antonius' 170 chapters appear within the *Philocalia*. See, for example, M. Spanneut in *Reallexikon für*

Antike und Christentum, V, 1962, cols. 662–64, s.v. "Epiktet." Cf. also the Christian reworking of Epictetus by Pseudo-Nilus, and an anonymous Christian paraphrase of his *Manual* in I. Schweighaeuser, *Simplicii Commentarius in Epicteti Enchiridion.* . . ., Leipzig, 1800, pp. 10–138. For an unpublished commentary on the paraphrase, cf. M. Spanneut, "Epiktet," cols. 667–70. In discussing pagan antecedents of less refined Christian literary genres we could also mention the so-called *Pseudo-Clementines* (being the story of St. Clement of Rome and of St. Peter; it dates from the fourth century in its two preserved forms) and of various apocryphal Acts of the Apostles, for these works do owe a debt, if of varying extent, to antique novel. The link between the romance episode inserted into an earlier (third century?) version of the *Pseudo-Clementines* and a lost Hellenistic novel, or at least novel motifs, is patent to all (this pre-Christian novel is now reflected in *Homilies* 12:8–14:12 [in Greek] and in *Recognitiones* 7:8–38; 9:32–37 [in Rufin's Latin]). As for sundry apocryphal Acts (especially those of St. Paul), the points of literary contact between them and antique fiction and its motifs are far less pronounced than the dependence of these writings on the canonical Acts of the Apostles. Cf., on the one hand, S. Trenkner, *The Greek Novella in the Classical Period*, Cambridge, 1958, pp. 101–102, and B. E. Perry, *The Ancient Romances* . . . , Berkeley and Los Angeles, 1967 (Sather Classical Lectures, 37), pp. 30–35, 285–93; and, on the other, R. Söder, *Die apokryphen Apostelgeschichten und die romanhafte Literatur der Antike*, Stuttgart, 1932 (Würzburger Studien zur Altertumswissenschaft, 3), *passim*, and the perceptive thesis by C. Milovanović, "Apokrifna Dela Pavlova i njihov odnos prema antičkom grčkom romanu i kanonskim Delima Apostolskim," *Zbornik radova Vizantološkog instituta*, XVII, 1976, pp. 297–416 (with French summary), esp. pp. 406–407, 415.

92. Cf. *Fourteen Early Byzantine Cantica*, C. A. Trypanis, ed., p. 22. E. Wellesz, "The 'Akathistos.' A Study in Byzantine Hymnography," *Dumbarton Oaks Papers*, IX–X, 1953, p. 154. On the date of the Acathist Hymn and the vexed question of the *kontakion's* Syriac roots, cf., most recently, J. Grosdidier de Matons, *Romanos le Mélode et les origines de la poésie religieuse à Byzance*, Paris, 1977, esp. pp. 16–27, 32–36. The author is an undisputed authority on the subject. I therefore regret to have to report that he is disinclined to admit much Syriac influence upon the *kontakion*; on the other hand, he is most convincing when he calls the Acathist one of the earliest *kontakia*.

93. The expression is πράττειν. Cf. *Pratum Spirituale*, chap. 77, Migne, *PG*, LXXXVII, 3, cols. 2930D and 2932C.

94. Cf. P. Gallay's edition of Gregory's letters, p. xlvi. S. Giet, *L'Hexaéméron de Saint Basile*, Paris, 1950, p. 74. The number of 150 for extant Moschus manuscripts has been established by Philip Pattenden subsequent to his "The Text of the Pratum Spirituale," *The Journal of Theological Studies*, XXVI, 1975, p. 36, where he counted "over one hundred."

95. For poems in iambics, see *Anthol. Palat.* 1. 120 and

121 (attributed to George of Pisidia). For those in hexameters, Corippus *In Laudem Iustini* 2. 52–69, Averil Cameron, ed., *Flavius Cresconius Corippus. In Laudem Iustini Augusti Minoris*, London, 1976, p. 46.

96. We can only make guesses as to Paul the Silentiary's views on authors such as Romanos and on the *kontakion*. We are fairly sure, however, that establishment figures at Justinian's court who were deciding on literary fare to be offered on state occasions were tolerant of new literary forms. About Christmas 562, and only at a few days' interval, two works were recited in the capital during the ceremonies rededicating the newly restored Hagia Sophia: Paul the Silentiary's ornate *ekphrasis* of the church, and a *kontakion*. We do know that Paul pronounced his work in front of Justinian. The *kontakion's* flattering allusions to the emperor of the day make it likely that Justinian heard the *kontakion* as well, perhaps during a procession. For the text of the *kontakion* on the rededication of Hagia Sophia (it is not by Romanos), cf. C. A. Trypanis, ed., *Fourteen Early Byzantine Cantica*, pp. 139–47. For Paul the Silentiary, his milieu and antecedents, cf., in addition to the exemplary discussion in the edition of his two *ekphraseis* by P. Friedländer (1912), T. Viljamaa, *Studies in Greek Encomiastic Poetry of the Early Byzantine Period*, Helsinki, 1968 (Commentationes Humanarum Litterarum. Societas Scientiarum Fennica, XLII), esp. pp. 60–62; 134–36.

97. *On Pentecost*, strophe 17, P. Maas and C. A. Trypanis, eds., Oxford, 1963, p. 265. Two recent writers detect high-style Hellenic sources of inspiration in individual *kontakia*, while a third does not. J. Grosdidier de Matons sees a "je ne sais quel" far-away reflection of Alexandrinism in the Acathist Hymn and describes the *kontakion* itself as the last poetic genre due to the fecundity of the "old Hellenic spirit." Cf. his *Romanos le Mélode*, pp. 36 and 65. Some passages in Romanos remind E. C. Topping of Aeschylus and Pindar. Cf. her "On Earthquakes and Fires: Romanos' Encomium to Justinian," *Byzantinische Zeitschrift*, LXXI, 1978, p. 30. For a different perspective (the true ancestor of Romanos and therefore of the *kontakion* was St. Ephrem the Syrian, the greatest poet of the patristic age, who knew no Greek), see R. Murray, *Symbols of Church and Kingdom. An Early Syriac Tradition*, Cambridge, 1975, p. 31.

98. Cf. *Heraclias*, I, 65–83, on the labors of Heracles; *Exped. Persica*, I, 65 ff., on Homer; *Bellum Avaricum*, 207–11, for the allusion to Odysseus. See A. Pertusi, ed., *Giorgio di Pisidia, Poemi*, Ettal, 1960, pp. 243–44 (cf. p. 265), 87, and 185 respectively. For a detailed summary of George of Pisidia's comparison between Heracles and Heraclius, cf. H. Hunger, "On the Imitation," p. 23.

99. Cf. *Historiae*, C. De Boor and P. Wirth, eds., Stuttgart, 1972, pp. 20–22. For further examples of the Sirens motif in a positive or neutral sense (time span: from Synesius in the late fourth century to Demetrius Cydones in the fourteenth), cf. H. Hunger, "On the Imitation," p. 29.

100. *Letter* 79, "Isocrates to Dionysius" (both names fictitious). For the nineteenth-century error, cf. *Oeuvres complètes d'Isocrate*, Le Duc de Clermont-Tonnerre, ed., Paris,

1864, III, 544. J. F. Boissonade, *Theophylacti Simocattae Opuscula*, Paris, 1835, p. 317, had already made fun of previous editors who put Letter 79 among Isocrates' works.

101. For a stimulating attempt to correlate the David plates with the poetry of George of Pisidia, cf. now J. Trilling, "Myth and Metaphor at the Byzantine Court. A Literary Approach to the David Plates," *Byzantion*, XLVIII, 1978, pp. 249–63. Attempts such as Mr. Trilling's, ought to be encouraged. The danger to avoid here is that of being more subtle than were the people who conceived the plates and wrote the poetry.

102. On the sparse use of "To Young Men" in Byzantium, the absence of a medieval Latin translation of the tract, and, above all, its popularity in the West during the Renaissance, cf. L. Schucan, *Das Nachleben von Basilius Magnus "ad adolescentes,"* Geneva, 1973. Note that Leonardo Bruni's Latin translation of ca. 1400 is preserved in about three hundred manuscripts. On Basil's tract as one of the three channels through which the story of Heracles at the crossroads penetrated into the artistic consciousness of Europe (e.g., paintings by Cranach and Carracci), cf. E. Panofsky, *Hercules am Scheidewege . . .* , Leipzig, 1930 (Studien der Bibliothek Warburg, XVIII), pp. 52–54.

103. Cf. F. Lefherz, *Studien zu Gregor von Nazianz*, pp. 86, 113–44, 132–33, and 161. For the lexicon to Gregory's prose, cf. J. Sajdak, "Anonymi Oxoniensis lexicon in orationes Gregorii Nazianzeni," *Symbolae grammaticae in honorem Ioannis Rozwadowski*, Cracow, 1927, I, esp. p. 159. Cf. also E. Follieri, "Ciriaco ὁ μελαῖος," *Zetesis, Album amicorum . . . E. de Strycker*, Antwerp-Utrecht, 1973, esp. pp. 524–26 on still unpublished lexica to Gregory's poetry.

104. Gregory's epigrams constitute the eighth book of the Palatine Anthology.

105. Psellos found that Gregory's pagan counterpart was Demosthenes. Gregory, however, had left Demosthenes behind when it came to the panegyric genre. Among other stylistic models that Gregory imitated (the terms Psellos used were μιμούμενος, ἐπαρύεται) or surpassed, Psellos quoted Thucydides, Isocrates, Lysias, Plato and—more appropriately—the shining light of the Second Sophistic, Aelius Aristides. For Psellos' first treatise (devoted exclusively to Gregory), cf., for example, P. Levy, *Michaelis Pselli de Gregorii Theologi charactere imdicium . . .* (Dissertation, Strassburg), Leipzig, 1912, esp. pp. 46–63. For the second treatise (in which Gregory was given the place of honor but was treated along with St. Basil, Gregory of Nyssa, and John Chrysostom), cf., for example, Migne, *PG*, CXXII, cols. 901–08. Cf. also Ja. N. Ljubarskij, "Mixail Psell i Grigorij Nazianzin," Vizantinovedčeskie ètjudy, Tbilisi: 1978 (Festschrift for S. G. Kauxčišvili), pp. 93–98 (inaccessible to me); idem, "Mixail Psell. Ličnost' i tvorčestvo . . . ," Moscow, 1978 (chapter on Psellos as literary critic); and the typewritten doctoral thesis by Č. Milovanovič on Psellos as theoretician of literature (presented at the University of Belgrade in 1979).

In the twelfth century, a Byzantine rhetorician put a fictitious harangue, in which he upbraided Emperor Julian for his edict against Christian professors, into the mouth of a "Christian lover of letters" (χριστιανὸς φιλόλογος). He saw the problem through the eyes of Gregory of Nazianzus, whose first invective against Julian (*Oration* 4) he quarried for words, style, and ideas. Cf. J. R. Asmus, "Die Ethopöie des Nikephoros Chrysoberges über Julians Rhetorenedikt," *Byzantinische Zeitschrift*, XV, 1906, pp. 125–36.

106. For a positive appreciation of the role of the fourth-century fathers in preserving the classics cf. C. Fabricius, *Zu den Jugendschriften des Johannes Chrysostomos*, p. 149, and, especially, idem, "Der sprachliche Klassizismus der griechischen Kirchenväter: ein philologisches und geistesgeschichtliches Problem," *Jahrbuch für Antike und Christentum*, X, 1967, pp. 187–99, esp. pp. 187–88. I chanced upon this stimulating article too late to make use of it in the present essay.

Except for two or three incidental remarks (cf. notes 11, 24, 81, above) I refrained from drawing parallels between the Greek and Latin Christian literature's classical heritage. For the Latin wing of the diptych, see the somewhat bland work by G. L. Ellspermann, *The Attitude of the Early Christian Latin Writers toward Pagan Literature and Learning*, Washington, D. C., 1949 (The Catholic University of America, Patristic Studies, LXXXII), and, most recently, the excellent collection of essays, M. Fuhrmann, ed., *Christianisme et formes littéraires de l'Antiquité tardive en Occident*, Vandoeuvres-Geneva, 1977 (Fondation Hardt. Entretiens sur l'Antiquité classique, XXIII). See particularly the contributions by Alan Cameron, pp. 1–40, and by J. Fontaine, pp. 425–72.

GEORGE M. A. HANFMANN

The Continuity of Classical Art:
Culture, Myth, and Faith

EVERYONE knows that the right person to discuss the continuity of classical art is the director of this symposium,[1] Kurt Weitzmann, whose books and collected articles on the subject form an indispensable commentary for the splendid exhibition he has masterminded.[2] You cannot surpass Weitzmann! I shall, therefore, attempt no more than some remarks prompted by this exhibition, remarks on three aspects of the decisive historical process by which an otherworldly faith accepted and transformed the heritage of classical anthropomorphic art.

A number of objects in the exhibition were grouped in a section designated as the "Classical Realm."[3] This realm, in turn, was subdivided into Science, Didactic Treatises, Literature, Mythology, and Mystery Cults. My three themes—culture, myth, and faith—were suggested by these groupings, but they are not three sharply separated divisions. Rather, I envisage them as one continuous arc that begins, at one pole, with the intellectual culture, with religiously neutral learning; then traverses the area of mythology, where literary culture and religious sentiment meet; and ends at the other pole, with works that are proclamations of religious faith.

By adopting this thematic-interpretative approach, I want to emphasize that the fate of the classical heritage was determined by the dialogue between *paideia* and *pistis*, between classical culture and Christian faith—a subject that has been treated in Professor Ševčenko's masterly discourse.[4] My arrangement is systematic, determined by the subject fields and meanings, as well as emotional connotations of art types, and not by development of style or by changes of iconography. The question I seek to answer is this: "What happened during late antiquity to that classical art which used to express pagan myth, pagan intellectual culture, and pagan faith?"

Viewed historically, the problem of the continuity of classical art has two major aspects: the survival of recognizably classical subjects, with or without their classical forms; and the transformation of classical art into Christian art—either with related meanings, often allegorical, attached to preexisting classical types, or with classical forms adjusted to an entirely new content.[5] My aim is to present a sampling of the process of survival and transformation, as well as of the different ways and gradations that characterize this process—from the straight survival of classical art, on the one hand, to its complete Christianization, on the other.[6]

In accordance with the triadic themes of culture, myth, and faith, my selection is influenced to some extent by the material in the exhibition.[7] We shall treat first the heroes of intellectual culture and the neutral didactic learning, then mythical heroes—pagan, controversial, and Christianized—and, finally, sacrifices and confessions of faith.

In describing my first theme as "culture," I have adopted a Ciceronian and a modern term for that educational and cultural heritage the French call *culture intellectuelle*.[8] For late antiquity, it is better described by the Greek term *paideia* or, as St. Basil called it, *paideusis*,[9] which puts the accent on education. Indeed, the survival of classical schools was fundamental to the survival of classical art. As Marrou observed, the Church did not immediately create an educational system of its own and therefore tolerated classical education. Papyrus scraps of school exercises prove that as late as the sixth century, Christian school children in Egypt practiced writing such objectionable mythological names as Europa and Pasiphae.[10] At the other end of the intellectual scale, great pagan and Christian literati met on common literary and philosophic ground. In the Greek-

speaking East, to be sure, Hellenic *paideia*, as Werner
Jaeger noted, "became a religion and an article of
faith" for pagans from Julian to Proclus.[11] But it was
also claimed as useful by St. Basil and other Church
fathers. In the West, this *réligion de culture* was sus-
tained not only by the pagan opponents to Christianity like Symmachus and Macrobius, but also by
Christians—nominal and real—from Claudian and

FIG. 1. Wall painting. Sappho.
  House 2, Room 12, Ephesus. (Photo: Österreichisches
  Archäologisches Institut)

FIG. 2. Ivory plaques. Authors and Muses.
  Musée du Louvre, Paris. (Photo: Giraudon)

Ausonius, Jerome and Augustine, to Sidonius Apollinaris, Boethius, and Cassiodorus.[12]

The ideal of a poet, a sage, a *mousikos aner*,[13] or
"man of the Muses," belonged to this culture and it
also persisted as an ideal in art. We illustrate here
two monuments, one from the Greek East, the other
from the Latin West. They are also reminders of that
seemingly unrelated coexistence of classicism and
Christianity which never ceases to amaze the student
of late antiquity.

Adorning the noblest room in an apartment in
Ephesus, there was a painting depicting Sappho, the
great poetess of love, as the tenth Muse, together
with Apollo and the nine Muses (Fig. 1). Her name
is inscribed. She floats on a little patch of ground
against a plain white background.[14] This simple kind
of illustration is known from literary papyri, and she
may be copied from one. Truly astonishing is the
classicistic style and the almost Pompeian face with
soulful eyes. Yet this painting, which glorifies a very

pagan woman, was painted in the fifth century of our era, perhaps in the very years when, only a half mile away at the Council of Ephesus (431), the Cyrillians and the Nestorians had their violent theological battle about a very different woman, the *Theotokos*, "the Virgin who gave birth to God."[15]

The quiet beauty of Sappho makes a rather striking contrast with an emphatic, dynamic Western representation of the Muses, made in the fifth century either in Italy or Gaul, that now comprises two parts of a famous ivory relief (Fig. 2). Originally, nine authors admired nine enthusiastically dancing Muses (only six survive).[16] The incongruous way in which the Muses whirl like nightclub dancers before the solemn but appreciative authors reminds one of another fifth-century work, a literary effort to combine traditional school learning and extravagant mythological ornamentation: Martianus Capella's fantastic

Wedding of Philology and Mercury, a work which evoked from C. S. Lewis the memorable remark that "this universe which has produced the bee-orchid and the giraffe has produced nothing stranger than Martianus Capella."[17] Probably, like Martianus Capella, the artist of the Louvre relief earnestly desired to portray a triumph of Muses and to glorify traditional learning. Yet, the scene could even be intended as humorous and joyful. In a comparable literary parade of tortuous mythology, all the Olympian gods twirl their attributes like jugglers—*quo quis pollebat lusit in officio*—while Orpheus leads in the Muses. This remarkable display occurs in the epithalamium written around 460 for Ruricius and Hiberia by Sidonius Apollinaris, sometime bishop of Clermont in Gaul. One wonders whether the Louvre ivories were not originally a marriage present.[18]

Poets and Muses constituted a popular general

FIG. 3. Colored glass panel from Kenchreai. Homer, detail.

Nauplion Museum (Photo: R.L. Scranton-Kenchreai Expedition)

FIG. 4. Drawing of Homer from Kenchreai

(Photo: R.L. Scranton-Kenchreai Expedition)

FIG. 5. Transfiguration mosaic. Christ.

St. Catherine's Monastery, Sinai (Photo: Courtesy of
Alexandria, Michigan, Princeton Expedition to Mt. Sinai)

symbol of intellectual culture, and the group of the
poet turning back to his Muse for inspiration eventually became a model for evangelists looking back
toward the hand of God, as Hugo Buchthal has shown
in a fine study.[19]

Let us turn now to the individual heroes of the
classical *paideia* and their transformations in Christian
art. The greatest heroes of classical Greek letters
were Homer and Plato. Homeric studies flourished
particularly in Alexandria; there, too, was the school
of the Neoplatonist Ammonius Saccas, who taught
Plotinus, the greatest Late Antique philosopher, as
well as the great Church father Origen.

A recent discovery has now given us Late Antique
portraits of Homer (Figs. 3 and 4) and Plato that, I
believe, were made in Alexandria. In the year 375,
a tidal wave swamped an apsidal hall in the sanctuary of the Egyptian goddess Isis on the waterfront of
Kenchreai, the eastern port of the cosmopolitan city
of Corinth. Shipped from Alexandria, the great glass-

making center of antiquity, and still packed in crates
and awaiting installation in the hall, were one
hundred panels of glass revetments. Among them
were inscribed, life-size portraits of Homer and
Plato[20] —the two unfortunately stuck face to face by
the deterioration of glass. The photographs had to
be taken from the backs (Figs. 3 and 7).

Emphasized by the linear inlay technique, the
standing figure of thundering Homer[21] displays a
dark intensity and an abstract spiritualization, suggesting that this type of Homer was a model not only
for prophets of the Old Testament, but even for the
bearded Christ himself, as he is seen, for instance, in
the magnificent Transfiguration mosaic of the Monastery of St. Catherine in Sinai (Fig. 5), a work done
in the later years of Justinian (545–65).[22] The drawing of the Alexandrian Homer, which shows him in
the correct, unreversed position (Fig. 4), reveals further resemblances to the Christ in the draping of the
garment and the placing of the right hand.

One may wonder, too, about a possible connection
between the Plato of Kenchreai, milder than Homer,
with well-groomed white hair (Fig. 7) and the white-
haired Moses of the Sinai Transfiguration (Fig. 6).
That great pioneer in the creation of Christian *paideia*, Clement of Alexandria, had described Plato as
an "Atticizing Moses"—*Moses Attikizon*.[23] Prompted
by such comparisons, an Alexandrian type of Plato
portrait might have influenced the visual portrayals
of Moses, resulting in a *Moses Platonikos*, a Platonic
Moses, so to speak.

Many years ago, Albert Friend argued in a famous study that the type of the standing sage used
to depict prophets and evangelists in Early Christian
art was adapted from classical models in Alexandria.[24] Now the Alexandrian portraits of Homer
and Plato lend new credibility to Friend's brilliant
hypothesis. The mosaicists of the Transfiguration
mosaic may well have been sent by Justinian from
Constantinople, as suggested by Weitzmann, but their
theological advisers at Sinai might have favored the
use of types derived from Alexandrian traditions.

What Homer was to the Greeks, Vergil became to
the Romans. Because in his fourth *Eclogue*, Vergil
had predicted the birth of the Savior Child, he was
thought by many to be a proto-Christian prophet.[25]
The emperor Constantine himself, according to the
report by Eusebius, had told the Council of Nicaea
(325) that Vergil "was acquainted with the blessed
mystery which gave to our Lord the name of Sav-
iour."[26] Thus even more than with Plato, there was
reason for adopting Vergil's portrait for representa-

tions of the evangelists, especially in Latin-speaking countries.

In the later of the two famous Vergil codices shown in the exhibition, the so-called Romanus (Vat. lat. 3867, ca. 500), there are three portraits of Vergil, of which I illustrate the one preceding the second Eclogue (Fig. 8). Vergil is seated frontally, drawn in rather linear, Western, Late Antique style, possibly in a North Italian scriptorium, such as Verona.[27] Following Francis Wormald, I should like to underline the probable importance of this type of Vergil portrait for the formulation of evangelist representations in the early medieval West.[28]

The Gospels of the luxurious Codex Aureus, now in Stockholm, were illuminated around 750 at Canterbury, the earliest center of the Roman Church in Anglo-Saxon England. Looking at the arrangement of drapery on the youthful St. John (Fig. 9), especially on his right shoulder and at the right leg, one

divines behind the dynamic linearism of this insular manuscript a model similar in type and style to the Romanus Vergil.[29] This model was not, of course, the Romanus Vergil itself. It was probably an evangelist illumination adapted in Italy from a Romanus-like Vergil type. Perhaps it had appeared in one of the books brought to Canterbury from Rome in 597 by St. Augustine, first bishop of Canterbury, or by one of his successors.[30] We perceive something of the ways by which a transformed classical heritage reached the new monastic centers in the West. Thus, the heroes of classical intellectual culture became the heralds of the Gospels.

We now turn to the didactic paideia and consider examples from botany, astronomy, and zoology.[31] From the point of view of religion, didactic and technical literature were the least controversial areas. A famous example of this "neutral" knowledge is the Vienna manuscript of the pharmaceutical treatise by

FIG. 6. Transfiguration mosaic. Moses.

St. Catherine's Monastery, Sinai (Photo: Courtesy of Alexandria, Michigan, Princeton Expedition to Mt. Sinai)

FIG. 7. Colored glass panel from Kenchreai. Plato, detail.

Nauplion Museum (Photo: R.L. Scranton-Kenchreai Expedition)

FIG. 8. Vatican Cod. Lat. 3867. Portrait of Vergil.
The Vatican Library, Rome (Photo: Vatican Library)

Right:
FIG. 9. Codex Aureus. St. John.
Royal Library, Stockholm (Photo: Royal Library, Stockholm)

Below:
FIG. 10. Vatican Cod. Gr. 1291. Helios.
The Vatican Library, Rome (Photo: K. Weitzmann)

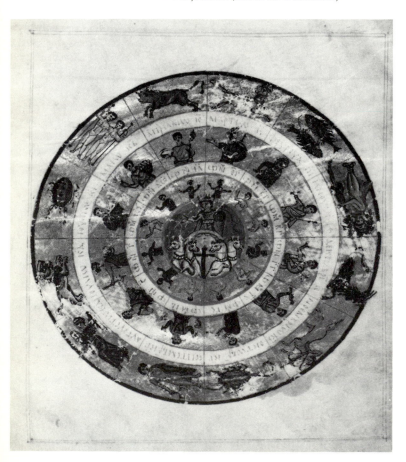

Dioscurides of Anazarbus, an army physician of the first century A.D. The glorious codex itself was written at Constantiople as a gift for Princess Juliana Anicia before 512. In one of its illuminations, a seated author, inscribed Dioscurides, is shown in a type rather similar to Vergil's. Some scholars conjecture that he is actually Crateuas, a Hellenistic botanist and predecessor of Dioscurides. He is being instructed by Heuresis, the very Greek personification of Discovery. The wondrous mandrake (*mandragora*) plant and a dog also appear in the picture.[32] The dog supposedly died as a result of digging up the mandrake. The illustrations were done with the same precise factual observation that characterized the descriptions by Dioscurides.[33] This herbal and its descendants enjoyed an enormous popularity in the Middle Ages, and their factual illustrations survived without provoking attempts at Christianization.[34]

With astronomy, we enter upon a more complicated field. Starting from abstract geometric diagrams,[35] the illustrators of astronomical treatises proceeded to diagrammatic representations that used mythological figures, human and animal, but were completely scientific in intent. Such an illustration is preserved in the Vatican Ptolemy *Handlists* (Fig. 10). In the center, the sun god Helios drives a chariot with four white horses through the blue sky. In the inner ring are personifications of the hours, in the median ring, the months, and in the outer ring, the signs of the zodiac. Since the moment of the entry of the sun into each sign of the zodiac is indicated to the minute, it was possible for Franz Boll to calculate that the original diagram was drawn around the middle of the third century of our era. The Vatican codex itself, however, was written and illuminated in Constantinople during the iconoclastic period, under Emperor Leo V, who ruled from 813 to 820. Thus, it provides cogent evidence for the actual survival and precise copying of scientific classical calendar illustrations.[36]

A popular spin-off from this scientific radial design was the radial type of calendar with the Sun god encircled by the zodiac and the months. The turning points of the year, the *tropai*, or the four seasons, were often placed in the corners. The earliest preserved example in a mosaic at Antioch dates ca. 120.[37] A mosaic calendar from the monastery at Scythopolis (Beth Shean) in northern Palestine is dated 569. Personifications of the Sun and the Moon are in the center; the months have Latin names written in Greek letters; and the number of days in each month is written in Greek (Fig. 11). The very fact that this calendar was used to decorate the floor of a hall in a

FIG. 11. Mosaic. Calendar.
Monastery, Beth Shean (Photo: A. Hay)

monastery[38] indicates that the design was readily accepted as part of neutral encyclopedic learning by Christians in the Eastern Empire.

At Scythopolis, the solar calendar was seen not in the chapel, but in a dining hall. The mosaic of Hamat Tiberias,[39] however, was in the nave of the synagogue hall itself (Fig. 12). Here and in other

FIG. 12. Mosaic. Helios and zodiac.

Synagogue, Hamat Tiberias (Photo: after Rosenthal, *Vergilius*, fig. 12)

FIG. 13. Medical manuscript, Lat. 7028. Helios and zodiac.

Bibliothèque Nationale, Paris (Photo: H.A. Bober)

synagogue mosaics dating from the fourth to the sixth century, the design no longer conveys neutral encyclopedic knowledge but illustrates instead God's creation of the sun and the moon, "and signs and days and years," as described in the first chapter of Genesis. This interpretation of the temporal *imago mundi* as a symbol of divine providence was also acceptable to Christians and appears in the medieval Octateuchs.[40] On the other hand, the radial, zodiacal *schema* could be interpreted by Christians as a symbol of un-Christian astrology and, hence, of evil. As early as 563, the Council of Braga anathemized the connection of the zodiac with parts of the soul or of the body. In a remarkable Latin medical manuscript of the late eleventh century (Fig. 13), discussed in Harry Bober's fine study of the zodiacal man,[41] we see a bearded Sun god in the center. The signs of the zodiac are related to various parts of the body by means of inscriptions. Then the whole design is labeled at top: "According to the delirious thoughts of

the astrologers" (*philosophorum*). And in the late Byzantine painter's guide from Mt. Athos, a radial design of this kind is captioned: "The Vain World" (*Ho mataios Kosmos*).[42] Thus, the same classical design could not only survive as a neutral, scientific calendar, but could also be Christianized in two directions—*in bonam* or *in malam partem*—as good or as evil.

In zoological illustrations, the battle of the stag and the snake presents us with an example of the straight survival of a classical motif and of a double transformation, involving the separate Christianization of both the story and the image.

The battle of the stag and the snake (Fig. 14)—from that extraordinary collection of classical motifs, the mosaic of a peristyle in the Great Palace of Constantinople—is a work placed by some scholars as late as 700.[43] This strange combination of disparate elements of reality, mythology, and animal lore probably illustrates a poem or an oration in praise

FIG. 14. Mosaic. Stag and snake.

"Great Palace," Istanbul (Photo: after Brett, *The Great Palace*, pl. 42)

of hunting read before the emperor. The representation of the stag and the serpent[44] follows the version of Greek writers on zoology. The stag "rends the snake . . . while it writhes about his knees and neck," as Pseudo-Oppian, a writer of Caracalla's time, says in his poem on hunting.[45] Our second illustration is from the Latin version of a famous book of animal lore known as the *Physiologus*. It was originally compiled in Greek, possibly in Alexandria.[46] In the *Physiologus* version, the stag flushes out the serpent, using water from a fountain, and then kills it. The illumination in the famous Carolingian codex, the Bern *Physiologus* (Fig. 15),[47] was painted by a certain Haecbertus, probably at Reims in the ninth century under Archbishop Ebo, 825–45. But the artist followed closely a Late Antique manuscript of the third or fourth century.

These illustrations presuppose a *Physiologus* text that was not yet Christianized. But the *Physiologus* text had been Christianized at a very early date. Already in the earliest preserved Greek version of the *Physiologus*, the story of the stag and the serpent is prefaced by the moving verses of Psalm 41: "As the hart panteth after the waterbrooks, so panteth my soul after thee, O God."[48] There is a string of Christian allegories attached to the story in the Greek and the Latin *Physiologus* texts, but Psalm 41 made a natural bridge to the authoritative interpretation of Jerome and Augustine; the stag is a symbol of the neophyte who defeats evil and attains life eternal through the waters of baptism. In Africa, this very Psalm was sung in the baptismal liturgy at Easter.[49]

No longer as an illustration of animal lore but as a symbol of baptism, the stag then appears in Early Christian and early Byzantine art. In the fifth- or sixth-century North African baptistery at Henchir Massaouda, the mosaic still portrays the stag's combat with the snake (Fig. 16) as a symbol of *abrenuntiatio Satanae*, the "renunciation of the devil," according to St. Augustine.[50] But in the standard versions, such as the glorious mosaics in the lunettes of the Mausoleum of the Empress Galla Placidia in Ravenna,[51] executed after 425, only the formal resemblance of the stag to the zoological illustrations of the *Physiologus* remains; the snake is omitted. In this case, the process of transformation went from the illustrations of scientific and pseudoscientific animal lore, to

FIG. 15. *Physiologus*, cod. 318. Stag and serpent.

Burgerbibliothek, Bern (Photo: Burgerbibliothek, Bern)

FIG. 16. Mosaic. Two stags with snakes at tree.

Baptistery, Massaouda, Tunisia (Photo: after Feuilles, *Cahiers Archéologiques*, 1949, p. 12, fig. 3)

FIG. 17. Mosaic. Phaedra, nurse,
Hippolytus. From Antioch, House of
the Red Pavement.
Antakya Museum, Antioch (Photo: Committee
for Excavation of Antioch)

FIG. 18. Silver dish. Phaedra.
Dumbarton Oaks Collection, Washington, D.C.
(Photo: Dumbarton Oaks)

Christian allegorization of both the story and the image, and ended with the creation of a new visual symbol for one of the sacraments of the Christian religion. Such then, were the fortunes of some of the illustrations of didactic learning.

We turn now to the vast and difficult subject of the myth. Ever since Homer had created the Greek gods and heroes, myth had remained a central fact of classical culture. It was a prime target of systematic Christian attacks on the immorality of polytheism. Yet, in fact, Late Antique attitudes toward myth varied from nearly neutral acceptance of mythology as part of the reading of famous authors in school, through moralistic allegorization by philosophic pagans and Christians, to partial Christianization or total rejection.[52] All through this period, Homer and Euripides remained the most popular school authors and their illustrated editions played a major part in the continuing survival of mythology in art.[53]

The silver dish at Dumbarton Oaks (Fig. 18) dates to the sixth century.[54] It is one of the latest mythological representations known from the period with which we are concerned, and the scene is derived, with some abbreviation, as Weitzmann has shown,

from the illustrations of Euripides' *Hippolytus* in a purple codex. Such illustrations were copied around 200 in the so-called Red Pavement mosaic at Antioch (Fig. 17) and in the late second century on the walls of the Theater Room in Ephesus.[55] The mosaic makes clear that the scene shows Hippolytus reading Phaedra's fatal confession of love. Weitzmann has suggested that the gesture of Phaedra grasping Hippolytus' garment already reflects the influence of Early Christian representations of Potiphar's wife grasping Joseph's garment.[56] To me, Hippolytus looks rather like a husband reading a detective story when his wife wants to go to bed.

The production of this kind of silver ware was controlled by high officials of the imperial court at Constantinople, and it thus reflects the taste of the court circles. One wonders about the reasons for the choice of subject. Certainly pride in showing off a knowledge of Euripidean drama was one reason, but conceivably the representation also denotes a moralistic interpretation in which Hippolytus becomes a *sophrosynes paradigma*, an example of chastity, as he is still called in the *Lexikon* of Patriarch Photius.[57] At any event, the relief documents the survival of the Hippolytus myth in literary illustration.

The Argive hero Bellerophon, tamer of the winged Pegasus and slayer of the fire-spitting Chimera, is a very controversial figure. Has Bellerophon ever become a Christian? In 1963, there was discovered in a rich Roman villa at Hinton St. Mary, Dorset, datable in the mid- to late fourth century, a mosaic pavement that contained a bust of Christ in one panel and a Bellerophon slaying the Chimera in another (Fig. 19). They appear upside down in relation to each other, and Jocelyn Toynbee has suggested that the pagans in the family lined up on one side and worshiped Bellerophon (Fig. 20), while the Christian side lined up opposite and worshiped Christ.[58] Marcel Simon has proposed that "Bellerophon chrétien" was allegorized by Christians as a slayer of evil.[59] As Ihor Ševčenko points out, around 300, Methodius, bishop of Olympus, identified the Chimera of the *Iliad* (6. 180–83) with the dragon of Revelations and stated that Christ slew the Chimera—thus implying that Christ was a new Bellerophon.[60] On the other hand, Hugo Brandenburg[61] argued that since several Bellerophon mosaics were found in dining rooms, the function of Bellerophon as a famous hunter was to provide dainty Chimeras as delicacies for the dining table.

There is no question that the slaying of the Chimera was a popular motif in late antiquity. Weitzmann has proved from Middle Byzantine illustrations that the scene probably appeared in a fifth- or sixth-century illustrated mythological handbook.[62]

FIG. 19. Mosaic. Bellerophon slaying the Chimera. Hinton St. Mary, Dorset.

British Museum, London (Photo: Royal Commission on Historical Monuments)

FIG. 20. Simplified diagram of the decorative scheme of the pavement, Hinton St. Mary, Dorset

(Photo: Royal Commission on Historical Monuments)

FIG. 21. Ivory. Bellerophon.

British Museum, London (Photo: Hirmer)

Somewhat similar to these painted versions is the openwork ivory in the British Museum (Fig. 21),[63] probably of the fifth century and carved in Syria, I believe. In the mosaic of the Imperial Palace in Constantinople, Bellerophon and the Chimera were represented in a hunting context as late as 700.[64] They still appeared among classical myths in the mosaics of the imaginery palace of Digenis Acrites, as described in the great Byzantine epic of the ninth or tenth century.[65]

Bellerophon was certainly popular, but it is not clear to what extent Methodius' interpretation of

FIG. 22. Coptic textile. Equestrian saint.

Cooper-Hewitt Museum, New York, Gift of J.P. Morgan, 1902–1–71 (Photo: Cooper-Hewitt Museum)

Christ as a new Bellerophon was widely held. Although we may consider it valid for the British Museum ivory (Fig. 21), it does not commend itself for the hunting ambience of the mosaic of the Imperial Palace in Constantinople. The subjects of the mosaics in Digenis Acrites' imaginary palace emphasized, by means of biblical and Homeric *exempla*, the theme of valor in general; and Eustathius, in the twelfth century, glosses Bellerophon as *phoneus kakias*, "killer of evil."[66]

FIG. 23. Ivory pyxis. Orpheus and the animals.

Museo Nazionale, Florence (Photo: Giraudon)

It has been suggested that Bellerophon provided not a moral prototype, but the artistic, visual model for equestrian saints, some of whom are attested by inscribed representations from Coptic Egypt in the sixth century and by somewhat earlier bronze phylacteries from Syria and Palestine.[67] Such a Coptic equestrian saint fighting a lion (rather than a Chimera) is seen in a fine textile at the Cooper-Hewitt Museum (Fig. 22).[68] There are, however, claimants other than Bellerophon as possible models for equestrian saints—for example, the emperor killing a lion, or defending Faith.[69] Thus, even the case for Bellerophon as a visual model for equestrian saints is not uncontested.

If Bellerophon's Christianization is doubtful, Orpheus enchanting the animals presents us with an incontrovertible example of a mythological image that passed into both Jewish and Christian iconography.[70] Some seventy late Roman and Late Antique mosaics,[71] as well as marble sculptures and ivories, attest to the great appeal of the subject. This popularity was perhaps caused by a universal longing for a world of peace, where "the cattle will not fear the great lions," as Vergil says (*Eclogue* 4. 22), or where "the calf and the young lion shall abide together," according to Isaiah (11:6). The survival of the pagan mythological Orpheus as late as 500 is witnessed by the ivory pyxis from Brioude (St. Julien), perhaps a Constantinopolitan work (Fig. 23).[72]

In 1965, there was discovered in a synagogue ruin at Gaza a mosaic dated by an inscription to the year 508–09.[73] An Orpheus-like musician, dressed in the manner of a Byzantine king, is inscribed "David" in Hebrew (Fig. 24).[74] The discovery suggests that in the synagogue frescoes at Dura Europos, painted around 245, the musician with Phrygian cap, whose identity has been much debated, may be David shown in the type of Orpheus, and not Orpheus or an unknown musician.[75] Clearly, not later than the third century, Jewish illustrators of the Bible had adopted the Orpheus type for David. They may have known the alleged Testament of Orpheus (*Diathekai*), a pseudo-Orphic poem, which pretended that Orpheus had been converted to Jewish monotheism.[76]

FIG. 24. Mosaic. David.

Gaza synagogue, Israel (Photo: after Ovadiah, *Qadmoniot*, 1968, p. 124)

Beginning with a painting in the catacomb of Callistus in Rome, datable around 220,[77] six Early Christian catacomb pictures and three pre-Constantinian Christian sarcophagi, studied by H. Stern,[78] depict an Orpheus-like musician. His central place on vaults and over arcosolia leaves no doubt that he is in some sense a symbol of salvation and/or of paradise and, hence, alludes to Christ. Is the Christian musician Orpheus, or David, or Christ? Does Orpheus prefigure David who prefigures Christ? The costume unmistakably indicates Orpheus himself as the immediate artistic prototype. As to the impulse that led Christians to adopt the type, the entire first book of Clement of Alexandria's *Protrepticus*, close in time to the Callistus catacomb painting, develops the idea of the New Song, sung by the New Musician, who enchants not animals but human souls and the universe—Christ as Logos, "who was from David and before David." Later on, Clement mentions Or-

pheus with approval as one who has glimpsed the truth.[79]

Seeking an artistic form to portray the Logos as the New Christian Musician, Christian artists took over Orpheus as the artistic type nearest to the Logos in content. For Christians, he was Christ. For those yet to be converted, this familiar image alluded to hopes of messianic peace. With the triumph of the Church, the need for such double-layered "allusive" or, as Professor Kitzinger calls it,[80] "signitive," imagery passed, and the Orpheus-Christ type does not reappear after 400.

Orpheus as David, on the other hand, was transmitted by fifth- or sixth-century Psalter illustrations, now lost, to the magnificent Psalters of the Macedonian Renaissance in the tenth and eleventh centuries. At that time, Orpheus *qua* Orpheus also reemerged in mythological illustrations.[81] In this way, surviving as Orpheus in his own recognizable artistic

FIG. 25.
Ivory diptych.
Nicomachorum and
Symmachorum.

Musée Cluny, Paris, and
Victoria and Albert Museum,
London (Photo: Hirmer)

FIG. 26. Mosaic. "Quodvoldeus" panel. Rheinisches Landesmuseum, Trier (Photo: Landesmuseum, Trier)

type, the mythical Thracian bard also came to signify the Psalmist of the Old, and the Logos of the New, Testament.

When we consider expressions of faith, and especially sacrifices, nothing can be more representative of the intellectualized religion of the late pagan aristocracy in Rome than the superlative Symmachi-Nicomachi diptych (Fig. 25).[82] It is a proclamation of faith, a credo issued by the two leading pagan families of Rome. Indeed, some scholars read the diptych as an invitation to the traditional sacrifices,[83] which since 382 had not been supported by the state. On the Nicomachorum side, a majestic priestess of Demeter or Ceres holds the torches of the venerable Eleusinian mysteries as she stands before a flaming altar; the pine tree (behind the altar) belongs to Cybele and Attis. On the better preserved Symmachorum part, the ivy-crowned priestess of Bacchus puts incense on an altar in front of Jupiter's oak. A little maid gives her a bowl and a kantharos with wine. This is not an official Roman state sacrifice with slaughter of bull, pig, and sheep, nor is it the bloody *taurobolium* offered to Cybele and Attis, in whose priesthoods so many of these late pagans held of-

fices. Only bloodless sacrifices are shown, and intentionally, I think. What then is the message? To an astonishing degree the diptych succeeds in recapturing the solemnity and beauty of the classic Hellenic, one might almost say "Parthenonian," age. Against Christian accusations, it proclaims that the old religion is decent, dignified, and beautiful. But it is Thought and Beauty, not intense religious emotion, that this sacrifice communicates.[84]

The mosaic found in the center of the imperial capital of Trier (Fig. 26) leads us into a different world, the world of popular mystery religions. Made around 380, the mosaic was a pavement for the small dining hall of an association formed to celebrate the mysteries of the Dioscuri, perhaps for a *collegium Castorum*.[85] On one side we see the sacred myth—the birth from one egg of the heavenly twins, inscribed *Castor* and *Polus*, and their sister Helen—*Aelena*. The embryo triplets are seen in the egg, two in profile, one from the back. Mother Leda—inscribed *Lyda*—is on the right, Agamemnon on the left. The eagle of the triplets' heavenly father, "of Jupiter"—*Iobis*—hovers above. The same story is represented in this exhibition by an engraved bronze plaque of the

FIG. 27. Arch of Constantine, Rome. *Congiarium* scene, detail. (Photo: Deutsches Archäologisches Institut)

fourth century [Cat. no. 215] showing Jupiter as a swan with Leda and a nymph (above); Leda on a childbirth couch (in the middle): and the newly born triplets in a neatly sliced half egg (below).[86]

The sacred ritual is shown on the other side of the Trier mosaic. A man with the Christian sounding name "What God wills" (*Quod/vol/deus*) holds a wine ladle and a bird. A devoutly kneeling figure on the left offers an egg. Will *Quodvoldeus*, fulfilling God's will, break the egg to parallel the breaking out of the egg of the heavenly triplets and announce the birth of the new Trinity?

All around the central scenes people bring food and implements for a sacramental meal, perhaps similar to the Christian *agape*. These mystics are not, I believe, high intellectuals, who composed Orphic hymns and speculated about the World Egg.[87] They put up quite cheerfully with misspellings like *Iobis* for *Iovis*, and substituted Agamemnon for Leda's husband Tyndareos. Yet the awkwardly designed ritual scene is permeated by a spirit of ponderous intensity and genuine devotion which explains why the mysteries were the most dangerous competitors of Christianity.

How did Christianity respond to these challenges? How could the supreme mystery of the Eucharist be shown, that bloodless sacrifice in which flesh and blood of Christ were offered to the faithful? The Riha paten,[88] a work of the time of Justin II (565–78), presents a grandiose, imaginative attempt to meet this challenge. Christ himself celebrates the Communion of the Apostles (Fig. 28). In correspondence to ancient Eastern liturgical practice, by which the priest offered bread and a deacon the wine, Christ is shown twice, once giving bread to the six apostles on the left, and again offering wine to the other six on the right. The altar is also the table of the Last Supper.

A spiritual experience of moving power is conveyed by the gesture of Christ—an urgent offering of a gift—and by the intent humility of the apostles. Their amazingly differentiated faces are unclassical to the point of ugliness. Yet this flaming symbol of Christian faith, which seems so unclassical, is yet also a witness to the continuity of classical art. This continuity stems, however, not from representations of pagan religious ritual, but from the Roman imperial realm. The architectural background and the massed grouping of the apostles is in the tradition of historic imperial reliefs. The thematic connection is with the imperial generosity of Constantine bestowing gifts upon the urgent, humble *plebs Romana*,[89] the Roman people on the Arch of Constantine (Fig. 27), and the boundless generosity of Christ giving himself and salvation to the *plebs Dei* represented by the apostles. This true analogy was adopted as a general formal design, perhaps through the mediation of a monumental composition in the Church of the Last Supper on Mount Sion at Jerusalem.[90]

I should like to end our discussion of the visual expressions of faith by pointing out one special aspect of classical survival that bears on the problem of the rise of the icon.[91] Starting from imperial allegorical scenes, Late Antique artists created an abstract design to represent abstractions as attributes of divinity. In the great tapestry depicting "Hestia of Many Blessings," now at Dumbarton Oaks, Hestia, traditionally the goddess of the hearth, but also the center of the Pythagorean and Platonic universe, has become a semiabstract empress. Her blessings, Wealth

FIG. 28. Silver paten from Riha. Communion of the Apostles.
Dumbarton Oaks Collection, Washington, D.C. (Photo: Dumbarton Oaks)

FIG. 29. Silver plate. Meleager and Atalanta.

State Hermitage Museum, Leningrad (Photo: The
Hermitage)

and Cheer (upper left and right), Praise and Abundance (mid-left and right), and Virtue and Progress (below), are given to angel-like putti. Her stately attendants are Light (*Phos*) and a sage reading from a scroll.[92]

The magnificent Coptic tapestry icon in Cleveland, showing *He Hagia Maria* with the archangels Michael and Gabriel surrounded by busts of apostles, is a product of the same textile atelier, as Dorothy Shepherd has shown [Cat. no. 477].[93] There is a genuine seriousness, an effort at intellectual adoration about the Hestia tapestry. Perhaps Paul Friedländer was right, after all, when in his beautiful book on documents of dying paganism he saw in the Hestia panel a Neoplatonic icon made for some last defender of intellectual religion similar to Proclus.[94] What a striking symbol of survival and transformation they would have offered—a Neoplatonic and a

FIG. 30. Transfiguration mosaic.

St. Catherine's Monastery, Sinai (Photo: Courtesy of
Alexandria, Michigan, Princeton Expedition to Mt. Sinai)

Christian icon being made side by side in the Christian Egypt of Justinian's time.

In the beginning of this paper I asked: "What happened during late antiquity to that classical art which used to express pagan intellectual culture, pagan myth, and pagan faith?" With examples taken from these three aspects of the classical realm, I have sought to illustrate the survival and the diversified transformation and Christianization of classical art. We have observed the straight survival of botanical, zoological, and astronomical illustrations and, to a lesser degree, of mythological subjects. We have found various degrees of transformations, ranging from purely verbal allegorization of zoological images, as in the stag and snake of the *Physiologus*, to the adaptation of an essentially true analogy in content and form—the musician Orpheus as the True Logos— to the creative reshaping of a scene of imperial largess into a symbol of profoundest Christian mystery. Only by combining an interpretative study of ideological and emotional connotations with the study of iconography and style can we do justice to the rich complexity that attended the transition from classical antiquity to the age of faith.

To sum up: by the end of the Late Antique period, the survival of classical art—in the strict sense of survival of ancient themes with their classical art forms— was limited and dwindling. In the West, "the monstrous cultural shrinkage" (in Wilhelm Koehler's phrase)[95] was taking an enormous toll of classical art, while in the Byzantine East "the Classical Realm remained a rather artificial concern of a small class of intellectuals cultivating a humanistic outlook," as Weitzmann has pointed out for a later age.[96] The amazing Meleager plate in Leningrad (Fig. 29) is a work of the seventh century[97] and, with its curious echoes of the Scopasian Meleager and the Phidian Amazon, was made for just such a limited, cultivated, courtly clientele.[98]

As for transformation, once the Christians conceded that God-become-man could be suitably represented in human form, once they began to extol not only Christ's humility but his power and his glory (as in the Transfiguration mosaic from Sinai, Fig. 30, which uses transformed classical motifs),[99] once they adopted the illustrated epic narratives of Homer and Vergil for the Old and the New Testaments, then Christianity had accepted the basic tenet of classical art: that the human form is art's central subject and can be glorious *ad imaginem Dei*. In this comprehensive sense, not only the demonstrable transformations which we have discussed, but all Christian figurative art, is a continuation of classical art.

NOTES

1. My paper was designed to mesh closely with the *Age of Spirituality* exhibition, held at the Metropolitan Museum, New York from November 1977 to February 1978. I presented the paper in its original character as a sketch intended to serve as a commentary on some aspects of the exhibition.

I gratefully acknowledge my debt to my colleagues Robert P. Bergman and Ernst Kitzinger, who let me draw freely on their great knowledge of the early medieval field. Ihor Ševčenko helpfully discussed some points of my paper. For help with slides, illustrations, and information of various kinds, I am indebted to H. A. Bober, F. M. Cross, M. K. Donaldson, P. C. Finney, M. E. Frazer, C. Kondoleon, K. E. McVey, S. Morgan, R. L. Scranton, V. M. Strocka, H. Vetters, K. Weitzmann. R. Weil rendered much valuable assistance with both the oral presentation and the written version of this paper. Through the kindness of M. E. Frazer, I was able to use the tentative checklist and descriptions of several items in the exhibition discussed in my paper. Because rich bibliographical selections appear in the catalogue, I exercise restraint in bibliographical citations.

2. A bibliography of Weitzmann's work through 1969 is found in Kurt Weitzmann, *Studies in Classical and Byzantine Manuscript Illumination*, H. L. Kessler, ed., Chicago,

1971, pp. 335–39. Other frequently cited works by Weitzmann: *Greek Mythology in Byzantine Art*, Princeton, 1951; *Late Antique and Early Christian Book Illumination*, New York, 1977; G. H. Forsyth and K. Weitzmann, *The Monastery of St. Catherine at Mount Sinai I. The Church and Fortress of Justinian*, Ann Arbor, 1968.

Directly germane to the subject of the symposium is E. Kitzinger's *Byzantine Art in the Making*, London, 1977. Unfortunately, it appeared after the symposium papers had been completed. For a collection of Kitzinger's other essays, see *The Art of Byzantium and the Medieval West*, W. E. Kleinbauer, ed., Bloomington and London, 1976. Valuable background for the social position and values of art, including its classical components, is given in P. Brown, *The World of Late Antiquity, A.D. 150–750*, London, 1971, as well as in his paper "Art and Society in Late Antiquity," pp. 17–27, above.

3. The division of the exhibition into five "realms" is discussed by K. Weitzmann in K. Weitzmann and M. E. Frazer, *Age of Spirituality: Late Antique and Early Christian Art, Third to Seventh Century* (Picture Book), based on the catalogue to the exhibition, New York, 1977, pp. 3–7. The Classical Realm is the second and is treated, with select examples, on pp. 23–45.

4. I. Ševčenko, "A Shadow Outline of Virtue: The Classical Heritage of Greek Christian Literature," pp. 53–73, above. A masterly sketch on *paideia* and *pistis* was given by W. Jaeger, *Early Christianity and Greek Paideia*, Cambridge, Mass., 1965.

5. Various methodological aspects of the problem of survival have been treated by K. Weitzmann, especially in "The Classical Heritage in the Art of Constantinople," *Studies in Classical and Byzantine Manuscript Illumination*, pp. 128–29 with references to previous articles; also "The Classical in Byzantine Art as a Mode of Individual Expression," ibid., pp. 151–75; and "The Survival of Mythological Representations in Early Christian and Byzantine Art and Their Impact on Christian Iconography," *Dumbarton Oaks Papers, XIV, 1960, pp. 43–68.* See also E. Kitzinger, "A Marble Relief of the Theodosian Period," *The Art of Byzantium and the Medieval West*, pp. 1–31; "On the Interpretation of Stylistic Changes in Late Antique Art," ibid., pp. 32–48; "Byzantine Art in the Period between Justinian and Iconoclasm," ibid., pp. 157–232; and his article "The Hellenistic Heritage in Byzantine Art," *Dumbarton Oaks Papers*, XVII, 1963, pp. 97–115.

6. My "functional" approach, which follows Weitzmann, is, in a sense, horizontal. I am looking for the final result rather than the developmental process within the period we are considering. The pioneering vertical analysis of transformation and survival of classical elements in Christian thought and art was given by M. Dvořák in terms of a dialectical process involving three major historical phases: the creation of catacomb art, a minority art sharply different from the classical art all around it, in the pre-Constantinian period, constitutes the thesis; a "classical reaction" after the Peace of the Church threatens to engulf an only ostensibly Christian art in its imperial classicizing aspect (antithesis); the final synthesis occurs in the service of the great Christian theological systems. (The synthesis, however, largely does away with classical elements as survivals.) See M. Dvořák, "Katakombenmalerei, Die Anfänge der christlichen Kunst" (1919), in *Kunstgeschichte als Geistesgeschichte*, J. Wilde and M. K. Swoboda, eds., Vienna, 1923, 1928, pp. 3–40, esp. pp. 19–26. E. Kitzinger's more complex dialectical model is indebted to Dvořák in some essentials. For Kitzinger's position, see *Byzantine Art in the Making*, introduction, esp. p. 4, and his paper, pp. 141–63, below.

7. My selection was based on the tentative preliminary listing, which did not completely coincide with the final subdivisions adopted in the exhibition and also contained some objects that proved to be unavailable.

8. For *culture intellectuelle*, see H. I. Marrou, *Histoire de l'éducation dans l'Antiquité*, Paris, 1958, pp. 19–25.

9. St. Basil, "Address to Young Men on Reading Greek Literature" (literally: "How They Might Derive Profit from Pagan Literature"), in *Saint Basil, The Letters*, IV, R. J. Deferrari and M. R. P. Maguire, eds., London and Cambridge, Mass., 1934 (Loeb Classical Library), pp. 363–465. St. Basil speaks of Hellenic literature as *paideusis*, and also *exothen*, or *thurathen mathemata* (3.1–2; 4.1). He uses *paideumata* for Christian teachings (2.8).

10. H. I. Marrou, *Histoire de l'éducation dans l'Antiquité*, chap. IX, "Le christianisme et l'éducation classique," esp. pp. 416 and 419.

11. W. Jaeger, *Early Christianity and Greek Paideia*, p. 72.

12. P. de Labriolle, *Histoire de la littérature latine chrétienne*, 3rd ed., Paris, 1947, pp. 1–43. C. N. Cochrane, *Christianity and Classical Culture*, London, 1944, parts II and III. P. Courcelle, *Late Latin Writers and Their Greek Sources*, H. E. Wedeck, trans., Cambridge, Mass., 1969. And the ever enjoyable D. Comparetti, *Vergil in the Middle Ages*, London, 1895, chaps. V–VII, pp. 88–101.

13. H. I. Marrou, *Mousikos Aner*, Grenoble, 1937. Consult also the interesting section on "The Poet and the Muses" in the *Age of Spirituality*, Cat. nos. 240–42.

14. V. M. Strocka, *Die Wandmalerei der Hanghäuser in Ephesos, Forschungen in Ephesos*, VIII, 1, Vienna, 1977, pp. 127 and 136, figs. 316, 317, 319, and 339. Strocka, pp. 133 and 137, dates the paintings of the Sappho Room, H 2/12, on stylistic grounds to the mid-fifth century (440–50). For Sappho as the tenth Muse, he cites Plato's epigram, *Anthologia Graeca* 9. 506, and the mixed Latin-Greek epigram by Ausonius (Epigram 51), which may or may not indicate the existence of another Late Antique set of Sappho and the Muses.

15. St. Cyril of Alexandria upheld the orthodoxy of the term *Theotokos* against Nestorius at the Council of Ephesus in 431. F. J. Dölger, "Zum Theotokosnamen," *Antike und Christentum*, I, 1929, pp. 118–23.

16. Cat. no. 242. W. F. Volbach, *Elfenbeinarbeiten der Spätantike und des frühen Mittelalters*, 3rd ed., Mainz, 1976, p. 58, no. 69, pl. 40: "5th century, made perhaps in Gaul." K. Weitzmann, by letter, suggests that the ivory plaques may have belonged to a bridal casket. He cites Cat. no. 309, the cosmetic box from the Esquiline for the subject, and no. 311, the bridal box in ivory from Saqqara for the type of object.

17. *Martianus Capella and the Seven Liberal Arts*, W. H. Stahl and R. Johnson, eds., New York, 1971. C. S. Lewis, *The Allegory of Love*, Oxford, 1936, p. 78, cited by Stahl and Johnson.

18. Sidonius Apollinarius *Praefatio Epithalamii dicti Ruricio et Hiberiae* 10. 9–17. W. B. Anderson, *Sidonius, Poems and Letters*, Cambridge, Mass., 1936 (Loeb Classical Library), I, p. 199, translates verses 9–10: "Then every god that was present laid aside his dreadfulness and exhibited a playful version of his special power."

19. H. Buchthal, "A Byzantine Miniature of the Fourth Evangelist and Its Relatives," *Dumbarton Oaks Papers*, XV, 1961, pp. 129–39. He discusses the Louvre ivory, fig. 9, on p. 134.

20. L. Ibrahim, R. L. Scranton, and R. Brill, *Kenchreai, Eastern Port of Corinth II. The Panels of Opus Sectile in Glass*, Leiden, 1976, pp. 268–69, for the *terminus ante quem* A.D. 375. The "Hieratic Panels," ca. 1.80 meters high, represented statues of Homer, Plato, Theophrastus, and a fourth sage, standing on pedestals, as well as six mythical and two secular (donor?) figures. A tentative reconstruction of the wall is given in Drawing LIV. Homer, Panel VI.3 A, 1.78 meters high, is inscribed OMEROS, ibid. pp. 168–74, figs. 32 and 139–46, Drawing XXIV; Plato, Panel VI.3 B, 1.78 meters high, is inscribed (Pla)TO(n). I am greatly indebted to R. L. Scranton for placing slides and photographs at my disposal.

21. Paulus Silentiarus *Descriptio Sanctae Sophiae* 617, P. Friedlaender, ed., *Johannes von Gaza und Paulus Silentiarus*, Leipzig, 1912, p. 244, speaks of "thundering strains ['mouths'] of Homer." "Thundering"—ἐϲίγδουπος—is an archaic Homeric epithet of Zeus. Paulus thus emphasizes Homer's Zeus-like character.

22. H. Forsyth and K. Weitzmann, *The Monastery of St. Catherine at Mount Sinai I*, pp. 11–13, plate vol., pls. 103–07, color; esp. pls. 104 and 139 (Christ), pls. 107 and 143 (Moses). K. Weitzmann, *Studies in Classical and Byzantine Manuscript Illumination*, pp. 163–65, figs. 140–42. E. Kitzinger, *Byzantine Art in the Making*, pp. 99–101, figs. 177–79.

23. *Stromateis* 1.22, following the Neopythagorean Numenius (second century A.D.). The idea stems from the Jewish contention that Moses had anticipated the philosophy of the Hellenes. See W. Jaeger, *Early Christianity and Greek Paideia*, p. 61; and note 76, below.

24. A. M. Friend, Jr., "The Portraits of the Evangelists in Greek and Latin Manuscripts," *Art Studies*, V, 1927, pp. 124–33, pls. I–VII. Some additional information on Friend's theories and the entire problem is given by R. P. Bergman, "Portraits of the Evangelists in Greek Manuscripts," in *Illuminated Manuscripts from American Collections, An Exhibition in Honor of Kurt Weitzmann*, G. Vikan, ed., The Art Museum, Princeton University, Princeton, 1972, pp. 44–50.

25. D. Comparetti, *Vergil in the Middle Ages*, pp. 96–103.

26. Eusebius, reporting Constantine's *Oratio ad Sanctos* 19. See D. Comparetti, *Vergil in the Middle Ages*, p. 100.

27. Vergilius Vaticanus Latinus 3867, Cat. nos. 204 and 225. Our Figure 8 is fol. 3ᵛ, after E. Rosenthal, *The Illuminations of the Vergilius Romanus*, Zurich, 1972, p. 80, pl. XVII. A recent comprehensive treatment of the manuscript, with a summary of previous opinions on its date and origin is given by C. Eggenberger, "Die Miniaturen des Vergilius Romanus," *Byzantinische Zeitschrift* LXX, 1977, pp. 58–90, pointed out to me by E. Kitzinger. In an informal discussion, J. P. Elder suggested that on paleographic grounds one might think of a North Italian scriptorium rather than of a scriptorium in Ravenna. The latter provenance is preferred by B. Bischoff, *Die Hofbibliotek Karls des Grossen*, Düsseldorf, 1965, p. 46, and C. Eggenberger, who ends up with "Rom oder Ravenna."

G. Rodenwaldt, "Sarkophag zu Ancona," *Archäologischer Anzeiger*, XLIX, 1934, p. 295, ill. 6, had already considered a North Italian origin for the Romanus. To me, the curious "Western" linearism of the Romanus has nothing to do with Ravenna. It comes from a North Italian school, and thus represents an important step toward the aggressive linear style found in the frescoes of St. Proculus at Naturns (south of Meran), which I recently had occasion to study. See C. Eggenberger, "Die Miniaturen des Vergilius Romanus," p. 70, and his article "Die frühmittelalterlichen Wandmalereien in St. Proculus zu Naturns," *Frühmittelalterliche Studien*, VIII, 1974, pp. 343–47.

Although the Vergil portraits of the Romanus may be copies from earlier models, they have no real connection with any previous iconographic tradition of Vergil portraits, such as the portrait on the mosaic from Sousse, proposed as an ancestor for *The Romanus Vergil* by F. Wormald, *The Miniatures in the Gospels of St. Augustine. Corpus Christi College MS. 286*, Cambridge, 1954. For possible reflections of a type similar to Vergil in tenth-century Byzantine manuscripts, see K. Weitzmann, *Studies in Classical and Byzantine Manuscript Illumination*, pp. 115–16, figs. 91–92.

28. F. Wormald, *The Miniatures in the Gospels of St. Augustine*, pp. 7, 9, 10, and pl. XII. W. R. Koehler, *Buchmalerei des frühen Mittelalters*, E. Kitzinger and F. Mütherich, eds., Munich, 1974 (Veröffentlichungen des Zentralinstituts für Kunstgeschichte in München, V), pp. 79–80, pointed to the connection of the St. Matthew in the Codex Aureus with the Romanus Vergil, but only as one of several parallels.

29. C. Nordenfalk, *Celtic and Anglo-Saxon Painting*, New York, 1977, pp. 27–29, 96, and pl. 37. F. Wormald, *The Miniatures in the Gospels of St. Augustine*, pp. 6–11, pl. XV: "the Evangelists [of the Codex Aureus] should be compared to such figures as those found in Codex Romanus in the Vatican (Lat. 3867). The style of the Codex Aureus suggests that its prototypes may have been nearer to the Romanus [than to the Gospels of St. Augustine]."

30. S. M. Kuhn, "From Canterbury to Lichfield," *Speculum*, XXXIII, 1948, pp. 591–629, has tried to dispute the association of the Codex Aureus Gospels with Canterbury, but not convincingly.

31. An invaluable survey of didactic illustrations is found in K. Weitzmann, *Ancient Book Illumination*, Cambridge, Mass., 1959 (Martin Classical Lectures, XVI), part I, "Scientific and Didactic Treatises," pp. 5–30.

32. Vienna, Österreichische Nationalbibliothek, Codex Med. Gr. 1, fol. 4, *De materia medica*, Cat. no. 179 showed fol. 4v, Dioscurides and Heuresis.

33. K. Weitzmann, *Studies in Classical and Byzantine Manuscript Illumination*, pp. 136–37, and figs. 111–12. For the hypothesis that the descriptions and plant illustrations in the herbal of Dioscurides go back to Crateuas (first century B.C.), see Pliny *Natural History* 25. 4: "Crateuas used to depict various plants in color . . . and add to them a description of their properties. . . ."

34. C. Singer, "The Herbal in Antiquity," *Journal of Hellenic Studies*, XLVII, 1927, pp. 1–52. K. Weitzmann, *Ancient Book Illumination*, pp. 12–14, figs. 12–15.

35. K. Weitzmann, *Ancient Book Illumination*, p. 6, fig. 2. In general, A. W. Byvanck, "De Platen in de Aratea van Hugo de Groot," *Koninklijke Nederlandsche Akademie van Wetenshappen, Mededelingen*, Afd. Letterkunde, n. s. XII, 2, 1949, pp. 169–235.

36. F. Boll, *Beiträge zur Überlieferungsgeschichte der Astronomie und Astrologie*, Munich, 1899 (Sitzungsberichte der Bayerischen Akademie der Wissenschaften, philosophisch-historische Klasse), part 1, p. 126. W. Kubitschek, *Die Kalenderbücher von Florenz, Rome und Leiden*, Vienna, 1915 (Denkschriften der Akademie der Wissenschaften, Wien, philosophisch-historische Klasse LVII, 3), gives the contents with calculations for sixteen different systems of calendars. Helios, zodiac, months, and hours are illustrated on fol. 9r. See K. Weitzmann, *Die byzantinische Buchmalerei des IX. und X. Jahrhunderts*, Berlin, 1935, pp. 1–5, pl. 1. A. W. Byvanck, "De Platen in de Aratea van Hugo de Groot," pp. 34 and 38–39. D. Levi, "The Allegories of the Months," *Art Bulletin*, XXXIII, 1941, pp. 252, 281, 290, and fig. 3. J. Beckwith, *The Art of Constantinople*, London, 1961, p. 60 and fig. 74. P. Brown, *The World of Late Antiquity*, p. 71 and fig. 50 (in color).

37. D. Levi, *Antioch Mosaic Pavements*, Princeton, 1947, pp. 36, 625, 295, and pl. 67c, dates the mosaic after A.D. 115. For a recent study of radial calendars, see R. Hachlili, "The Zodiac in Ancient Jewish Art: Representation and Significance," *Bulletin of the American Schools of Oriental Research*, CCXXVIII, 1977, pp. 61–78 and fig. 12 (Antioch).

38. G. M. Fitzgerald, *A Sixth Century Monastery at Beth Shan (Scythopolis)*, University Museum, Pennsylvania, Palestine Section IV, Philadelphia, 1939, pp. 2–3, 5–7, 16 (date), and pls. VI–X. R. Hachlili, "The Zodiac in Ancient Jewish Art," p. 73, fig. 12. Another mosaic from the monastery was displayed in the exhibition, Cat. no. 343. Our Figure 11 is a photograph by A. Hay, obtained through the kind services of R. Hachlili.

39. Cat. no. 342. M. Dothan, "The Synagogues at Hammath-Tiberias," *Qadmoniot*, I, 1968, pp. 16–23, and "The Representation of Helios in the Mosaic of Hammath Tiberias," *Quaderno dell'Accademia Nazionale dei Lincei, Roma*, CV, 1968, pp. 99–104. B. Goldman, *The Sacred Portal*, Detroit, 1966, pp. 59–61 and fig. 19. R. Hachlili, "The Zodiac in Ancient Jewish Art," p. 62, fig. 2 (recent photograph). E. Rosenthal, *The Illuminations of the Vergilius Romanus*, p. 16, fig. 12, upper part.

40. Genesis 1:14. For the Octateuchs and medieval calendars, see G. M. A. Hanfmann, *The Season Sarcophagus in Dumbarton Oaks*, Cambridge, Mass., 1951, I, pp. 199–202, and II, chap. VIII, notes 351 and 355.

41. H. Bober, "The Zodiacal Miniature of the Très Riches Heures of the Duke of Berry, Its Sources and Meaning," *Journal of the Warburg and Courtauld Institutes*, XI, 1948, p. 14, pl. 3b, with a survey of ancient and Early Christian debates on the zodiac and the zodiacal man. See also G. M. A. Hanfmann, *The Season Sarcophagus*, II, chap. VIII, note 356.

42. *Dionysiou Hieromonachou Hermeneia tes Zographikes*, A. Papadopoulos-Kerameus, ed., Athens, 1909, pp. 213–14. G. M. A. Hanfmann, *The Season Sarcophagus*, I, p. 202 and II, chap. VIII, note 405.

43. The late date of ca. 700 is proposed by P. J. Nordhagen, "The Mosaics of the Great Palace of the Byzantine Emperors," *Byzantinische Zeitschrift*, LVI, 1963, pp. 53–68. Cf. E. Kitzinger, *Byzantine Art in the Making*, p. 112, "of the seventh century or even as late as 700." The only uncontested evidence is the probable terminal date of 520–40 for the pottery found under the mosaic, as determined by J. W. Hayes, *Late Roman Pottery*, Rome, 1972, p. 418. Nordhagen argues that no building activity is recorded for this part of the palace under Justinian and Heraclius and equates the mosaic peristyle with the *Ioustinianon* dated to 694. I do not believe that our documentation of the palace is sufficiently complete to permit dogmatism; and I am doubtful of Nordhagen's handling of archaeological evidence. Stylistically, either the reigns of Justinian or Heraclius appear possible. The compositional principle is the same as that in late mythological silver reliefs: elements taken from earlier traditions are put side by side without any real unification.

44. G. Brett, *The Great Palace of the Byzantine Emperors*, London, 1947, p. 76, pl. 32.

45. Pseudo-Oppian *Cynegetica* 2.248–49. A. W. Mair in his edition and translation of *Oppian, Colluthus, Tryphiodorus*, Cambridge, Mass., 1928 (Loeb Classical Library), p. lxx, cites firsthand testimonials of Argentine gauchos on the deer (*cervus campestris*) as a snake-hater and snake-killer; as well as the ancient authors, p. 77. K. Weitzmann, *Illustrations in Roll and Codex*, 2nd ed., Princeton, 1970, pp. 138–39, fig. 22, suggests that the eleventh-century illustration in the Marciana Pseudo-Oppian goes back to the original manuscript of the third century and that this original illustration was copied in the Physiologus.

46. *Physiologus*, F. Sbordone, ed., Milan, 1936. Origen already knew the collection; cf. *In Jerem. Homil.* 18.9. H. C. Puech, "Le Cerf et le serpent," *Cahiers Archéologiques*, IV, 1949, pp. 30–31.

47. Cat. no. 192. H. Woodruff, "The Physiologus of Bern," *Art Bulletin*, XII, 1930, p. 250, fig. 38. C. von Steiger and O. Homburger, *Physiologus Bernensis, Voll-Faksimile Ausgabe des Codex Bongarsianus 318 der Burgerbibliotek Bern*, Basel, 1964, p. 20 (date), p. 40 and fol. 17r (stag and serpent).

48. For the *Physiologus* versions, see *Physiologus* F. Sbordone, ed., p. 97, text no. 30. For Psalm 41 (Douay), I give the translation according to King James' version (where it is Psalm 42:1) because "waterbrooks" is closer to the Greek than the "fountains" of Douay version. The Greek text reads:

Ὄν τρόπον ἐπιποθεῖ ἡ ἔλαφος ἐπὶ
τὰς πηγὰς τῶν ὑδάτων, οὕτως
ἐπιποθεῖ ἡ ψυχή μου πρὸς σὲ ὁ θεός.

49. H. C. Puech, "Le Cerf et le serpent," pp. 30–52, has a carefully documented discussion. The earliest interpretations are by Jerome, *Breviarium in Psalmos*, and Augustine, *Enarratio in Psalm 41*, written in 414. For other references, see T. Velmans, "Quelques versions rares du thème de la fontaine de vie dans l'art paléochrétien," *Cahiers Archéologiques*, XIX, 1969, p. 38. This article, brought to my attention by C. Kondoleon, has much interesting material on stags in baptisteries, e.g. fig. 4, a mosaic at Ohrid.

50. C. L. Feuilles, "Une mosaïque chrétienne de l'Henchir Massaouda," *Cahiers Archéologiques*, IV, 1949, pp. 9–15, fig. 3, from which our Figure 16 is taken. B. Brenk, *Tradition und Neuerung in der christlichen Kunst des ersten Jahrtausends*, Graz, Vienna, and Cologne, 1966 (Wiener Byzantinistische Studien, III), p. 193, fig. 22. H. Stern, "Le décor des pavements et des cuves dans les baptistères paléochrétiens," *Studi di Antichità Cristiana*, XXII, 1957, pp. 386–87, fig. 3, and fig. 4, a mosaic at Salona inscribed with Psalm 41:2.

51. F. W. Deichmann, *Ravenna. Hauptstadt des spätantiken Abendlandes. Geschichte und Monumente*, Wiesbaden, 1969, pp. 158–60, figs. 250–51. Ibid., *Kommentar*, I, Wiesbaden, 1974, pp. 70 (restoration), 79–80, and 96 (interpretation) based on Psalm 41:2.

52. For Late Antique attitudes toward the myth, cf. the studies cited above, notes 4–5 and 8–13. Also K. Weitzmann, *Greek Mythology in Byzantine Art*, and especially, "The Survival of Mythological Representations," pp. 43–68, with literature p. 45, note 4.

53. K. Weitzmann, "Euripides Scenes in Byzantine Art," *Hesperia*, XVIII, 1949, pp. 159–210. Idem, *Ancient Book Illumination*, pp. 31–40 and 63–80. S. Charitonides, L. Kahil, and R. Ginouvès, *Les Mosaïques de la maison du Ménandre à Mytilène*, Bern, 1970 (Antike Kunst, Supp. 6). Important new evidence for Euripides and Menander illustrations appears in paintings of the late second century A.D. in Ephesus. I believe that they copy illuminated codices written on purple vellum. V. M. Strocka, "Theaterbilder aus Ephesus," *Gymnasium*, LXXX, 4, 1973, pp. 363–80, pls. 16–20. Idem, *Die Wandmalerei der Hanghäuser in Ephesos*, pp. 45–56, pls. 54–77.

54. Cat. no. 217. D. Levi, *Antioch Mosaic Pavements*, pp. 36–37. K. Weitzmann, "The Survival of Mythological Representations," p. 54, fig. 16.

55. For the Theater Room at Ephesus, see V. M. Strocka, "Theaterbilder aus Ephesus," and *Die Wandmalerei der Hanghäuser in Ephesus*.

56. K. Weitzmann, "The Survival of Mythological Representations," pp. 53–55, figs. 14 and 18, compared the mosaic of San Marco. See also the same scene in the Vienna Genesis, illustrated in Weitzmann, *Studies in Classical and Byzantine Manuscript Illumination*, p. 161, fig. 138.

57. Photius *Lexicon*, s.v. "Hippolytos," S. A. Naber, ed., Leiden, 1864, p. 296.

58. J. M. C. Toynbee, "A New Roman Mosaic Pavement Found in Dorset," *Journal of Roman Studies*, LIV, 1964, pp. 7–14. Our Figure 20 is after the drawing in Toynbee, fig. 1. K. S. Painter, "The Roman Site at Hinton St. Mary, Dorset," *British Museum Quarterly*, XXXII, 1967, pp. 13–31.

59. M. Simon, "Bellérophon chrétien," *Mélanges offerts à Jérôme Carcopino*, Vendôme, 1966, pp. 889–903, with earlier literature. K. S. Painter has even proposed a reconstruction of a hypothetical church apse with a bust of Christ above and an equestrian St. Bellerophon below: "The Design of the Roman Mosaic of Hinton St. Mary," *The Antiquaries Journal*, LVI, 1976, pp. 49–54, figs. 1–2, pls. VII–IX.

60. I. Ševčenko kindly made available to me the manuscript of his study published on pp. 53–73, above. He cites (note 32) V. Buchheit, "Homer bei Methodios von Olympos," *Rheinisches Museum für Philologie*, XCIX, 1956, pp. 23–24. Methodius *Symposium* 8.12–14 (A.D. 203–10), N. G. Bonwetsch, ed., Leipzig, 1917, p. 97.

61. H. von Brandenburg, "Bellerophon christianus?" *Römische Quartalschrift*, LXIII, 1968, pp. 48–86, and pp. 64–67 for Bellerophon in dining rooms.

62. K. Weitzmann, *Greek Mythology in Byzantine Art*, pp. 24–26, 106–07, figs. 23–24 (Pseudo-Nonnus), and p. 112 (Pseudo-Oppian).

63. Cat. no. 143. K. Weitzmann, *Greek Mythology in Byzantine Art*, fig. 113. W. F. Volbach, *Elfenbeinarbeiten*, p. 57, no. 67, pl. 39.

64. G. Brett, *The Great Palace of the Byzantine Emperors*, London, 1947, p. 72, pl. 28.

65. *Digenis Acrites* 7.42–44. C. Mango, *The Art of the Byzantine Empire 312–1453*, Englewood Cliffs, 1972, p. 216: "golden ceilings upon which he represented in mosaic the victories of all those men of yore, who shone in valor . . ." Samson, David, Achilles, Odysseus, Bellerophon, Alexander, Moses, and Joshua are cited.

66. Eustathius *Ad Iliadem* 6. 162, 181. The etymological argument deriving Bellerophon from *ellera-kaka* is probably from an earlier source.

67. K. Lehmann-Hartleben, "Bellerophon und der Reiterheilige," *Römische Mitteilungen*, XXXVIII–XXXIX, 1923–24, pp. 264 ff. W. F. Volbach, "Un medaglione d'oro con l'imagine di S. Teodoro," *Archivo storico per la Calabria e la Lucania*, XIII, 1943–44, pp. 61–72, figs. 1–2. Concerning phylacteries, an example antedating A.D. 325 was found at Beth Shan. See C. Bonner, *Studies in Magical Amulets*, Ann Arbor, 1950, pp. 219, 221, pl. 17, no. 324. Bonner dated the group that mixes pagan and Christian elements from the fourth to the seventh century. M. C. Ross, *Catalogue of the Early Byzantine and Early Medieval Antiquities in the Dumbarton Collection*, Washington, D.C., 1962, I, p. 53 and pl.

53, no. 60, with an inscription from Psalm 91. Ross also cites recent literature. I owe this and several other references on equestrian saints to E. Kitzinger.

68. Verein Villa Hügel, Essen, *Koptische Kunst: Christentum am Nil*, Essen, 1963, pp. 337–38, no. 351. The Walters Art Gallery, *Early Christian and Byzantine Art, An Exhibition Held at the Baltimore Museum of Art*, Baltimore, 1949, p. 159, no. 813, pl. 112.

69. Another claimant is Horus killing a crocodile. See M. W. Williams, "Whence came St. George?" *Bulletin de la Société Royale d'Archéologie d'Alexandrie*, IX, 1936, pp. 102–04, fig. 9. For the emperor killing a lion, see W. F. Volbach, *Elfenbeinarbeiten*, pp. 47 and 61, nos. 48, 77, pls. 26, 44.

70. J. Wilpert, *Roma sotterranea: Le pitture delle catacombe Romane*, Rome, 1903, I, pp. 222–25. H. Stern, "Orphée dans l'art paléochrétien," *Cahiers Archéologiques*, XXIII, 1974, pp. 1–16, with literature.

71. H. Stern, "La mosaïque d'Orphée de Blanzy-les-Fismes (Aisne)," *Gallia*, XIII, 1955, pp. 41–77. M. A. del Chiaro, "A New Orpheus Mosaic in Yugoslavia," *American Journal of Archaeology*, LXXVI, 1972, pp. 197–200, pls. 47–48. R. M. Harrison, "An Orpheus Mosaic in Ptolemais," *Journal of Roman Studies*, LXII, 1962, pp. 13–18.

72. Cat. no. 161. W. F. Volbach, *Elfenbeinarbeiten*, p. 70, no. 92, pl. 51, with literature.

73. A. Ovadiah, "The Synagogue at Gaza," *Qadmoniot*, I, 1968, pp. 124–27. Idem, "Excavations in the Area of the Ancient Synagogue at Gaza," *The Israel Exploration Journal*, XIX, 1969, pp. 193–98, pls. 15–18. H. Stern, "Un nouvel Orphée-David dans une mosaïque du VIe siècle," *Comptes Rendus de l'Academie des Inscriptions*, Paris, 1970, pp. 63–79, figs. 1–6.

74. A. Ovadiah, "The Synagogue at Gaza," p. 124. Idem, "Excavations in the Area of the Ancient Synagogue at Gaza," p. 193. H. Stern, "Un nouvel Orphée-David," p. 68, fig. 5, after Ovadiah. Our Figure 24 is a photograph of the mosaic taken from Ovadiah, "Excavations," p. 124, before the head of David was destroyed.

75. C. H. Kraeling, *The Synagogue. The Excavations at Dura-Europos. Final Report VIII, Part I*, New Haven, 1956, pp. 62ff., 214ff.: H. Stern, "Un nouvel Orphée-David," pp. 72–78, figs. 8–10.

76. H. Stern, "Orphée dans l'art paléochrétien," pp. 8–9, with literature. Orpheus had been adopted by Jewish propagandists as far back as Aristobulus of Alexandria (second century B.C.). A survey of Jewish-Orphic traditions is about to be published by P. C. Finney, under the title, "Orpheus-David: A Connection in Iconography between Greco-Roman Judaism and Early Christianity?", with a "Note on Psalm 151 (11 QPs²)" by K. E. McVey. The authors generously permitted me to consult the article in typescript. The alleged equation of Orpheus and David in

Qumran Psalm 151A, first proposed by J. Sanders, "Ps 151 in 11 QPs²," *Zeitschrift für alttestamentliche Wissenschaft*, LXXV, 1963, pp. 81–85, appears to have been rejected by a majority of competent philologists. In addition to K. E. McVey's discussion, I have profited by a note of my colleague F. M. Cross, "David, Orpheus, and Psalm 151:3–4," *Bulletin of the American Schools of Oriental Research*, No. 211, October 1978, pp. 69–71.

77. J. Wilpert, *Le pitture delle catacombe Romane*, I, pl. xxvii. H. Stern, "Orphée, dans l'art paléochrétien," pp. 1–2, fig. 1.

78. Ibid., pp. 1–16, figs. 1–10.

79. Clement of Alexandria *Protrepticus* 1. 5, 3 and 7. The *Protrepticus* was written under Septimius Severus (ca. 193–203). See Clement d'Alexandrie, *Le Protreptique*, C. Mondésert, ed., Paris, 1942, pp. 12–13.

80. E. Kitzinger, *Byzantine Art in the Making*, p. 20, following W. Weidlé, *The Baptism of Art*, n.d. See also Kitzinger's remarks, pp. 141–63, below.

81. K. Weitzmann, *Greek Mythology in Byzantine Art*, pp. 6, 67–68, figs. 82–85. H. Stern, "Orphée dans l'art paléochrétien," pp. 14–15, figs. 13–16, 17–19, largely after Weitzmann.

82. Cat. nos. 165–66. W. F. Volbach, *Elfenbeinarbeiten*, p. 51, no. 55, pl. 29.

83. W. F. Volbach, *Elfenbeinarbeiten*, p. 51.

84. E. Kitzinger, *Byzantine Art in the Making*, pp. 34–35, fig. 63, has an interesting discussion of the piece as an example of "other-directed" art; but I cannot agree with his emphasis on its "chilly, academic quality." The artist did look at Hadrianic art (the Hadrianic sacrifices in the medallions of the Arch of Constantine are particularly relevant); but he penetrated beyond Hadrianic classicism to a genuinely classical reverence for dignified beauty. The piece is unemotional only in terms of the fourth century.

85. H. Eiden, "Ein spätrömisches Figurenmosaik am Kornmarkt in Trier," *Trierer Zeitschrift*, XIX, 1950, pp. 52–71, fig. 1, pls. 7–14, Beilage 6–9. R. Egger, "Ein *Collegium Castorum* in Trier," *Trierer Zeitschrift*, XXII, 1953, pp. 56–63, fig. 1. J. Moreau, *Das Trierer Kornmarktmosaik*, Cologne, 1960 (Monumenta Artis Romanae, II, H. Kähler and J. Moreau, eds.).

86. G. M. A. Richter, "Department of Classical Art. Accessions of 1913," *The Metropolitan Museum of Art Bulletin*, IX, 1914, pp. 93–94, fig. 5. K. Parlasca, "Das Trierer Mysterienmosaik und das ägyptische Ur-Ei," *Trierer Zeitschrift*, XIX, 1950, p. 113, pl. 7. J. Moreau, *Das Trierer Kornmarktmosaik*, p. 16, pl. 13.

87. K. Parlasca, "Das Trierer Mysterienmosaik," pp. 109–25, figs. 1–2, pls. 5–8.

88. Cat. no. 547. M. C. Ross, *Catalogue of the Byzantine and Early Medieval Antiquities in the Dumbarton Oaks Collection*, I, pp. 12–15, no. 10, pls. 11–13. The paten was made under Justin II (565–78), probably in Constantinople. For the connection with Eastern liturgical practice, see E. Lucchesi Palli in *Lexikon der christlichen Ikonographie*, I, E. Kirschbaum, ed., Freiburg, 1968, pp. 174–75, s.v. "Apostelkommunion." K. Wessel in *Reallexikon zur Byzantinischen Kunst*, I, Stuttgart, 1963, pp. 239–42, s.v. "Apostelkommunion."

89. Cat. no. 58. H. P. L'Orange and A. von Gerkan, *Der spätantike Bildschmuck des Konstantinsbogens*, Berlin, 1939, pp. 90 ff., pl. 17, fig. 12. G. M. A. Hanfmann, *Roman Art*, New York, 1975 p. 124, fig. 141. T. Kraus, *Das römische Weltreich*, Berlin, 1967, p. 243, pl. 253a. E. Kitzinger, *Byzantine Art in the Making*, p. 7, fig. 4.

90. G. de Jerphanion in *Nouvelle Revue Théologique*, LXVI, 1939, pp. 461 ff., cited by K. Wessel, "Apostelkommunion." W. C. Loerke, "The Monumental Miniature," *The Place of Book Illumination in Byzantine Art*, K. Weitzmann, ed., Princeton, 1975, pp. 94–95, argued for a composition in the dome. I am grateful to R. B. Bergman for referring me to this article.

91. For the general problem, see E. Kitzinger, "The Cult of Images before Iconoclasm," *The Art of Byzantium and the Medieval West*, pp. 85–156; and for the impact of iconoclasm on art, *Byzantine Art in the Making*, pp. 104–07.

92. P. Friedländer, *Documents of Dying Paganism*, Berkeley and Los Angeles, 1945, pp. 1–26, color plate. R. Bianchi Bandinelli, *Hellenistic-Byzantine Miniatures of the Iliad*, Olten, 1955, p. 155, fig. 231, compares a Virgin from Bawît. P. Brown, *The World of Late Antiquity*, p. 79, fig. 57, "Our Lady of Many Blessings."

93. D. G. Shepherd, "An Icon of the Virgin," *The Bulletin of The Cleveland Museum of Art*, LVI, 3 (March 1969), pp. 90–120, color plate and details.

94. P. Friedländer, *Documents of Dying Paganism*, pp. 4–5 and 12–14.

95. B. Bischoff and W. Koehler, "Eine illustrierte Ausgabe der spätantiken Ravennater Annalen," *Medieval Studies in Memory of A.K. Porter*, W.R.W. Koehler, ed., Cambridge, Mass., 1939, p. 137: "in ungeheuerlichem kulturellen Schrumpfungsprozess."

96. K. Weitzmann, "The Survival of Mythological Representations," p. 68. E. Kitzinger, *Byzantine Art in the Making*, pp. 110–12, fig. 196, sees a classicizing revival directed by Heraclius and his court.

97. Cat. no. 141. L. A. Matzulevitsch, *Byzantinische Antike*, Leningrad, 1929, pp. 2–3, 9–17, figs. 1, 2, pl. 1. E. C. Dodd, *Byzantine Silver Stamps*, Washington, D.C., 1961 (Dumbarton Oaks Studies, VII), pp. 176–77, pl. 94, dated 613–29. A. Banck, *Byzantine Art in the Collections of the USSR*, Leningrad and Moscow, 1966, no. 94. For evaluations, see K. Weitzmann, "The Classical Heritage in the Art of Constantinople," *Studies in Classical and Byzantine Manuscript Illumination*, pp. 132–34, fig. 109. E. Kitzinger, *Byzantine Art in the Making*, pp. 107, 110, figs. 191, 196.

98. H.-G. Beck, pp. 29–37, above, speaks of the sterile atmosphere of Constantinople and I. Ševčenko, p. 63 above, of "deadly antiquarians"; these were the people whose taste was presumably responsible for the classical character of the Constantinopolitan silver. For art historical assessments of the impact of this group see the opinions of Weitzmann and Kitzinger, cited in note 96, above.

99. H. Forsyth and K. Weitzmann, *The Monastery of St. Catherine at Mount Sinai I*, plate vol., pp. 11 ff., pls. 103 and 136–37.

MASSEY H. SHEPHERD, JR.

Christology: A Central Problem of Early Christian Theology and Art

THEOLOGY is a conceptual reflection upon the data of religious experience of the numinous, of a transcendent presence and power in either or both the natural orders of creation and the dynamic processes of history. This experience, which is essentially one of worship, cannot be fully grasped or expressed in rationally definable terms. It is apprehended and communicated in symbolic, mythological, or analogical language. Unlike theology, art is not limited to a particular kind of experience; but insofar as it lends itself to express and illuminate religious experience it finds itself in the same dilemma as that of theology. It cannot portray or comprehend in either symbolic or iconic forms a full, final expression of numinous reality.

In any age, the language of theology and the forms and styles of art are culturally conditioned. This does not preclude, as history shows, original insights of thinkers and artists that reach beyond the accepted ideology, and modes of expressing it, in their own times. This is true particularly of the doctrine of the person of Jesus Christ that has been at the center of theological reflection and teaching and, from the third century on, of artistic illustration down to the present time. It is this doctrine that separated Christianity most acutely from its Jewish parentage, from its ancient Greco-Roman competitors, and later from its close relative of monotheistic faith, Islam. It is this doctrine that has dominated Christian apologetic and missionary activity, both in antiquity and in later ages, over and against all polytheistic, dualistic, and purely monistic religions of the human race.

In this paper we shall first trace the origins, the development, and the theologians' varied resolutions of the Christological problem. No single resolution

ultimately prevailed, as evidenced by the schisms that have persisted in Christianity to our own day. Secondly, we shall sketch the evolution of Christian art, especially in the portrayal of the doctrine of Christ, as it attempted to resolve the problem. Yet, this resolution was only partially successful, since Eastern and Western Christian art developed their own respective ways of implementing it.

It may seem strange and arbitrary to treat the theological and the artistic developments separately. But theological speculation did not affect the beginnings of Christian art. The latter emerged two centuries after theologians had marked out the boundaries and issues of their own problems, often with expressed hostility to any artistic portrayal of their faith. Christian art developed its own history, its own speech. Not until the reign of Justinian (527–65) did Christian theology and art interlock in a struggle over a proper interpretation of Christ the God-Man.

Our sketch covers eight centuries and thus extends beyond the chronological limits of this exhibition and symposium. Yet some discussion of the origins and denouement of our theme may help to clarify the central issues of the period selected for more concentrated attention.

I. *Christology and Theology*

About the year A.D. 29 or 30, in the reign of the Roman emperor Tiberius, a Palestinian Jew known as Jesus of Nazareth, a popular itinerant prophet, teacher, and worker of healing and other miracles, was crucified as a messianic pretender by Pontius Pilate, Tiberius' governor of Judaea. This might well have been the end of him and of his name, forgotten in recorded history.[1] Within three days after Jesus' cruel and ignominious death, however, his disciples, who "hoped that he was the one to redeem Israel" (Luke 24:21), had an experience that would change the course of history. They believed that God had vindicated Jesus by raising him from the dead and exalting him to heaven, whence he would soon return to judge the living and the dead. He would then establish a new age of righteousness and peace, a kingdom of the one and only God promised by the Hebrew prophets of old, in which not only Israel but all the nations would acknowledge and obey God's sovereign rule and unite in a common worship.[2]

Thus there emerged in the Greco-Roman world of "gods many and lords many" (1 Cor. 8:5) a new religious movement with a unique and startling claim. Jesus alone was the bringer of salvation. He was the true Messiah, Son of Man, Son of God, Lord, and Savior to all who called upon his name. "There is salvation in no one else," said an early proclamation attributed to St. Peter, "for there is no other name under heaven given among men by which we must be saved" (Acts 4:12). Later, St. Paul, at first a persecutor and then a convert to this faith, would write: "All the promises of God find their Yes in him. . . . For God has put his seal upon us and given us his Spirit in our hearts as a guarantee" (2 Cor. 1:20–22).

The earliest adherents of the new faith about Jesus included both Aramaic-speaking and Greek-speaking Jews. The latter group, known as Hellenists, held unorthodox opinions about the Jewish Law and the Jewish Temple in Jerusalem;[3] and they were soon scattered by persecution from the Jewish authorities. Some of them initiated a mission of surprising success among Samaritans and Gentiles. A new base of operation was formed at Antioch, where they were soon joined by their erstwhile persecutor Paul of Tarsus. Their novel experiment in evangelization brought tensions within the movement by their admission of newly won Gentile converts into full fellowship in the Church without requiring them to become full-fledged Jewish proselytes.[4]

Within a decade of the death of Jesus, the disruptive activities of these Hellenists in Jewish communities brought them to the attention of Roman authorities, who named them *Christiani*, partisans of the Christ, from the Greek word *Christos* ("the anointed one"), a translation of the Hebrew term "Messiah." First applied in Antioch and a few years later in Rome, the title "Christians" suggests that the Roman authorities were becoming cognizant of the new religious sect as something distinct from the

Jewish messianic expectations, which had political connotations. These they could contain. But the messianic proclamation of the new movement had no revolutionary intention, and hence it was the more dangerous because it was the more intangible.[5] Nero's attack on the Christians in Rome in the year 64 showed, at least, that the Roman state was aware of Christianity as a new and identifiable religious entity. His police action on a fraudulent charge of arson established a precedent for persecution—but without a clearly defined and unambiguous legal basis, other than an assumption of crimes associated with profession of the name of Christian.[6]

In the Christian communities, the conflict over the terms of admission of Gentile converts was resolved in a council of apostles and elders held in Jerusalem about the year 48, which decided in favor of the freedom of the Gentiles from the obligations of the Jewish Law. This decision alienated the majority of Jews, and indeed many Jewish-Christians, and made the separation of Christianity from its Jewish parent inevitable.[7] So it came about that Hellenistic Jewish and Gentile converts to Jesus as the unique and final bringer of salvation would be, for the wider Greco-Roman world, the transmitters and adapters of the original oral traditions and interpretations about Jesus that stemmed from his disciples.[8]

In order to make this gospel intelligible to the Gentiles, they had at hand Greek versions of the Old Testament books and a wide variety of other Jewish writings of more or less authority, especially those of an apocalyptic or wisdom character.[9] From these writings, they derived the honorific titles and metaphorical images, prophetic oracles and narrative types, fulfilled in Jesus. They also produced all the extant Christian writings of the first and early second centuries, beginning with the letters of St. Paul. These works were composed in Greek in response to internal needs of instruction and edification of the early Greek-speaking Christian communities. There is no conclusive evidence that any of these early Christian writings were primarily designed for outsiders.[10]

Certain shifts of emphasis occurred in this transmission. The Jewish title "Messiah," when translated into Greek as *Christos* (sometimes mispronounced *Chrestos*, "the useful one"[11]), was either unintelligible to Gentiles or was of little interest to them. Already in St. Paul's letters, the title took on the connotation of a proper name, although certainly St. Paul and the Gospel writers knew what it meant.[12] Another Jewish title of eschatological significance was "Son of

Man." Although Jesus himself may have used it, the title soon passed out of circulation in its original meaning. St. Paul ignored it altogether and substituted the concept of Jesus as the "new Adam."[13] More significant for Gentile converts were other titles that stemmed from the original Aramaic-speaking Church: "Lord," "Son of God," and "Savior." More abstract titles, such as "Power," "Wisdom," and "Word" (*Logos*), also had their root meaning in Jewish writings.[14] All of these titles would be the basis of Christological development.

Scholars have dissected these Christian writings minutely for indications of the consciousness of Jesus himself about his person and mission, and for the evolution of Christological doctrine in this early period. At the same time, they have ransacked Jewish and Hellenistic texts (not always with care for precise dating) for sources and parallels of savior-god ideology and devotion as a background for the early Christian proclamation about Jesus. They have illuminated a plethora of myths, speculations, and cults, coalescing and competitive, that offered innumerable benefits—singly or in combination, whether material or spiritual—dependent upon the seekers' quests. There were gods, supernatural powers, or angelic beings who for a time mingled or appeared among men for the specific purposes of aid or revelatory knowledge; mortals endowed with divine powers and wisdom, some of whom (such as Heracles and Asklepios) attained the rank of immortal gods; dying and rising deities of the mystery cults; and the divine epiphanies in the presence and virtue of rulers.[15]

Hellenistic Judaism also had its own peculiar "divine men"—Enoch, the patriarchs, Moses, etc.—who had preexisted in heaven before creation, had been endowed with the divine Wisdom during their earthly life, and had then returned to their heavenly state. Though lesser than God, they were greater than men. They personalized the more abstract concepts of the eternal Wisdom or Word of God, which was embodied and revealed in the Torah (the Law) or in the "mystery of Israel," and which indwelt and glorified certain "holy souls" and made them the "friends of God."[16] In no case, however, was any one of these figures the object of a cult; nor did their honor impinge upon God's transcendence.

This massive research does not prove that early Christian writers consciously borrowed from pagan sources. The parallels were mediated through Hellenistic Judaism.[17] The scandal of Christology to both Jews and Gentiles was not that the Christ preexisted as Power, Wisdom, Word, or even Angel with God, or that he descended in the form of a man for revelatory purposes and then returned exalted to heaven. It was the claim that the Revealer was at one with the God revealed, that his descent into the world was not a mere condescension, but rather a self-humiliation, that his ignominious death was a sacrifice which atoned for the sins of the whole world, and that, being exalted, he would return to judge the living and the dead.[18] In this Jesus of Nazareth "there was salvation in no one else" (Acts 4:12). A crucified Messiah was "a stumbling block" to the Jew; a crucified Jew who was raised from the dead was "a folly to the Greek" (1 Cor. 1:23; cf. Acts 17:32).

In none of the early Christian writings was there a systematic exposition of the titles and claims about Jesus; nor were the authors conscious that these titles and claims implied any deviation from the strict monotheism inherited from Judaism. Yet by the later first and second centuries there appears the simple confessional equation that Jesus was God.[19] A recent study has shown that the equation—or the confusion, as the case may be—stemmed in large measure from Christian copies of the Septuagint, that is, the Old Testament in Greek.[20] It is well known that pious Jews never pronounced the Name of God revealed to Moses (Exodus 3:15) in the tetragram YHWH—usually transcribed as *Yahweh*—but substituted the word *Adonai* ("my Lord") or some phrase such as the one common in rabbinic writings: "the Holy One, Blessed is He."[21] In Jewish versions of the Old Testament in Greek, now confirmed by fragments from the Dead Sea scrolls, the tetragram was simply transcribed in Hebrew letters or in some other recognizable, symbolic notation. But in the Septuagint of the Church, the divine Name was regularly translated as *Kyrios*, the Greek equivalent of *Adonai*. Thus, Christians who were unfamiliar with Jewish custom often understood *Kyrios* in their Greek Bibles to refer either to God or to the Lord Jesus Christ. This explains some textual variants in New Testament books between *Theos* ("God") and *Kyrios* ("Lord").[22]

The confession that the man Jesus was God set the stage for the later developments, arguments, and proposed solutions about Christology, which attempted to explicate a deep personal experience and belief that in Jesus Christ "there is salvation in no one else." The contention was not, as many suppose, about appropriate philosophical terminology to explain the mystery and the paradox of the union of divine and human realities in Jesus Christ. There was much of this, to be sure, among the theologians. Yet they always used philosophy to support their biblical exegesis and the tradition of faith as the Church had received it from the apostles.

A simple explanation, congenial to Gentile religiosity, had emerged by the early second century. It is generally called *Docetism*, from the Greek verb meaning "to seem"; and it was especially developed by Marcion and the Gnostics, each in their own way. Harnack rightly called Docetism "the acute Hellenization of Christianity," since it sought to divorce the person of Christ from his Jewish roots.[23] Basically dualist, Docetism appealed to those who felt themselves trapped or enmeshed in an evil material creation and who yearned for release from it.

Marcion, a native of Pontus, was less speculative than the Gnostics, with whom he is often allied. He simply cut the Gordian knot by affirming that the creator God of the Old Testament was in no way the God and Father of Jesus Christ. Christ came to reveal the true God, the God of love and goodness, and to redeem man from the power of the evil and vengeful creator of the material universe. Marcion denied that Jesus was humanly born; he was a man only in semblance. Yet strangely, he taught that the Christ really died for our redemption as a ransom to the creator God. His Resurrection was in a spiritual form, whereby he opened the way to man's escape from all the evils of material existence. To support his views, Marcion resorted to a radical biblical criticism. He rejected the Old Testament *in toto*. Among Christian writings, he accepted only the Pauline letters and the Gospel of Luke, Paul's companion; but from these he expurgated all passages that suggested a relationship of Jesus to the creator God. Thus he pushed to an extreme the Pauline antitheses of law and grace, of flesh and spirit.[24]

Unlike Marcion, the Gnostics elaborated a cosmic mythology to explain the predicament of man. An accident within the supreme and unknowable Godhead led to the creation of the material world by an inferior power. As a result, certain seeds of the Godhead became lost in this world in a forgetfulness of their true origin. Then Christ, in whom "all the fullness of God was pleased to dwell" (Col. 1:19), was sent by the unknowable Father to reveal to these lost spirits the saving knowledge (*gnosis*) of their true origin and destiny. Valentinus, the most Christian of the Gnostics, said of the Christ in his *Gospel of Truth*:

> What exists in him is knowledge, which was revealed so that forgetfulness might be destroyed and that

they might know the Father. Since forgetfulness existed because they did not know the Father, if they then come to know the Father, from that moment on forgetfulness will cease to exist.

> That is the gospel of him whom they seek, which he has revealed to the perfect through the mercies of the Father [as] the hidden mystery, Jesus the Christ.[25]

In the Gnostic systems there was no place for redemption from sin but only from unavoidable error. Their appeal lay in the promise of salvation through Christ from the misery of this life to those chosen ones who were "in the know." The descent of Christ, in the semblance of a man, from the Father, to reveal a saving knowledge, and his reascent to the Father were assurance to the elect of a similar destiny. The shock of the Gnostic "redeemer-myth" was traumatic to Church leaders. Yet they held fast to the apostolic *kerygma* or "proclamation," about Jesus by a careful exegesis of the Scriptures according to a "rule of faith" transmitted to them.[26] The Gnostic mythology dissolved any relevance of God either to creation or to history. Their redeemer was not really involved in either; and he offered no universal gospel. In fact, Gnosticism soon disintegrated into numerous esoteric sects, each with its bizarre, syncretistic, and incongruous elaborations of the basic myth.

At the opposite pole from docetic Christology was one generally known as *Modalism*—also a development of the second and third centuries. It was a gospel for simple Christians who read the Bible literally and prayed to Jesus as God. We know of it chiefly from the philosophically trained theologians who were offended by its lack of discrimination. One of its proponents was a man named Noetus, a native of Smyrna, who taught that "Christ was the Father himself, and that the Father himself was born and suffered and died." When called to book and examined by the presbyters of the Church, he answered simply: "What evil am I doing in glorifying Christ?"[27]

The Modalist doctrine of the undifferentiated oneness of God was widespread in both the East and the West. Some scholars consider it to have been a reaction or an indifference by ordinary Christians to the sophisticated speculations of the theologians. One of its more astute advocates was Sabellius, who was active in Rome in the episcopates of Zephyrinus (ca. 200–217) and Callistus (ca. 217–22); and he seemed to have had some influence upon these popes, if we can trust the reports of their archenemy, the presbyter-theologian Hippolytus. Sabellius turned to his own account the prevalent, dispensational views of the theologians with respect to God's revelation of himself for our salvation.[28] He affirmed that God is one and had revealed himself successively as Father, Son, and Holy Spirit; yet in his eternal, essential being there are no such distinctions.

According to Hippolytus, Pope Zephyrinus affirmed:

> I know one God, Jesus Christ; nor except him do I know any other that is begotten and susceptible to suffering. . . . Yet the Father did not die, but the Son.

This equivocal statement was more nuanced in that of Zephyrinus' deacon and successor, Pope Callistus:

> I will not say that there are two Gods, Father and Son, but one. For the Father who existed in him, after he had taken unto himself flesh, raised it to the nature of deity, by bringing it into union with himself and made it one; so that Father and Son are styled one God, and that this God being one Person, cannot be two.[29]

Another, independent form of Modalism is called *Adoptionism*. Its roots were in Jewish Christianity; and the major center from which it spread seems to have been Antioch. Its proponents also favored a literal interpretation of Scripture rather than the allegorical method used by the philosophical theologians. They did not deny that the Christ was the Word of God and that he preexisted with the Father; but the Word was an attribute of the Godhead and not a distinct person (*hypostasis*) within it. Nor did they deny the miraculous birth of Jesus from the Virgin by the will and purpose of the Father. From the conception of Jesus in St. Mary, the Word of God was conjoined with him to inspire and uphold him, so that by his sinless life and perfect obedience to the Father's will Jesus was adopted as God's Son and given divine honor and status.[30]

The most subtle of the Adoptionists was Paul of Samosata, a politician no less than a theologian, the "prime minister" (*ducenarius*) of Queen Zenobia of Palmyra, and the Bishop of Antioch, ca. 260–70. His views are clearly expressed in the following excerpt:

> A human being is anointed; the Word is not anointed. The Nazarene, our Lord, was anointed. For the Word is greater than the Christ [i.e., the anointed one], since Christ became great through Wisdom. The Word is from above; but Jesus Christ is man from hence. Mary did not give birth to the Word, since Mary was not before the ages. Mary received the Word; Mary is not older than the Word but gave birth to a man like unto us, though better in every

way since he was of the Holy Spirit. From both the promises and the scriptures, grace [was] upon him.[31]

These early attempts to understand the mystery of Jesus—docetic, modalist, and adoptionist—although discredited as inadequate and heretical, nonetheless left an enduring mark on later Christological formulations. These heresies were deeply rooted in popular devotion and influenced the philosophical theologians even as they combatted them.[32] Docetic and modalist overtones remained in Alexandrian Christology, with its emphasis upon the assumption of humanity by the divine Son of God and his coessential being with the Father. Antiochene theologians, on the other hand, started from the two natures that were united in the one person of Christ, a doctrine that the Alexandrians considered too close to Adoptionism if the union was merely one of a concord of will.

Philosophical Christology had its origin in the work of the second-century apologists. Their primary concern was not merely to combat heresy but, more positively, to defend the faith from the calumnies of the populace, the unjust persecution of the government, and the contempt of the educated. About the year 160, a pagan philosopher named Celsus wrote a book called the *True Word*, in which he attacked Christianity as a shameful and foolish religion that affirmed "that some God or son of God has come down to the earth as judge of mankind." He went on to say:

> What is the purpose of such a descent on the part of God? Was it in order to learn what was going on among men? Does he not know everything? If, then, he does know, why does he not correct men, and why can he not do this by divine power?[33]

Celsus had at least taken the trouble to read the Bible and to learn something of Christian teachings. He was not always clear in distinguishing Jews, Christians, and Gnostics. He could see nothing about Jesus that was not true of other magicians and wonder-workers. Other pagans of more distinction than Celsus wrote against Christianity in this period: the rhetorician Fronto and the physician Galen, both of them friends of the philosopher-emperor Marcus Aurelius—who, incidentally, dismissed the Christians' acceptance of martyrdom as a mere spirit of opposition and a theatrical gesture.[34] Another opponent was the Sophist Lucian of Samosata, whose *Death of Peregrinus* included a satire on the gullibility of Christians who aided an imposter posing as a confessor.[35]

The apologists joined this attack by positing Christianity as the only true philosophy. They had a valuable tool in the wisdom books of the Greek Old Testament and in the identification of Jesus with the *Logos*—the Word, reason, and mind of God—in the prologue of the Gospel of John. These texts were admirably suited to the Stoics' conception of the *Logos* immanent and the *Logos* expressed. From the latter were derived the "seminal *logoi*" in all reality and in the mind of man as a ruling principle. More useful were the Middle Platonists who posited a supreme, transcendent, unchanging, and contemplative Mind from whom emanated a second and active Mind that formed and ruled the universe, and in turn a World Soul that gave intelligence to all living beings.[36]

These pagan philosophers, according to the apologists, came close to the truths of Christianity; but they lacked its "more heavenly wisdom": namely, that the Word became flesh. One could quote many passages; but the following from Justin Martyr (d. ca. 165) may suffice:

> . . . with all my strength I strive to be found a Christian—not because the teachings of Plato are different from those of Christ, but because they are not in all respects similar, as neither are those of the others, Stoics, poets, and historians.

> For each man spoke well in proportion to the share he had of the spermatic word, seeing what was related to it. But they who contradict themselves on the more important points appear not to have possessed the heavenly wisdom, and the knowledge which cannot be spoken against. Whatever things were rightly said among all men are the property of us Christians.

> For next to God, we worship and love the Word who is from the unbegotten and ineffable God, since also he became man for our sakes; that, becoming a partaker of our sufferings, he might bring us healing. For all the writers were able to see realities darkly through the sowing of the implanted word that was in them. . . . But quite another is the thing itself, of which there is participation and imitation according to the grace that is from him.[37]

Two outstanding theologians of the early third century laid the groundwork for all later Christology: Origen of Alexandria and Tertullian of Carthage. The former was more Platonic and subtle, the latter more Stoic and matter-of-fact. Both were staunch trinitarians and incarnationists. God is one Being from all eternity in three distinguishable *hypostases* or *personae*, who neither divide his essence

nor are in any way created. The Father alone is unbegotten and unoriginated. From him the Son eternally is begotten and the Spirit eternally proceeds. They are therefore subordinate and may be termed second and third God, comparable to the sun and its rays, the fountain and its streams. Yet the three are of one essence, of one substance.

Origen anticipated the later Nicene Creed with his stress on the "eternal begetting of the Son" who was "of one essence" (*homoousios*) with the Father and his affirmation that "there was never when he was not."[38] Tertullian wrote that the Son was both Wisdom and Word: Wisdom before all creation, Word manifested in creation. But the Trinity is of "one substance and one status and one power . . . one substance in three who cohere," one from the other. They are *unum*, not *unus*—i.e., one Godhead, not one Person.[39] Tertullian's formula *una substantia, tres personae* would remain unchanged in the Latin Church.

The theology of these two fathers concerning the Incarnation was basically similar, except for Origen's peculiar doctrine of the eternity of God's creation of a world of spiritual beings. Both men were the first to note with greater precision that the union of God the Son with the man Jesus Christ was more than a Spirit-flesh or a Word-flesh union; it was a union of the Son with a complete man, possessing a rational soul and a fleshly body. Origen was the first to use the term *theanthropos*, the God-Man.[40] The eternal Son, the Word, entered wholly and fully into a perfectly created rational soul, as the intermediary of redemption, that it might assume a body, so that "the soul and the body of Jesus formed . . . one being with the *Logos* of God."[41] For Tertullian, the Son of God did not transform himself but "clothed" himself in human nature, lest there be a mixture, a *tertium quid*, of the two substances that made Christ both God and man. In this union of two substances, each maintained its own full properties within a single subject: "a twofold state, not confused but conjoined in one person Jesus, God and Man."[42]

Since theological reflection is an individual enterprise, theologians will differ in both their comprehension and their expression of similar beliefs and experiences. With the conversion of Constantine, however, a new factor of momentous consequence emerged. Now, emperors of Christian conviction were determined to achieve a dogmatic unity of doctrine to support the political unity of their power. Basic theological differences were abhorrent to them, since they were displeasing to the divine favor bestowed upon their terrestrial reign and responsibility. Thus, when theological arguments and ecclesiastical schisms developed, there began the long series of councils and counter-councils, of creeds and counter-creeds, approved and enforced by the emperors—and even theological statements produced on their own initiative, such as the *Henoticon* of Zeno (482) and the *Ecthesis* of Heraclius (638). In his address to the bishops at the First Ecumenical Council of Nicaea in 325, Constantine said: "In my judgment, intestine strife within the Church of God is far more evil and dangerous than any kind of war or conflict."[43] In the long run, the interferences and manipulations of emperors in theological disputes failed to coerce those who in sincere conscience could not submit to what they believed to be false teaching. What was at stake was how the Savior saved us.

We shall not pursue in detail the long-drawn-out conflicts over Christology in the next five centuries; but a few observations will be made. The first major issue was the relation of the Son to the Father. Was it by essence or by grace? The dogmatic decision of Nicaea in 325 was for the former; and it was basically one of Alexandrian theology. Unless the Son was of "the same essence" (*homoousios*) as the Father—"true God from true God"—his mediatorship of salvation in the Incarnation could not be a complete and secure access of mankind to God himself but only to a lesser god.

On the contrary, the Alexandrian presbyter Arius, who was trained in Antioch, insisted that "there was when [the Son] was not," that he was created a divine being, and that his knowledge of the Father was imperfect since he was capable of change as are all creatures.[44] Those who agreed or sympathized with him—many for political reasons—were trying to say that unless the Savior was himself saved, he could not be the "author and perfecter of our faith" (Heb. 12:2).[45] In a recent study this conflict was summarized as follows: "Against Arianism, orthodoxy here affirmed a fiercely held boundary—not just between the creature and God—but between the Savior and creatures."[46] But Constantine's son, the emperor Constantius II, kept the Church in turmoil for two decades by favoring the Arian interpretation, which held that the emissary of the supreme ruler bears his authority, but only by grace and not by congenital relationships or co-rulership.[47]

The Second Ecumenical Council of Constantinople in 381 affirmed the Nicene definition of the essential unity of the Son with the Father. But theologians were now faced with the problem of how a divine nature and person could be united with a human nature and person. It condemned the solution of Apollinarius, a friend of Athanasius, who was Arianism's most indefatigible opponent. The fear of Adoptionism led Apollinarius to posit that in the Incarnation the Word of God replaced the human mind of Jesus, lest there be two persons in Christ—i.e., two centers of consciousness and will. This solution was virtually a denial of the complete humanity of Jesus; for a human being without a rational mind was little less than an animal.[48]

The conflict that ensued was chiefly between the Antiochene and the Alexandrian theologians, with the Roman see acting as arbiter, since both sides needed its support. The issue was whether in the Incarnation there was an assumption of one nature by the other or the conjoining of the two natures. First one view, then the other, were ascendant. At the Third Ecumenical Council of Ephesus in 431, the Alexandrians under Bishop Cyril won the day. The divine nature assumed the human nature; and Christ's human mother was affirmed as *Theotokos*, the "God-bearer." But in 451 the Fourth Ecumenical Council of Chalcedon promulgated a creed, based upon a *Tome* of Pope Leo I, that was a victory for neither side, although it leaned more in the Antiochene direction. This creed stated that two natures were united *in* the one Person of Christ "without confusion, without change, without division, without separation."[49]

The paradox remained; it was not resolved. For many, a real stumbling block was the affirmation of two natures in one person. To them a "nature" (*physis*) meant not the constitution and function of a thing, but a concrete embodiment or personality. Hence arose Monophysitism,[50] taking as its watchword the formula, although not the nuances, of Cyril of Alexandria: "one nature (*physis*) of the Word of God incarnate." The union in Christ was therefore *of* two natures, not *in* two natures; for God the Word was the personal subject of the incarnate Christ.

All attempts to conciliate the Monophysites only alienated the Western Church, which stood firmly loyal to Pope Leo's *Tome*. At the Fifth Ecumenical Council of Constantinople in 553, the emperor Justinian's compromise—to maintain the Chalcedonian definition but condemn the propositions of three pre-Chalcedonian, Antiochene theologians (the "Three Chapters")—drove the Monophysites into schism. Justinian's humiliation of Pope Vigilius—he forced the pope to sign the compromise—only deepened suspicions in the West about imperial intentions. The emperor Heraclius' edict of 638, the

Ecthesis, which affirmed the two natures but only a single, divine will in Christ (what is known as Monothelitism), was a last desperate effort at conciliation that signally failed. Before the Sixth Ecumenical Council of Constantinople in 680–81 condemned it as heretical, large areas of the Eastern provinces, where Monophysitism was strong, had been lost to the Arabs.

The last Christological conflict began with the attack on the veneration of images by the emperor Leo III in 727. Whatever political or ecclesiastical motives the emperor may have had, the theological issue again centered on the Chalcedonian definition, the two natures doctrine. The last of the ecumenical councils, that held at Nicaea in 787, reaffirmed this doctrine by pronouncing that created natures, including the human nature of Christ, could be pictorially portrayed, but not the uncreated, divine natures of the three Persons of the Godhead. Further outbreaks of iconoclasm ensued; but by 843 iconodule orthodoxy had prevailed.[51] Two-dimensional images or icons might receive reverence (*proskynesis*) but not worship (*latreia*). Eastern orthodoxy has remained faithful to this decision. In the West, although Pope Hadrian I accepted the Council of 787, its decision ultimately came to be ignored insofar as it legitimatized only two-dimensional images.[52]

In this last Christological struggle of the ancient Church, the principles of theology and art became inextricably mixed.

II. *Christology and Art*

The earliest Christians had no interest in the arts. Their expectation of the imminent return of Jesus at the end of the age precluded concern for artistic works. The music of their "psalms, hymns, and spiritual songs" (Col. 3:16; Eph. 5:19) is largely unknown to us.[53] The scant remains of their places of assembly before the time of Constantine—the house churches and meeting halls—have little or no architectural significance.[54] Their neglect of, and opposition to, pictorial and plastic arts, even after Christianity became Hellenized, has generally been attributed to the legacy of Judaism, which would not compromise with polytheism and idolatry. This may well be true. But the discovery of the wall paintings in the synagogue at Dura Europos [Cat. no. 341] and the mosaic pavements of Palestinian synagogues [Cat. nos. 342–43], no less than the smaller *objets d'art* so thoroughly researched by the late Erwin R. Goodenough, have shown that the strictures of the Second Commandment of the Decalogue were not so faithfully observed by Jews in the Roman world.[55]

The portrayals of Christ in Early Christian art are all symbolic or imaginary.[56] Neither the Gospels nor other early Christian writings preserve any reminiscence of his human features, such as we have of St. Paul in the apocryphal Acts of Paul and Thecla from the second century.[57] The early Church fathers utilized the Suffering Servant song of Isaiah 53 to stress Jesus' lack of human comeliness and beauty. Tertullian, for example, argued against the docetic view of the Gnostics that Christ's flesh was in some way of celestial glory. On the contrary, he said that had not Christ's body been of a very terrestrial and ignoble aspect, men would not have dared to revile it and spit upon it.[58] Yet the popular view, expressed in apocryphal works, recounted that his risen body was young and beautiful and, indeed, of surpassing size.[59]

Persecution, with its demand that Christians sacrifice before the image of "Lord Caesar," reenforced the Church's abhorrence of idolatry.[60] The scurrilous charge of the populace that Christians were atheists, since they had neither temples nor images, was still being met by apologists of the third century.[61] Minucius Felix stated categorically:

> What image of God shall I make, since, if you think rightly, man himself is the image of God? What temple shall I build to him, when this whole world fashioned by his work cannot contain him?[62]

So also Origen wrote:

> . . . there are some who make images of the supreme God in a superior way and according to perfect knowledge, so that there is no comparison between the Olympian Zeus wrought by Pheidias and him who is made in the image of God who created him. But of all the images in the whole creation by far the most superior and pre-eminent is that of our Saviour who said, "My Father is in me."[63]

Hippolytus, in his account of the screening of candidates for instruction prior to baptism, gave these directives among others:

> If a man be a sculptor or a painter, he shall be taught not to make idols. If he will not desist, let him be rejected. . . .

> If a man be a priest of idols or a keeper of idols, either let him desist or let him be rejected.[64]

Nonetheless—and despite the opposition of theologians—works of art designed for Christians began to appear by the turn of the third century. No extant examples can be dated before that time. Simple and ambiguous in execution as they were, they did not escape the strictures of theologians. Clement of Alexandria, the most Hellenistic in his sympathies of all the early fathers, would allow the faithful nothing more than ambiguous figures on the seals of signet rings: a dove, a fish, a ship, an anchor, a fisherman.[65] A Christian would know their hidden significance; a pagan friend would not. The puritan Tertullian was scandalized by the depiction of the Good Shepherd on glass cups (*calices*) and considered it little less than a prostitution of the sacrament.[66]

The figure of the Good Shepherd was one of the most common and widespread portrayals of Christ in this Early Christian art [Cat. nos. 364, 462–63]. Iconographically, the figure was derived from pagan art, where it was a symbol of philanthropy. There are many examples in painting and sculpture; but without adjoining contextual symbols, it is difficult to decide whether the figure is pagan or Christian.[67] For the Christian believer, the figure recalled not only the parable and allegory of the Good Shepherd in John 10, but more particularly the parable of the lost sheep in Luke 15:4–7, in which the shepherd, rejoicing in having found his lost sheep, carries it on his shoulders back to the fold. The popularity of this figure in funerary art, in baptisteries,[68] and possibly in free sculptured form in the patios of private dwellings, is a poignant example of believers' faith that, although they were lost, in Christ they were found.

All of the surviving art from the period before Constantine belongs, with one exception, to the funerary paintings in underground chambers of the catacombs or to carved sarcophagi whose original location is not always known, although they were undoubtedly in cemeterial places. These paintings and sarcophagi belonged to the private sector, to Christians of sufficient wealth to afford them.[69] It is possible, although not provable, that Church authorities accepted or tolerated this art, for it is unlikely that they would resist the desires of their more affluent members. In many cases, the tombs or crypts belonged to families of mixed religious allegiance or to those who became Christian in the course of the third century.[70] One cemetery was officially Christian from the beginning: the plot (*area*) owned by Pope Zephyrinus (d. 217) on the Via Appia and administered by his deacon and successor Callistus, from whom the catacomb beneath the plot would take its name.[71]

Related to this funerary art is the baptistery of the house church in Dura Europos, discovered by the Yale expedition to the site in the winter of 1931–32 [Cat. no. 360]. The date of the building is sometime between A.D. 232 and 256.[72] We do not know who was the patron of this house church on the borders of eastern Syria or whether it belonged to a particular Christian sect. Except for a scene of the women approaching a monumental tomb, the wall paintings of this baptistery do not materially differ in subject matter or design from those of the Roman catacombs. There is no indication that other rooms of the house, including the enlarged room for congregational worship, had any decoration of significance. A baptistery, however, was a very private room, inaccessible to those who were not initiated, lest the mystery of the sacrament be profaned. In a sense, too, a baptistery was a tomb where the convert had died to the old life of sin and alienation from God so as to be reborn to a new life in Christ.[73]

The cryptic, abbreviated, and impressionistic art of the early Christians reminded believers of their assurance of salvation.[74] The Old Testament scenes—probably derived from illuminated manuscripts[75]—were understood typologically as referring to Christ. They were relevant to times of threatened or actual persecution: deliverance from death (Noah in the Ark, the Sacrifice of Isaac, Moses striking the rock [Cat. no. 381]); from wild beasts (Daniel in the lions' den); from false accusation (Susanna); or from ordeals by fire (the Three Hebrews in the Fiery Furnace [Cat. no. 383]). Scenes from the story of Jonah, common to both paintings and sarcophagi [Cat. nos. 361, 365–69], recalled the saying of Jesus in Matthew 12:40: "As Jonah was three days and three nights in the belly of the whale, so will the Son of Man be three days and three nights in the heart of the earth" (cf. Jonah 1:17). The story is unique in being portrayed as a sequence of scenes: Jonah is cast into the sea; swallowed and then vomited out by the great fish or dragon; and, finally, he rests under the gourd vine. The sequence may have been taken from illuminated manuscripts with certain apocryphal features; but the final scene has affinities with pagan scenes of the sleep of Endymion.[76]

In New Testament scenes Jesus appears simply dressed in a tunic and without special distinction—as a teacher (the Samaritan woman at the well), a healer (the paralytic and the woman with the issue of blood [Cat. nos. 401–02, 397–98]), and a savior from death (Peter walking on the water and the Raising of Lazarus [Cat. nos. 360, 403–04]). He is identifiable only by an outstretched arm or by a wonder-worker's rod. These scenes may have been original compositions or adaptations of Old Testament ones. It is unlikely that at this early date there were illuminated manuscripts of New Testament books.[77]

Other scenes, often called "sacramental," are also symbolic of the experience of salvation: 1) the Baptism of Jesus [Cat. no. 395], or, it may be, of the believer, with or without the descending Dove of the Holy Spirit,[78] and 2) a banquet of persons seated about a sigma table, in which often one of them reaches out a hand to bless the platters of loaves and fish and the wine cups. Many of the banquet scenes also have baskets of loaves and jars of wine either before or adjacent to the table, thereby recalling the miracles of the Feeding of the Multitude and the changing of water into wine at Cana [Cat. no. 396].[79] The banquet scene has variously been interpreted as a Eucharist, a funerary *agape*, or a representation of the messianic banquet of the redeemed in heaven.

In the third-century crypt of Lucina, later incorporated into the catacomb of Callistus, there is a unique symbol: two fish facing each other, on each of which rests a basket of loaves, within which is seen a cup of wine. It is difficult not to perceive in this symbol a sacramental reference, since the fish is one of the earliest cryptic symbols of Christ.[80] As St. Ignatius of Antioch said: "The breaking of the one bread is the medicine of immortality, the antidote that we should not die but live for ever in Christ."[81]

A few images anticipate theological concerns of the post-Constantinian era. Figures of the Madonna and scenes of the Adoration of the Magi, generally dated to the third century, exhibit an interest in the Incarnation.[82] A singular example of great significance occurs in the ceiling mosaic of Tomb M of the Julii family, found in the excavations under St. Peter's in Rome [Cat. no. 467]. The family apparently became Christian sometime in the late third or early fourth century. This is confirmed by the wall mosaics with scenes of Jonah, the Fisherman, and the Good Shepherd. The ceiling mosaic, partially destroyed, shows a man ascending in a chariot drawn by two horses—two others, making a quadriga, belonged to the missing portion of the mosaic. Christ has a nimbus, behind which issue rays of the sun.[83]

The portrayal of Christ as the sun god, whether Apollo or Helios, inevitably calls to mind the visions of Constantine that led to his conversion, his change from a monotheistic sun-worshiper like his father to a believer in Christ, the "Sun of righteousness" (Malachi 4:2). The precise date of the mosaic cannot be determined. Originally, it may have been an actual portrayal of the Sun god that was allowed to remain or was retouched sometime in the early fourth century before the foundations of St. Peter's Basilica were laid. Its iconography is similar to representations of the apotheosis of an emperor at his death, which later was used as a model for the portrayal of the ascension of Elijah.[84]

After the conversion of Constantine, Christian art became public and monumental through the beneficence of imperial and wealthy lay patrons and, much later, of wealthy ecclesiastics. Church leaders were not prepared for the new situation. Some opposed, some acquiesced, others settled for a didactic rather than a theological interpretation. Few could resist the trend. Bishop Eusebius of Caesarea, a thoroughgoing Origenist in his theology and an unsurpassed admirer of Constantine, was shocked when the emperor's sister requested from him a portrait of Christ. Such a thing, he said in a letter, was contrary not only to the second commandment, but to the glorified, transformed splendor of the exalted Lord.[85] One wonders what he might have thought had he ever visited the Lateran basilica in Rome. According to the inventory of the *Liber Pontificalis* ("The Book of the Popes"), Constantine gave the church a silver *fastigium*, erected behind the altar, which portrayed on the front and sides Christ among his apostles and, on the back, Christ among the angels.[86]

The Church had no iconographic tradition for the triumph of Christ; hence it adopted forms based upon imperial ideology and choreography. Christ was Victor, Lawgiver, and Judge.[87] As Victor he was often presented in symbolic form by a wreathed cross or Chi Rho monogram (reminiscent of Constantine's conversion experience), supported by angels or accompanied by two or more phoenixes.[88] By the fifth century he was also represented by the jeweled encasement of the relic of the True Cross in the cathedral complex at Jerusalem.[89]

The scene of Christ standing or enthroned among his apostles takes many forms. Although Christ is usually holding an open scroll—less often, a codex—it is perhaps too simple an explanation to see him here in a teaching role comparable to numerous pagan portrayals of the philosopher-teacher.[90] The picture becomes increasingly complex, majestic, and monumental, with overtones of Christ commissioning the apostles, his proclamation with and through them of his universal gospel, and perhaps also their part in his final Judgment.[91] Christ is depicted either as a youth or as a bearded figure of Jovian aspect. Closely associated with, and often overlapping, this scene is the more restricted one of Christ delivering the Law (i.e., his universal message) to Peter and Paul—and sometimes to all the apostles.[92] The model of such scenes is imperial—the allocution of the emperor in public or at a palace consistory, when he receives or dispenses gifts. It is depicted on the Arch of Constantine in Rome [Cat. no. 58] and on the Missorium of Theodosius I, dated 388 [Cat. no. 64], where the emperor is portrayed seated in a tribunal as he delivers a codicil to an official, with his two sons and two soldiers on either side of him. In the Christian scene, Christ receives or delivers crowns of victory and may be accompanied by archangels instead of soldiers.[93] The scene is in heaven, not on earth.

Much of this symbolism and more is brought together in the apse mosaic of Sta. Pudenziana in Rome, dated ca. 400 (Fig. 13, p. 46, above). It is still impressive, despite later renovations and repairs. The lower part of the mosaic is framed by a semicircular, roofed ambulatory cut by doors, which places the scene in an imperial audience court. In the center, Christ with a golden nimbus and golden garments is seated on a cushioned, jeweled throne as he teaches his apostles, seated on either side of him. Two female figures, symbolic of the Church of the Jews and the Church of the Gentiles, hold crowns over the heads of Peter and Paul, on the right and left, respectively. This symbolism is confirmed in the upper portion of the mosaic by the great churches of Bethlehem on the right and of Jerusalem on the left. In the center of this upper sphere, directly above Christ, rises the Mount of Calvary on which stands the jeweled case of the True Cross reaching up into heaven, where are placed the symbols of the four evangelists.[94]

Less rich in symbolism—but more "oriental" in the frontality of its figures—is the apse mosaic of S. Vitale in Ravenna, which dates from the time of Justinian [Cat. no. 505]. Christ in a purple garment and a cross-inscribed nimbus sits on the orb of the world. An angel or archangel stands on either side of him. To his left stands the martyr Vitalis dressed as a court official, to whom Christ proffers a crown; and on the right stands the bishop in ecclesiastical dress as he holds and offers a model of the church.[95]

Such majestic scenes as those at Sta. Pudenziana and S. Vitale combine theology with historical allusion. They show how the futuristic eschatology of pre-Constantinian funerary symbolism was now realized; for the kingdom of the eternal Christ came to be seen in the image of the imperial Church. In similar ways the scenes of catacomb painting and sar-cophagus sculpture were greatly enriched to portray the history of salvation from both the Old and the New Testaments. Also included are scenes from apocryphal stories of the apostles and from the lives of the martyrs, for the history of salvation continues in the life of the Church. This larger repertory of scenes possibly had its inspiration from frescoes or mosaic plaques along the clerestory walls of churches.[96]

Of special interest to our theme is the appearance of narrative series depicting the life of Christ in a great variety of artistic media—mosaic, sculpture, carved wood and ivories, illuminated manuscripts, and silver—intended either for liturgical or personal use.[97] Among the examples are the so-called Passion sarcophagi with scenes of the arrest and trial of Jesus. The actual Crucifixion, however, is not exhibited, but is replaced (at the center) by a victory symbol.[98] Another series included Nativity stories, and combines the narratives of Matthew and Luke. Several ivory plaques used as covers for Gospel books reflect the principal lections of the two main cycles of the Church year: Christmas-Epiphany and Lent-Easter. On one, the central panel is the *Theotokos* (Virgin and Child); on another, it is Christ enthroned or symbolized by the jeweled cross or a lamb. Around each central panel are smaller scenes of the Nativity, including some apocryphal ones from the life of the Virgin, and of the miracles of Christ [Cat. nos. 457–61 and Cat. fig. 64].[99]

How this flowering of Christian art related to the dogmatic controversies of the theologians is difficult to say—other than that both had a common, absorbing interest in the person and work of Christ. He is the central, dominant figure, whether young or old, whether in historical manifestation or in celestial glory. It is impossible, however, to identify the portrayals of him according to the theological positions held—Nicene or Arian, Chalcedonian or Monophysite.

One of the so-called Dogmatic sarcophagi scenes has commonly been supposed to portray the doctrine of the Trinity, although this view has recently been challenged. Three bearded men of similar visage engage in the Creation of Man. The center one (probably the Father) is seated with his right arm in blessing, while the one on his right (probably the Son) lays a hand on the diminutive but erect figure of Eve. An equally diminutive figure of Adam lies asleep on the ground.[100]

From the fifth century on, the Trinity is more often portrayed typologically or symbolically in such scenes as the three angelic visitors to Abraham (Genesis 18), or the hand of God and the Dove of the Holy Spirit in the Baptism of Christ. The doctrine of the Incarnation is, of course, implicit in representations of the Virgin and Child, especially after the Third Ecumenical Council of Ephesus in 431 affirmed the Virgin to be the *Theotokos*, the "Bearer of God." But the divine-human nature of Christ also finds expression in scenes of the Ascension of Christ, or in varied forms of visions of the glorified Christ in an aureole, adored by evangelist symbols and figures of prophets and saints.[101]

In the imperial iconography of Christ, he is never dressed in imperial regalia, even when seated on an imperial throne. He wears only a sleeved tunic and a pallium of gold or royal purple. There is no jeweled ornament or diadem. A nimbus or halo identifies his holiness; but this also came to be used for martyrs and saints. Bishops wear the insignia of their office (the pallium); and at times martyrs are clothed like court personages. Christ gives or receives crowns; he himself is never crowned, and his hair is free of ornament. He may, however, hold a jewel-covered book or a globe. In such ways, artists sought to portray Christ's two natures: a man simply dressed but no less majestic and glorious. We cannot differentiate the images designed for either orthodox or heretical definitions. For example, the Christological scenes in both the baptistery and the cathedral built in Ravenna by the Arian king Theodoric (493–526) were not changed when these and other Arian churches were taken over by the orthodox in 556.[102]

By the time of the emperor Justinian in the sixth century, the veneration of images of Christ and the saints was becoming widespread. In some ways, it was an extension of the long-established veneration of relics. But in the case of images of Christ, a more potent source was the veneration accorded to images of the emperor. Some of these images were supposed to be miraculous—"not made with hands" (*acheiropoietai*). Three of them, dating from the later sixth century, were considered to have been impressions of Christ's face made by him on a cloth.[103] Most, if not all, of these were destroyed during the iconoclastic controversy.[104]

For one phenomenon in Early Christian art I have no simple solution: the late appearance of pictorial representations of the Crucifixion of Jesus. From early times, Christians used the gesture of the sign of the cross as a means of identifying their faith or, apotropaically, to ward off evil demons.[105] Various symbols suggesting the cross were enumerated by

Justin Martyr and others: the sail of a ship, a plow, a tree, an anchor, even the erect form of a man with arms outstretched.[106] Occasionally, on grave inscriptions in the catacombs, one finds a simple cross or other symbol, but never any picture of the Crucifixion itself.[107]

Perhaps it was too much to ask that Christians openly represent the instrument of shame in times of persecution and ridicule. One thinks of the satirical graffito of the late second century, found in the Palatine, depicting a clothed man with the head of an ass affixed to a Tau cross and inscribed "Alexamenos worships his god."[108] After the Constantinian peace the same reticence continued, possibly because paganism remained legal and pagan officials were needed in government. Constantine and his successors in the fourth and early fifth centuries promoted the cross as a sign of victory and success, not of humiliation and failure. Consequently, for this reason no less than for pious sentiment, Constantine changed Roman law by forbidding punishment by crucifixion.[109]

The two oldest surviving Crucifixion portrayals come from the West, both dated to the early fifth century; and they were probably made in Italy. The first is on one of the four Passion plaques in the British Museum [Cat. no. 452]; the other is a panel of the wooden doors of Sta. Sabina in Rome [Cat. no. 438]. Although differing in iconographic detail, both have in common a Christ, nude save for a loincloth, shown in a rigid, frontal position. They exhibit little familiarity with the manner of crucifixion. Had it been forgotten already?

Later, in the sixth and seventh centuries, we have examples from the East. For the most part, they occur on small objects—ampullae, reliquary boxes, jewelry—that pilgrims brought home as souvenirs from Palestine. Their iconographic models were probably monumental portrayals at the "holy places":[110] a miniature from the Rabbula Gospels in Syriac (dated 586);[111] a painting on the lid of a wooden box in the Museo Cristiana of the Vatican;[112] a wall painting in Sta. Maria Antiqua in the Roman Forum;[113] and, with fewer figures, a silver dish in the Hermitage, Leningrad,[114] and an enamel inlay in a silver-gilt reliquary in The Metropolitan Museum of Art, New York [Cat. no. 574]. In all of these images, Christ is clothed in a dark tunic, called a *colobium*, and in all but the last, the scene includes the two thieves and the two soldiers, one with the sponge on a reed and the other with a spear. Some also have St. Mary and St. John near the cross. The eyes of

Christ are open, although the spear wound in his side, from which gush the streams of water and blood, indicates that Jesus is dead. For it was good patristic theology that the Godhead did not die, but only the human form in which it was incarnated.

The earliest icon of the crucified but dead Christ—i.e., with his eyes closed, a form that later became common in the East and the West—comes from St. Catherine's Monastery on Mount Sinai. It is dated to the eighth century, during the iconoclastic controversy, by which time St. Catherine's was beyond the reach of the Byzantine emperor.[115] It has been proposed that the representation of the crucified and dead Christ was a new affirmation of the two natures doctrine of the Chalcedonian Council, reaffirmed at the Seventh Ecumenical Council of 787 by its approval of the veneration of images.[116]

Yet the larger question remains regarding the late representation of the Crucifixion as a historical scene. No doubt, the end of paganism in public cult worship and the ban on crucifixion as a form of punishment, removed any danger of serious blasphemy or ridicule concerning the image. It may also be that the troubles of the Empire—first in the West with the barbarian migrations and their disruptions, and then in the East with its schisms and, later on, the Persian and Arab invasions—made the Crucifixion a relevant image for the Church's external and internal sufferings.

The great Christological acclamation in the liturgy, the *Trisagion*, first attested at the Council of Chalcedon—

> Holy God,
> Holy and Mighty,
> Holy Immortal One,
> Have mercy on us . . . [117]

was twisted by the Monophysites for their own theological stance by an insertion after the third line: "Who was crucified for us." The Chalcedonians were annoyed by this insertion (after all, the divine nature was not killed); hence, they reinterpreted the *Trisagion* as a Trinitarian acclamation. Thus official, imperial theology prevailed over the deepest, most ancient and widespread form of popular piety, whether Modalist or Monophysite, that felt, if it could not precisely articulate, the experience of the mystery: in Jesus Christ, God himself had entered fully and perfectly in all the suffering that humanity endures, even unto death itself.

NOTES

1. The precise date of Jesus' birth and death are much debated because of the contradictory notices in the Gospels. For the year of his death, Western patristic sources favored the date of A.D. 29, the fifteenth year of Tiberius in the consulate of L. Rubellius Geminus and C. Fufius Geminus. Modern scholars are more inclined, from astronomical data, to the year A.D. 30. See G. B. Caird in *The Interpreter's Dictionary of the Bible*, New York and Nashville, 1962, I, pp. 602–03. J. Jeremias, *The Eucharistic Words of Jesus*, N. Perrin, trans., New York, 1966, pp. 36–41. On the basis of data in the Gospel of John, a strong argument has been made for the year A.D. 33 by P. L. Maier, "Sejanus, Pilate, and the Date of the Crucifixion," *Church History*, XXXVII, 1968, pp. 3–13.

2. Isa. 2:2–4, Mic. 4:1–4. Cf. 1 Cor. 15:24–28, Heb. 12:25–29.

3. Acts 6:1, 9:29, 11:20. M. Simon, *St. Stephen and the Hellenists in the Primitive Church*, London, 1958.

4. Acts 11:22–23, 15:1–5; Gal. 2:1–16, 5:2–12; Phil. 3:2–10.

5. Acts 11:26, 26:28; 1 Pet.4:16 ; Tacitus *Annals* 15.44, 3–4. These passages all show that the term "Christian" was given by pagans. Ignatius of Antioch (d. 115) was the first Christian author to adopt the term; see *Magnesians* 10.3, *Philadelphians* 6.1. See my article, "The Occasion of the Initial Break between Judaism and Christianity," *Harry Austryn Wolfson. Jubilee Volume on the Occasion of his Seventy-Fifth Birthday*, Jerusalem, 1965, English Section 2, pp. 703–17.

6. W. H. C. Frend, *Martyrdom and Persecution in the Early Church*, Oxford, 1965, pp. 167–69, 218–25.

7. The so-called "apostolic decree" in Acts 15:28–29 was based upon the ritual requirements for strangers dwelling among Jews in Lev. 17:8. It was probably not a decision of the Council but a later regulation of the Jerusalem Church. St. Paul never referred to it (cf. Acts 21:25); but the alienation of most Jews from the Christian gospel is nonetheless attested by him in Romans 9–11. See E. Haenchen, *The Acts of the Apostles. A Commentary*, B. Noble and G. Shinn, trans., revised by R. McL. Wilson, Philadelphia, 1971, pp. 468–72. For the various sects of Jewish-Christians that developed and for their relation to both Judaism and Christian groups, see H. J. Schoeps, *Jewish Christianity*, D. R. A. Hare, trans., Philadelphia, 1969.

8. No writings of Aramaic-speaking Christians have come down to us. It has been conjectured that they gathered "testimonies" from the Old Testament that were prophetic of Christ. This theory has been revived by the discovery at Qumran of a fragment of messianic prophecies. See J. M. Allegro, "Further Messianic References in Qumran Literature," *Journal of Biblical Literature*, LXXV, 1956, pp. 182–87. J. A. Fitzmyer, "'4Q Testimonia' and the New Testament," *Theological Studies*, VIII, 1957, pp. 513–37. For a contrary opinion, J. P. Audet, "L'Hypothèse des Testimonia," *Revue Biblique*, LXX, 1963, pp. 381–405. The tradition of Papias of Hierapolis (ca. 130), preserved in Eusebius *Hist. eccl.* 3. 39, 16, that "Matthew arranged the oracles (*logia*) in the Hebrew language, and each one translated them as he was able," lacks context. It has been variously interpreted as referring to Old Testament prophecies, the sayings of Jesus, or a written Gospel. See W. R. Schoedel, *The Apostolic Fathers. A New Translation and Commentary*, R. M. Grant, ed., Camden, N. J., 1967, V, pp. 109–10.

9. A. C. Sundberg, Jr., *The Old Testament of the Early Church*, Cambridge, 1964 (Harvard Theological Studies, XX).

10. The Jewish-Christian "Gospel according to the Nazareans," probably written in Aramaic in the early second century, was a targumistic rendering of the Greek Gospel of Matthew. See E. Hennecke, *New Testament Apocrypha*, W. Schneemelcher, ed., R. McL. Wilson, trans., London, 1963, I, pp. 139–53. The destination of Luke-Acts and the Gospel of John may have been intended for Gentiles or Jews, no less than for Christians. In the case of Luke-Acts, much depends upon one's view of the person of Theophilus, to whom the work is dedicated. See the survey in W. G. Kümmel, *Introduction to the New Testament*, 14th rev. ed., A. J. Mattill, Jr., trans., Nashville and New York, 1965, pp. 113–15. For the Gospel of John, see A. Wind, "Destination and Purpose of the Gospel of John," *Novum Testamentum*, XIV, 1972, pp. 26–69; and my comments, "The Jews in the Gospel of John, Another Level of Meaning," *Gospel Studies in Honor of Sherman Elbridge Johnson*, M. H. Shepherd, Jr., and E. C. Hobbs, eds., *Anglican Theological Review*, suppl. ser. 3, 1974, pp. 101–03. Cf. Kümmel, pp. 161–65.

11. Suetonius *Claudius* 25. 4; Tacitus *Annals* 15. 44, 3, in the Codex Mediceus 68 II; Tertullian *Apologia* 3. 5. Other references in H. Fuchs, "Tacitus über die Christen," *Vigiliae Christianae*, IV, 1950, pp. 69–74.

12. W. Kramer, *Christ, Lord, Son of God*, B. Hardy, trans., Naperville, 1966 (Studies in Biblical Theology, L), pp. 203–06.

13. Rom. 5:14, 1 Cor. 15:22, 45. Outside of the Gospels, the only use of "Son of Man" in the New Testament is Acts 7:56.

14. In addition to W. Kramer, *Christ, Lord, Son of God*, other comprehensive treatments of New Testament Christology will be found in R. Bultmann, *Theology of the New*

Testament, K. Grobel, trans., New York, 1951, 1955, I, pp. 26–37, 42–53, 121–33, and 292–306; II, pp. 33–69, 155–202. O. Cullmann, *The Christology of the New Testament*, S. C. Guthrie and C. A. M. Hall, trans., Philadelphia, 1967. R. H. Fuller, *The Foundations of New Testament Christology*, London, 1965. J. Knox, *Jesus Lord and Christ: A Trilogy Comprising The Man Christ Jesus, Christ the Lord, On the Meaning of Christ*, New York, 1958. V. Taylor, *The Names of Jesus*, London, 1953.

15. For surveys, with copious bibliography, see M. Hengel, *The Son of God: The Origin of Christology and the History of Jewish-Hellenistic Religion*, J. Bowden, trans., Philadelphia, 1976. B. M. Metzger, "Considerations of Methodology in the Study of the Mystery Religions and Early Christianity," *Harvard Theological Review*, XLVIII, 1955, pp. 1–20. M. Smith, "Prolegomena to a Discussion of Aretalogies, Divine Men, the Gospels and Jesus," *Journal of Biblical Literature*, XC, 1971, pp. 174–99. C. H. Talbert, "The Concept of Immortals in Mediterranean Antiquity," ibid., XCIV, 1975, pp. 419–36, and "The Myth of a Descending-Ascending Redeemer in Mediterranean Antiquity," *New Testament Studies*, XXII, 1976, pp. 418–40. See also notes 16 and 18 below.

16. Wisdom 7:27; cf. James 2:23. See E. R. Goodenough, *By Light, Light: The Mystic Gospel of Hellenistic Judaism*, New Haven, 1935. J. Z. Smith, "The Prayer of Joseph," *Religions in Antiquity: Essays in Memory of Erwin Ramsdell Goodenough*, J. Neusner, ed., Leiden, 1968 (Studies in the History of Religions, supplements to *Numen*, XIV), pp. 253–94.

17. The few quotations of pagan authors in the New Testament (1 Cor. 15:33, Acts 17:28, Titus 1:12) are not based on direct knowledge of pagan literature, but are phrases from the common parlance. If there was any mediation, it was probably by way of Hellenistic Judaism. Cf. E. Haenchen, *The Acts of the Apostles*, p. 525. Similarly, the legend of the phoenix in 1 Clement 25 came from Hellenistic-Jewish sources (so J. B. Lightfoot, *The Apostolic Fathers*, Part I. S. Clement of Rome, London, 1890, II, p. 85), although R. M. Grant considered it to come from Roman sources: *The Apostolic Fathers, A New Translation and Commentary*, New York, 1965, II, p. 51.

18. This paragraph condenses insights from A. D. Nock, *Essays on Religion and the Ancient World*, Z. Stewart, ed., Cambridge, Mass., 1972, II, pp. 928–39. M. Hengel, *The Son of God*, pp. 21–83. F. Young, "Two Roots of a Tangled Mass?" in *The Myth of God Incarnate*, J. Hick, ed., London, 1977, pp. 87–121. C. H. Talbert, "The Concept of Immortals," p. 434.

19. John 20:28, Titus 2:13, 2 Pet. 1:1, 2 Clement 1:1, and esp. Ignatius *Ephesians* inscr., 1:1, 7:2, 15:3, 18:2, 19:3; *Romans* inscr., 3:3, 6:3; *Smyrneans* 1:1; *Polycarp* 8:3.

20 G. Howard, "The Tetragram and the New Testament," *Journal of Biblical Literature*, XCVI, 1977, pp. 63–83.

21. G. F. Moore, *Judaism in the First Centuries of the Christian Era. The Age of the Tannaim*, Cambridge, Mass., 1927, II, pp. 424–31.

22. Examples in G. Howard, "The Tetragram and the New Testament," pp. 78–82.

23. The phrase is that of A. von Harnack, *Lehrbuch der Dogmengeschichte*, 4th ed., Tübingen, 1909, I, p. 250. It has been aptly applied to Docetism by M. Hengel, *The Son of God*, p. 41.

24. The principal patristic refutation of Marcion is Tertullian *Adversus Marcionem*, E. Evans, ed. and trans., Oxford, 1972 (Oxford Early Christian Texts). The basic modern studies are A. von Harnack, *Marcion. Das Evangelium vom fremden Gott*, 2nd ed., Leipzig, 1924. E. C. Blackman, *Marcion and His Influence*, London, 1948.

25. Trans. by W. W. Isenberg, in *Gnosticism. A Sourcebook of Heretical Writings from the Early Christian Period*, R. M. Grant, ed., New York, 1961, p. 147.

26. Summaries of the "rule of faith" may be found in Irenaeus *Adversus haereses* 1. 10, 1–2; Tertullian *De praescriptione haereticorum* 13, *Adversus Praxean* 2, *De virginibus velandis* 1, 3; Origen *De principiis* praef.

27. Hippolytus *Contra Noetum* 1.

28. On the range of meaning of "dispensation" (Greek, *oikonomia*), see G. L. Prestige, *God in Patristic Thought*, London, 1952, pp. 57–69 and 98–102. A. Grillmeier, S. J., *Christ in Christian Tradition*, 2nd rev. ed., J. Bowden, trans., Atlanta, 1975, index s.v. "oikonomia."

29. Hippolytus *Refutatio omnium haeresium* 9. 11–12.

30. On the early Adoptionists, see Eusebius *Hist. eccl.* 5. 28 and 7. 27–30. G. L. Prestige, *God in Patristic Thought*, pp. 114–15 and 202–05.

31. Text in G. Bardy, *Paul de Samosate. Etude historique*, Louvain, 1929 (Spicilegium sacrum Lovaniense, Etudes et documents, IV), pp. 56–57.

32. J. Lebreton, "Le désaccord de la foi populaire et de la théologie savante," *Revue d'histoire ecclésiastique*, XIX, 1923, pp. 481–506, and XX, 1924, pp. 5–37. H. J. Carpenter, "Popular Christianity and the Theologians in the Early Centuries," *Journal of Theological Studies*, n.s. XIV, 1963, pp. 294–310.

33. Origen *Contra Celsum* 4. 3, H. Chadwick, trans., Cambridge, 1953, pp. 185–86.

34. Marcus Aurelius *Ad se ipsum* 11. 3.

35. Lucian *De morte peregrini* 11–16.

36. P. Merlan, "The Later Academy and Platonism," *The Cambridge History of Later Greek and Early Medieval Philosophy*, A. H. Armstrong, ed., Cambridge, 1967, pp. 53–83, esp. p. 66 on the "triad" of Albinus. R. A. Norris, Jr., *God and World in Early Christian Theology*, New York, 1965.

37. Justin Martyr *Apologia* 2. 13, trans. in *The Ante-Nicene Fathers*, I, Buffalo, 1886, pp. 192–93.

38. Origen *De principiis* 1. 2 and 4. 1. Origen's use of *homoousios* is extant only in a fragment of his commentary on the Epistle to the Hebrews. For a translation, see J. Quasten, *Patrology*, II, Westminster, Md., 1953, p. 78. For an interpretation, see J. N. D. Kelly, *Early Christian Creeds*, London, 1950, p. 245.

39. Tertullian *Adversus Praxean* 2, 12, 25. Cf. *De pudicitia* 21.

40. Origen *De principiis* 2. 6, 3, and *In Ezek. homilia*, 3. 3.

41. Origen *Contra Celsum* 2. 9.

42. Tertullian *Adversus Praxean* 27.

43. Eusebius *Vita Constantini* 3. 12.

44. Athanasius *Oratio contra Arianos* 1. 9.

45. The soteriology of Arius was considered by his bishop, Alexander of Alexandria, to be comparable to that of the Adoptionists in his encyclical letter to the Eastern bishops (Theodoret *Hist. eccl.* 1. 4). This charge had a basis in Arius' *Thalia*: "he that is without beginning made the Son a beginning of things originated, and advanced him as a Son to Himself by adoption." See Athanasius *De synodis Arimini et Seleuciae* 15; and cf. his *De decretis Nicaenae Synodi* 22.

46. R. C. Gregg and D. E. Groh, "The Centrality of Soteriology in Early Arianism," *Anglican Theological Review*, LIX, 1977, p. 273.

47. G. H. Williams, "Christology and Church-State Relations in the Fourth Century," *Church History*, XX, 1951, no. 3, pp. 3–33, no. 4, pp. 3–26.

48. C. E. Raven, *Apollinarianism. An Essay on the Christology of the Early Church*, Cambridge, 1923. A. Grillmeier, *Christ in Christian Tradition*, pp. 329–40.

49. G. L. Prestige, *Fathers and Heretics*, London, 1940 (The Bampton Lectures for 1940), pp. 249–368, on Nestorius and Cyril. R. V. Sellars, *The Council of Chalcedon. A Historical and Doctrinal Survey*, London, 1953. A. Grillmeier, *Christ in Christian Tradition*, pp. 345–557. The most extensive treatment of all aspects of Chalcedon and its aftermath is A. Grillmeier and H. Bacht, eds., *Das Konzil von Chalkedon*, 3 vols., Würzburg, 1951–54.

50. W. H. C. Frend, *The Rise of the Monophysite Movement. Chapters in the History of the Church in the Fifth and Sixth Centuries*, Cambridge, 1972. R. C. Chesnut, *Three Monophysite Christologies*, Oxford, 1976.

51. In the extensive literature on the iconoclastic controversy, two works are fundamental in scope and reference: E. Kitzinger, "The Cult of Images in the Age before Iconoclasm," *Dumbarton Oaks Papers*, VIII, 1954, pp. 83–150 (reprinted in *The Art of Byzantium and the Medieval West: Selected Studies by Ernst Kitzinger*, W. E. Kleinbauer, ed., Bloomington, 1976, pp. 91–156). P. J. Alexander, *The Patriarch Nicephorus of Constantinople. Ecclesiastical Policy and Image Worship in the Byzantine Empire*, Oxford, 1958. To their bibliographies should be added: J. Kollwitz, "Zur Frühgeschichte der Bilderverehrung," *Römische Quartalschrift*, XLVIII, 1953, pp. 1–20. H. von Campenhausen, "The Theological Problem of Images in the Early Church," *Tradition and Life in the Church. Essays and Lectures in Church History*, A. V. Littledale, trans., London, 1968, pp. 171–200. P. Brown, "A Dark-Age crisis: aspects of the Iconoclastic Controversy," *The English Historical Review*, CCCXLVI, January 1973, pp. 1–34. P. Henry, "What Was the Iconoclastic Controversy About?" in *Church History*, XLV, 1976, pp. 16–31.

52. On the Western reaction, see F. Kempf et al., *The Church in the Age of Feudalism*, A. Biggs, trans., New York, 1969 (Handbook of Church History, III), pp. 78–80, 113, and literature, p. 506.

53. For survivals of Jewish melodies in early Christian chant, see E. Werner, *The Sacred Bridge: The Interdependence of Liturgy and Music in Synagogue and Church during the First Millenium*, New York, 1959.

54. J. Lassus, *Sanctuaires chrétiens de Syrie*, Paris, 1947 (Institut français d'archéologie de Beyrouth, Bibliothèque archéologique et historique, XLII), pp. 1–22. R. Krautheimer, *Early Christian and Byzantine Architecture*, Baltimore, 1965 (The Pelican History of Art), pp. 1–15.

55. E. R. Goodenough, *Jewish Symbols in the Greco-Roman Period*, 12 vols., New York, 1953–65 (Bollingen Series, XXXVII). C. H. Kraeling, *The Synagogue. The Excavations at Dura-Europos. Final Report VIII, Part I*, New Haven, 1956. E. Kitzinger, *Israeli Mosaics of the Byzantine Period*, London, 1965 (Fontana Unesco Art Books).

56. V. Schultze, "Christus in der frühchristlichen Kunst," *Strena Buliciana. Commentationes gratulatoriae Francisco Bulic . . .* , Zagreb and Split, 1924, pp. 331–36. G. de Jerphanion, *La voix des monuments*, Rome, 1938 (Etudes d'archéologie, Nouvelle Série), pp. 1–26. J. Kollwitz, *Das Christusbild des dritten Jahrhunderts*, Münster, Westf., 1953 (Orbis Antiquus, IX). Idem in *Reallexikon für Antike und Christentum*, III, 1955, pp. 1–24, s.v. "Christusbild."

57. E. Hennecke, *New Testament Apocrypha*, II, p. 354.

58. Tertullian *De carne Christi* 9.

59. *Acts of John* 87, *Acts of Peter* (Vercelli Ms.) 5, *Acts of Andrew and Matthias* 33. For Christ's surpassing size, see the *Gospel of Peter* 10, *Acts of John* 89. Cf. Hermas, *The Shepherd*, Sim. 9:6 and 12.

60. Pliny *Epistulae* 10. 96; Tertullian *Apologia* 32; Origen *Cohortatio ad martyrium* 7.

61. For references, see my article, "The Early Apologists and Christian Worship," *The Journal of Religion*, XVIII, 1938, pp. 60–79.

62. Minucius Felix *Octavius* 32.

63. Origen *Contra Celsum* 8. 17, H. Chadwick, trans., pp. 464–65.

64. Hippolytus *The Apostolic Tradition* 16. 11, 16, G. Dix, trans., London, 1937, pp. 25–26.

65. Clement of Alexandria *Paedagogos* 3. 11.

66. Tertullian *De pudicitia* 10. It is disputed whether these *calices* were for sacramental use or—more likely—for private, domestic use. For the texts of both Clement and Tertullian, see T. Klauser, "Studien zur Entstehungsgeschichte der christlichen Kunst," *Jahrbuch für Antike und Christentum*, I, 1958, pp. 20–27.

67. This is cogently argued by Klauser, pp. 27–44, to which is appended a catalogue of sculptured examples. With regard to a number of third-century sarcophagi often considered to be Christian, cf. Klauser's articles in the *Jahrbuch für Antike und Christentum*, III, 1960, pp. 112–33, and VIII–IX, 1965–66, pp. 126–70. See also Cat. nos. 364 and 462.

68. The Good Shepherd as a symbol of salvation has been discussed by J. Quasten, "Das Bild des Guten Hirten in den altchristlichen Baptisterien und in den Taufliturgien des Ostens und des Westens," *Pisciculi. Studien zur Religion und Kultur des Altertums*, T. Klauser and A. Rücker, eds., Münster, Westf., 1939, pp. 220–44. See also L. de Bruyne, "La décoration des baptistères paléochrétiens," *Miscellanea liturgica in honorem L. Cuniberti Mohlberg*, Rome, 1948 (Bibliotheca "Ephemerides Liturgicae," XXII), I, pp. 189–220, and the remarks of C. H. Kraeling, *The Christian Building. The Excavations at Dura-Europos. Final Report VIII, Part II*, New Haven, 1967, pp. 180–83.

69. A Grabar, *Early Christian Art*, New York, 1968, pp. 10–12 and 81.

70. The oldest strata of the ancient Roman catacombs of Domitilla, Priscilla, and Praetextatus contain pagan and Christian burials in close proximity. Of unusual interest is the mixed pagan and Christian catacomb of the fourth century, discovered in 1956 on the Via Latina outside of Rome. See A. Ferrua, S. J., *Le pitture della nuova catacomba di Via Latina*, Vatican City, 1960 (Monumenti di antichità cristiana, II Serie, VIII). This was the private cemetery of a few families and was unknown to later Christian pilgrims. See also below, note 83.

71. Hippolytus *Refutatio omnium haeresium* 9. 2. It is not known how Zephyrinus acquired the property. His tomb, according to pilgrim itineraries, was above ground. For the evolution of the extensive catacomb, in which no pagan

burials have been found, see P. Styger, *Die römischen Katakomben*, Berlin, 1933, pp. 34–62. E. Josi, *Il cimitero di Callisto*, Rome, 1933 (Collezione "Amici delle catacombe," II).

72. C. H. Kraeling, *The Christian Building*. See also the review of Kraeling's book by A. von Gerkan, "Zur Hauskirche von Dura-Europos," *Mullus. Festschrift Theodor Klauser*, in the *Jahrbuch für Antike und Christentum*, Ergänzungsband I, 1964, pp. 143–49.

73. J. Quasten, "Der gute Hirte in frühchristlicher Totenliturgie und Grabeskunst," *Miscellanea Giovanni Mercati*, Vatican City, 1946 (Studi e testi, CXXI), I, pp. 373–406. Architectural historians had already suggested that Early Christian baptisteries were not only developed from baths, but also from tombs. See P. Styger, "Nymphäen, Mausaleen, Baptisterien, Problem der Architekturgeschichte," *Architectura. Jahrbuch für Geschichte der Baukunst*, I, 1933, pp. 50–53. R. Krautheimer, "Introduction to an 'Iconography' of Mediaeval Architecture," *Journal of the Warburg and Courtauld Institutes*, V, 1942, pp. 20–33.

74. F. Gerke, "Ideengeschichte der ältesten christlichen Kunst," *Zeitschrift für Kirchengeschichte*, LIX, 1940, pp. 1–102. W. Weidlé, *The Baptism in Art. Notes on the Religion of the Catacomb Paintings*, Westminster, n.d. P. du Bourguet, S. J., *Early Christian Painting*, London, 1965, pp. 28–34.

75. C. H. Kraeling, *The Synagogue*, pp. 392–402. K. Weitzmann, *Illustrations in Roll and Codex. A Study of the Origin and Method of Text Illustration*, 2nd ed., Princeton, 1970, pp. 130–33, 228–29, and 240. Idem, *Late Antique and Early Christian Book Illumination*, New York, 1977, pp. 15–24. On the other hand, T. Klauser (*Jahrbuch für Antike und Christentum*, IV, 1961, pp. 128–45) believes that the abbreviated style of catacomb painting and Early Christian sarcophagi was primarily derived from gems and signet rings, whether Jewish or pagan. Ibid., pp. 130–34 for a comprehensive survey of the pre-Constantinian scenes with their locations and with bibliographical notes.

76. E. Stommel, "Zur Problem der frühchristlichen Jonasdarstellungen," *Jahrbuch für Antike und Christentum*, I, 1958, pp. 112–13. A unique set of four sculptures of the Jonah story (three of them in the round) and one of the Good Shepherd (Cat. nos. 364–68) belong to The Cleveland Museum of Art. See W. D. Wixom, "Early Christian Sculpture at Cleveland," *The Bulletin of The Cleveland Museum of Art*, LIV, March 1967, pp. 67–88.

77. No extant, illustrated Christian Bibles or Gospel books can be dated prior to the fifth century. (See references above, note 75.) The fifty copies of the Scriptures that Constantine ordered Bishop Eusebius of Caesarea (*Vita Constantini* 4. 36–37) to prepare for the churches in Constantinople were to be written on parchment; but they probably had no miniatures.

78. The earliest examples are in the crypt of Lucina and the so-called "sacrament chapels" (*cubicula* A2 and A3) in the catacomb of Callistus. See J. Wilpert, *Die Malereien der Katakomben Roms*, Freiburg i. Br., 1901, pls. 27.3, 29.1, and 39.2. On the sarcophagi, the oldest one is in Sta. Maria Antiqua in Rome: F. W. Deichmann, G. Bovini, and H. Brandenburg, *Repertorium der christlich-antiken Sarkophage*, I, Wiesbaden, 1967, no. 747, pl. 117. For pagan antecedents, see J. Leipoldt, *Die urchristliche Taufe im Lichte der Religionsgeschichte*, Leipzig, 1928.

79. The early examples of banquet scenes are more numerous than scenes of baptism. See, for instance, J. Wilpert, *Die Malereien der Katakomben Roms*, pls. 15.1–2, 27.2, 41.1–3, 57, 65.2, 132.1, 133.1, distributed in the catacombs of Priscilla, Callistus, and Peter and Marcellinus. For late third-century sarcophagi, cf. the lid of the sarcophagus of Baebia Hertofila in the Museo Nazionale Romano in Rome. F. W. Deichmann et al., *Repertorium der christlich-antiken Sarkophage*, I, no. 778, pl. 124.

80. J. Wilpert, *Die Malereien der Katakomben Roms*, pls. 27.1 and 28. For the fish symbol of Christ, see J. Engemann in *Reallexikon für Antike und Christentum*, VII, 1968, cols. 1022–97, s.v. "Fisch, Fischer, Fischfang."

81. Ignatius *Ephesians* 20:2.

82. For Madonna and child images, cf. the two in the catacomb of Priscilla—one with a figure pointing to a star, usually identified as Balaam (cf. Num. 24:17), the other in the *cubiculum* of the Velatio; reproduced in J. Wilpert, *Die Malereien der Katakomben Roms*, pls. 22 and 81. In the Coemeterium Maius (ibid., pls. 207–09) the scene may be a portrait of the deceased with her child—the two Chi Rho monograms suggest a date after 312. For Adoration of the Magi scenes, cf. those in the catacombs of Domitilla and Massimo; ibid., pls. 116.1, 141, 212, and 239. On sarcophagi, the scene does not appear until the first third of the fourth century. For examples, see F. W. Deichmann et al., *Repertorium der christlich-antiken Sarkophage*, I, nos. 662, 670, 803, 835, and 887.

83. E. Kirschbaum, S. J., *The Tombs of St. Peter and St. Paul*, J. Murray, S. J., trans., London, 1959, pp. 34–42, pl. 3. J. M. C. Toynbee and J. B. Ward-Perkins, *The Shrine of St. Peter and the Vatican Excavations*, London, 1956, pp. 72–74, 116–17, pl. 32.

84. For texts and references to monuments, see L. Koep and A. Hermann in *Reallexikon für Antike und Christentum*, III, 1955, cols. 284–94, s.v. "Consecratio II (Kaiserapotheose)." Eusebius *Vita Constantini* 4. 73, mentions coins struck at Constantine's death showing the emperor with head veiled, sitting in a chariot drawn by four horses as he ascended into heaven. L. Koep, "Die Konsekrationsmünzen Kaiser Konstantins und ihre religionspolitische Bedeutung," *Jahrbuch für Antike und Christentum*, I, 1958, pp. 94–104, pl. 6b. The pagan tradition is preserved in an archaizing ivory diptych leaf of the fifth century [Cat. no. 60] in the British Museum. The adaptation for the ascension of Elijah is portrayed on the sarcophagus in S. Ambrogio, Milan, and on the wooden doors of Sta. Sabina, Rome. See W. F. Volbach, *Early Christian Art*, New York, 1961, pls. 46 and 104.

85. Eusebius' letter is extant only in excerpts read at the Council of 787. See H. Koch, *Die altchristliche Bilder-frage nach den literarischen Quellen*, Göttingen, 1917 (For-schungen zur Religion und Literatur des Alten und Neuen Testaments, N. F., X), pp. 42–43.

86. *Le Liber Pontificalis*, L. Duchesne, ed., with correc-tions by C. Vogel, Paris, 1955 (Bibliothèque des écoles françaises d'Athènes et de Rome), I, p. 172. See M. T. Smith, "The Lateran *Fastigium*. A Gift of Constantine the Great," *Rivista di Archeologia Cristiana*, XLVI, 1970, pp. 149–75. U. Nilgen, "Das Fastigium in den Basilica Con-stantiniana und vier Bronzesäulen des Lateran," *Römische Quartalschrift*, LXXII, 1977, pp. 1–31.

87. A. Grabar, *Christian Iconography. A Study of Its Origins*, London, 1969 (The A. W. Mellon Lectures in the Fine Arts, 1961), pp. 124–27. Y. Christe, "Victoria-Imperium-Judicium. Un schème antique de pouvoir dans l'art paléo-chrétien et médiéval," *Rivista di Archeologia Cristiana*, XLIX, 1973, pp. 87–109.

88. A fine example, with angels, is the sarcophagus of a child in the Archaeological Museum of Istanbul; repro-duced in W. F. Volbach, *Early Christian Art*, pl. 75. Three Passion sarcophagi in the Museo Pio Cristiana (see below, note 98) show a wreathed monogram surmounting a cross, with two phoenixes above the crossarm and two soldiers below it, thus making a symbol of the Resurrection of Christ. The pediment of one end of the sarcophagus in S. Ambrogio, Milan, shows the wreathed monogram with phoenixes and with an Alpha and Omega; W. F. Volbach, *Early Christian Art*, pl. 47.

89. The relic is first mentioned by Cyril of Jerusalem *Catecheses* 4. 10, 10. 19, and 13. 4 (ca. 350). The *Itinerarium* of Egeria, sec. 37 (ca. 400), speaks of a gilded silver casket in which it was kept. The jeweled encasement may have been a gift of Theodosius II (408–50). Two monumental representations of the True Cross relic are in the apse mosaic of Sta. Pudenziana, Rome, and S. Apollinare in Classe, Ravenna—the former of the early fifth, the latter of the mid-sixth century. See W. F. Volbach, *Early Christian Art*, pls. 130 and 173. Ibid., pls. 101 and 245, for smaller objects—an ivory plaque in the Cathedral Treasury of Milan (mid-fifth century) and a silver plate in the Hermi-tage, Leningrad (late sixth century). The cross as a sign of victory is well known in the hymn *Pange lingua* of Venantius Fortunatus (569).

90. The earliest painting of Christ in this form is probably the one in the syncretistic hypogeum of the Au-relii on the Viale Manzoni, Rome, which may be a scene of Christ teaching the apostles (*gnosis?*). A. Grabar, *Early Christian Art*, p. 209, no. 230. (See note 91 below.)

91. Catacomb paintings of the fourth century begin to reflect more monumental sources: in Domitilla, and Mark and Marcellinus (J. Wilpert, *Die Malereien der Katakomben Roms*, pls. 148.2, 193, and 177), and in Jordani (P. du Bourguet, *Art paléochrétien*, Paris, 1970, p. 121). Sar-cophagi portrayals often show Christ seated or standing

on a mount, with the rivers of paradise flowing from it, or on the *caelus*, a mythological figure holding the dome of heaven. A typical example is the sarcophagus of Probus in the Grottoes of St. Peter's; F. W. Deichmann et al., *Reper-torium der christlich-antiken Sarkophage*, I, no. 678, pl. 107. For the image on smaller objects, see the caskets repro-duced in W. F. Volbach, *Early Christian Art*, pls. 86, 95, and 111; in apsidal mosaics, ibid., pls. 130 and 138.

92. The *traditio legis* scenes are numerous in many me-dia, beginning with the mid-fourth-century mosaic in Sta. Costanza, Rome (P. du Bourguet, *Art paléochrétien*, p. 129). An inventory of the scenes, some thirty-four in all, with an acute critique, is given in F. Nikolasch, "Zur Deutung der 'Dominus-legem-dat' Szene," *Römische Quartalschrift*, LXIV, 1969, pp. 35–73.

93. A type of sarcophagus known as "wreath and star" shows the wreathed monogram above a cross with the phoenixes and soldiers in the center and, on either side, six apostles with crowns over their heads interspersed with stars (see above, note 88). Thus Christ the Victor bestows the crowns in the heavenly region. For examples in Arles, Manosque, Rome (S. Sebastiano), and the Palermo cathe-dral, see J. Wilpert, *I sarcofagi cristiani antichi*, Rome, 1929, I, pls. 12.4, 18.5; II, pls. 192.6, 238.7, 239.2. In the ceiling mosaic of the Arian Baptistery in Ravenna, ca. 500, the apostles, in two semicircles, carry their crowns to the cush-ioned throne on which stands the jeweled cross (*hetoimasia*), symbol of Christ; reproduced in W. F. Volbach, *Early Christian Art*, pl. 149. Soon after, the originally Arian church, now known as S. Apollinare Nuovo, had mosaics installed, showing a procession of male martyrs on the lower frieze of the right wall who bring their crowns to Christ en-throned. (On the left wall is a similar procession of female martyrs who bring their crowns to the enthroned *Theoto-kos*.) See the illuminating commentary in O. von Simson, *Sacred Fortress*, Chicago, 1948, pp. 81–98, pls. 30 and 34.

94. W. F. Volbach, *Early Christian Art*, pl. 130. E. Dass-mann, "Das Apsismosaik von S. Pudentiana in Rom. Phi-losophische, imperiale und theologische Aspekte in einem Christusbild am Beginn des 5. Jahrhunderts," *Römische Quartalschrift*, LXV, 1970, pp. 67–81.

95. W. F. Volbach, *Early Christian Art*, pl. 158. Cf. pl. 33, the mid-fourth-century mosaic in Sta. Costanza, Rome, where Christ, seated on the orb of the world, gives the keys to St. Peter.

96. Discussion of the propriety, intent, and meaning of pictures in churches engaged many of the Church fath-ers in the late fourth and early fifth centuries. Cf., for ex-ample, the description by Paulinus of Nola *Carmina* 27–28, of the Old and New Testament scenes in his churches. See H. Koch, *Die altchristliche Bilderfrage*, pp. 58–77. E. Kitzin-ger, "The Cult of Images in the Age before Iconoclasm," pp. 88–95. A. Ferrua, *Le pitture della nuova catacomba di Via Latina*, pp. 96–97. A. Grabar, *Christian Iconography*, pp. 87–106. K. Weitzmann, *Late Antique and Early Christian Book Illumination*, pp. 18–21.

97. Only a few notable examples can be listed here. The earliest extant narrative mosaics are in Sta. Maria Maggiore, Rome, ca. 432–40—the Nativity cycle on the triumphal arch, Old Testament scenes on the nave walls. See C. R. Morey, *Early Christian Art*, Princeton, 1942, pp. 146–55, and A. Grabar, *Christian Iconography*, pp. 47–49, pls. 130–44. Later mosaics are in S. Apollinare Nuovo, Ravenna, with miracles of Christ on the left, Passion scenes on the right; O. von Simson, *Sacred Fortress*, pp. 76–79, pls. 30, 32–35, and 42. Notable examples on sarcophagi are those of Adelphia, Museo Nazionale, Syracuse, ca. 340, and of Junius Bassus [Cat. no. 386], Grottoes of St. Peter's, dated 359; reproduced in W. F. Volbach, *Early Christian Art*, pls. 37–39 and 41–43. The two front alabaster columns of the ciborium of S. Marco, Venice, early fifth century, have scenes from the life of Christ; reproduced in ibid., pls. 82–83. Cf. also the carved wooden doors of Sta. Sabina, Rome, early fifth century, with Old and New Testament scenes [Cat. no. 438]. For ivories, cf. the late fourth-century casket (lipsanothek) in the Museo Civico, Brescia, with scenes of the Old and New Testaments; W. F. Volbach, *Elfenbeinarbeiten der Spätantike und des frühen Mittelalters*, 3rd ed., Mainz, 1967, no. 107. For ivory Gospel covers, see below, note 99. Lastly, among the ivories, the episcopal throne of Archbishop Maximianus (545–53), Museo Arcivescovile, Ravenna [Cat. fig. 65]. For illuminated manuscripts, see K. Weitzmann, *Late Antique and Early Christian Book Illumination*, with bibliography and color plates. In silver, cf. the reliquary casket in S. Nazaro Maggiore, Milan, from the end of the fourth century; reproduced in W. F. Volbach, *Early Christian Art*, pls. 110–15.

98. F. W. Deichmann et al., *Repertorium der christlich-antiken Sarkophage*, I, nos. 49, 57–59, 61, 106, 151, 164, 171, and 174.

99. There are five, possibly six, pairs of these ivory covers, only three of which are complete and in the same museum. Each of them is, or was originally, a five-part diptych, with a large central panel showing either the *Theotokos* or Christ, two horizontal panels at the top and the bottom, and two vertical panels on either side of the central one. For the two fifth-century examples, see W. F. Volbach, *Elfenbeinarbeiten*, nos. 112–13—a pair of vertical panels from a five-part diptych, one in Berlin, the other in Paris—and no. 119, a complete pair in the Cathedral Treasury, Milan. The extant sixth-century diptychs show one common feature: the top horizontal panel has a wreathed cross supported on each side by an angel. See ibid., nos. 142 and 145, for the two complete diptychs in the Bibliothèque Nationale, Paris, and the Matenadaran, Yerevan, Armenia; and no. 125, for the diptych leaf in the Museo Nazionale, Ravenna. A group similar to the Ravenna leaf, with the *Theotokos* in the center, was put together for the Metropolitan Museum's exhibition from various museums; see Cat. nos. 457–61 (Volbach, *Elfenbeinarbeiten*, nos. 126–29). Finally, a panel of the *Theotokos*, in the British Museum, London, ibid., no. 131, was undoubtedly at one time part of such a diptych.

100. F. W. Deichmann et al., *Repertorium der christlich-antiken Sarkophage*, I, no. 43, pl. 14, in the Museo Pio Cris-

tiana. In 1974, a similar sarcophagus was discovered in Trinquetaille near Arles (now in the Musée d'Art Chrétien in Arles), with the same creation theme, but with four rather than three figures. Hence, doubts as to the Trinitarian dogma of the scene have been cogently raised by J. Engemann, "Zu den Dreifaltigkeitsdarstellungen der frühchristlichen Kunst: Gab es im 4. Jahrhundert anthropomorphe Trinitätsbilder?" in *Jahrbuch für Antike und Christentum*, XIX, 1976, pp. 157–72, pls. 10–20. He argues that the third and fourth figures are assisting angels.

101. See the general discussion, with examples of Trinitarian and Incarnational portrayals, in A. Grabar, *Christian Iconography*, pp. 112–46. As early as Justin Martyr (*Dialogus cum Tryphone* 56 and 128) and Irenaeus (*Adversus haereses* 4. 7, 4) one of the three visitors to Abraham in Gen. 18 was considered to be the *Logos* (the Son). This interpretation seems to be accepted in the upper portion of the nave panel of the scene in Sta. Maria Maggiore, Rome. Cf. C. R. Morey, *Early Christian Art*, pp. 146–47. On the other hand, St. Augustine *De Trinitate* 2. 10–11, rejects this interpretation and states that the three were a theophany of the one God who spoke to Abraham. This accords with the mosaic of the scene in S. Vitale, Ravenna, where all three visitors are alike and have halos (O. von Simson, *Sacred Fortress*, pl. 14). On the visions of the glorified Christ in an aureole, Grabar rightly points to the fifth-century mosaic in the chapel of Hosios David in Thessalonike (W. F. Volbach, *Early Christian Art*, pl. 134). The same may be true of the obscure panel (second row, far right) on the doors of Sta. Sabina, Rome (ibid., pl. 103).

102. O. von Simson, *Sacred Fortress*, pp. 69–71.

103. E. Kitzinger, "The Cult of Images in the Age before Iconoclasm," pp. 90–115.

104. E. Kitzinger, "On Some Icons of the Seventh Century," *Late Classical and Mediaeval Studies in Honor of Albert Mathias Friend*, K. Weitzmann, ed., Princeton, 1955, pp. 132–50.

105. Tertullian *Adversus Marcionem* 3. 22, and *De corona* 3; Minucius Felix *Octavius* 9; Lactantius *Institutiones divinae* 4. 27; Origen *Selecta in Ezekielem*, quoted in F. J. Dölger, "Beiträge zur Geschichte des Kreuzzeichens II," *Jahrbuch für Antike und Christentum*, II, 1959, pp. 15–16.

106. Justin Martyr *Apologia* 1. 55, and *Dialogus cum Tryphone* 86–91 (on Old Testament types of the cross).

107. A cross sign is very rare. There is one in the third-century hypogeum of the Aurelii on the Via Manzone, Rome, belonging to a syncretistic sect. Its interpretation is disputed. See C. Cecchelli, *Il trionfa della croce. La croce e i santi segni prima e dopo Costantino*, Rome, 1954, fig. 54. Others known to me are the one inscribed on a *loculus* beneath the names (in Greek letters) of Rouphina and Eirene in a third-century gallery of the catacomb of Callistus (E. Josi, *Il cimitero di Callisto*, fig. 20); and a graffito on a third-century columbarium in the catacomb of S. Sebastiano, in which a Tau cross is inserted after the first letter of the

Greek word for fish, ICHTHYS (G. P. Kirsch, *The Catacombs of Rome*, Rome, 1946, fig. 51). These, along with the more common symbol of the anchor, are illustrated in P. Testini, *Archeologia cristiana*, Rome, 1958, figs. 54, 64, 157, 186, 206, 232, and 233. The cross marks on Jewish ossuaries in Talpioth and the necropolis "Dominus flevit" near Jerusalem do not prove that they contained the remains of Jewish-Christians. See the full discussion, with a catalogue of all known examples, in E. Dinkler, *Signum Crucis. Aufsätze zum Neuen Testament und zur Christlichen Archäologie*, Tübingen, 1967, pp. 1–54.

108. Ibid., pp. 150–53, pls. 13 and 33a, for a discussion of various interpretations. The scandalous charge was known to Tertullian *Ad nationes* 1.14, and *Apologia* 16; and to Minucius Felix *Octavius* 9.

109. Sozomenus *Hist. eccl.* 1. 8, 13. This law was probably promulgated after the defeat of Licinius, when Constantine became sole emperor. It is not in the Theodosian Code; but an earlier law of 314 (or 320–23) prescribed crucifixion for slaves and freedmen who accused their masters or patrons of high treason, *Codex Theodosianus* 9. 5, 1; English trans. by C. Pharr, *The Theodosian Code and Novels and the Sirmium Constitutions*, Princeton, 1952, p. 230.

110. A. Grabar, *Ampoules de Terre Sainte (Monza-Bobbio)*, Paris, 1958. J. Engemann, "Palästinensische Pilgerampullen im F. J. Dölger-Institut in Bonn," *Jahrbuch für Antike und Christentum*, XVI, 1973, pp. 5–27, for a wider survey of examples. K. Weitzmann, "*Loca Sancta* and the Representational Arts of Palestine," *Dumbarton Oaks Papers*, XXVIII, 1974, pp. 31–55, esp. pp. 40–41. It should be noted, however, that the ampullae only rarely show Christ, clothed, affixed to the cross; more often a bust of Christ surmounts the cross.

XXVIII, 1974, pp. 31–55, esp. pp. 40–41. It should be noted, however, that the ampullae only rarely show Christ, clothed, affixed to the cross; more often a bust of Christ surmounts the cross.

111. Florence, Biblioteca Laurenziana, cod. Plut. I, 56 [Cat. no. 445].

112. F. van der Meer and C. Mohrmann, *Atlas of the Early Christian World*, fig. 321. A. Grabar, *Christian Iconography*, fig. 260. Cf. C. R. Morey, *Early Christian Art*, p. 122.

113. It probably dates from the time of Pope Zacharias (741–52), the last of the Greek popes. See P. Romanelli and P. J. Nordhagen, *Santa Maria Antiqua*, Rome, 1964.

114. D. V. Ainalov, *The Hellenistic Origins of Byzantine Art*, E. and S. Sobolevitch, trans., C. Mango, ed., New Brunswick, 1961, pp. 257–59, fig. 117.

115. K. Weitzmann, *The Monastery of Saint Catherine at Mount Sinai. The Icons, I, From the Sixth to the Tenth Century*, Princeton, 1976, pp. 61–64, pl. 25.

116. J. R. Martin, "The Dead Christ on the Cross in Byzantine Art," *Late Classical and Mediaeval Studies in Honor of Albert Mathias Friend, Jr.*, K. Weitzmann, ed., Princeton, 1955, pp. 189–96.

117. For the history of the *Trisagion*, see J. M. Hanssens, S. J., *Institutiones liturgicae de ritibus orientalibus*, III, 2, Rome, 1932, pp. 110–23.

RICHARD KRAUTHEIMER

Success and Failure in
Late Antique Church Planning*

I'M GOING to start with a church right in the midst of Rome and well known—by hearsay, since with a succession of excuses it has been closed to visitors these last twenty-five years—Sto. Stefano Rotondo (Fig. 1).[1] Were you to enter, you would see a tall cylindrical center nave (A) over 21 meters (70 Roman feet) in height as well as width. Carried by twenty-one gray granite columns with crude Ionic capitals and surmounted by an architrave, this nave was lit by windows, twenty-one originally, high up in the clerestory wall (Fig. 2). In the window zone, you might notice a setback in the wall; it has been explained by Deichmann, rightly I think, as the springing for a dome of light material, planned but never built;[2] and from the interpenetration of the window arches into the foot of the dome you'd realize that the vault would have been scalloped—a pumpkin dome. You would also see a triple arcade thrown across the nave in the twelfth century and resting on top of huge red granite columns. Leaving the nave, you would walk into a wide enveloping ambulatory (B), its wall articulated by colonnaded arcades divided into eight groups—four with five higher arches, and four with six lower ones. All are now blocked, except for the group of five to the east, which opens into a tall and deep chapel (C), and one to the west, which opens toward a small medieval apse. Were you to penetrate into the garden around the building, you would notice that the arcades of the ambulatory are blocked with characteristic medieval masonry. You would also encounter, 10.40 meters (35 Roman feet) from the arcaded ambulatory wall, another circular wall built of brick like the rest of the structure. You would notice that three chapels like the one to the east (C) originally extended north, west, and south to the outer ring wall—traces of their side

walls remain (Fig. 3); that the sectors between the chapels were each divided by a low wall into a narrow section (E) adjoining the outer ring and a wider inner part (D) hugging the arcaded ambulatory; that each of the outer sections (E) originally were to be entered by two wide doors; that in the inner D sections a strip of small hollow tubes still runs above the blocked arcaded colonnades; and that from the chapels a door led to the outer E sections, while a triple "Palladian" arch opened to the inner D sections.

Under the circumstances, it seemed reasonable to envision the building with a round center nave planned to be domed, an ambulatory, four radial chapels (C) linked to one another by vaulted sections (D), and with narrow outer atria in the sections (E). However, Spencer Corbett years ago suspected the reverse arrangement, that is, courtyards in the inward D sections and corridors in the outward E sections, the dividing wall presumably opened by columns or piers rising from a low parapet (Fig. 4). His reconstruction has meanwhile been confirmed: the late Carlo Ceschi observed that the hollow tube band of the D sections continues at the same level and at a right angle on the outside south wall of the surviving eastward radial chapel (C). Corbett had also noticed that in at least three of these courtyards there were cisterns, presumably to feed fountains. In short, standing in the well-lit center nave (A), an early visitor would have found himself in a cylindrical space planned with a scalloped dome and brightly illuminated by comparatively small windows. Rather than see walls whitewashed, as at present, he would

*This is the text of the lecture presented at the symposium, November 22, 1977. It is slightly enlarged, and I prefer to retain the lecture style.

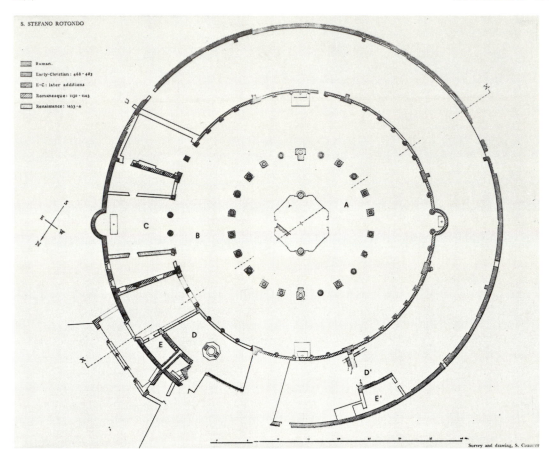

FIG. 1.
Sto. Stefano
Rotondo,
Rome. Plan
(Drawing: S.
Corbett)

FIG. 2.
Sto. Stefano
Rotondo,
Rome. View
of nave from
ambulatory
(Photo: Renzetti)

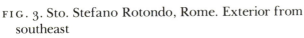

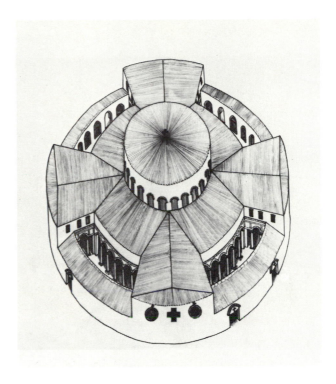

FIG. 3. Sto. Stefano Rotondo, Rome. Exterior from southeast

(Photo: S. Corbett)

FIG. 4. Sto. Stefano Rotondo, Rome. Reconstruction of exterior

(Drawing: S. Corbett)

have seen them covered by a colorful *opus sectile*, articulated by pilasters and inlaid with green and purple plaques and roundels, with bunches of grapes and leaves of mother-of-pearl. A drawing attributed to Cronaca shows the marble revetment from the architrave to the clerestory zone (Fig. 5), albeit too low in proportion. Fifteenth-century visitors, too, speak of the *opus sectile* and mosaic decoration. Vestiges of marble revetment and stucco moldings survive to this day in the outer zone, marble pavement and marble mosaic floors throughout the building. The visitor, then, would have looked through a number of successive screens, all resplendent with stucco, mosaic, and marble decoration: the colonnade of the nave, the arcades leading from the ambulatory into the courtyards and, further, the one separating the courtyards from the corridors. He would also have been struck by the alternation of well-lit and shadowed zones—the bright nave, the dim ambulatory, the darkish chapels, the sunlit courtyards against the background of the dark outer corridors; and by the

complexity and playfulness of the plan as well as of the alternating open and closed spaces of different heights (Fig. 6).

It's a strange structure and it does not fit into the common concept of Early Christian church building. In fact, for many centuries it was believed to be an ancient Roman building, either a *macellum* or a temple. But it *is* a church and a church of the late fifth century. Documentation, technique of construction, and stylistic elements coincide. The *Liber Pontificalis* and inscriptions read by early visitors tell us that it was erected between 468 and 482 by Pope Simplicius, with work on the decoration continuing until the late twenties of the sixth century. Excavations, soon to be published by Mrs. Lissi Caronna, have uncovered in recent years a number of Roman structures buried underneath—a private residence, barracks and, from the end of the fourth century, a mithraeum with beautiful paintings—all unconnected with the structure of the church.

Whitewashed and fragmented as it is today, Sto.

FIG. 5. Sto. Stefano Rotondo, Rome. Interior, as seen in a 15th-century drawing (Cronaca?)

(Photo: after Bartoli, *I monumenti antichi nei disegni degli Uffizi*, 1915, I, pl. V)

Stefano nonetheless remains, to me anyhow, the most fascinating church in Rome. To visualize it as planned—domed nave, ambulatory, chapels, court-yards, corridors, all interlocking in a *rondo* and re-splendent in colorful marble revetment and mosaic articulated by classical pilasters and profiles—almost defeats imagination. Still, the architectural historian, while overwhelmed by the sheer beauty of the de-sign, feels disturbed. Obviously, it is a design of Late Antique flavor; but he is unable to assign the plan and the principle from which it grew to a specific place in Late Antique architecture, pagan or Christian, secular or religious. Certainly, he cannot fit it into the ambience of Late Antique—call it Early Christian—church planning, whether in Rome or elsewhere. How would the liturgy of Rome, well-cod-ified by the fifth century, work out in such a build-ing? Historians of architecture have, after all, a conscience; and that conscience remains uneasy in the face of questions unsolved and perhaps insoluble.

All church planning within the borders of the Em-pire, from the fourth to the early sixth century, stands firmly rooted in the architectural concepts and the building categories of the Roman-Hellenistic world as they survived, modified and enriched, in late an-tiquity.[3] Also, since antiquity thought in terms of specific building types and categories for specific functions, Christian patrons and church leaders from the outset drew automatically on such categories to create variants suitable for, or adaptable to, the ex-ternal requirements of Christian worship. Likewise, church planning naturally remained for a time ex-perimental both in the choice of the categories and types on which they drew and in the variants that they created. And, as is in the nature of experiments, not all of them were successful. Some succeeded fully. Others succeeded in part and gradually gave way to more successful solutions. Others still were just failures and died out.

The most successful experiment in church planning was evolved at the very beginning of Constantine's reign, or possibly a few years earlier, simultaneously in both the east and the west of the Empire. This was the basilica, as it appears at Tyre around 314 and a year or so before in Rome, when Constantine—I think in the winter of 312–13—founded a cathedral at the Lateran for the Roman Christian community and completed it probably by 318.[4] Remodeled through the Middle Ages and incorporated since 1646–50 into Borromini's grand design, Constantine's Lateran cathedral nonetheless can be clearly envisioned (Fig. 7). A nave over 91

FIG. 6. Sto. Stefano Rotondo, Rome. Reconstruction of interior
(Drawing: S. Corbett)

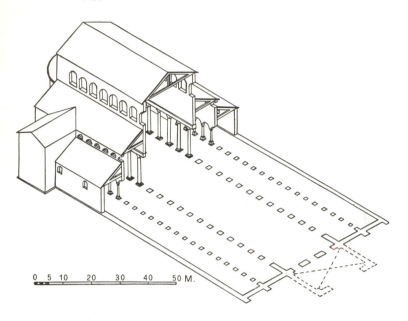

FIG. 7. S. Giovanni in Laterano, Rome.
Reconstruction (S. Corbett-P. Waddy-J. Lloyd)

meters (300 Roman feet) long and proportionately wide and high rested on trabeated columns, nineteen on either side, and was lit by clerestory windows; twin aisles flanked it right and left, separated by an arcade supported by splendid green columns; an apse terminated the nave to shelter bishop and clergy; and, in place of the present transept added in medieval times, two short wings—the foundations of only one have been excavated—projected sideways from the chancel area, possibly serving as depositories for offerings. Just as clear as the overall plan and elevation is the splendor of the original decoration: a colored marble floor; green columns in the aisles; huge red ones in the nave; the spandrels of the aisle arcades sheathed in marble; the apse vault gilded and aniconic; a silver *fastigium*, screen or canopy, on the chord of the apse, carrying silver-sheathed statues of Christ, angels, and apostles (a remarkably early case of figural church decoration); and lighting fixtures of silver and gold all through the building.[5]

There is no need to dwell on the break the Lateran cathedral made with the structures that so far had apparently served, and for a time continued to serve, Christian worship: the *domus ecclesiae*, which we would translate as community centers. *Domus ecclesiae* were houses of local type. Slightly altered for the needs of the smallish Christian congregations, they housed offices, clergy quarters, storerooms,

classrooms for instruction, rooms for the baptismal rite, another for divine service—all behind the facade of an ordinary house. They emphatically proclaimed their private and utilitarian character, whether found in a small provincial town in the East, such as the one at Dura Europos, datable as early as 231–32 [Cat. no. 580], or in Rome, in one of the large tenements of the metropolis, presumably a remodeled apartment or a sizeable workshop. The Lateran cathedral was of a different kind. Designed for worship only, it held three thousand or more faithful. Clergy quarters, offices, and installations for baptism were relegated to separate structures. Above all, the cathedral claimed assertively public rather than private standing; and it was monumental rather than utilitarian. Constantine's church, then, broke decidedly with past Christian building. By no means, though, did it break with the past altogether. On the contrary, it was deeply embedded in the soil of Roman public architecture. And within that framework, it seems to me, the choice was limited. Plan, design, and overall function were evolved within the appropriate *genus* of public building—the assembly hall, or *basilica*, to use the Latin term. Basilicas had risen for half a millenium or longer all over the expanding commonwealth of Rome in ever new variants in form and function: timber-roofed as a rule—the Basilica of Maxentius [Cat. no. 103] was an unsuccessful attempt at breaking away from the established category—they were essentially a covered extension of the market place. Modest or lavish, depending on their specific function, the financial means available, and the prestige striven for, they could be as grand as Trajan's Basilica Ulpia, where law courts met in colonnaded hemicycles at either end, with the nave, aisles, and galleries given over to doing business and spreading the news. Or they could be ordinary market basilicas, single-naved or with aisles, with or without galleries; or military drill halls, spartan and bare and lacking both aisles and galleries; or elegantly appointed meeting places for religious sects—synagogues, for instance; or reception halls in the mansions of the great, such as the Basilica of Junius Bassus, once on the Esquiline in Rome, where the clientele gathered before their patron; or, in imperial palaces and villas, audience halls where the Divine Majesty, present in the flesh or in effigy, revealed himself to his subjects, as at Piazza Armerina [Cat. no. 105]. Religious overtones, inherent in any basilica through the obligatory presence of a divinity's or the emperor's effigy, were naturally strongest in such imperial audience halls. And with the growing importance of the emperor cult, by the early fourth century their type was gaining ascendancy within the *genus*—single-naved, apsed, profusely lit, the walls sheathed in marble, and surmounted by painted plaster or mosaic: witness the *sedes iustitiae* in Trier, Constantine's own audience hall built but a few years before the Lateran cathedral (Fig. 8).[6]

Traditionalism is inherent in all government architecture; the more so in the climate of political and cultural conservatism that was cultivated through the fourth and fifth centuries by the Roman aristocracy and the imperial court.[7] When commanded to design a hall—a *basilica*—for the gatherings of the Christian congregation of Rome, Constantine's architect could only envision a variant on the age-old type, adapted to its new function and particular standing. Conscious of the emperor's wish to set up a grand structure speedily, proclaiming through its size and splendor both the status of the Church and the generosity of its exalted patron, he would devise a huge building, simple in plan and elevation, inexpensive to erect, but resplendent with precious pilfered columns and with huge wall surfaces to display marble, mosaic, painting, and gilding. Informed of the Christian ritual as practiced in Rome, he would plan the building to be longitudinal, culminating in the altar and the bishop's chair, like an audience hall; particularly since he could hardly fail to know that the new faith viewed Christ, in Eusebius' phrase, as the sovereign King of the Universe, greater than all earthly rulers and with all the attributes of a Roman emperor: lawgiver supreme, ever righteous, all-powerful, ever victorious.[8] Around 390, the apse mosaic at Sta. Pudenziana (see p. 46, Fig. 13) still reflects this concept. The Lateran cathedral, then, was an audience hall where faithful subjects would assemble before Christ, the *basileus*; and since a single-naved hall, even one as large as the *sedes iustitiae* at Trier, was too narrow to hold a congregation as numerous as the one to be gathered in the Roman cathedral, the structure was expanded sideways by double aisles. The profusion of precious materials and furnishings would stun the congregation and satisfy the ambitions both of the imperial donor and the Church leaders.

By trial and error and, as a rule, independent from one another, variants different from the Lateran cathedral were evolved for Christian worship on the parent type—the traditional assembly hall—during Constantine's lifetime and later. Indeed, such variants may well have existed prior to his reign. All were adapted to local ritual requirements, local building practice and, when necessary, to religious functions, other than divine service in the narrowest sense: basilicas with nave and two aisles; single-naved basilicas with or without apse; funerary basilicas, U-shaped with the aisles enveloping the apse; basilicas with a transept, as at St. Peter's, to house in it the *memoria* of the apostle. Whatever the variant, however, all Christian basilicas in design and function clearly belong to the parent *genus* meeting hall, as the form was given new life among both pagans and Christians by the early fourth century.

Nothing either in plan or elevation sets a Christian basilica fundamentally apart from any other variant—synagogue, audience hall, market basilica—except, that is, the changes in plan or elevation required by its specific function as a church: the layout of the chancel area, and the aisles, at times multiplied to provide additional space for the congregation. Likewise, Christian and non-Christian building, religious and secular, appropriates the stylistic

FIG. 8. Basilica, Trier. Interior
(Photo: Fototeca Unione)

FIG. 9.
Old St. Peter's,
Rome. Nave as of
1534–36, as seen
in M. van
Heemskerck's
drawing
(Photo: after Hülsen-
Egger, 1916, II, pl. 69)

FIG. 10.
Sta. Maria
Maggiore, Rome.
Reconstruction of
nave
(S. Corbett)

changes that mark all Constantinian architecture. The sculptural modeling of the spatial envelope by projecting columns and cornices, so dear to the architects of the Tetrarchy, was abandoned—the so-called Tempio della Siepe in Rome, known from engravings, was a prime example. Instead, from about 310 on, interiors were simple in plan, but filled with light from huge windows and delimited by the thin membrane of shimmering surfaces sheathed with marble and often mosaic.[9] At the same time, the order, that mainstay of classical antiquity, was treated in an offhand way.[10] Either its members—columns, pilasters, entablatures—were embedded as two-dimensional features into the wall revetment; or colonnades and their pertinent elements were composed of spoils taken from older buildings. Devaluation of the classical order, both in the three-dimensional strength of its members and their homogeneity, appears to be a hallmark of Constantinian design. Using spoils had long become common and, within the framework, the members of the order—column shafts, bases, capitals, and entablatures—need not and often could not conform to each other, and were re-used in contexts alien to their original meaning. Where a uniform set of splendid columns was at hand, it would be employed as a matter of course, as in the aisles of the Lateran. At St. Peter's [Cat. no. 581], the nave columns differed vastly in size and material. Heemskerck's *veduta* shows that the builders only took care in the nave to match right and left column groups (Fig. 9). In both Christian and non-Christian buildings, patrons and architects rejected the classical past and searched for new, yet decidedly Late Antique solutions.

Only a hundred years later, the Roman Church emphatically revived the classical tradition. Sta. Maria Maggiore, begun about 425 and completed 432–40 by Sixtus III, is still the best example of this renascence—and it is a renascence, recent objections notwithstanding.[11] Remodeled more than once, Sta. Maria Maggiore nonetheless retains its main features (Fig. 10): the Roman standard plan—nave, apse, and two aisles, as evolved from the late fourth century on; and the elevation, decidedly nonstandard—a set of uniform Ionic columns, an entablature and, in the clerestory, an order of pilasters, bonded with the wall and corresponding to the Ionic columns below. Between the pilasters, the series of Old Testament mosaics, one in each bay, were framed by colonnaded aediculae; two orders of stucco colonnettes, twisted clockwise and counterclockwise, framed the windows; and the upper order was sur-

mounted by a rinceaux frieze of superbly classical flavor. A small stretch of that frieze survives and suggests an originally coffered ceiling over the nave, much like the Renaissance ceiling now in place. The sculptural articulation of the envelope by pilasters, aediculae, colonnettes, friezes, and the classical tenor of the vocabulary—as it appears in Corbett's reconstruction (Fig. 10)—coincides so strikingly with the classical proportions of the nave that for a long time Sta. Maria Maggiore was believed by some to be a second-century building. But, of course, it was built three centuries later, at a time when classical antiquity was long a thing of the past; a renascence—nobody could fail to see that, one should think—out of step with the mainstream of contemporary thought and created by and for the benefit of Christian aristocrats, laymen, and Church leaders, eager to salvage classical culture in the framework of the new faith.

In recent years, Charles Piétri and Peter Brown have brought out the background of the phenomenon that twenty years ago I could but sketch: the Christianization of cultivated Roman circles from the latter fourth century on and the resulting Romanization of the Church and her assimilation of the classical heritage.[12] Sta. Maria Maggiore, then, reflects a Christian renascence in Rome that had started in the late fourth century, competing with the pagan revival of the same decades. Nostalgically looking back to a world forever lost, both pagan and Christian aristocrats and intellectuals battled forlornly for its survival. Once more, that vocabulary and the concept of the classical order are present at Sto. Stefano Rotondo in the trabeated nave colonnade, the stucco cornices, and the mosaic pavements and *opus sectile* revetment that once covered the building.

Whether renouncing or reviving the classical vocabulary and whatever the variants of the plan—in Rome, in Syria, at Constantinople, or in North Africa—the Christian basilica was no doubt the most successful adaptation of an antique building type to the needs of the Church. Essentially unchanged, it conquered the West and East and, in the West, retained its predominance up to and into the Renaissance. In the Greek East, of course, from the sixth century on, the basilica gave way to church plans of central shape. This is not the place to discuss the reasons. However, the monopoly of the basilica in church planning was challenged, if sporadically, from the start. A few years after the Lateran basilica and St. Peter's had been completed, still in Constantine's lifetime, central plan structures of Roman, though

FIG. 11.
SS. Sergios and Bacchos,
Constantinople. Interior
(Photo: Powell)

FIG. 12.
S. Vitale, Ravenna. Interior
(Photo: Deutsches Archäologisches Institut)

not classical, antiquity began to exert their impact on monumental church building.

Monumental churches on a central plan are best known, to be sure, from Constantinople and its sphere of influence in the early reign of Justinian, between roughly 527 and 540.[13] There is the church of SS. Sergios and Bacchos (Fig. 11),[14] begun shortly after 527—I still disagree with Professor Mango on both the date and circumstances of the foundation. The nave is an octaconch, its niches, screened by columns in two tiers, billowing into an enveloping ambulatory and gallery—a double-shell design, the center dome scalloped, of light material, its foot pierced by windows, the ambulatory and gallery groin- and barrel-vaulted. There is S. Vitale in Ravenna, laid out at the same time, although completed only in the forties, more slender in proportion, ambulatory and gallery unvaulted, but otherwise on the same plan (Fig. 12).[15] Finally, there is the crowning glory of the group, the Hagia Sophia (Fig. 13).[16] To be sure, the nave, rather than an octaconch, is formed by the square main bay and two semi-circles, east and west, each expanding in screened, two-tier conches, the whole surmounted by that miraculous ascending sequence of quarter-domes, half-domes, and main dome. As at S. Vitale and SS. Sergios and Bacchos, space billows sideways, lengthwise, diagonally, and upward; column screens connect the nave with, and separate it from, the enveloping aisles and galleries; light and shade form complex patterns; multicolored marble plaques, mother-of-pearl inlay, and mosaic sheath walls, piers, arcades, and vaulting; and the nave, fully intelligible to those standing in it, becomes unintelligible except in fragments when viewed from the enveloping zones.

One is apt to think of these churches as the perfect product of sixth-century Eastern planning. However, their roots, both in the East and in the West, go far back into Constantinian times and beyond. The Great Church at Antioch, built near the Imperial Palace between 327 and 341, is known only from early descriptions: it had an octagonal nave, surmounted, it seems, by a dome, possibly wooden and gilded—hence the popular name of the church, the Golden Octagon—and was enveloped by *exedrae* (niches) and *oikoi* (colonnaded aisles) in two tiers, that is, an ambulatory and a gallery. Wayne Dynes has convincingly interpreted the sources as referring to a double-shell octaconch much like S. Vitale in Ravenna.[17] So far, the Antioch Octagon remains the only *octa*conch church known to have been built prior to Justinian. But one early church on a related

*tetra*conch plan, and that in the West, has survived—S. Lorenzo in Milan [Cat. no. 584].[18] Laid out, I submit, shortly before 378, it remains intact, if disguised by a sixteenth-century remodeling (Fig. 14): a tall square nave, four expanding niches, the two-tiered envelope of ambulatory and gallery, outer walls, and four towers rising from the corners. Whether the center bay, now surmounted by the overly tall sixteenth-century drum and dome, was originally groin-vaulted or covered by a dome of light material is to me still a moot point.

Irving Lavin, nearly twenty years ago, outlined the background from which such polyconch church plans appear to have sprung.[19] Reception rooms—*triclinia, salutatoria,* or whatever the term used for such glorified *saloni* in villas, mansions, and palaces—from early times constituted in both function and form a specific genus with a broad spectrum of variants. By the second century A.D. the genus appears to have sprouted a category of increasing importance. It is a pavilion architecture, as known first in Hadrian's villa at Tivoli, in a variety of shapes. An octagonal

FIG. 13. Hagia Sophia, Constantinople. Interior (Photo: G. E. Kidder Smith)

FIG. 14. S. Lorenzo, Milan. Interior
(Photo: Sopraintendenza ai Monumenti di Lombardia)

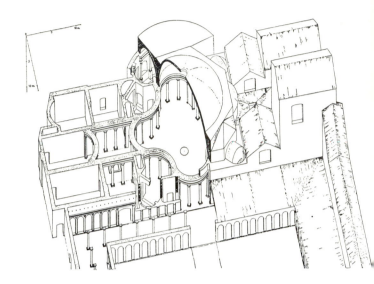

FIG. 15. Piazza d'Oro, Tivoli. Reconstruction of Octagon
(Photo: after Kähler, pl. 16)

core expands in four niches at the corners, while the intervening sides curve inward, convexly; or, again, concave and convex curves alternate; and there are other variations (Figs. 15, 16). Whatever the plan, though, the core frequently is covered by a scalloped dome; the walls are thin membranes dissolved in columnar screens; and these screens, more often than not, open toward adjoining spaces, frequently courtyards sheltering pools or fountains.[20] Regardless of variations, the genus playfully combines architectural elements, landscaping, and water. And it works with interlocking inner and outer spaces, with overlapping column screens, with zones of alternating light and shade. Frank Brown has suggested that Hadrian himself may have had a hand in developing the type. For Dio Cassius tells how Apollodorus, Trajan's architect, irritated by Hadrian's criticism, told him to go off and draw his pumpkins; Apollodorus was obviously not referring to a still life, but presumably to pumpkin domes—scalloped domes, as we would call them.[21]

Such pavilions appear to have been forerunners of the vaulted polyconch *saloni* customary in Late Antique and early Byzantine palace and villa plan-

ning, and one wants to remember that in late antiquity and in Byzantium palaces and villas had become interchangeable. Whether in the city or in the country, such lordly mansions were laid out as groups of pavilions, loosely scattered in parks and linked by courtyards, pools, and colonnaded porticoes—the Alhambra is a late descendant, the Imperial Palaces in Constantinople were an earlier case in point. In Rome, around 320, the so-called Minerva Medica in the gardens of Licinius, by then imperial property, is just such a pavilion (Fig. 17). A decagonal nave, covered by a ribbed dome and lit by large windows, shoots forth nine low niches; the rear of the nave was filled by a heatable platform. Of the niches, the four in the transverse axis opened in triple colonnaded arcades toward outdoor pools of but slightly later date.[22] Obviously, then, the pavilion was for use both in summer and in winter. And if, as has been suggested, the heatable platform was intended for the emperor's state banquet, the *coenatio Jovis*, it would have served as a *salone* with religious connotations. A century after the Minerva Medica, a polyconch *salutatorium* appears in Constantinople—in the entrance lobby of the palace of Antiochos north of the Hip-

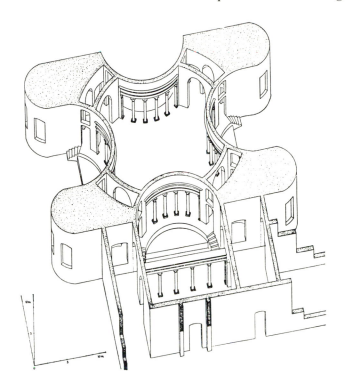

FIG. 16. Small Palace, Tivoli. Reconstruction of garden hall

(Photo: after Kähler, pl. 14)

FIG. 17. Temple of Minerva Medica, Rome. Engraving by T. W. Kobell

(Photo: GFN)

podrome, dating 420–36: a hexagon, whose five niches alternating with small circular closets open in column screens toward adjoining rooms.[23] Such *saloni*, from triconches to octaconches, are documented in Byzantine and Umayyad palaces into the ninth century and beyond.

The central plan, double-shell churches—from the Great Church at Antioch and S. Lorenzo in Milan, to SS. Sergios and Bacchos and the Hagia Sophia—thus would appear to be variants on a genus of Late Antique architecture, just as the Lateran cathedral and other Constantinian churches were variants on the antique genus basilica. Still, there are differences.

Christian basilicas grew without effort, as it were, from the parent genus; a genus unsophisticated in plan and construction on a simple builder's and carpenter's level; with roots deeply sunk into the Roman past, preclassical, classical, and postclassical; designed to hold large popular assemblies, and therefore emphatically public in status and easily adapted to variations in plan and function, the latter including Christian worship. Neither patrons nor architects would have viewed the Lateran cathedral or St. Peter's as innovative. And the Christian people would have felt at home in these structures—a building type they were accustomed to gathering in, although glorified by size and glittering splendor.

On the contrary, the Golden Octagon at Antioch and S. Lorenzo in Milan had sprung from a parent genus anything but deeply rooted, ubiquitous, or unsophisticated. Niched pavilions and palace lobbies were decidedly innovations of *late antiquity*, and perhaps of a specific moment and place, such as Hadrian's villa at Tivoli. And while for centuries these types lived on in Late Antique palace planning, they never became popular. Nor were they ever public buildings. Dreamed up by a sophisticated architect (or the imperial dilettante Hadrian), they were designed for the use, enjoyment, and understanding of a sophisticated minority—pieces of luxury architecture embedded in the comparative privacy of a palace or villa. Correspondingly, the migration of the niched pavilion type into church planning took place not through a natural, easy evolution, but through pruning, as it were: an artificial transfer from the parent genus, in function as well as in plan. *Salutatoria* or *triclinia*, whether or not on a pavilion plan, were not designed, after all, for large popular assemblies. They were laid out for the reception of the intimates of the master of the house, or, in an imperial palace, of the high charges of the court. Hence, they were comparatively small. Even the Minerva Medica would have held but a hundred-odd courtiers gathered in front of the podium. That difficulty, though, was the least. Enlarged and transformed, the free-standing polyconch pavilion was turned into the center core of the church plan and enveloped by the outer shell of a two-tier ambulatory. The latter provided the additional space that the size of a larger gathering—the Christian congregation of Antioch, for instance—would require.

Nevertheless, the transfer of such double-shell polyconches into church planning left architect and patron with problems hard to solve. The placing of altar and celebrant created difficulties: if placed in the center of the nave, they would be in the midst of, rather than dominating, the congregation; if removed into a chancel attached to the center nave, as at S. Vitale, they would disappear from the view of a large part of the congregation. On a broader plane, tetraconch or octaconch double-shell structures were not designed to appeal to the masses, except through size, splendor, and their miraculous statics. They were a challenge to the intellect and the sensitivity of the sophisticated—a Procopius, a Paul the Silentiary. Problems galore remain open. Why did the genus, apparently rare in the fourth century, come to the fore with such vigor around 500 apparently in Syrian tetraconch churches? Why in Justinian's reign did it reach that remarkable degree of perfection in Constantinople and her sphere of influence? And why did just such central plan, double-shell churches so often rise near an imperial, bishop's, or governor's palace? These questions have been discussed frequently and sometimes with virulence during the last years, but, alas, to my mind, are still open.

In sum, the Christian basilica presents a mere variant on an old antique genus of assembly halls, designed on a simple level of construction and on a simple plan. Easily adapted to any new function, it successfully solved the transition from secular to ecclesiastical Christian use by incorporating the necessary liturgical adjustments, as well as the imperial connotations it carried. Christian basilicas thus remain within their proper ancestral genus. Double-shell churches, on the other hand, on a tetraconch or octaconch plan, were rooted in the high class, sophisticated genus of pavilions designed for small intimate gatherings. Their very transfer to the alien category of church planning represents an innovation. And, artificial as it is, this transfer is only partially successful. It succeeds superbly in the perfection of its design—one need but recall Hagia Sophia. Yet it teeters on the brink of failure in its structural features—the dome of Hagia Sophia, after all, collapsed more than once. And it is at best only partially successful in adjusting the plan to the requirements of the service: the chancel reserved for the sacrifice of the Mass, Christ's revelation in the flesh; the nave given over to the processions of the clergy, to readings and sermons—Christ in the Word; the congregation, on the other hand, including the emperor, relegated to the aisles and galleries and thus unable to follow the service and participate in the sacrifice, except in fragments.

Failures, then, or near failures are as frequent in architectural history (and in history altogether) as success. The transfer into church planning of building types from antiquity is full of such failures. Sto. Stefano Rotondo is, I think, a conspicuous example. For performing the liturgy of the Roman rite it has always been bothersome, not to say unfit; hence, the recent proposals to turn it into an ecumenical church, a "church of the light," and the like. Where, indeed, would Mass be celebrated? If in the nave, the faithful would crowd around the celebrant, a custom frowned upon in Early Christian times. In any case, no trace of an altar has ever been found in the nave of Sto. Stefano. In 1583 Gregory XIII placed a chancel there, but no altar. If Mass was performed in one of the chapels—in the one to the east an altar has stood since the seventh century—there was room for only the smallest congregation. And, in that case, why four chapels, all alike, whether or not with altars, all accessible both through the ambulatory and to those coming from the outside through the flanking courtyards and corridors, and all opening onto them by wide doors and triple "Palladian" arches? But then, what was Sto. Stefano's intended liturgical function? It was not a parish church; it had no clergy of its own—no *presbyter sancti Stephani in Caelio Monte* signed the minutes of the synods of 499 and 595. Presumably it was a dependency of the Lateran, ten minutes' walk away, and serviced by the clergy of the cathedral. It might have been a martyrium. But there is not a shred of evidence that any important relic was ever venerated there; at least not until 642–49, when Pope Theodore brought the bones of Sts. Primus and Felicianus from the catacombs.

Forty years ago, I suggested that we see in Sto. Stefano Rotondo a copy of the Anastasis Rotunda in Jerusalem; "copy" in the sense given the term from antiquity through the Middle Ages—a selective re-shuffling of elements shared with the model and crossed with alien features.[24] Indeed, some main features coincide: the circular plan, composed of center room and ambulatory; the niches—chapels at Sto. Stefano—projecting from the ambulatory; and the similar dimensions, of the naves' diameter, both around 21 meters. These resemblances, then, remain significant, despite the absence at the Anastasis Rotunda of an outer corridor, not to mention the presence of courtyards at Sto. Stefano Rotondo. The link between Sto. Stefano and the Anastasis, therefore, need not be eliminated. But it wants to be seen within a context quite different in nature.

Whatever the specific liturgical function intended, Sto. Stefano is cast in an idiom that has neither forerunners nor parallels in church planning. The vocabulary, to be sure, is the same as that employed in many contemporary and earlier churches in Rome. The Ionic capitals, their trabeation, and the classical stucco profiles of the courtyards find their counterparts in Sta. Maria Maggiore and in the Lateran baptistery as remodeled by Pope Sixtus III (432–40). The *opus sectile* revetment of the nave, as known from Cronaca's drawing (Fig. 5), recalls the decoration that once covered the walls of the baptistery. The arcaded colonnades of the ambulatory, opening to the outdoors, are reminiscent of a striking feature of fourth- and early fifth-century church planning in Rome: the arcaded open facade of the nave as found at S. Clemente, S. Vitale, SS. Giovanni e Paolo, and at S. Pietro in Vincoli, in its first building phase. The open courtyards, too, with their entrance corridors skirting the outer wall, are obviously adapted—the former from traditional atria, the latter from *quadriporticus*, whole or fragmented, as at Old St. Peter's prior to A.D. 500.[25] However, all these features, rather than hallmarks of church building, were also elements of non-Christian building: an Ionic order, at the Temple of Saturn; *opus sectile* walls in the hall that later became SS. Cosma e Damiano; arcaded facades, to list a few, in the triconch at Piazza Armerina [Cat. no. 105], in the reception hall of the mansion of Fortuna Annonaria at Ostia, and in the garden hall excavated below S. Pietro in Vincoli, the flanks of which are similarly pierced by arcades; and, finally, courtyards and *quadriporticus* in any sizeable villa, town mansion, or palace.[26]

In brief, the vocabulary was a common fund drawn on by religious building, pagan or Christian, and by secular architecture, mansions and villas in particular. More than anything else, therefore, the idiom of

Late Antique villa and palace design permeates the design of Sto. Stefano Rotondo, both in its overall concepts and in individual elements: the fourfold repetition of atria, courtyards, corridors, and chapels; the alternation of covered and open spaces and of grouped arcades, of tall chapels and low porticoes; the overlapping of column screens in the nave and ambulatory and the resulting complex views; the fountains and perhaps pools in the courtyards. Time and again one is reminded of Hadrian's villa, of Piazza Armerina [Cat. no. 105], of the Villa dei Quintili on the Via Appia. Were one to look for specific parallels—not models by any means—the dining hall in Hadrian's villa might come to mind, opened as it is in column screens on four open-air spaces, one filled by a pool, the others bordered by colonnaded porticoes (Fig. 18).[27] Moreover, the scalloped dome planned over the nave of S. Stefano likewise belongs to the tradition of Late Antique palace and villa planning.

Thus, Sto. Stefano would seem to represent a transfer from secular Late Antique architecture into church building. More precisely, it represents a

FIG. 18. Hadrian's Villa, Tivoli. Reconstruction of dining hall

(Photo: after Kähler, pl. 10)

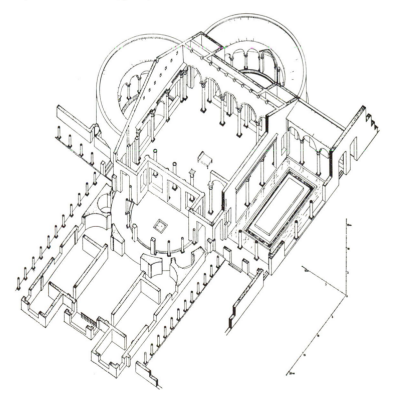

transfer from villa and palace planning. However, the transfer is different in kind from that from which spring church plans like the Golden Octagon or SS. Sergios and Bacchos. Rather than lift a building type, a pavilion like the Minerva Medica, from villa planning and turn it into the core of a double-shell church design, the architect of Sto. Stefano seems to have recomposed disparate elements and concepts from villa planning—courtyards, arcaded corridors, overlapping column screens, a scalloped dome—into a wholly new church plan that was without forerunners and remained without issue.

One is tempted to work out some ingenious theory to explain the phenomenon. But common sense offers a simple solution linked to the topography of the neighborhood. All along the crest of the Celian Hill, from Sto. Croce in Gerusalemme and the Lateran, to Sto. Stefano and, further west, to S. Gregorio Magno, there extended a vast stretch of the greenbelt of ancient Rome.[28] Here, the *domus* of the great—often imperial property by the fourth century—were scattered in parks, pavilion fashion: far east, the *Horti Spei Veteris*, where the Sessorian Palace rose, including the core of the church of Sto. Croce in Gerusalemme; near the Lateran cathedral and its palace, the mansions of the Laterani and the Pisones, and the *domus Faustae*, whatever and wherever that was; below the hospital of S. Giovanni, the villas of the family of Marcus Aurelius, that of his mother, Domitia Lucilla, and his grandfather, Annius Verus; westward toward Sto. Stefano, the *domus* of L. Martius Maximus Perpetuus and that of the Valerii, one of the great Roman families in the fourth and early fifth centuries; finally, on the westernmost slope of the hill, the mansion of the Anicii, Gregory the Great's ancestors.

In the course of the fifth century, many of these *domus* had fallen to the Church and were turned into hostels or convents, such as the *domus* of the Valerii into the convent of S. Erasmo. But the neighborhood retained its greenbelt character, as it does to this day. One villa or palace pavilion, extraordinarily Hadrianic-looking and presumably of second- or third-century date, survived near the Lateran baptistery until 1588. Dedicated to the Holy Cross by Pope Hilary (461–68), it is known from sixteenth-century drawings and descriptions: cross-shaped, the corners filled with octagonal closets, all parts vaulted in hollow tube construction (Fig. 19). The walls were sheathed in multicolored *opus sectile*; the main vault was covered by a mosaic showing four half-naked male caryatids that supported a wreath enclosing a

cross. This cross may well have been the only alteration made by Pope Hilary. The villa character of the neighborhood at that time is also reflected in the courtyard laid out by Hilary in front of the chapel. Demolished along with the chapel by Sixtus V, it is known from Bufalini's map and from a lengthy, if unclear, description in Hilary's biography in the *Liber Pontificalis*.[29] Enveloped on three sides by colonnades, the courtyard sheltered some kind of water display. The papal biographer lists a porphyry basin and a strigilated trough, presumably a sarcophagus, in its center; two more strigilated conches; fluted porphyry columns and colored marble columns; entablatures inlaid in mosaic; and gables, possibly crossed arches like those over Constantine's shrine of St. Peter. The whole courtyard was tiny in size, sophisticated in intent, and in all likelihood crude in execution, notwithstanding the grandiloquent and confusing pseudoclassical terminology of the biographer's account. One cannot help recalling the canopy and the *Pigna* placed in the atrium of Old St. Peter's by Pope Symmachus forty years after Pope Hilary: the porphyry columns with emperors' busts; the grills rising from the architrave; the peacocks; the bronze dolphins; the marble slabs with griffons enclosing the basin—all spoils gathered from far and near, such as those found in Late Antique villas, placed together so as to form a playful, light ensemble. In Hilary's courtyard at the Lateran, the association with villa design becomes even clearer, being transposed into vestpocket format—an association in conformity with the greenbelt character of the neighborhood, with the remains of the great villas, presumably preserved in large part. It seems that Pope Hilary and his contemporaries had a very particular predilection for villa design, for a design playful in character that fused landscape, fountains, and architectural elements. It can hardly be by chance that among all the biographies in the *Liber Pontificalis*, only Hilary's own mentions at length the construction near S. Lorenzo of a convent and country house with a bath and an open-air swimming pool and, perhaps, two libraries, obviously a Greek and a Latin one as would be appropriate through late antiquity for a Roman grand seigneur's mansion.[30]

Is it then possible that this climate of villa building also underlies the planning of Sto. Stefano Rotondo under Hilary's successor, Pope Simplicius? Clearly such a suggestion is entirely in the realm of conjecture, but I feel it should be entertained. The details of the plan, the courtyards under the sky, the arcaded openings of the ambulatory toward the

FIG. 19. S. Giovanni in Laterano, Rome. Chapel of The Holy Cross. Drawing by Giuliano da Sangallo
The Vatican Library, Rome (Barb. lat. 4424)

outdoors, the fourfold redundancy of chapels, courtyards, and entrance corridors, all point in that direction. Obviously, the pope and his architect experimented. And they failed. The design was perfect, but the function of the structure as a church was treated with benign neglect. The liturgy of Rome, as codified by the fifth century, simply would not work in that building. To be sure, all four chapels might have been planned to shelter altars. But, the total lack of evidence aside, such an arrangement would only have repeated the same inconvenience four times: insufficient space for a congregation inside the chapel; the difficulty for a congregation assembled outside to participate in the service; and the needless redundancy of courtyards and entrances. Indeed, while still under construction, the plan was changed. The entrances from the outside to three of the courtyards were blocked, thus condemning their function as atria. The lightweight dome was never put in place over the nave. In addition, by the twelfth century, the cylinder wall of the nave had to be strengthened by a diaphragm wall thrown across. Failure, then, all over. Still, the transfer to church building of elements and concepts rooted in the realm of Late Antique villa and palace planning turned Sto. Stefano Rotondo, I propose tentatively, into the beautiful freak that it is.

NOTES

1. Cat. no. 589. R. Krautheimer, S. Corbett, and W. Frankl, *Corpus Basilicarum Christianarum Romae* (hereafter, *Corpus*), IV, Vatican City, 1970, pp. 199—240, with bibliography to date of publication.

2. F. W. Deichmann, "Die Eindeckung von S. Stefano Rotondo," *Miscellanea Giulio Belvederi*, Vatican City, 1954–55, pp. 437–50.

3. R. Krautheimer, "The Constantinian Basilica," *Dumbarton Oaks Papers*, XXI, 1967, pp. 115–40.

4. R. Krautheimer, S. Corbett, and A. K. Frazer, *Corpus*, V, Vatican City, 1977, pp. 1–92.

5. Whether or not the inner aisles rose with overhead windows above the outer ones, as I believe they did, is still a matter of contention. Likewise, it remains open whether the *fastigium* described in the *Liber Pontificalis* (L. Duchesne, ed., Paris, 1889, I, p. 172) was a gabled double colonnade across the apse opening, as suggested by M. Teasdale Smith, "The Lateran Fastigium . . . ," *Rivista di Archeologia Cristiana*, XLVI, 1970, pp. 149–75; or a baldacchino, perhaps with crossed arches as at St. Peter's, as suggested by U. Nilgen, "Das Fastigium in der Basilica Constantiniana . . . ," *Römische Quartalschrift*, LXXII, 1977, pp. 1–31. The aniconic gold mosaic of the apse vault gave way to a figural mosaic, presumably in the fifth century.

6. Cat. no. 102.

7. J. F. Mathews, *Western Aristocracies and the Imperial Court*, Oxford, 1975, *passim*. P. Brown, *Religion and Society in the Age of St. Augustine*, New York and London, 1972, *passim*.

8. Eusebius *Eccl. History* 10. 4, 16, K. Lake, trans., London and New York, 1932 (Loeb Classical Library), II, pp. 406–07.

9. A. K. Frazer, *Four Late Antique Rotundas . . .* , Ph.D. Dissertation, New York University, 1965, *passim*.

10. F. W. Deichmann and A. Tschira, "Die frühchristlichen Basen und Kapitelle von S. Paolo fuori le mura," *Römische Mitteilungen*, LIV, 1939, pp. 99–111. F. W. Deichmann, "Säule und Ordnung in der frühchristlichen Architektur," ibid., LV, 1940, pp. 114–30. Idem, *Die Spolien in der spätantiken Architektur*, Munich, 1975 (Sitzungsberichte der Bayerischen Akademie der Wissenschaften, philosophisch-historische Klasse, fasc. 6), *passim*.

11. R. Krautheimer, "The Architecture of Sixtus III: A Fifth-century Renascence?" *Studies in Early Christian, Medieval, and Renaissance Art*, New York and London, 1969, pp. 181–96. See, however, F. W. Deichmann, "Die Spolien in der spätantiken Architektur," pp. 20–21.

12. C. Piétri, "Concordia Apostolorum et Renovatio Urbis," *Mélanges d'Archéologie et d'Histoire de l'Ecole Française à Rome*, LXXIII, 1961, pp. 275–322. Idem, *Roma Christiana*, Rome, 1976, *passim*. P. Brown, *Augustine of Hippo*, Berkeley, 1967, *passim*. Idem, *Religion and Society in the Age of St. Augustine, passim*.

13. R. Krautheimer, *Early Christian and Byzantine Architecture*, Harmondsworth, 1975 (The Pelican History of Art), pp. 215–30, 233–37, 244–48, with bibliography.

14. Cat. no. 249. For the date, R. Krautheimer, ibid., pp. 508–09, with reference to Mango's contrary opinion.

15. Cat. no. 593.

16. Cat. no. 592.

17. W. Dynes, "The First Christian Palace-Church Type," *Marsyas*, XI, 1962–64, pp. 1–9.

18. R. Krautheimer, *Early Christian and Byzantine Architecture*, pp. 82–85, with bibliography. For reasons to be explained in a forthcoming publication, I prefer the date "shortly before 378" to that formerly accepted—"between 355 and 373."

19. I. Lavin, "The House of the Lord," *Art Bulletin*, XLIV, 1962, pp. 1–27.

20. H. Kähler, *Hadrian und seine Villa bei Tivoli*, Berlin, 1950, *passim. Ricerche sull'architettura di Villa Adriana*, C. F. Giuliani, ed., Rome, 1975 (Quaderni dell'Istituto di Topografia Antica dell'Università di Roma, VIII), *passim*. Also, F. Rakob, "'Litus Beatae Veneris Aureum', Untersuchungen am 'Venustempel' in Baiae," *Römische Mitteilungen*, LXVIII, 1961, pp. 114–49.

21. F. E. Brown, "Hadrianic Architecture," *Essays in Memory of Karl Lehmann*, Locust Valley, N. Y., 1964 (*Marsyas*, Supplement I), pp. 55–58.

22. M. Stettler, "St. Gereon in Köln und der sogenannte Tempel der Minerva Medica in Rom," *Jahrbuch des Römisch-Germanischen Zentralmuseums Mainz*, IV, 1957, pp. 123–28. A. K. Frazer, *Four Late Antique Rotundas*.

23. R. Naumann and H. Belting, *Die Euphemia-Kirche am Hippodrom zu Istanbul und ihre Fresken*, Berlin, 1966 (Istanbuler Forschungen, XXV), *passim*.

24. R. Krautheimer, "Sto. Stefano Rotondo a Roma e la chiesa del Santo Sepolcro a Gerusalemme," *Rivista di Archeologia Cristiana*, XII, 1935, pp. 51–102.

25. Pope Symmachus' remodeling (498–514) of the *quadriporticus* was apparently confined to the entry part of the atrium and to the narthex at the front of the church (*Corpus*, V, pp. 267–68).

26. R. Krautheimer, *Early Christian and Byzantine Architecture*, pp. 181 and 502, note 8. Also, A. Boethius and J. B. Ward-Perkins, *Etruscan and Roman Architecture*, Harmondsworth, 1970 (The Pelican History of Art), p. 335. G. Matthiae, *S. Pietro in Vincoli*, Rome, ca. 1965 (Chiese Illustrate, LIV), figs. 1 and 2, pp. 12–13.

27. H. Kähler, *Hadrian und seine Villa bei Tivoli*, pp. 122–28, pls. 9 and 10.

28. A. M. Colini, *Storia e topografia del Celio*, Vatican City, 1944 (Memorie della Pontificia Accademia Romana di Archeologia, VII), pp. 253 ff. and pls. XIII, XIX, and XXIV. V. Santa Maria Scrinari, "Per la storia e la topografia del Laterano," *Bollettino d'Arte*, L, 1965, pp. 38–44. Idem, *Egregiae Lateranorum Aedes*, Rome, 1967, *passim*. Idem, "Scavi sotto Sala Manzoni," *Rendiconti della Pontificia Accademia Romana di Archeologia*, XLI, 1969, pp. 167–89. Idem, "Nuove Testimonianze per la 'Domus Faustae,'" ibid., XLIII, 1971, pp. 207–22. E. Nash, "Convenerunt in domum Faustae," *Römische Quartalschrift*, LXXI, 1976, pp. 1–21.

29. *Liber Pontificalis*, L. Duchesne, ed., I, pp. 242–43. The chapel was frequently drawn by fifteenth- and sixteenth-century artists, e.g. Giuliano da Sangallo, Barb. lat. 4424, f. 31, and Baldassare Peruzzi, Uffizi, dis. arch. 438. See A. Bartoli, *I monumenti antichi nei disegni degli Uffizi*, II, Rome, 1915, pl. CVIII.

30. *Liber Pontificalis*, L. Duchesne, ed., I, p. 245. The passage regarding the two libraries has been recently referred not to the country house at S. Lorenzo fuori le mura, but to the Lateran. See G. Scalia, "Gli 'Archiva' di Papa Damaso e le biblioteche di Papa Ilaro," *Studi Medievali*, ser. 3, XVIII, 1977, pp. 39–54.

ERNST KITZINGER

Christian Imagery: Growth and Impact

THE PERIOD in the history of art to which this splendid exhibition is devoted does not come across easily. Whether considered in terms of content or of style, it lacks a tangible unity and a palpable inner development. Previous speakers in this symposium have had much to say about legacies from antiquity being inherited, sifted, phased out, transmuted, and reinterpreted. What was accomplished in these respects during the centuries under discussion was vitally important and bears significantly on the subsequent fortunes of the visual arts in the Western world. But only in one area was there a consistent—one might almost say systematic—progression. Christian religious imagery is the only field of artistic endeavor in which one can readily perceive a process of steady and organic growth.

It is a story with a beginning, a middle, and an end, and with its own peculiar dynamics. It begins—slowly and gropingly—early in the third century; it ends in the eighth century when the imperial government in Constantinople puts a stop to the making of religious images. That measure, of course, was effective only within the Byzantine domain, and even there it was to be rescinded eventually. But the outbreak of iconoclasm in Byzantium unquestionably constitutes a landmark in the history of art, the more so since it coincided with two other major developments—the emergence of the art of Islam, on the one hand, and of Christian art in Northern Europe, on the other.

The iconoclastic crisis of the eighth century is indeed generally recognized as a dramatic hiatus. By contrast, scholars do not always face up squarely to the even more radically negative situation at the beginning of the history of Christian art. During the first two centuries, Christians rejected art altogether as an element of religious life. The fact is well attested in writings of the period and borne out by all

the archaeological evidence we have. Many scholars believe that the root cause of this negative attitude was the Old Testament commandment against graven images, which Christians continued to observe. This, however, was a tabu within a larger tabu that associated the making of religious images—or, for that matter, the erection of shrines and altars—not only with pagan cult practices but with a whole way of life in Greco-Roman society. By the same token, the emergence of Christian art early in the third century was part of a process of coming to terms with the Greco-Roman way of life.[1] But the process was slow and gradual, and the aftereffects of the negative beginnings were to be felt for a long time. Indeed, the issue of the graven image never quite came to rest during the period under review. Eighth-century iconoclasm was, in a sense, a return to the concerns and attitudes of the early Church. The violence and magnitude of the iconoclastic reaction would, however, be inexplicable were it not for the intervening development of Christian imagery. This is what I meant when I spoke of the dynamics of that development.

Taking a very broad view and allowing oneself a certain amount of oversimplification, one can distinguish in the rise of Christian religious iconography three major stages: first, the era of tentative beginnings in the third century; then, starting with the triumph of Christianity under Constantine and continuing to the reign of Justinian, the great era of expansion; and, finally, the most critical and least well-defined stage, which lasts from the middle of the sixth to the early eighth century and which, for want of a more elegant term, I shall call the era of potentiation. To characterize these three stages as succinctly and graphically as possible, I shall illustrate each of them with a few representative objects—primarily objects that are in the exhibition.

FIG. 1. Sarcophagus. Good Shepherd, orant, and married couple.

Museo Pio Cristiano, The Vatican, Rome (Photo: Deutsches Archäologisches Institut)

The handsome sarcophagus from the Via Salaria in Rome, probably carved about A.D. 260, can serve to pinpoint many of the essential characteristics of the first stage (Fig. 1).[2] Its central figure is the Good Shepherd, the most common of all subjects in third-century Christian art. The motif of the *kriophoros* is, of course, age-old. But it gained enormous popularity among Christians because it called to mind the Gospel parables of the lost sheep (Luke 15) and of the shepherd who gives his life for his sheep (John 10).[3] That is to say, it epitomized central tenets of the faith—remission of sins and redemption through Christ's self-sacrifice. It did not, however, depict the historical Jesus. It evoked a verbal simile. To be sure, Christ had used this simile in reference to himself. But it was still only a simile that in turn illustrated an idea. It was thus twice removed from an actual portrayal of the divine person. It was a pictograph, a shorthand cipher for a concept. In the case of our sarcophagus, the figure appears yet further removed from "reality" by its context, in which it plays the part of a mental image only. On the left, the deceased is seated reading from a scroll. He is characterized as a man of intellect—a *mousikos aner*—and is attended by two men of similar type. His wife, with her attendants, is seated opposite. The figure of the shepherd is introduced as the subject of their discourse. We are meant to "read" it in the manner of indirect speech. It is the embodiment of the true philosophy that has governed the couple's life and will assure their afterlife.

Nearly all the earliest Christian images are of this "signitive" kind (an apt term applied to them by Wladimir Weidlé).[4] The shepherd may be replaced by other figures from the traditional repertory, such as Orpheus or Helios.[5] Though not capable of convey-

ing Christian concepts as patently and succinctly as the *kriophoros*, these figures are similarly charged. When represented at the tomb they, too, speak in metaphorical terms of Christ as the bringer of peace, security, and eternal life. Again, the episodes from the Old Testament and the Gospels that form part of this earliest repertory[6] are not depicted for their own sakes. They are selected in seemingly random fashion and make sense only in relation to a common underlying theme—the theme of deliverance and redemption through divine power. It is not by chance that the ordeal and deliverance of the prophet Jonah is the story most frequently represented (Fig. 2).[7] Christ himself had likened the three days the prophet spent in the belly of the fish to his three days in the tomb (Matt. 12: 40). The Jonah story becomes an earnest of resurrection and eternal life, and the point is emphasized by giving special prominence to a motif that is not really warranted by the biblical text, namely, the prophet ultimately coming to a peaceful and idyllic rest under the gourd tree. The Jonah story thus takes the form of a brief narrative cycle. Most of the biblical deliverance stories, however, are depicted in a much more drastically abridged form consistent with their role as signs or pictographs. The prophet Daniel, for instance, whom the Lord protects in the lions' den, is simply an *orans* figure with two docile little animals at his feet; and it is important to note that he may take the place of the Good Shepherd as a central motif. Such is the case in one of the earliest painted decorations in the Roman catacombs, a frescoed chamber in the catacomb of St. Callistus, where Daniel appears in the center of the ceiling and the figure of the shepherd (repeated twice) is relegated to the periphery (Fig. 3).[8] As ciphers the two motifs are coequal.

FIG. 2.

Painted ceiling. Good Shepherd, orants, and the story of Jonah.

Catacomb of SS. Pietro e Marcellino, Rome (Photo: Pontificia Commissione di Archeologia Sacra)

FIG. 3.

Painted ceiling. Daniel in the Lions' Den, Good Shepherds, and orants.

Catacomb of St. Callistus, Rome (Photo: Pontificia Commissione di Archeologia Sacra)

The "signitive" method was not a Christian invention. One can find it in pagan religious and funerary contexts, too.[9] What was new was the amount of content packed into these modest images. There was a vast imbalance here between the weight and complexity of the message and the visual form that carried the message. This surely had to do with the fact that pictorial representation was questionable in principle. It was justifiable only by the urgency of what these images had to say. The direct relevance of this earliest Christian representational art to those for whom it was made is indeed obvious. It was an art keyed essentially to personal concerns. It spelled assurance, protection, and peace; and therein lay its justification. A sign language entirely, it was worlds apart from the detested idols of the pagans, against which Christian apologists never ceased to inveigh.

Yet, it was the thin end of the wedge. Once the image had gained admittance, its function and uses proved difficult to delimit and control. Gradually, often imperceptibly, the safeguards with which it was hedged at this early stage were dropped or lost sight of. From the cipher that merely evoked, from the sign that consistently pointed beyond itself, there ultimately developed the icon that lent itself to contemplation and worship.

The period of Constantine marks a first major turning point in this development. In the reliefs of the so-called frieze sarcophagi, which are a characteristic product of this period, the "signitive" method is used à outrance (Fig. 4).[10] The largest possible number of drastically abridged "deliverance" stories are crammed together on these tombs. Often the episodes are grouped around a central *orans*, whom we see invoking these "precedents" of divine intervention, so that once again the sacred subjects and holy persons are introduced only by way of "indirect speech." The repertory of salvation miracles remained popular throughout the fourth century and beyond. In this exhibition, there are many objects from this period that show such scenes singly or in groups. But new themes expressive of new concerns soon came to the fore, and with them different modes of representation.

A fragmentary sepulchral relief in the Metropolitan Museum shows in an elaborate columnar setting Christ surrounded by the apostles and handing an open scroll to St. Peter, who approaches reverently from the right (Fig. 5).[11] This is the so-called *traditio legis*, a scene in which Christ hands to the apostle the New Law that he has come to promulgate and that has replaced the law of Moses.[12] The scene exemplifies a new kind of ceremonial art certainly created under official auspices. It was devised some time in the fourth century, probably for the apse of a church, and we see it here adopted—quite late in the century—for an individual tomb. (It appears in other

FIG. 4. Sarcophagus. Miracles of Christ and scenes from life of St. Peter.
Museo Pio Cristiano, The Vatican, Rome (Photo: Vatican Museums)

FIG. 5. Sepulchral relief. *Traditio legis.*

The Metropolitan Museum of Art, New York, Gift of Ernest and Beata Brummer in memory of Joseph Brummer, 48.76.2 (Photo: The Metropolitan Museum of Art)

media as well, for instance, on glass vessels with decorations in gold leaf which are a characteristic product of this period.[13])

"Christ the Lawgiver" might still be thought of as a metaphor, comparable to Christ as Shepherd, Orphic musician or rising Sun. But the image now conjured up is that of the ruler of the world in all his majesty; and the message it carries is public and communal rather than private and personal. It has to do not with individual survival and redemption, but with the ordering of the universal polity, which has become the means and the guarantee of the individual's welfare. For the earthly world is now being governed on Christ's behalf. The Roman emperor has assumed the role of Christ's representative and rules in imitation of him. It is on the complete harmony and correspondence of the heavenly and the earthly regimens that salvation depends.[14] Quite logically, then, the ceremonial of the imperial court gets projected into heaven. If the emperor's rule mirrors that of Christ, the reverse must also be true. This is the thought underlying the *traditio legis* theme. Christ's celestial court is visualized in terms familiar to the Roman citizen—with subordinates acclaiming their overlord and receiving from him their charges and privileges. A famous silver dish in Madrid [Cat. no. 64][15] depicts an official receiving from Emperor Theodosius I the document of his appointment in much the same way that Peter receives the Law from Christ. The metaphor (if metaphor it may still be called) has thus been invested with a degree of reality that goes well beyond a mere "sign." The majes-

tic presence at the center of an elaborate multifigured composition *is* Christ in a sense that the shepherd boy carrying his sheep had not been.

Concomitantly, biblical history also becomes impersonal and objective. More and more, the events recorded in the Old and New Testaments are presented simply as history, rather than on grounds of immediate personal relevance. They are the enactment of the divine plan on which the Christian world order rests. Accordingly, stories from the Pentateuch, from the Gospels, from the Acts of the Apostles, and from apocryphal books as well are now often depicted in chronological order and in circumstantial detail. The biblical person, the hero, becomes an object of biographical interest.

I cite as an example a group of four ivory reliefs in the British Museum. The little panels that once were part of a box illustrate in sequence and in considerable detail the story of Christ's Passion and Resurrection (Fig. 6).[16] The subject first appeared in cyclical form on sarcophagi in the late or post-Constantinian period.[17] This fully developed cycle, which includes one of the earliest known nonsymbolic renderings of the Crucifixion, is of the first half of the fifth century. The story begins with Pilate washing his hands and ends with the incredulity of Thomas. The artist dwells on incidentals such as the brazier providing warmth in the scene of Peter's denial of Christ and the pieces of silver scattered on the ground beneath the tree on which Judas has hanged himself.

Cyclical narrative of this kind found a major application in the illustration of texts. Among illumi-

FIG. 6. Four panels of an ivory casket. Scenes of Christ's Passion and Resurrection.
British Museum, London (Photo: Hirmer Fotoarchiv)

nated biblical manuscripts of this period—all great rarities—I single out the Itala fragment from Quedlinburg, dating from the early decades of the fifth century (Fig. 7).[18] It is the earliest extant example of biblical book illumination, and an extraordinarily detailed illustration it is. The page I am showing illustrates in four scenes a sequence of only some twenty verses from a single chapter in the first Book of Samuel. The painter was directed to follow the text blow by blow, clearly with no other purpose than to bring it to life visually.

We have come a long way here from "signitive" art, in which biblical stories were reduced to shorthand ciphers, interchangeable with quite dissimilar subjects such as the Good Shepherd. Epic narration has become a distinct category in Christian art, as it had always been in Greco-Roman art.[19] There is, in fact, a close resemblance between the rendering of Old Testament episodes in the Quedlinburg miniatures and episodes from the *Aeneid* in a famous illustrated Vergil manuscript in the Vatican [Cat. no. 203].[20] It is possible that both were painted in the same atelier in Rome.

Christian art, then, was being normalized in Greco-Roman terms. Evolving, as it did, ceremonial scenes like the *traditio legis*, on the one hand, and extensive narrative cycles, on the other, it created its own equivalents of two age-old categories in the religious art of the pagans (as well as in Roman imperial art, which had long since assumed a quasi-religious status). Another major category of ancient art that also assumed a distinct and important role in Christian contexts in the course of the fourth century was portraiture (Fig. 8).[21] Simple, straightforward portrayal became a frequent means of honoring divine or holy persons. This was perhaps the most momentous development of all. More than the other categories of which I have spoken, the portrait involved an outright rejection of the "signitive" method. Lacking a specific message, the image became its own justification entirely. It was there simply to be beheld and contemplated. Ultimately, and perhaps inevitably, it would be worshiped.

One aspect of this expanding Christian art that an exhibition such as this cannot fully convey is its increasingly comprehensive and systematic character. On portable objects the imagery is often confined to just one of the several categories I have mentioned. It is in monumental art primarily, and above all in the pictorial decoration of churches, that one finds these categories combined and integrated. The walls of S. Apollinare Nuovo, King Theodoric's court church in Ravenna, which were decorated in mosaic about or soon after the year 500, may serve as an example (Fig. 9).[22] In its three registers, the decoration of these walls combines solemn ceremonial processions (originally of the king and his retinue, though these were later replaced by corteges of martyrs); a most impressive series of simple, statuesque portraits of holy persons (presumably Old Testament prophets); and finally, at the top, an extensive cycle of scenes of the life of Christ. The Christian world order is palpably and factually presented to the faithful both in its historical unfolding and in its present reality.

We turn to our third stage, which begins in the middle of the sixth century and lasts through the

FIG. 7. Quedlinburg Itala, Cod. theol. lat. fol. 485. Illustrations to the First Book of Samuel, chap. 10.

Staatsbibliothek, Berlin (Photo: after Degering-Boeckler)

FIG. 8. Marble statuette of Christ.

Museo Nazionale, Rome (Photo: Moscioni)

FIG. 9. S. Apollinare Nuovo, Ravenna. South wall of nave (Photo: Alinari)

seventh and into the eighth. One of its hallmarks is that large systematic programs such as those in the Ravenna church become scarce. Few comprehensive church decorations are known from this period. It is primarily an era of devotional images, of isolated and easily accessible panels, either in a fixed position on a church wall (Fig. 10)[23] or of a movable kind. In some ways the shift is comparable to that which was to take place later in Western art of the Middle Ages, particularly in the fourteenth century, when the great systems of cathedral decoration gave way to the altarpiece and the votive statue. The shift reflects a need for a more direct and intimate communication with the heavenly world. No longer is it sufficient for the beholder to perceive the image as a factual or

historical record, or as part of a self-contained system. It must serve him here and now. It must receive, and be responsive to, his appeals. It becomes a means of harnessing the heavenly powers to clear and present needs. This is the process I have in mind when I speak of "potentiation."

The reasons for so profound a change are bound to be complex. It cannot be adequately explained in terms of a single and direct cause-and-effect relation. Let us remind ourselves, however, that the late sixth and seventh centuries were a period of mortal peril and convulsive change in the Mediterranean world. Successive invasions—Persian, Slavic, and Arabic—tore that world apart. In the face of multiple intrusions of unbelievers, there was an unprecedented need for Christians not only to assert their religious identity but also to secure divine help. The government itself assumed a leading role in this. Increasingly, in the stress of the times, it made use of religious images in a variety of secular contexts to proclaim the authority of Christ, the Virgin, and the saints over human affairs.[24]

One of the significant developments in the art of this period is a proliferation of simple, straightforward portraits of holy persons. Scholars may disa-

gree about the dating of this or that example. But unquestionably there was a marked overall increase in the making of images of this kind—and of portable ones in particular (Fig. 11).[25] As I indicated earlier, the portrait's true function is "representation" in the literal sense. It exists to make present that which is absent. It conveys no message and illustrates no story. Inactive itself, it is correspondingly receptive. A holy person represented in this manner is ready to accept homage and listen to pleas and—particu-

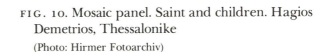

FIG. 10. Mosaic panel. Saint and children. Hagios Demetrios, Thessalonike

(Photo: Hirmer Fotoarchiv)

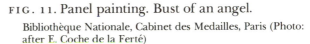

FIG. 11. Panel painting. Bust of an angel.

Bibliothèque Nationale, Cabinet des Medailles, Paris (Photo: after E. Coche de la Ferté)

FIG. 12. Apse mosaic. St. Agnes and papal donors.
Sant' Agnese fuori le mura, Rome (Photo: Anderson)

larly when the image is portable—may serve the votary in concrete situations of need.

From literary sources we know that well before the period we are now considering images of saints were expected to act vicariously on behalf of the saints themselves. We learn that in the fifth century pictures of St. Symeon Stylites were placed at the entrance of workshops in Rome to ward off evil.[26] But it is also clear from literary sources that the frequency and intensity of such practices increased greatly in the late sixth and seventh centuries.[27] The fact that simple portrayals of holy persons in portable form proliferated during this period is surely related to this phenomenon. Christ, the Virgin, the saints and, indeed, the angels became as familiar, as real, and as accessible in their portraits as a local bishop or abbot of saintly renown. Equally significant is the presentation of the saint, still and motionless, in monumental isolation as a central figure in the apse of the church that houses his or her burial. Portraits had always had special meaning in relation to tombs. In that context most particularly they conjure up a spiritual presence, a presence which gains a heightened degree of reality from the physical proximity of the body. When a saint's image is placed in a central position over the altar of his or her tomb church, as was done by Pope Honorius I (625–38) in Sant' Agnese in Rome (Fig. 12),[28] these inherent powers of the funerary portrait are brought fully into play. The image presides over the holy rites. The saint is palpably present to serve the faithful as a conduit to the heavenly world.

It was not only in simple portrayals, however, that this enhanced role, this new centrality of the image in religious life, manifested itself. The development affected the narrative category as well. I propose to discuss this aspect in somewhat more detail.

Once again, I can draw on the riches of this exhi-

FIG. 13, a–d. Gold marriage ring. Scenes from the life of Christ.
Dumbarton Oaks Collection, Washington, D.C. (Photo: Dumbarton Oaks)

bition. From Dumbarton Oaks comes a heavy ring in solid gold and niello, one of several such rings made in the seventh century, evidently for well-to-do people (Fig. 13).[29] On the bezel, a husband and wife are represented with Christ and the Virgin blessing them. The word *omonia* ("Concord") is inscribed below. On the other seven facets of the octagonal hoop are seven tiny scenes representing events from the life of Christ, beginning with the Annunciation and ending with his appearance to the women after his Resurrection. To say that the events are "represented" really overstates the case. Each scene is reduced to a formula recognizable only to those who already know the iconography. We are back here to ciphers and pictographs. But these ciphers, unlike those of the third century, make a single sequence, a complete life of Christ, whose help for the wearer is invoked in an inscription on the edge of the bezel.

There is no doubt that the life of Christ is here recited as a charm. It is worn around the finger as a protection. Octagonal rings in themselves were credited with beneficent properties.[30] That the cycle of Christ's life has acquired the role of an amulet is proved conclusively by another group of personal

FIG. 14, a–b. Silver bracelet. Scenes from the life of Christ and apotropaic emblems.
Egyptian Museum, Cairo (Photo: after J. Maspero)

ornaments of the same period (not represented in the exhibition), namely, silver bracelets with a sequence of formulaic scenes very similar to those on our ring. The cycle begins with the Annunciation and ends with the Ascension, and is here interspersed with patently apotropaic devices (Fig. 14).[31]

Essentially the same cycle was also represented on a number of objects that pilgrims in the late sixth and early seventh centuries acquired on visits to the holy sites in Palestine. Prominent among such objects are little lead flasks filled with oil from the lamps that burned at Christianity's most sacred shrines. Some of these flasks are adorned with a sequence of seven (or in one case nine) scenes neatly arranged in a pattern of medallions. The scenes epitomize the life of Christ through practically the same major events that we found represented on the rings and bracelets (Fig. 15).[32] The pilgrim himself has trodden the ground where these events had taken place. The images thus relate to an intensely concrete and personal experience. It is from this, not from any elaborate rendering, that they derive their "reality." At the same time, a protective element is

FIG. 15. Pilgrims' ampulla. Scenes from the life of Christ.

Cathedral Treasury, Monza (Photo: after A. Grabar)

present as well. Some of the flasks bear inscriptions invoking divine assistance and could be—and clearly were—worn around the neck as amulets [Cat. nos. 525–26].[33]

These cycles are a far cry from the epic narrative that simply records and evokes past history. This is sacred history powerfully and palpably related to the here and now in terms of the beholder's—or should one say user's?—experiences and needs. The image serves as a link with the divine presence along with the hallowed oil inside these flasks. Completeness of the cycle evidently was important in this connection. The story, however abridged, must go from the beginning to the end of Christ's life. And it must be presented as a closed ring or a self-contained pattern.

There is no precedent in earlier Christian art for a picture cycle so conceived and thus charged. It is an innovation of the late and post-Justinianic age. On the other hand—and this should be noted at least in passing—there are threads that lead from these cycles to the so-called feast cycle that was to become an important element in Byzantine art of later centuries. The limits of the validity of that term need not concern us here. Unquestionably, there was in mature Byzantine art a core sequence of scenes that encompassed the life of Christ and was intimately tied to the liturgy.[34] It is also undeniable that between our cycles and this standard set of later times there are connecting links.[35] In other words, at a certain point in the history of these cycles the emphasis shifted from the reality of the holy sites to the reality of the liturgy in which Christ's life was reenacted and in which every believer was a participant. In either case the cycle was actualized in terms of personal experience.

The emergence of the closed or patterned cycle can thus be seen to have great long-range significance. But individual scenes from Christ's life were similarly "recharged" in the course of the sixth century. The majority of the little oil flasks from the Holy Land are adorned not with complete cycles but with selected single scenes that carried associations with specific places the pilgrim had visited—the site of the Nativity at Bethlehem, the site of the Crucifixion on Golgotha, the Holy Sepulcher adjacent to it; and most of these representations are not purely historical. There are anachronisms, such as pilgrims genuflecting at the foot of Christ's cross in the Crucifixion, or the architecture of the Church of the Holy Sepulcher providing the setting for the Marys' encounter with the angel (Fig. 16).[36] Although topographic references of this kind are not unknown in

FIG. 16, a–b. Pilgrims' ampulla. Crucifixion (obverse) and Holy Women at the Tomb (reverse).

Dumbarton Oaks Collection, Washington, D.C. (Photo: Dumbarton Oaks)

earlier Christian art, they became prominent only in the period that concerns us.[37] Clearly they served as a means of relating the events depicted to the here and now.

On the famous eucharistic paten from Riha, a work of the period of Justin II (565–78), a comparable result was achieved by means of the liturgy (Fig. 17).[38] Liturgical references again are nothing new in Christian iconography. But on the Riha paten the liturgical interpretation of a biblical event has been carried very far indeed. The Last Supper has become a Communion of the Apostles with Christ officiating as the priest administering the sacraments. He is represented twice—dispensing the bread to six of his disciples and the wine to the other six. The action he performs was, of course, profoundly

FIG. 17. Silver paten from Riha. Communion of the Apostles.

Dumbarton Oaks Collection, Washington, D.C. (Photo: Dumbarton Oaks)

FIG. 18. Transfiguration mosaic.

St. Catherine's Monastery, Sinai (Photo: Courtesy of Alexandria, Michigan, Princeton Expedition to Mt. Sinai)

real and familiar to every communicant. Seeing it represented on the plate from which he himself received the host, the communicant must indeed have felt the past merging with the present. In all probability, the scene was not originally devised for a liturgical vessel. It has numerous parallels in later apse mosaics and frescoes; and the suggestion has been made that its prototype was a monumental painting in the Church of Holy Sion in Jerusalem, where pilgrims of this period were shown the very room of the Last Supper.[39] It is possible, therefore, that the image on the paten was charged with topographical as well as liturgical actuality.

In the apse mosaic of the church of St. Catherine's Monastery at Mount Sinai (Fig. 18),[40] executed late in Justinian's reign, we have an actual example of a Gospel scene thus monumentally displayed at a *locus sanctus* and acquiring special power from its local association. The subject here is the Transfiguration, an

event in which Moses was a prime participant. It is he, of course, who provides the local link. We are at the very site where God had revealed himself to Moses—two subsidiary mosaic panels on the wall above the apse represent these earlier theophanies recorded in the Book of Exodus—and in the Transfiguration he was a witness to the divinity of Christ. Placed before us in this particular spot, the scene acquires an extra dimension of reality.

Events from the Gospels and the life of Christ came to be singled out elsewhere in church decorations during our period; and the connection with the here and now of the beholder's experience is not always as self-evident as it is in the case of the Sinai mosaic. In Sta. Maria Antiqua in Rome, for instance, one finds side by side with clearly devotional images of saints (which, as I said earlier, are a characteristic phenomenon of the period) self-contained panels depicting events such as the Annunciation and

Christ's Descent into Hell.[41] So far as the Annunciation is concerned, the explanation may not be far to seek. We are, after all, in a church dedicated to the Virgin, and the choice of this scene may have been dictated simply by devotion to her. In the case of the Descent into Hell, however, the motivation is not so clear.[42] And the elaborately framed and clearly self-contained mosaic panel with Christ's Presentation in the Temple discovered some years ago in Istanbul poses a similar problem (Fig. 19).[43] The mosaic, which is certainly a work of the period before iconoclasm, was in an accessible position in the sanctuary area of a church of unknown dedication. In later Byzantine art such panels—whether fixed or movable—would be called feast icons. The reference, in other words, would be liturgical. But to relate this mosaic specifically to the feast of the Hypapante on February 2nd—or those Roman frescoes of the Descent into Hell to the celebration of Easter—could well be an unwarranted anticipation of a development belonging to a subsequent age. The problem that lurks here is of some importance for the very reason that the single New Testament scene was to have a considerable future in Byzantine art. Given their context (or, if you will, lack of context), panels such as these are likely to have their *raison d'être* in some specific element relating them to the beholder's world. But for the moment, at least, the nature of this experiential reference remains in doubt.

I shall close my discussion of "potentiated" narrative scenes with one more object from the exhibition—the beautiful enamel staurotheca that once belonged to the Fieschi family in Genoa and came to the Metropolitan Museum with the Morgan collection (Fig. 20).[44] While the date of its manufacture may well be somewhat beyond the avowed chronological limits of the show, the Fieschi-Morgan reliquary is an extraordinarily telling example of the development I have described. It is a container for a relic of the True Cross; and the Crucifixion scene displayed on its sliding lid acquires special weight and heightened reality from its physical association with that relic. But on the inside of the lid—visible only to him who is privileged to open the box—are four more scenes, engraved in niello, and one of them is the Crucifixion again, in a rendering very similar to that on the outside. The repetition seems puzzling, the more so since there is no reason to doubt that the niello work is part of the original design. But I think it becomes intelligible in the light of what we saw earlier about cyclical illustrations of Christ's life on rings, bracelets, and pilgrims' flasks. Brief as this particular cycle is, it is an epitome of that life in its entirety—from the Annunciation to the Anastasis. While the image on the outside refers to the relic enshrined in the box (bringing that relic to life and in turn being energized by it), the cycle on the inside is protective and apotropaic.[45] Images thus appear in two different functions on the same object, and these functions are clearly differentiated by technique, scale, and degree of visibility. In addition, the decoration comprises a large number of tiny busts of saints, all with their names inscribed. There are fourteen such busts framing the Crucifixion on the outside and the same number again on the edges. It has long been recognized that they constitute a litany, a prayer of intercession in pictorial form.[46] In effect, then, this small and exquisitely wrought object brings into play all three of the realms that in our third period became important in relating religious images to the beholder's own experience—the realm of relics, the realm of charms and apotropaia, and the realm of prayer and ritual.

FIG. 19. Mosaic. Presentation of Christ in the Temple.

Kalenderhane Djami, Istanbul (Photo: George E. Thomas, Kalenderhane Archaeological Project)

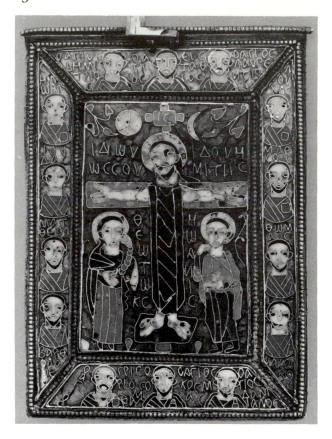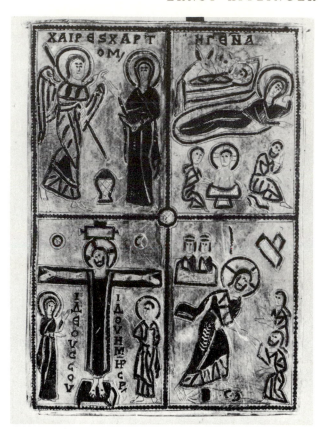

FIG. 20, a–b. Reliquary for fragment of the True Cross: a. top, showing sliding lid with Crucifixion and busts of saints in enamel; b. inside of lid, with scenes from the life of Christ in niello.

The Metropolitan Museum of Art, New York, Gift of J. Pierpont Morgan, 17.190.715 (Photo: The Metropolitan Museum of Art)

All of these factors—let me stress this once more—had played a role in earlier Christian art. But there is no doubt that they came to the fore with unprecedented strength during the last of our three stages; and quite often more than one of them became operative in the same image or object simultaneously. What they all had in common was that they involved the divine presence in the here and now. That presence was palpably experienced in relics, tombs, and holy sites which literally put the faithful in touch with the persons and the events that had made redemption a reality; it was similarly experienced in the liturgy in which God's redemptive work was reenacted; and it was experienced by sheer intensity of desire in every ardent act of prayer or invocation. To whichever of these experiences the image was related, it ceased to be merely a record, an objective statement, and became a conduit or receptacle of divine power. Quite evidently, visual form was felt to have special properties which enabled it to hold or attract that power.

I called this paper "Christian Imagery: Growth and Impact." I hope I have succeeded in giving some idea of the extraordinary process whereby Christian imagery grew—from its signitive beginnings in the third century to its stage of potency in the seventh. I have left myself little time to speak about its impact on subsequent developments. But what I want to say on this score can be said very quickly.

In my introduction, I spoke of the eighth century as a turning point in the history of Western art. In trying to evaluate the momentous new departures of that time, it is important to bear in mind what the image had then become in Christian society. The image of which the Byzantine government of Leo III and Constantine V made such a burning issue was not the image of the catacombs, nor even that of the great mosaic systems we know from Ravenna. It was the potent image of our third stage. And it was this same image that confronted the newly acculturated Moslems and the newly converted peoples of northern Europe.

FIG. 21. Wall mosaic with architectural landscape.
Great Mosque, Damascus (Photo: Courtesy of O. Grabar)

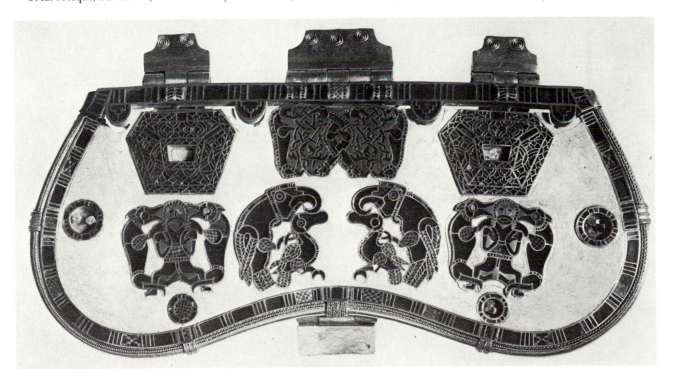

FIG. 22. Purse-lid with inlaid ornaments, from the Sutton Hoo ship burial.
British Museum, London (Photo: British Museum)

FIG. 23. Gilt-bronze plaque with Crucifixion, found at Athlone.

National Museum of Ireland, Dublin (Photo: National Museum of Ireland)

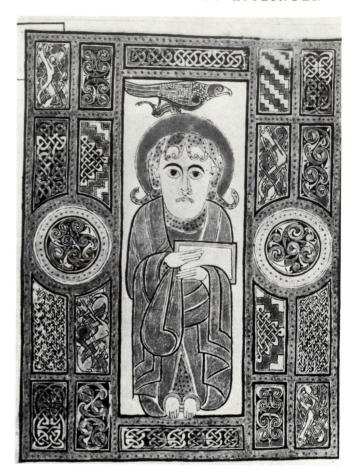

FIG. 24. St. John the Evangelist.

Stiftsbibliothek, St. Gall, Cod. 51 (Photo: after Duft and Meyer

Byzantine iconoclasm[47] is an unintelligible phenomenon if it is not viewed in the light of what had happened in the sphere of religious images in the preceding age. Iconoclasm constituted a reversal of the imperial government's own previous policy, and no doubt there were good reasons for this reversal. Other issues, especially social and economic ones, may well have been involved; and at a certain point doctrinal and specifically Christological questions became important. But the image and its function in society was and remained central to the controversy. Ultimately, however, iconoclasm was only an interlude. Byzantine art of the ninth and tenth centuries is often thought of in terms of an entirely fresh start. Actually, much of it was a restoration of the *status quo*; and this involved a reattachment to our third stage. To what extent the role of the religious image in Byzantine society was tempered by the iconoclas-

tic crisis is an interesting question. Officially, at least, the image was never again credited with quite the potency that it had attained in the seventh century. But it certainly regained a central role in religious life.[48]

The Moslems, on the other hand, rejected the image, at least in the religious sphere, for good and all. Whatever their attitude to representational art in general, they settled a potentially sensitive issue by eschewing altogether the representation of animate beings in religious and, more broadly, in official contexts.[49] It is the monuments rather than the texts that speak most loudly and clearly. I have in mind the pointedly nonfigural coins of the Umayyad caliphs and the great mosaic decorations of the Umayyad mosques, in which representation is limited to inanimate objects (Fig. 21).[50] The very fact that these monuments depended heavily on Byzantine antecedents (to say nothing of Byzantine skills and materials used in their production) suggests that the Christian experience had a great deal to do with shaping the Moslem attitude. Potentiation, then, had as negative an effect here as in Byzantium itself in the eighth century. Byzantine iconoclasm and Moslem nonfigural art are two reactions to the same phenomenon, whether or not the former was actually influenced by the latter, which is an eternally controversial question.

As for the peoples of the far North, the situation there was very different. Images came with the conversion to Christianity; and, whatever the role that the ecclesiastic leadership may have envisioned for them in the life of the newly established churches, there was fertile ground there for the potent image. The Germanic peoples had an artistic tradition of their own going back many centuries, a tradition bound up with the decoration of their weapons,

FIG. 25. Fifth-century ivory plaque. Detail of Christ healing the paralytic and the man possessed.

Musée du Louvre, Paris (Photo: Hirmer Fotoarchiv)

FIG. 26. Carolingian ivory plaque. Detail of Christ healing the paralytic and the man possessed.

Bodleian Library, Oxford (Photo: Münchow)

utensils, and personal ornaments (Fig. 22); and, although we tend to consider this rich and intricate repertory of forms as being indeed just "ornament," there is no doubt that much of it was, in fact, protective and amuletic and was credited with beneficent powers.[51] These northern peoples, therefore, were predisposed to endow the image with a role comparable to that which it had slowly and gradually assumed in the life of Mediterranean Christendom during the sixth and seventh centuries. This explains the speed and ease with which the seemingly alien art brought by the missionaries was absorbed and assimilated by Germanic and Celtic craftsmen (Fig. 23).[52] Christian imagery was not turned into "ornament." Rather, it was invested with the same powers that spirals, knot-work, and zoomorphic interlace had possessed all along. It was integrated into the repertory of potent signs, to which it added a new force and a new, quite specific content. There is a literary counterpart to this in an author such as the Venerable Bede, for whom prayer and devotional practice were very much a matter of keeping Satan and unclean spirits at bay.[53] Thanks to these deeply ingrained attitudes and traditions, Christian artists in the North very rapidly evolved visual forms more fully adequate to the notion of the potent religious image than anything ever achieved by their brethren in the Mediterranean world. It was in the British Isles in the eighth century that the potent image received its fullest aesthetic realization (Fig. 24).[54]

There was, however, in the transalpine North, a formidable reaction, and that reaction came with Charlemagne. His was an era of enlightenment. The cultural program that he and his advisers instituted and pursued so vigorously and systematically was predicated on a firm belief in the power of knowledge and the importance of education.[55] Thus, it is not surprising that in matters of art they turned back to our second stage with its emphasis on recording, on explication, and on straight historical narrative. With diligence and purposefulness, craftsmen were directed to school themselves on works of the fourth and fifth centuries (Figs. 25, 26).[56] The corresponding policy statement may be found in the *Libri Carolini*, an official treatise on the subject of images written at the behest of Charlemagne himself. However dubious the political motivation of that document and however muddled its content, it amounts to an indictment of the potent image and its role in religious practice. Works of art were "removed from the realm of the 'numinous'."[57] What Charlemagne and his advisers proclaimed was the commemorative and didactic, as well as the decorative, function of pictorial art. As a result of this Carolingian reaction, the scope and range of Northern pictorial art were enormously and lastingly expanded. With the spell of potency broken, the medieval West was ready to enter into the fullness of the Mediterranean artistic heritage—a fullness superbly displayed in this exhibition.[58]

NOTES

1. Since this lecture was written two articles have appeared that challenge the proposition that in the period about A. D. 200 a major change occurred in the Christian attitude toward the visual arts as an element of religious life: P. C. Finney, "Antecedents of Byzantine Iconoclasm," *The Image and the Word*, J. Gutmann, ed., Missoula, Montana, 1977, pp. 27–47; Sister Charles Murray, "Art and the Early Church," *Journal of Theological Studies*, N.S. XXVIII, 1977, pp. 303–45. This is not the place to take issue with these studies. The principal evidence on which my statements rest is summarized very briefly in my recent book, *Byzantine Art in the Making*, London, 1977, pp. 19–20, and notes 31–33.

2. Cat. no. 462. F. W. Deichmann, G. Boivini, and H. Brandenburg, *Repertorium der christlich-antiken Sarkophage*, I, Wiesbaden, 1967, pp. 62–63, no. 66, and pl. 21.

3. T. Klauser, in his "Studien zur Entstehungsgeschichte der christlichen Kunst," has provided a healthy

corrective to a tendency, rife at times in earlier scholarship, to interpret in Christian terms any and all *kriophoroi* in Late Antique art. See, especially, *Jahrbuch für Antike und Christentum*, VIII–IX, 1965–66, pp. 126–70, and X, 1967, pp. 82–120 (with references to his earlier articles). But undoubtedly he went much too far. For a more balanced view, see H. Brandenburg, *Überlegungen zum Ursprung der frühchristlichen Bildkunst*, IX Congreso Internazionale di Archeologia Cristiana, Rome, 1975, p. 11.

4. W. Weidlé, *The Baptism of Art. . .* , Westminster, n.d., pp. 10–11.

5. For Orpheus as a motif in Early Christian funerary art, see the paper by G. M. A. Hanfmann above, pp. 87–88. Christ-Helios is the central theme of a well-known mosaic that adorns the ceiling of a small mausoleum in the necropolis beneath St. Peter's in Rome [Cat. no. 467]. See A. Grabar, *Le premier art chrétien*, Paris, 1966, p. 80, fig. 74. Cf. E. H. Kantorowicz, "Oriens Augusti—Lever du Roi,"

Dumbarton Oaks Papers, XVII, 1963, pp. 117–77, esp. pp. 143–45 and fig. 30.

6. See T. Klauser, "Studien zur Entstehungsgeschichte der christlichen Kunst, IV," *Jahrbuch für Antike und Christentum*, 1961, pp. 128–34. H. Brandenburg, *Überlegungen*, pp. 5–8.

7. See the statistics given by T. Klauser, "Studien . . . , IV," p. 133. For the ceiling decoration with the story of Jonah illustrated in fig. 2, see G. P. Kirsch, "Un gruppo di cripte dipinte inedite del Cimitero dei Ss. Pietro e Marcellino," *Rivista di Archeologia Cristiana*, VII, 1930, pp. 203–34, esp. pp. 226–32.

8. J. Wilpert, *Roma sotterranea: Le pitture delle catacombe romane*, Rome, 1903, pl. 25.

9. See, for example, G. M. A. Hanfmann, *Roman Art*, Greenwich, Conn., n.d., pp. 107 and 195 (basilica under Porta Maggiore, Rome).

10. Cat. no. 374. E. Kitzinger, *Byzantine Art in the Making*, pp. 22–24. For the sarcophagus illustrated in Fig. 4, see F. W. Deichmann et al., *Repertorium der christlich-antiken Sarkophage*, pp. 6–7, no. 6, and pl. 2.

11. Cat. no. 502. B. Brenk, "Ein Scheinsarkophag im Metropolitan Museum in New York," *Kolloquium über spätantike und frühmittelalterliche Skulptur*, II, Mainz, 1971, pp. 43–53.

12. C. Davis-Weyer, "Das Traditio-Legis-Bild und seine Nachfolge," *Münchner Jahrbuch der bildenden Kunst*, XII, 1961, pp. 7–45.

13. Ibid., p. 12. Cat. no. 503.

14. See, in particular, a famous passage in chapter 2 of Eusebius' oration on the Tricennalia of Constantine in A.D. 336 (*Eusebius. Werke*, I, I.A. Heikel, ed., Leipzig, 1902, p. 199); cf. F. Dvornik, *Early Christian and Byzantine Political Philosophy*, Washington, D.C., 1966, II, pp. 616–18, with English translation.

15. E. Kitzinger, *Byzantine Art in the Making*, pp. 31–32 and figs. 57–59.

16. Cat. no. 452. W. F. Volbach, *Elfenbeinarbeiten der Spätantike und des frühen Mittelalters*, 3rd ed., Mainz, 1976, pp. 82–83, no. 116, and pl. 61.

17. E. Kitzinger, *Byzantine Art in the Making*, p. 26 and fig. 44.

18. Cat. no. 424. H. Degering and A. Boeckler, *Die Quedlinburger Italafragmente*, Berlin, 1932. K. Weitzmann, *Late Antique and Early Christian Book Illumination*, New York, 1977, pp. 40–41.

19. See the chapter "The Historical Scene" in A. Grabar's *Christian Iconography*, Princeton, 1966, pp. 87–106.

20. J. de Wit, *Die Miniaturen des Vergilius Vaticanus*, Amsterdam, 1959.

21. Cat. no. 469. See, in general, A. Grabar, *Christian Iconography*, pp. 60–86. For the marble statuette of Christ in the National Museum in Rome, illustrated in Figure 8, see F. Gerke, *Christus in der spätantiken Plastik*, Mainz, 1948, pp. 38, 97, and figs. 56–59.

22. F. W. Deichmann, *Ravenna. Hauptstadt des spätantiken Abendlandes*, I, *Geschichte und Monumente*, Wiesbaden, 1969, pp. 171–200; II, *Kommentar*, 1, Wiesbaden, 1974, pp. 125–89; III, *Frühchristliche Bauten und Mosaiken von Ravenna*, 2nd ed., Wiesbaden, n.d., pls. IV–VII, pp. 98–213.

23. Cat. no. 500. For the mosaics on the chancel piers of Hagios Demetrios in Thessalonike (Fig. 10), which are outstanding examples of this category, see E. Kitzinger, *Byzantine Art in the Making*, pp. 105–06, with note 19, and figs. 189, 190.

24. E. Kitzinger, "The Cult of Images in the Age before Iconoclasm," *Dumbarton Oaks Papers*, VIII, 1954, pp. 83–150, esp. pp. 110–12 and 121–28. See also the postscript accompanying the reprint of this article in E. Kitzinger, *The Art of Byzantium and the Medieval West*, W. E. Kleinbauer, ed., Bloomington and London, 1976, pp. 390–91. Also, A. Cameron's recent work on Corippus' *In laudem Iustini*, especially the comments on pp. 150–51 of her edition of the poem, London, 1976.

25. Cat. no. 483. See, especially, some of the early encaustic icons in the Sinai Monastery, now splendidly published by K. Weitzmann, *The Monastery of Saint Catherine at Mount Sinai. The Icons*, I, Princeton, 1976, pls. 1–2, 8–10, 11, 12, 14, 15, 17, etc. My own view concerning the dates of certain of these icons differs somewhat from Professor Weitzmann's. See my *Byzantine Art in the Making*, pp. 117–18 and 120–21. For "portrait" icons in general, see E. Kitzinger, "On Some Icons of the Seventh Century," *Late Classical and Mediaeval Studies in Honor of Albert Mathias Friend, Jr.*, Princeton, 1955, pp. 132–50, esp. pp. 143–44. See also the postscript accompanying the reprint of this article in *The Art of Byzantium and the Medieval West*, p. 393. The panel with the bust of an archangel illustrated in Figure 11 was published by K. Parlasca, *Mumienporträts und verwandte Denkmäler*, Wiesbaden, 1966, p. 210 and pl. 53,2.

26. E. Kitzinger, "The Cult of Images," p. 94, note 32.

27. Ibid., *passim*.

28. E. Kitzinger, *Byzantine Art in the Making*, pp. 103–04, and fig. 187.

29. Cat. no. 446. M. C. Ross, *Catalogue of the Byzantine and Early Mediaeval Antiquities in the Dumbarton Oaks Collection*, II, Washington, D.C., 1965, pp. 58–59 and pls. E, 43, 44.

30. Alexander of Tralles, a sixth-century physician, recommended the wearing of an octagonal ring, appropriately inscribed, as a remedy for colic. Cf. G. Schlumberger, "Amulettes byzantins anciens destinés à combattre les maléfices et maladies," *Revue des études grecques*, V, 1892, pp. 73–93, esp. p. 87.

31. J. Maspero, "Bracelets-amulettes d'époque byzantine," *Annales du service des antiquités de l'Égypte*, IX, 1908, pp. 246–58 and figs. 1, 2 (at end of volume).

32. A. Grabar, *Les ampoules de Terre Sainte*, Paris, 1958, pp. 18–20, 40–43 and pls. 5–7, 46, 47–49, 50–52.

33. J. Engemann, "Palästinensische Pilgerampullen im F.J. Dölger-Institut in Bonn," *Jahrbuch für Antike und Christentum*, XVI, 1973, pp. 5–27, esp. pp. 12–13.

34. For the feast cycle, see K. Weitzmann, "Byzantine Miniature and Icon Painting in the Eleventh Century," *The Proceedings of the XIIIth International Congress of Byzantine Studies, Oxford, 5–10 September 1966*, London, 1967, pp. 207–24. I cite this article after the reprint in K. Weitzmann, *Studies in Classical and Byzantine Manuscript Illumination*, Chicago and London, 1971, pp. 271–313, esp. pp. 292–93. Cf. also idem, *Catalogue of the Byzantine and Early Mediaeval Antiquities in the Dumbarton Oaks Collection*, III, Washington, D.C., 1972, pp. 45–47. The term "feast cycle" tends to be used too freely, particularly in relation to the sequence of scenes from the life of Christ in Byzantine church decorations of the eleventh and twelfth centuries. Nevertheless, these monumental cycles are also "liturgical," as A. Grabar has pointed out in "Un rouleau liturgique constantinopolitain et ses peintures," *Dumbarton Oaks Papers*, VIII, 1954, pp. 161–99, esp. pp. 189–90.

35. I have in mind particularly sequences of scenes such as those on the silver cross in the Pieve of Vicopisano—see E. Lucchesi Palli, "Der syrisch-palästinensische Darstellungstypus der Höllenfahrt Christi," *Römische Quartalschrift*, LVII, 1962, pp. 250–67, esp. pp. 256–62 and pls. 18b, 19a—and the small gold cross discovered in 1973 at Pliska, for which see L. Dontcheva, "Une croix pectorale—reliquaire en or récemment trouvée à Pliska," *Cahiers archéologiques*, XXV, 1976, pp. 59–66; for the date, see below note 44. Both these objects combine the function of a reliquary with that of a personal ornament of an amuletic kind. Both are adorned with series of scenes that correspond largely to those of the pilgrims' ampullae but with significant changes. The Visitation and the Women's Visit to the Sepulcher have been dropped in favor of the Presentation in the Temple and the Descent into Hell. In addition, the Pliska cross shows the Transfiguration. All three of these scenes were to become part of the normal liturgical cycle of the life of Christ in mature Byzantine art. For the staurotheca in the Metropolitan Museum, whose iconography is likewise transitional in this sense, see below pp. 155–56 and note 44. See also note 45 for the reliquary box from the Sancta Sanctorum that is adorned with a patterned cycle of scenes corresponding exactly to those on the ampullae (Cat. Fig. 76). As K. Weitzmann has pointed out, here, too, we have a preliminary stage "of what, in the

Middle Byzantine period, was to become the widespread collective icon with the twelve major feasts of the Orthodox Church" ("*Loca Sancta* and the Arts of Palestine," *Dumbarton Oaks Papers*, XXVIII, 1974, pp. 31–55, esp. p. 45).

36. Cat. no. 524. M. C. Ross, *Catalogue of the Byzantine and Early Mediaeval Antiquities in the Dumbarton Oaks Collection*, I, Washington, D.C., 1962, pp. 71–72 and pl. 48.

37. See, in general, K. Weitzmann, "*Loca Sancta* and the Arts of Palestine."

38. Cat. no. 547. M. C. Ross, *Catalogue . . . Dumbarton Oaks Collection*, I, pp. 12–15 and pls. 11–13.

39. W. C. Loerke, "The Monumental Miniature," in K. Weitzmann et al., *The Place of Book Illumination in Byzantine Art*, Princeton, 1975, pp. 61–97, esp. pp. 94–95.

40. G. H. Forsyth and K. Weitzmann, *The Monastery of Saint Catherine at Mount Sinai. The Church and Fortress of Justinian*, Ann Arbor, n.d. [1973], pp. 11–16 and pls. 103–28, 136–86.

41. P. Romanelli and P. J. Nordhagen, *S. Maria Antiqua*, Rome, 1964, pls. 20, 21, 30, 31, 32, 34, and 35.

42. On this problem see P. J. Nordhagen, "Kristus i Dødsriket," *Kunst og Kultur*, LVII, 1974, pp. 165–74.

43. C. L. Striker and Y. D. Kuban, "Work at Kalenderhane Camii in Istanbul. Third and Fourth Preliminary Reports," *Dumbarton Oaks Papers*, XXV, 1971, pp. 251–58, esp. pp. 255–56 and fig. 11. Cf. also ibid., XXIX, 1975, pp. 312–13 and fig. 10. E. Kitzinger, *Byzantine Art in the Making*, pp. 115–16 and fig. 206.

44. Cat. no. 574. M. Rosenberg, *Geschichte der Goldschmiedekunst auf technischer Grundlage: Zellenschmelz*, III, Frankfurt a. M., 1922, pp. 31–38. Idem, *Niello bis zum Jahre 1000 nach Chr.*, Frankfurt a.M., 1924, pp. 61–67. Rosenberg's attribution of the reliquary to the period ca. 700, with Jerusalem as a likely place of origin, has been widely accepted. A. Frolow, however, argued for a date ca. 1000 in *La relique de la vraie croix*, Paris, 1961, pp. 249–50. While so late a date is not plausible, the date proposed by Rosenberg may indeed be too early. The four scenes engraved in niello on the inside of the lid are very similar to the corresponding scenes on the Vicopisano and Pliska crosses (for which see above, note 35). The similarity in the rendering of the Descent into Hell is particularly striking. Now the Pliska cross is said to have been found in an archaeological stratum that belongs to the ninth or tenth century (L. Dontcheva, "Une croix pectorale—reliquaire," p. 66). One must hope for a detailed publication of the stratigraphical data associated with this important find.

45. For the placing of a pictorial epitome of the life of Christ on the inside of a lid of a receptacle for relics, there is an interesting precedent in the wooden box from the Sancta Sanctorum in the Museo Sacro of the Vatican, previously referred to in note 35 (C. R. Morey, "The Painted

Panel from the Sancta Sanctorum," *Festschrift zum sechzig-sten Geburtstag von Paul Clemen, 31.Oktober 1926*, Düsseldorf and Bonn, 1926, pp. 151–67). Five scenes, from the Nativity to the Ascension, are here displayed in a patterned arrangement, while the outside of the lid is adorned with a cross. Generally attributed to the second half of the sixth century, the Vatican reliquary is certainly a good deal older than the staurotheca in the Metropolitan Museum. See, most recently, K. Weitzmann, "*Loca Sancta* and the Arts of Palestine," p. 35 and *passim*.

46. M. Rosenberg, *Zellenschmelz*, III, pp. 34–38.

47. For a recent summary of the sequence of events, see the historical introduction by C. Mango in *Iconoclasm*, A. Bryer and J. Herrin, eds., Birmingham, 1977, pp. 1–6.

48. See—despite its unpromising title—H.-G. Beck's study *Von der Fragwürdigkeit der Ikone*, Munich, 1975 (Sitzungsberichte der Bayerischen Akademie der Wissenschaften, philosophisch-historische Klasse, fasc. 7). The author rightly points out that the icon never became an integral, let alone an essential, part of the Byzantine liturgy (p. 33). But he also stresses its renewed importance in Byzantine religious life in the centuries after iconoclasm (cf. pp. 28, 35, and *passim*). If no writer of these later centuries, when dealing with the subject of images, mustered the fervor of a John of Damascus or a Theodore of Studios, this is not surprising. At all times the theoretical defense of images was a function of attacks upon them. Cf. E. Kitzinger, "The Cult of Images," pp. 86–87.

49. O. Grabar, *The Formation of Islamic Art*, New Haven and London, 1973, p. 91 and *passim*. Also, the same author's "Islam and Iconoclasm" in *Iconoclasm*, A. Bryer and J. Herrin, eds., pp. 45–52, esp. p. 47.

50. For the mosaics of the mosque at Damascus (Fig. 21), see O. Grabar, *The Formation of Islamic Art*, pp. 92–93 and 131–34; for the coinage, pp. 94–96.

51. H. Vierck, "Ein Relieffibelpaar aus Nordendorf in Bayerisch Schwaben: Zur Ikonographie des germanischen Tierstils I," *Bayerische Vorgeschichtsblätter*, XXXII, 1967, pp. 104–43. G. Haseloff, "Goldbrakteaten-Goldblattkreuze," *Neue Ausgrabungen und Forschungen in Niedersachsen*, V, 1970, pp. 24–39. For the purse lid from the Sutton Hoo ship burial (Fig. 22), see R. L. S. Bruce-Mitford, *The Sutton Hoo Ship-Burial: A Handbook*, London, 1968, pp. 63–64 and pl. C.

52. For the openwork plaque with the Crucifixion, found in Athlone (Fig. 23), probably a work of the eighth century,

see F. Henry, *Irish Art in the Early Christian Period (to 800 A.D.)*, Ithaca, New York, 1966, p. 114 and pls. 46, 48.

53. *Epistola Bede ad Ecgbertum Episcopum*, 5. 15, in *Venerabilis Baedae opera historica*, C. Plummer, ed., Oxford, 1896, I, pp. 408–09 and 418–19.

54. The figures of the evangelists in Ms. 51 in the library of St. Gall (Fig. 24) are outstanding representatives of this achievement. For this Gospel book of ca. 750, see J. Duft and P. Meyer, *Die irischen Miniaturen der Stiftsbibliothek St. Gallen*, Olten, Bern, and Lausanne, 1953, pp. 69–71, 87–101 and pls. 1–14, 20–25. The art exemplified by the St. Gall evangelists can be seen *in statu nascendi* in the carvings on the coffin reliquary of St. Cuthbert in Durham (698), carvings that at the same time testify to the magic function of such imagery in the Hiberno-Saxon world. See E. Kitzinger, "The Coffin-Reliquary," in *The Relics of Saint Cuthbert*, C. F. Battiscombe, ed., Oxford, 1956, pp. 202–304, esp. pp. 279–80 and 303–04. Cf. also W. Koehler, *Buchmalerei des frühen Mittelalters*, E. Kitzinger and F. Mütherich, eds., Munich, 1972, pp. 69–73 and, more generally, pp. 7–8.

55. *Karl der Grosse II: Das geistige Leben*, B. Bischoff, ed., Düsseldorf, 1965; see especially W. von den Steinen's introductory essay, "Der Neubeginn," pp. 9–27.

56. Cat. no. 407. This is particularly evident in the ivory carvings of Charlemagne's court school. Cf. H. Fillitz, "L'arte alla corte di Carlo Magno nei suoi rapporti con l'antichità," *Rendiconti della Pontificia Accademia Romana di Archeologia*, XXXVIII, 1965–66, pp. 221–36. Idem, "L'arte alla corte di Carlo Magno ed i suoi rapporti con l'antichità," *Colloqui del Sodalizio*, Rome, 1966–68 (Sodalizio tra studiosi dell'arte, 2nd ser., 1), pp. 45–58. I illustrate the relationship with a detail from a Carolingian ivory plaque in Oxford (Fig. 26) and the corresponding representations of two of Christ's miracles on a fifth-century relief in the Louvre (Fig. 25). For this comparison, see pp. 223–24 of Fillitz' first article, and pp. 49–50 of the second.

57. S. Gero, "The Libri Carolini and the Image Controversy," *The Greek Orthodox Theological Review*, XVIII, 1973, pp. 7–34, esp. pp. 18–19.

58. I wish to thank Nicholas Gendle, Anna Kartsonis, Lawrence Nees, Natasha Staller, and William Tronzo for their advice and criticism, from which I benefited in preparing this lecture for publication. References to the catalogue of the exhibition, published in 1979, were added editorially.

Index